THE CIGARETTE

THE CIGARETTE

A Political History

Sarah Milov

Harvard University Press

Cambridge, Massachusetts, and London, England · 2019

For My Mother

Library of Congress Cataloging-in-Publication Data

Names: Milov, Sarah, 1984– author.
Title: The cigarette : a political history / Sarah Milov.
Description: Cambridge, Massachusetts : Harvard University Press, 2019. |
    Includes bibliographical references and index.
Identifiers: LCCN 2019002275 | ISBN 9780674241213 (alk. paper)
Subjects: LCSH: Cigarettes—United States—History—20th century. |
    Tobacco industry—United States—History—20th century. | Tobacco—
    United States—History—20th century. | Smoking—Law and legislation—
    United States—History—20th century.
Classification: LCC HD9149.C43 U663 2019 | DDC 338.4/76797309730904—
    dc23 LC record available at https://lccn.loc.gov/2019002275

Contents

Introduction   1

1   Tobacco in Industrializing America   11

2   Tobacco's New Deal   46

3   Cultivating the Grower   78

4   The Challenge of the Public Interest   118

5   Inventing the Nonsmoker   160

6   From Rights to Cost   201

7   Shredding a Net to Build a Web   241

Conclusion: "Weeds Are Hard to Kill":
The Future of Tobacco Politics   279

Notes   297

Acknowledgments   377

Index   381

Introduction

ON A COLD SATURDAY IN JANUARY 1964, a morning press conference garnered international attention. To the chagrin of some of the assembled journalists, "no smoking" signs had been hastily affixed to the auditorium walls in advance of the release of the much-anticipated *Surgeon General's Report on Smoking and Health*. The auditorium doors were locked and uniformed guards blocked doors leading to other parts of the building.[1] Inside, Luther Terry, John F. Kennedy's choice as surgeon general, who was now serving at the pleasure of Lyndon Johnson, and the other members of the committee responsible for the report fielded questions from hundreds of journalists who had just got their hands on it. The nearly 400-page report concluded that cigarettes caused death—death from lung cancer, bronchitis, emphysema, and coronary artery disease. After reviewing the accumulated evidence on the relationship between cigarette smoking and disease, two of the committee members had quit smoking altogether. Terry himself had switched from cigarettes to an occasional cigar or pipe. Some of the reporters expressed their anxiety over the government's findings in a rather different way—by sheepishly smoking in the halls.

The theatrics of the report's release—the lock-and-key treatment, the Saturday morning presser—were intended to minimize the effects upon the stock market. The committee needn't have worried. The Royal College of Physicians had published a similar report two years earlier.[2] On the eve of the report's release, stock market analysts were recommending that investors purchase tobacco stocks, as their prices already reflected the damning news and would only rise again in the future.[3] It was sound advice. In the United States, sales fell 20 percent in the months after the report's issue, only to rebound spectacularly in 1965, when companies posted their highest profits to date.[4] Politicians, experts, and everyday Americans increasingly knew that cigarettes were deadly, and yet 42 percent of Americans smoked.[5] And they smoked everywhere, lighting up at work and at play: offices, public buildings, retail establishments, sporting facilities, and even hospitals permitted indoor smoking. Some high schools even allowed students to smoke on campus.[6] But enlightenment alone cannot effect a widespread change in behavior. Laws and institutions must change as well. People must be compelled.

Cigarettes were central to American political institutions throughout the twentieth century. At home and abroad, the U.S. government encouraged people to smoke. And for four decades after the surgeon general determined that cigarette smoking was dangerous, the government continued to subsidize tobacco production. Although the big cigarette firms were among the most powerful American companies by mid-century, tobacco's political privilege lay less in the machinations of industry than in the everyday workings of American government. For a literal representation of the crop's importance to American politics, one need look no further than the Capitol building's grand Hall of Columns, where tobacco leaves sit atop the Corinthian columns, holding the building together.

By the mid-1970s, however, Americans were smoking less. By 1974, the percentage of smoking adults had fallen to 37 percent, and it has continued downward in a sustained descent right through the present day.[7] A transformation in the way that Americans understood and demanded an entitlement to public space catalyzed this change in behavior. Beginning in the 1970s, more and more Americans identified themselves by their rejection of smoking. Drawing inspiration from the civil rights and environmental movements, a group of nonsmoking activists extinguished the public hold of cigarettes—achieving their goal of making smoking socially unacceptable. Under the banner of nonsmokers' rights, grassroots activists organized and won restrictions on smoking in a variety of public places.

Nonsmokers, a group that had once been, in the words of Richard Nixon's surgeon general, Jesse Steinfeld, the true silent majority, began to speak. They found success not in Congress—which journalist Elizabeth Drew characterized in 1965 as the industry's "best filter yet"—but in local ordi-

nances and voluntary rules imposed by employers.[8] The power of the tobacco lobby in Congress pushed nonsmokers' rights activists to seek regulatory solutions at lower levels of government, where the industry had less
power.[9] Beginning in the early 1970s, city councils around the country
began to pass legislation that regulated public smoking. At the same time,
lawyers in Washington, D.C., petitioned and sued regulatory agencies, reasoning that expanding the purview of administrative agencies offered "the
greatest potential return for our legal action and efforts."[10] By 1974, both
the Civil Aeronautics Board (CAB) and the Interstate Commerce Commission (ICC) had implemented rules restricting smoking on flights and interstate buses. The history of the cigarette is the history of government's complex machinery, its levers of power differentially accessible to organized
business, farmers, and activists.

Smoking, Citizenship, and the State

The movement of tobacco from the center to the periphery of American political life highlights two competing conceptions of government at work
during twentieth century: one concerned with the prerogatives and economic rights of producers, the other with the broad social costs of such producerism.[11] For most of the twentieth century, the federal government had
an active hand in shoring up the cigarette economy: soldier's rations helped
to popularize the cigarette in wartime, surplus export programs boosted
farmers' incomes and global cigarette consumption, and a generous price
support system stabilized the agricultural economy of the Southeast until
2004—long after the surgeon general had proclaimed the cigarette lethal.

The political economy of tobacco production and consumption was
rooted in a New Deal–era vision of supply management. The New Deal ushered in an expansive program of agricultural regulations.[12] And no crop
was more regulated than tobacco.[13] Responding to the desires of elite
growers and their interest groups, the federal government imposed a rigid
program of supply control, tightly regulating the areas in which tobacco
could be cultivated.[14] The tobacco program outlasted other New Deal agricultural initiatives—a fact that challenges frameworks in political history
that emphasize the fall of the New Deal order under the conservative jug-
gernaut of the 1980s.[15] The staying power of the tobacco program lay largely

in the fact that its operations went unnoticed by the broader public and were closely stewarded by long-serving officials whose leadership of the tobacco economy straddled the public and private sectors.[16]

Associationalism is the term that scholars use to describe the achievement of public policy goals through private means.[17] From the first, faltering attempts by tobacco producers to organize cooperatives in the 1920s to the bailout of tobacco farmers by cigarette manufacturers in the 1990s, the tobacco economy has been organized by interest groups endowed with coercive, decision-making power. The global proliferation of American cigarette tobacco after the Second World War provides a case in point. Facing postwar surpluses and an unprecedented opportunity to expand the reach of their crop, a group of prominent tobacco growers sought and received special legislation from the North Carolina General Assembly. The bill authorized the creation of a private export promotion organization called Tobacco Associates, whose mission would be to promote the consumption of U.S.-grown cigarette tobacco around the world. It also compelled tobacco growers to tax themselves to finance the organization, resulting in a double interweaving of public and private. During the second half of the twentieth century, Tobacco Associates helped to secure the integrity of the domestic tobacco program by making sure surplus stocks of tobacco found disposal abroad, rather than, at mounting taxpayer expense, at home. In so doing, Tobacco Associates—and the hundreds of thousands of growers that financed it—helped to accelerate the global epidemic of cigarette-related disease.[18] The role of organizations like Tobacco Associates in the history of the cigarette has largely been obscured by the fact that associational government operates "out of sight"—its public face obscured by the long shadow cast by private sector support.[19]

The premises of tobacco associationalism came under sustained assault by the public interest movement of the 1960s and 1970s. Grassroots activists—led mostly by women—and Washington-based lawyers ushered the arrival of the nonsmoker as a rights-bearing political subject. For these activists, rights were a powerful rhetorical tool—laden with moral heft in the wake of the rights revolutions of the 1960s.[20] For such activists, nonsmokers' rights contained a critique, not only of the ubiquity of smoke in public places, but also of the smoke-filled chambers that endowed tobacco with political power. What political scientist Ira Katznelson has evocatively called a "southern cage"—the contouring of policymaking around the racist, segregationist prerogatives of southern Democrats—was also a smoking section.[21] For nonsmoker activists, dethroning tobacco from its political perch was part and parcel of a quest for broader political representation.

The language of rights also dovetailed with the emergent public interest critique emanating from the environmental and consumer protection movements of the 1960s and 1970s. Public interest reformers were skeptical of the state's capacity to reflect more than the narrow economic interests of business. They sought to democratize what they understood as a managerial corporate state, and did so by insisting on greater opportunities for citizen participation in administration:[22] by acting as agency watchdogs, by advocating an expanded concept of judicial standing, and by suing.[23] The new social regulations of the 1970s, which led to the creation of the Environmental Protection Agency (EPA), the Consumer Product Safety Commission, and the Occupational Safety and Health Administration (OSHA), reflected a keen appreciation for the unseen, latent risks of modern society—a precautionary sensibility especially common in the environmental movement.[24]

Like these movements, the nonsmokers' rights movement drew attention not only to the negative externalities of modern American life—pollution, industrial poisoning, lung cancer, and heart disease but also to the sclerotic decision-making structures that privileged the organized few at the expense of the disorganized many. It sought to embed calls for nonsmokers' rights within the broader struggle to make political processes more inclusive. As such, the political history of the cigarette highlights the connections between the politics of the body and those of the body politic.

Moreover, the relative power of smokers versus nonsmokers was, foremost, a political rather than a scientific question. Rights-based demands for smoking restrictions preceded scientific evidence of the dangers of secondhand smoke by more than a decade. But science played a crucial role in contouring politics in the 1970s and 1980s. The air quality and workplace safety standards enforced by the EPA and OSHA legitimated nonsmokers' demands. If the government could regulate emissions from factory pollution, why couldn't it regulate pollutants from "human smokestacks"? Why should nonsmokers be subjected to the unnecessary risk of a stranger's idling cigarette when OSHA had established permissible exposure limits for some of the dangerous compounds in tobacco smoke, including carbon monoxide, nitric oxide, benzene, and formaldehyde?[25] Yet it was not until the early 1980s that a body of epidemiology began to specify the risks that cigarettes posed to nonsmokers.[26] And only in 1986 did the surgeon general devote an entire edition of the *Surgeon General's Report* to the "health consequences of involuntary smoking."[27] By then, the movement for smoking restrictions was well under way. Proof of physical harm from secondhand smoke intensified, but did not originate, calls for nonsmokers' rights.[28]

The meaning of nonsmokers' rights changed as such claims migrated into new settings. At workplaces, nonsmokers' rights became corporate risk mitigation. In the late 1970s, an estimated three fourths of all employers allowed unrestricted smoking at the worksite.[29] Finding that appeals to the bottom line were more persuasive to their employers than simply registering their distress and discomfort, nonsmokers embraced the business case for smoking restrictions at work. Smokers, they argued, were bad employees: they had higher rates of absenteeism than their nonsmoking colleagues; they were less productive, took frequent breaks, cost more to insure, dirtied equipment, and caused accidents. In clearing the air at work, nonsmokers offered the argument that a cheap employee is a good employee.

Businesses embraced this argument, out of deference to the bottom line and the desire to mitigate liability should a nonsmoking employee bring suit. A nationwide business survey conducted in 1987 found that 54 percent of responding businesses had adopted workplace smoking restrictions—and 85 percent of them had adopted such policies within the past three years.[30] In appealing to management, nonsmokers' rights activists collided with organized labor, which the tobacco industry recognized as an ally in the fight to preserve the smoke break and the acceptability of smoking employees. But the new expectation of smoke-free air at work did not represent the straightforward triumph of an individual rights–based vision of liberalism over the collective vision guarded by unions.[31] Ideas about health and the environment had expanded the realm of the contestable, galvanizing previously unorganized constituencies to make the state reflect their interests.[32]

Pressing upon business and government to consider the myriad social costs of smoking, nonsmokers' rights activists constructed a vision of citizenship focused on cheapness and efficiency: the best workers, citizens, and taxpayers were those who kept costs down and productivity up.[33] This politics of bodily evaluation dovetailed with market-centric judgments of the body politic. The state's performance was increasingly subject to market metrics, such as cost-benefit analysis and balanced budget requirements; its governance marked by market techniques such as privatization, lowered trade barriers, deregulation, and means testing.[34]

The federal tobacco program chafed against this paradigm of personal and fiscal prudence. To many, the tobacco program proved the very folly of government intervention into private markets. It was wastefully hypocritical, a residue of southern political domination of Congress. Fearful that the program would be axed completely during the early, zealous years of Reagan budget cutting, tobacco state members of Congress and growers assented to program reform in 1982. By levying an assessment on tobacco held in government storage, the legislation shifted financial liability for the tobacco program from taxpayers to tobacco producers themselves. Under the new law, farmers would have to fashion their own safety net as federal price supports were lowered in the name of achieving a more "market-oriented" program. Many could not afford to do so, and left tobacco production. Others clung desperately to what remained, unable to imagine their futures without the program that had been the salvation of their parents and grandparents.

In 2004, the program was terminated. Only growers who had enough capital or access to credit to expand their operations and ramp up production continued to grow tobacco.[35] These bigger, highly capitalized farms now rely heavily on poorly paid migrant labor—working and living under conditions that some have described as squalid and slave-like.[36] These farmers appear to be the consummate capitalists: they control land, invest in sophisticated machines, and oversee the labor of workers who live in trailers on the growers' property.[37] But these modern growers face the perils of modern capitalism as surely as their pre–New Deal forebearers did. They sell their tobacco directly on contract to the cigarette manufacturers—and the companies set the terms of the contract. As one grower lamented, it is a struggle to negotiate with "multibillion-dollar, multinational companies on a one-on-one basis."[38]

At the beginning of the twenty-first century, a symmetry unites smokers and tobacco farmers. Within the "narcotic tobacco haze of capitalism," to borrow Allen Ginsberg's phrase in *Howl*, the smoker stands alone on a street corner and the farmer stands alone against the cigarette giants.[39] Their exile represents the transformation of a political economy that was once guided by economic stability and unbridled consumption, and which has now been replaced by one of efficiency and prudence. By looking at the cigarette, we see our state and ourselves.

Beyond Big Tobacco

Historians, legal scholars, and political scientists have been exceptionally attentive to cigarettes.[40] Explanations for the rise, persistence, and fall of smoking have largely centered on the goals and machinations of the cigarette manufacturers known as Big Tobacco. There is a cinematic quality to this narrative, complete with greedy villains, secret meetings, and smoke-filled rooms. In one such room, at the Plaza Hotel in December 1953, the major cigarette manufacturers "launched the formal conspiracy" agreeing to form the Tobacco Industry Research Committee (TIRC). From the mid-1950s until the 1998 Master Settlement Agreement (MSA) formally disbanded the organization, TIRC spent more than $300 million on "smoking and health research" intended to mislead while maintaining a veneer of corporate responsibility and concern.[41] It was, in short, a decades-long conspiracy to publicly deny what they privately admitted: that cigarettes were deadly and addictive.

Historians have resoundingly shown—to the public and in the courts—how the tobacco industry successfully exploited the idea of scientific uncertainty to subvert regulation.[42] An infamous 1969 memo penned by a vice-president of marketing at Brown & Williamson encapsulated the industry's duplicity with Orwellian elegance. Surveying the "aggressive," "orderly," and "accelerating" momentum of the anti-cigarette forces, the executive proposed a reformulation of the company's sales priorities. "In thinking over what we might do to improve the case for cigarettes, I have looked at the problem somewhat like the marketing of a new brand," he wrote. "Doubt is our product since it is the best means of competing with the 'body of fact' that exists in the mind of the general public."[43] Doubt's greatest virtue was that it stoked public perception that a "controversy" existed around what should have been a dispositive scientific fact: smoking was the leading cause of preventable death in the United States. The industry enlisted scientists, physicians, statisticians, social scientists, and even historians in an expert-driven campaign to subvert regulation and keep people smoking.[44]

But the history of the cigarette does not begin and end with Big Tobacco. By expanding our gaze beyond the perfidy of corporations, attorneys, and public relations flacks, we can see the extent to which tobacco was a normal part of American political economy—and one enabled by the United States' postwar economic hegemony. Government bureaucracies working hand-in-hand with agricultural interest organizations were coconspirators in making the cigarette century.[45] This relationship—and the broader tobacco industry's power—was not a matter of capture or corruption, but a result of associational state-building.

Just as a Manichean assumption of a state-business binary underlies most histories of tobacco, so too is there a tendency to view questions of consumption as divorced from practices of production. Government policy conscripted tobacco producers into the project of expanding demand for cigarettes—a task that growers took to with alacrity, exploiting the umbrella of U.S. power to promote the consumption of their leaf during the Cold War. Indeed, the cigarette's mid-century status as the "ultimate symbol of a democratized consumer ethic" rested upon elaborate bureaucratic structures of production.[46] Through the history of the cigarette, we can see power that producers continued to wield in the consumer's republic.[47] At the same time, looking beyond Big Tobacco illuminates surprising interconnections between social movements—such as the environmental movement and the nonsmokers' rights movement—and among unexpected bedfellows, such as labor unions and cigarette manufacturers.[48] By embedding the cigarette within multiple narratives of political, economic, and legal change, we can better understand a paradox not easily resolved by business-centric histories: the power of the tobacco industry waned at the precise moment that other large American businesses saw their political power increase along with the fortunes of the New Right.[49]

———

Tobacco forces us to strip away sentimentalities about the twentieth century. Nobody who understands the damage that cigarettes do to a body would wish to live in the smoky world of mid-century America. Even with the substantial reduction in smoking rates, more people die every year from tobacco-related disease than murder, suicides, alcohol, automobile accidents, and AIDS combined.[50] Reckoning with the demise of that world and the origins of our own—where self-quantification is promoted by employers and government as a technique for achieving "wellness"—requires historians to reconcile an appreciation for a smoke-free world with an assessment of the market-oriented politics that produced it. A nonsmoking world is one that "we cannot not want."[51] Our less smoky present, forged through the assertion of nonsmokers' rights, is also a harsh and stigmatizing one. It is one in which the death of a smoker can be met with the thought—sometimes tactlessly expressed aloud—"What did he expect?"[52]

Since the 1970s, smokers have tended to be less educated and affluent than nonsmokers. Recent research suggests that they spend more time unemployed, are less likely to get hired, and earn less than those who abstain.[53] While social scientists puzzle over whether smoking status is a cause or consequence of poverty and educational attainment, Americans are less discerning in their judgments. In a 2016 Gallup survey, 40 percent of respondents—and nearly 50 percent of nonsmokers—said that they think more negatively of smokers simply because they smoke.[54]

Such judgments reside within a broader political culture in which the space between virtuous citizenship and market success grows ever narrower, where understandings of human nature once "thick with context, social circumstance, institutions, and history gave way to conceptions of human nature that stressed choice, agency, performance, desire."[55] This is as true for the smokers—exiled outside to furtively feed an addiction that they, more than likely, do not want—as it is for the tobacco farmers now "free" to sell as much tobacco as they can, but at prices they do not control.[56] Cleared of smoke, the individual's path to prosperity and health is obvious. The consequences of deviation are his or hers alone.

1

Tobacco in Industrializing America

> Which purposes and ideals . . . is to make those son-a-bitching
> buyers pay me what my tobacco's worth?
> —Robert Penn Warren, *Night Rider*

AT THE TURN OF THE TWENTIETH CENTURY, tobacco farmers were weak and angry.[1] Their sweat had made men like James B. Duke wildly rich. But growers were not sharing in the spoils of the profitable tobacco industry. Robert Penn Warren gave ominous voice to these frustrations in his novel *Night Rider,* a fictionalization of the violence that erupted in the tobacco regions of Tennessee and Kentucky in the first decade of the twentieth century. In real life, growers banded together and vowed to withhold the sale of their tobacco until Duke's American Tobacco Company (ATC) raised the price of leaf. Finding inadequate success through persuasion alone, some members of the growers' association began night riding—destroying the tobacco fields of farmers who refused to boycott the ATC, setting entire warehouses full of tobacco ablaze at night.

The novel's protagonist, an idealistic lawyer named Percy Munn, finds himself in the middle of forces he cannot control: the economic power of the tobacco companies that kept farmers disorganized and poor, the violence of the growers' association that was supposed to be the farmers' salvation, and the complicity of the law in vigilantism. Percy Munn marvels at his own descent into violence: he rapes his wife, murders a client, nearly murders a political rival, and leads a raid on a tobacco warehouse. These acts of passion coincide with Percy's increasing involvement with the Association of Growers—an abstraction that bound thousands of faceless men, "all different from each other in their own ways, but drawn together by the fact that their names were on the pieces of paper."[2]

By the 1920s, such collective action by farmers to raise the price of their crops formed the centerpiece of federal agriculture policy. The First World War had enabled economists, policymakers, and reformers to imagine greater large-scale organization across every sector of the economy. The passage of the Capper-Volstead Act in 1922 exempted agricultural cooperatives from provisions of the Sherman Anti-Trust Act. Its goal was to enable farmers to harness some of the power of organization that had for decades worked toward the benefit of big business, and, to a lesser extent, organized labor. It was also an implicit acknowledgment of farmers' relative weakness vis-à-vis buyers, processors, distributors, corporations, and consumers. In North Carolina, the top producer of cigarette tobacco by the 1920s, violence in the name of the cooperative never came close to the night riding that Warren described. Yet even with legal protections and the encouragement of the farm press, agriculture officials, and area businessmen, cooperative marketing of tobacco failed. Farmers could not overcome short-term market incentives to subvert the cooperative and sell to the tobacco companies, or the mismatch between oligopoly and small farmer when it came to the relative cost of organizing.

Until the New Deal's direct intervention into the agricultural marketplace, establishing a price floor and production quotas for tobacco, farmers failed to strengthen their hand against the cigarette manufacturers. But in their attempts to organize, growers and sympathetic public officials began to articulate and practice a producerist political economy centered on regulating tobacco output as a means both of combating the power of organized capital and of valorizing the sweated labor of white farmers.[3] In the early decades of the twentieth century, farmer organization did not just mean higher prices on commodities. It was an index of the strength of democracy itself. From Gilded Age businessmen to social reformers to tobacco farmers, myriad Americans found that in thinking about tobacco, they were really thinking about the distribution of wealth and power in society—as well as the obligations and capacities of government to change it. Perhaps they also contemplated the weight of their individual voices in a political world that was changing almost as rapidly as the economy that defined their fortunes.

This chapter sets the scene for understanding the rise of tobacco in public life. The story of tobacco in the twentieth century is rolled into the history of the cigarette; and the fate of tobacco farmers is inextricable from it. Although cigarettes were a quintessentially modern product—mass produced, heavily advertised, and consumed by urban dwellers—they did not appeal to all Americans. Temperance reformers, eugenicists, nativists, and industrial efficiency advocates waged war on "the little white slavers."[4] Before the First World War, they succeeded in urging numerous states to pass laws restricting the purchase, sale, or manufacture of cigarettes. The Great War was a major turning point in the history of tobacco, as cigarettes were reimagined as emblems of patriotism rather than symbols of foreignness. The postwar economic boom of the 1920s accelerated the adoption of the cigarette. Tobacco companies, awash in capital, spent handsomely on advertisements, assiduously courting women by the end of the decade.

The 1920s were good for the cigarette business, but they were bad for farmers. The policies and dynamics that had made business big in the 1920s made farmers small by comparison. But in seeking to enlarge their presence in the marketplace and in the political sphere, farmers emulated a tactic they saw working to the advantage of labor and capital: organization.[5] Tobacco growers in the tobacco belt of Virginia and the Carolinas also tried their hand at organizing. The Tri-State Tobacco Growers Cooperative Association (TGCA) was formed during the agriculture depression of the early 1920s. The premise was simple: if the cooperative had a monopoly over tobacco, it could dictate prices to the cigarette companies. Within five years, the venture had failed. Geographically scattered and too poor to consider economic strategies that did not offer immediate cash, tobacco growers never were able to achieve the level of organization that could improve their position in the marketplace. And in the 1920s, as cigarettes grew in popularity and the prices for other commodities sagged, an increasing number of farmers grew tobacco, making it harder for the cooperative to achieve monopoly control over the harvest.

Nevertheless, the process of corralling tens of thousands of scattered farmers into a shared economic vision paved the way for the New Deal's overhaul of farm economies and laid the foundations for the New Deal's system of associationalism, which transformed farmers into state administrators. The political discourse of the 1920s, suffused with discussion of the neighborly virtues of "farmer self-help," was premised on a working consensus between the rural government and select citizens. In the tobacco belt, state officials and tobacco growers came to share the same vision of the moral worth of cooperation, and the economic importance of collective action. The improbability of the cooperative's success—and the necessity of direct state intervention to raise tobacco prices—can only be appreciated when seen against the power of farmers' great adversaries: the cigarette manufacturers.

"Donating Fealty in Money and in Manhood to James B. Duke"

The most obvious source of farmers' disempowerment, and most frequent target of their invective, was the Tobacco Trust—James B. Duke's enormous and powerful tobacco monopoly that controlled the vast majority of the domestic and global tobacco trade.[6] In popular memory, the Tobacco Trust has taken a backseat to John D. Rockefeller's Standard Oil Trust, J. P. Morgan's U.S. Steel, and even the Beef Trust made famous by Upton Sinclair's *The Jungle*. But between its founding in 1890 and its dissolution in 1911, the Tobacco Trust controlled between 75 and 90 percent of all cigarette sales in the United States. One Kentucky congressman described the ATC as so intransigent in its operations that it could "make any convict feel like an honest man in comparison."[7]

The Trust was dissolved by Supreme Court decree in 1911, but the successor companies continued to operate as an oligopoly. R. J. Reynolds, Liggett & Myers, and Lorillard, as well as a pared-down American Tobacco, were divided but not competitive—especially not at the auction houses where company representatives bid on the price of farmers' tobacco. In the words of Louis Brandeis, the most famous lawyer in Progressive-Era America, the tobacco industry was but "an illegal trust legalized."[8] As any cigarette addict can tell you: old habits are hard to break. In 1941, these companies would be found guilty of price fixing in violation of the Sherman Anti-Trust Act.

The American Tobacco Company's roots were deep in the soil of the hilly North Carolina Piedmont. Prior to the Civil War, Washington Duke's farm was a large, diversified operation, growing wheat, corn, oats, sweet potatoes, and just a little bit of tobacco. Duke relied on the labor of enslaved people to turn a profit, but with the exception of one housekeeper, Caroline, he rented the work of slaves from the owners of nearby plantations. In 1863, however, Wash Duke converted all of his operations to tobacco. After a one-year stint in the Confederate Army, in spring 1865, he was captured by Union troops and imprisoned in Richmond.

After Robert E. Lee's surrender at Appomattox, Duke returned home to North Carolina and assessed his prospects. When he arrived back at the homestead after a 130-mile trudge from New Bern, where he had been held briefly by Union troops, Duke decided to give up farming altogether. Perhaps it was the labor "problem" posed by emancipation, or perhaps Duke imagined brighter economic prospects in factories rather than in fields. Regardless of his precise motives, his timing was fortuitous, for two technological innovations were essential for Duke's entry into the tobacco business.[9] First, in 1854, the North Carolina Railroad laid track through the tiny hamlet of Durham Station, whose population numbered less than one hundred.[10] And second, the flue-cured method of processing tobacco emerged. Flue-curing helped make cigarettes both popular and deadly because it made them more inhalable.[11]

The end product of flue-curing is a bright yellow tobacco leaf—a result of the steady application of heat to the mature green plant. This technological process was so closely associated with the Piedmont of North Carolina and Virginia that by the late nineteenth century, only those regions were considered climatologically hospitable to the variety tobacco farmers had taken to calling "Bright Leaf" or just "Bright." Americans first smoked bright leaf tobacco in pipes, or in roll-your-own cigarettes. And it was in the sale of this "smoking tobacco" that Washington Duke first entered the tobacco-manufacturing business. Along with his daughter, Mary, and two sons, Benjamin and James Buchanan (the Duke family's famed Republicanism postdated the birth of "Buck"), Washington Duke transformed their homestead into a factory of sorts. The family sold the tobacco in burlap sacks under the brand "Pro Bono Publico."

By 1881, W. Duke Sons & Company began producing cigarettes—encasing a blend of Bright Leaf and Burley tobacco within a cylinder of paper. This was a labor-intensive business—and one whose profitability paled in comparison to the manufacture and sale of chewing or smoking tobacco for pipe or roll-your-own consumption. To make money in cigarettes would require novel business techniques. Rather than innovate,

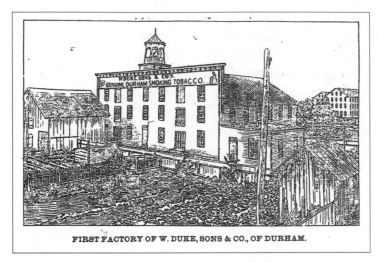

FIRST FACTORY OF W. DUKE, SONS & CO., OF DURHAM.

Figure 1.1 Sketch of Duke's first factory, Durham, North Carolina. (*Raleigh News and Observer*, April 5, 1896, p. 15)

Buck Duke, who took over the family business in the early 1880s, engaged in strong-arm tactics in order to dominate the regional tobacco industry.

Young, aggressive, and just rich enough to imagine copying the techniques of contemporary barons, Duke invested in machines and the manufacture of desire, two essential ingredients in the modern cigarette. At the time, the firm of Allen & Ginter was the leading producer of rolled cigarettes, employing 450 young women and girls as rollers in its Richmond factory. This dwarfed Duke's labor force of sixty.[12] But Duke saw a chance to make inroads on his Richmond competitor emerge from labor unrest at a New York City cigarette factory.[13] Tobacco workers at Goodwin & Company went on strike when the firm lowered their wages. Duke brokered a meeting with the leader of the striking workers. He offered the 125 strikers employment at his Durham factory, and promised to pay their old wages as well as relocation expenses (see Figure 1.1).

In Durham, the tobacco rollers, nearly all of whom were Jewish immigrants from Eastern Europe, established their own neighborhood—Yiddishe Streetal—with a synagogue above a drug store.[14] Some historians have speculated that Duke's antipathy to labor organizing soured him on this strike-prone Eastern European labor pool.[15] "We have never had any trouble in the help except when 125 Polish Jews were hired to come down to Durham to work in the factory," Washington Duke recalled. "They gave us no end of trouble."[16] In any case, as the business grew, Duke turned toward local sources of labor, advertising for "twenty-five white girls to make cigarettes."[17] Child labor was surely more pliable than the ideologically suspect Jewish rollers. But machines were more pliable still. And like other industrialists, Duke fantasized about a device that never complained or went on strike, even if the initial investment required more capital.

Ironically, a cigarette-rolling machine originally developed for Allen & Ginter allowed Duke to compete with the Richmond pioneer. In the late nineteenth century, machines transformed where and how Americans worked, relaxed, consumed, and even conceived of themselves. In agriculture, to take just one example, tractors and combines dramatically reduced the need for human and animal labor, rendering "every farm a factory." In California, where large-scale, capital-intensive agriculture developed earliest, in the middle of the nineteenth century, it took sixty hours of human labor to cultivate an acre of wheat; by 1900, it took just three.[18] Although immigration kept labor costs low, as a seemingly unending flow of immigrants rushed to fill low-wage jobs, many manufacturers in labor-intensive industries still sought to harness machine power.

In 1876, Allen & Ginter offered a prize of $76,000 to anybody who could devise a reliable cigarette machine. This sum was motivation enough for James Bonsack.[19] The teenage Bonsack, the son of a Roanoke textile magnate, had observed from a young age the jerky choreography of roller, frame, belt, and tube involved in textile manufacturing. In 1881 the twenty-one-year-old patented the Bonsack Cigarette Machine (see Figure 1.2). Allen & Ginter was, naturally, the first firm to install the device, which was estimated to equal in output a day's work of forty-eight hand rollers. At the time, conventional wisdom suggested that consumers would reject machine-made cigarettes, just as they had done with machine-made cigars.[20] But cigarette manufacturers, imagining a new market opened by Congress's recent reduction in the cigarette tax, were undeterred.[21]

By 1884 there were seven such machines humming in the United States, and seven more in Europe, each paying James Bonsack royalties. Buck Duke

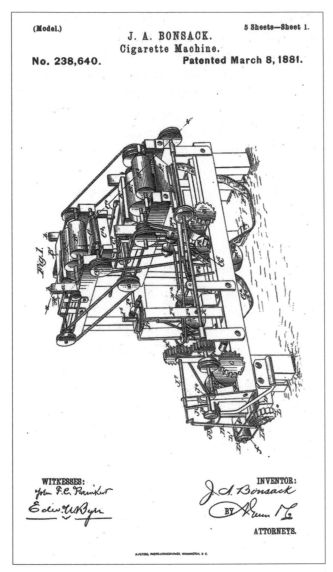

Figure 1.2 James Bonsack's patent for a "Cigarette Machine," 1881. (Patent No. 238,640, March 8, 1881, United States Patent and Trademark Office)

acquired one of the devices, and hired a full-time mechanic to attend to its hiccups and sputters. A few months after the first Bonsack was installed in Durham, tobacco workers voted to form a union—a decision that likely redoubled Duke's commitment to machines. Duke's investment began to pay off within a few years, as the Bonsack machine became more reliable.[22] By 1887, Duke was manufacturing more cigarettes than any other company in the world—as many cigarettes as all of his competitors combined.[23] But Duke did not want any competition, which was so frequently wasteful, inefficient, and needless. He imagined control.

Duke's dreams were enabled by changes in the legal status of the corporation—though his own mythologizing, later echoed by historians, would attribute his success to an elemental ruthlessness.[24] "Hit your competitors in the pocketbook. Hit 'em hard," Duke explained his philosophy. "Then you either buy 'em out or take 'em with you."[25] In reality, Duke's ascendancy to the top of the tobacco trade was far more contingent. After a plan to incorporate the American Tobacco Company in Virginia fell through, ATC was incorporated in New Jersey in 1890. This was a happy accident for Duke, as that state had recently loosened its incorporation laws, essentially freeing corporations from the regulation of monopoly. After the passage of the Sherman Anti-Trust Act in 1890, the state would become a refuge for businesses seeking to pool capital in the form of "holding companies."[26] At the same time, courts began to reimagine the corporation's scope. In 1886, the Supreme Court ruled that a corporation was a person under the Fourteenth Amendment, giving ATC's lawyers a new set of arguments with which to defend the trust against its opponents.[27]

The first move of the American Tobacco Company was to buy the five leading cigarette companies, essentially neutering Allen & Ginter as a competitor.[28] Immediately, the Tobacco Trust became responsible for 90 percent of cigarette sales.[29] ATC further absorbed 250 separate companies to dominate the plug, snuff, and smoking tobacco markets.[30] By 1910 its assets had grown to $350 million from an original capitalization of $25 million in 1890. By another metric of wealth, every $1,000 invested in 1890 brought $36,000 in profit in 1908.[31]

Duke was hardly alone in his zeal to "hit 'em hard" and "take 'em with you." It was the era of the Great Merger Movement, a period in which highly capitalized firms responded to economic uncertainty—rapid expansion of industry, "ruinous competition," and the Depression of 1893—by trying to monopolize the market.[32] As thousands of small to mid-sized firms disappeared, there arose a handful of Frankenstein-like businesses: oversized, stitched together, and frightful to many Americans who conceived of commerce on a human scale. It is not surprising that some of the results of these great mergers—Standard Oil, U.S. Steel, General Electric, DuPont—were sometimes imagined and described as monsters, menacing the republic, sucking the life out of the farmers and workers on whose labors they rested. Duke consolidated vertically and horizontally; he eliminated rungs on the supply chain, circumventing independent leaf dealers with a "leaf department" of company buyers. From Duke's perspective, cutting out the middlemen also had the added benefit of eliminating competition over the price of leaf from farmers. The Trust simply dictated the price.

Duke also integrated distribution. Drummers—traveling salesmen who drummed up the trade, taking orders for specific cigarette brands from retail tobacconists—were replaced with a system of independent, urban distribution centers.[33] Duke took over firms that produced inputs needed to make a cigarette or chew—licorice paste businesses, wooden-box firms, cotton-sacking businesses, tobacco paper concerns. He used price-cutting techniques in order to weaken competitors in the plug and snuff businesses—forcing smaller companies into his empire.[34]

And this integration did not stop at the U.S. border. In 1901, Duke bought Ogden's, a British cigarette manufacturer, and with that toehold in the British cigarette business set off a merger movement in Britain that resulted in the formation of the Imperial Tobacco Company. American Tobacco and Imperial Tobacco—monopolies both—entered into an agreement. They promised not to compete in the other's domestic market, and together they created a joint entity, British American Tobacco (BAT), which would sell tobacco products to the rest of the world.[35] BAT's influence was especially strong in China, where hundreds of white North Carolinians and Virginians, valued for their artisanal knowledge of tobacco, were imported to reproduce American-style cultivation, curing, processing, cigarette manufacture, and distribution.[36]

An early example of a multinational corporation, BAT forged an empire with American capital and through American management. And, of course, in the final analysis it operated through the Chinese bodies that supplied inexpensive labor and were the ultimate receptacle for tobacco itself. Duke's visions of the China market were contemporaneous with the McKinley administration's promotion of American empire achieved through trade and commerce.[37] Aided by federal and state laws that transformed the nature of the corporation, Duke came to preside over an unrivaled machine for buying, processing, distributing, and selling tobacco in less than a decade.

Unrivaled did not mean unchallenged. The American Tobacco Company and the Sherman Anti-Trust Act were born the same year. As legal historian Morton Keller put it, "the land of the trust was also the land of the anti-trust."[38] Courts took a constrained view of Congress's powers to regulate the size and operations of big business during the 1890s. With the 1895 E. C. Knight decision, the Supreme Court all but curtailed the ability of the federal government to regulate manufacturing as interstate commerce. Under the business-friendly McKinley administration, it seemed that there was little the federal government would do to halt the horizontal and vertical integration that characterized the Great Merger Movement—until, that is, the McKinley administration unexpectedly became the Roosevelt administration.

The prospect of a Teddy Roosevelt presidency was a source of dread for the business community at the turn of the century. As governor of New York, Roosevelt had burnished his reputation as a reformer by railing against excesses of large corporations. Allies of McKinley believed they were marginalizing the unpredictable New Yorker when they nominated him as vice-president. "I told William McKinley it was a mistake to nominate that wild man," Mark Hanna, McKinley's campaign manager and political adviser, recalled to a journalist while en route on the slain president's funeral train. "Now look, that damned cowboy is president of the United States."[39] In reality, Roosevelt's vision of the relationship between business and government was more complex than simple opposition. Roosevelt was skeptical of the Sherman Act and believed that the efficiencies of certain trusts could be harnessed and put to public use—that is, it was possible to discern a difference between "bad trusts" and "good trusts."[40] His preferred instrument of business regulation was not competition between smaller firms, but "continuous administrative action" on the part of the federal government.[41]

In 1904, the Court handed down the *Northern Securities* decision, dismantling a J. P. Morgan–backed railroad monopoly under the Sherman Act,
and inaugurating bolder federal scrutiny of the giant trusts. The Bureau
of Corporations opened an investigation on the American Tobacco Company the following year. The findings of the Bureau of Corporations, a fore-
runner to the Federal Trade Commission (FTC), provided the empirical
underpinnings to the suit against American Tobacco Company brought by
the Department of Justice in 1908. Charging that the Trust had been formed
"with enlarging purpose to restrain trade and acquire monopolies," the government sought the dissolution of Duke's behemoth.[42]

In May 1911, on the very same day as it handed down a similar ruling
against Rockefeller's Standard Oil, the Supreme Court ordered the dissolution of the American Tobacco Company. "The history of the combination
is so replete with the doing of acts which it was the obvious purpose of the
statute to forbid," Chief Justice Edward White wrote for the majority. Citing
examples of Duke's business decisions "designed to injure others," the Court
ordered that the combination be dissolved, and that successor companies
be re-created "out of the elements now composing it."[43]

The Court's spasmodic commitment to the antitrust principles laid
down by the Sherman Act did not resolve the tensions at the heart of early
twentieth-century political economy. The ruling in *United States v. American
Tobacco Company* broke up the Duke Trust, but did not force successor companies to compete in how they sourced tobacco. Cigarette companies
would be investigated multiple times for collusion in upcoming decades.
Debt-ridden and dispersed, farmers faced a many-headed hydra when they
hauled their tobacco for sale at auction. At every tobacco market in the
southeastern United States, a pantomime of competition testified to inequalities of wealth and power.

From "Little White Slaver" to Soldier's Friend

Although the Trust and its successor companies dominated the cigarette
market, cigarettes hardly predominated in Americans' demand for tobacco.
At the turn of the century, cigarettes accounted for just 2 percent of the total
tobacco products market. Demand for cigarettes surged amid unprecedented advertising expenditures, as Americans were exhorted to "reach for

a Lucky instead of a sweet" while also being reassured that "druggists and pharmacists stand ready to help" customers purchase Chesterfield cigarettes. Yet cigarettes still only accounted for 40 percent of total tobacco consumption in 1930.[44]

Public relations for cigarette companies routinely highlighted tobacco's foundational presence in colonial and revolutionary Virginia. But at the turn of the century, the cigarette was a decidedly foreign object. Cigarette production was based in New York and cigarettes were rolled by immigrant—largely Jewish—laborers.[45] The tobacco they rolled was most frequently imported from Turkey, where farmers had grown a dark, aromatic leaf for centuries. Camels—the name itself an orientalist fantasy—was the first nationally recognized packaged cigarette brand introduced by R. J. Reynolds in 1913. It used Turkish paper to wrap a blend of Turkish and Bright Leaf tobacco. Cigarette consumption in the United States trailed other nations, where tobacco rolled in paper was the cheapest way of getting a nicotine fix. In 1912, Britons consumed 428 cigarettes per capita, per year; Spaniards, 238; Russians, 235; Germans and Japanese, 172 and 145, respectively. Americans, by contrast, consumed just 138 cigarettes per capita yearly.[46] And even though Italian cigarette consumption lagged behind that of Americans, the press didn't miss an opportunity to connect Italians' hot-blooded passion to the cigarette: a "lovelorn Italian" committed suicide by smoking a cigarette and using the smoldering butt to ignite a stick of dynamite around his neck; two Italian immigrants in Brooklyn engaged in a deadly battle over a five-cent pack of cigarettes.[47] Given these global patterns of consumption, it is unsurprising that immigrants in America's growing cities smoked cigarettes to a greater extent than their native-born neighbors.[48]

Most Americans did not consume any form of tobacco at the turn of the century.[49] Those who did were more likely to chew it, burn it in a pipe, or nurse a cigar than they were to smoke a cigarette. Indeed, it was not until 1908 that sales of smoking tobacco exceeded sales of chewing tobacco.[50] Part of the reason lay in the concerted efforts of activists. In the decades prior to the First World War, moral reformers tirelessly inveighed against the cigarette. These reformers embodied the eclecticism of the Progressive Era. They were a mixture of evangelical Christians, efficiency evangelists, science and health advocates, suffragists, nativists, and eugenicists. Though largely forgotten in comparison to the more spectacular campaign against alcohol, the movement against cigarettes was strong at the turn of the century. Between 1890 and 1930, fifteen states had enacted laws to ban the sale, manufacture, use, or possession of cigarettes. Twenty-two states and territories considered such legislation, while municipalities carved out further restrictions, with some making it illegal, for example, for women to smoke in public.[51]

Lucy Page Gaston, an activist who had begun public advocacy in the Women's Christian Temperance Movement (WCTU), formed the Anti-Cigarette League, which emulated the Anti-Saloon League's tactics against alcohol. With chapters across the United States and in Canada, the Anti-Cigarette League had over 300,000 members by 1901. Gaston was a formidable woman, strident and steadfast in her opposition to both liquor and tobacco. Though she was easily caricatured as a sanctimonious scold and spinster-suffragette, Gaston also had a sense of humor about her unrelenting hostility to cigarettes. Coarse-featured and over six feet tall, Gaston once said that her qualifications for leading the anti-cigarette crusade lay in her physical resemblance to Abraham Lincoln. If he could free the slaves, she could emancipate the nation from the cigarette scourge.[52] The *Journal of Education* once described her as "making men more trouble than any other woman of her time"—a description she likely would have relished.[53]

Reformers like Gaston ascribed various social and moral failings to cigarettes. For some, cigarettes brought about juvenile delinquency. "The boy who smokes cigarettes need not be anxious about his future," warned David Starr Jordan, a eugenicist biologist and the first president of Stanford University. "He has none." Others expressed more direct fears about how cigarettes would blur the lines demarcating the sexes. Men who smoked cigarettes were described as effeminate, while the relatively few women who did smoke received special scorn and attention.[54] They risked the "premature degeneration of the sex glands," in the words of the homeopath physician-turned-cereal magnate John Harvey Kellogg.[55] Or, worse yet, in "unsexing" women, cigarette smoking would sap them of the very moral superiority that gave them purchase in the public sphere—the superiority that, for women like Gaston and WCTU president Frances Willard, helped to justify their quest for the ballot.

Underlying these concerns about the vitality of men, women, and children was a eugenic fear of the threat to the nation posed by new immigrants. "It's the Dutchmen, Italians, Russians, Turks and Egyptians who smoke cigarettes and they're no good anyhow," remarked the celebrity boxer John Sullivan.[56] For moral reformers steeped in the language of Anglo-Saxonism, cigarettes, more than other forms of tobacco use, posed a dual threat to the nation. Cigarettes were vectors of degeneracy whose use was accelerated by immigration. Their users (not to mention their manufacturers) tended to be urban and foreign-born. The city of New York alone accounted for 25 percent of national cigarette consumption in 1896.[57]

Asserting that cigarettes reduced worker output, some businessmen opposed cigarette use—and made abstention a condition of employment. The contention that cigarettes reduced the efficiency of workers would later reappear in the late-twentieth-century anti-tobacco movement. Between 1914 and 1916, Henry Ford famously published a four-volume pamphlet entitled *The Case against the Little White Slaver.* Ford maintained that he never knowingly hired cigarette smokers—an employment policy he shared with Thomas Edison and Department store magnate John Wanamaker. "We believe that men who do not smoke cigarettes or frequent the saloon can make better automobiles than those that do," read one testimonial from the Cadillac Company cited in Ford's pamphlet.[58] By emphasizing the "efficient" and "scientific" anti-cigarette policies already adopted by big business, Ford reframed abstention rather than consumption as a marker of modernity. Irving Fisher, the Yale economist, likewise suggested that cigarette consumption was irrational. Tobacco "takes away our money but gives us in return little or nothing except illusion and distress," he wrote.[59]

The cigarette posed a threat to the ordering institutions of society, weakening the fiber of the nation, slowing down work, and squandering family resources. It allowed all manner of ideologues to project their fears about a changing nation onto a single concrete object. For xenophobes and nativists, the foreignness of the cigarette was damning; for capitalists, it was its inefficiency—a smoky spanner in the works; for temperance reformers, it was its capacity to dissipate, leading men astray from the obligations of church and family. In the years before the First World War, as the tide of moral reform crested, the cigarette's rise was anything but certain.

The First World War changed the history of the cigarette. The urgency of moral reform waned as the nation mobilized for war. The federal government assumed a leading role as a tobacco merchant as Congress appropriated money to buy cigarettes for soldier's rations, and to subsidize their sale at post exchanges (PXs) and canteens. The War Industries Board (WIB), the agency responsible for overseeing industrial conversion to war, deemed the tobacco industry an "essential industry." This allowed manufacturers to secure preferential access to transportation networks, scarce materials, and, just as importantly, labor.[60] General John J. Pershing, commander of the American Expeditionary Force, regarded cigarettes as being as vital a necessity as food—"tobacco as much as bullets."[61] Able-bodied soldiers were given pouches of smoking tobacco and rolling papers with which they could fashion their own cigarettes. Manufactured, "ready-made" cigarettes were reserved for the infirm, who were sequestered at hospitals and medevac trains (see Figure 1.3).[62]

Figure 1.3 An American Red Cross worker distributes cigarettes to wounded American soldiers, 1918. (American National Red Cross photograph collection / Library of Congress / LC-A6196-6935)

Like a live virus inoculating recipients against a deadly infection, cigarettes were to vaccinate soldiers against more serious types of vice— "intoxicating liquors and lewd women."[63] The YMCA, which only a few years earlier had aligned itself with Gaston in the crusade against the cigarette, became one of its largest distributors during the war. Tobacco companies seized on the fervor to align their product with patriotism, presaging the iconic "Lucky Strike green has gone to war" campaign of the Second World War. American Tobacco Company led manufacturers in establishing "smoke funds." With sponsors ranging from the Forestry Association to the *New York Sun* to the Pennsylvania Railroad, businesses on the American home front raised money to send cigarettes to troops overseas.[64] As Cassandra Tate has argued, the valorization of the cigarette at war made possible its assimilation at home. Wartime songs like "Don't Be a Slacker, Send Some Tobaccer" and "Don't Forget the Smoke" aligned soldiers' cigarette use with sacrifice, portraying civilian support as a home front duty. "So eve'ry time you take a smoke, boys / Send one somewhere in France."[65] When soldiers smoked cigarettes overseas—their minor vice forgiven by the proximity of death—they helped make the world safe for all Americans who took up the habit.

After the war, cigarettes assumed a central role in American consumer culture. There were simply more of them around—between fingers, on posters, in magazines, and between the lips of Hollywood celebrities. In 1915, the United States produced roughly 18 billion cigarettes; in 1920, it produced 47 billion; by 1930, that figure stood at nearly 124 billion.[66] To the consternation of temperance advocates, cigarettes were eclipsing other forms of tobacco consumption. By 1920, cigarettes accounted for 20 percent of total tobacco consumption in the United States, as compared to 7 percent in 1914. In 1927, Kansas became the last state to repeal its prohibitions on the sale of cigarettes.[67]

Amid a rising stock market and a decade of tax cuts, tobacco companies poured millions of dollars into cigarette advertising.[68] Restoration of competition was an intended consequence of the court-ordered dissolution of the Tobacco Trust. The nature of that competition—occurring largely in the realm of advertising among successor firms—was perhaps less desired. American Tobacco, R. J. Reynolds, Liggett, and Lorillard did not compete on retail price; nor did they in buying tobacco at auction. But they did embrace what ATC president George Washington Hill called a program of "quality"—meaning the repetition of phrases, images, or catchwords intended to cement the association of brands and traits in the brains of would-be smokers.[69] Hill, who was installed as president of ATC in 1925, is perhaps best remembered for his stewardship of the company during some of its most iconic ad campaigns. He hired legendary admen Albert Lasker and Edward Bernays—the nephew of Sigmund Freud. In an era in which boyish thinness came to symbolize modernity and emancipation, ATC urged women to "Reach for a Lucky Instead of a Sweet" beginning in 1928. That year, American spent $7 million to advertise the best-selling brand, and was outspent only by General Motors' hawking of that other emblem of modernity and mass production: the personal car.[70] Awash in capital, the modern advertising industry grew alongside the cigarette.

The prewar reproach of woman smokers was not entirely gone: Amelia Earhart lost her job as a columnist at *McCall's* after appearing in an advertisement that claimed, "Lucky Strikes were the cigarettes carried on the 'Friendship' when she crossed the Atlantic."[71] But repeated attempts by cities to restrict where women could smoke in public were beaten back during the 1920s. In short, cigarettes had become domesticated. They were naturalized through wartime service; they lost their foreign accent after the passage of the restrictive Immigration Act of 1924; and they were incessantly advertised as an instrument of individualism in an era of novel, unending consumer choice. By the end of the decade, native and foreign-born Americans living in big, diverse cities and in tiny, homogenous hamlets were united by a national consumer culture that touted cigarettes as central to a range of human motivations, emotions, experiences, and states of being: excitement, relaxation, sensuality, concentration, urbanity, simplicity, health, risk taking, masculinity, and femininity—just to name a few. For many Americans in the 1920s, the cigarette was both a symptom of and a cure for modern times.

"Nothing but Low Prices"[72]

Tobacco farmers also experienced the paradoxical effects of the cigarette. Even though demand for cigarettes was growing, prices for tobacco leaf fell. Part of the problem lay in the inscrutable auction system—a method of selling wrapped so gauzily in the veil of memory that it is easy to forget all the frustration it occasioned.[73] But during the 1920s, the auction was a rapid-fire demonstration of just how little power farmers possessed, and just how much representatives from the companies colluded to keep them that way.

And then there was the growing popularity of cigarettes themselves, inducing more farmers to try their hands at tobacco production while simultaneously making it harder for growers to organize. Between 1911 and 1925, tenancy rose in North Carolina faster than in any other state except Texas, and after 1925 it was third only to Texas and Oklahoma.[74] Induced by the wartime boom in cigarettes and the waning fortunes of weevil-infested cotton, growers planted a record crop in 1920—and witnessed plummeting prices.[75] Production surged over the course of the 1920s, with particularly rapid increases in the Coastal Plain of North Carolina, as well as new tobacco cultivation in South Carolina, Georgia, and Florida. Between 1919 and 1929, pounds produced rose from 476,884,000 to 750,012,000. Tobacco that brought 44 cents per pound in 1919 fetched 18 cents a pound in 1920.[76]

Both the rising demand for cigarettes and the auction method intensified the concentrated power of industry over farmers. The breakup of the Tobacco Trust was supposed to restore competition between firms in the purchasing of leaf. But a tobacco auction was merely a simulacrum of competition, an elaborate staging of supposed rivalry between bidding firms. There was, perhaps, no better metaphor than a tobacco auction for the vagaries of the capitalist marketplace: the lone farmer awaiting a verdict by a corporate cabal on the value of a year's worth of family labor. The destruction of the auction market system was *the* primary objective of the cooperative movement.

Inside the auction warehouse, piles of tobacco were arranged across the floor, with farmers supervising their heaps. Clumps of well-dressed men—the tobacco buyers—huddled around the piles as an auctioneer rapidly sang out an indecipherable chant. "Sweet as honey, honey, gimme thirty, gimme thirty." There were winks, gestures. "Thirty and a quarter." In the blink of an eye—sometimes *by* the blink of an eye—the farmer's crop was sold.[77] The name of the manufacturer who won the auction punctuated the end of the transaction. Later, many mid-century Americans would be unexpectedly familiar with the auction system; American Tobacco Company introduced radio listeners to the most famous auctioneer in the United States, "Speed" Riggs, whose voice rounded out the advertisements for Lucky cigarettes with a signature "Sold American!" singsong refrain. Lightning rapidity characterized these transactions, as auctioneers and warehouse owners took fees for each sale. In the 1930s, rules were imposed to *decrease* the speed of auction to 360 piles an hour—six sales a minute, or ten seconds per pile (see Figure 1.4).[78]

Trailing behind the buyers were the "lightning calculators."[79] After a few seconds of their rapid arithmetic—price per pound by pounds sold—the calculation sheets were run over to the warehouse's bookkeeping office, where a weighing fee, an auction fee, and a warehouse commission were deducted from the farmer's gross earnings. Farmers then dashed over to the pay window, where, in exchange for a ticket of sale, they received cash on the spot. According to one early twentieth-century observer, it was "common for no more than ten minutes to pass between sale and payoff."[80] Meanwhile, warehouse hands helped buyers hoist the purchased tobacco leaf

Figure 1.4 Buyers inspect piles of tobacco at auction, Durham, North Carolina, 1939. (Farm Security Administration-Office of War Information Photograph Collection / Library of Congress/LC-USF33-030673-M5)

onto the flatbeds of trucks headed for manufacturer-owned processing plants. There, the loose-leaf tobacco would be re-dried, de-stemmed, and prepared for aging and several years of storage before its ultimate reconstitution inside of a cigarette.

Only a sliver of the auction floor's action, however, had anything to do with competitive bidding. Instead, the warehouse was a space in which whiteness and wealth mattered a great deal, and where powerful figures in the tobacco industry exerted their dominance over others. Physically, the buyers were in control in suits and hats and with a look of easy assurance; farmers, by contrast, were recognizable for their awkwardness in cheap "town" clothes, or maybe just because they were dressed in overalls.[81] Jim Crow was the real force behind much of the auction floor action. African Americans were employed by the warehouses only in the most menial of positions—arranging tobacco on the floor or hauling it to buyers' trucks. When they sold their tobacco, black farmers generally received less for their crop than whites and were sometimes the victims of auction-floor swindles and speculations.[82] Frequently, poor farmers deemed it prudent to pay their wealthier neighbors a few dollars to market their tobacco for them. Buyers often "shaded up" the price for influential farmers, which is why tenants sometimes asked their landlords to sell in their stead—further reducing the amount of control poor farmers exercised in the marketplace.[83]

Despite the official dissolution of the Tobacco Trust, there was very little competition in bidding at auction. Farmers suspected buyers representing different companies of agreeing to not bid above a predetermined price. Middlemen formally unaffiliated with any of the major companies rounded out the pack of perambulating bidders. But even though they purchased about 25 percent of the leaf on the auction floor, the presence of presumably independent buyers did not add any layer of competition to the process. Frequently, they operated under instructions from manufacturers, just as company buyers did. A 1920 FTC inquiry noted that these dealers often purchased tobacco for multiple companies, which had "a tendency to lower prices in that competition is eliminated in proportion to the number of companies involved."[84] The investigation tepidly concluded that "many of the independent dealers and warehousemen were unequivocal in their statements . . . that they did not observe . . . that there was collusion on the part of manufactures and large dealers in the buying of leaf tobacco." There were, however, "many who expressed a contrary opinion."[85] Five years later, the FTC continued to find domination by the major tobacco firms on the Virginia and Carolina auction markets.[86] Despite these observations, the pro-business FTC of the 1920s was uninterested in pursuing restraint of trade charges against tobacco firms.[87] The FTC, to which farmers might have looked for relief, took a hands-off approach. It acknowledged the possibility of collusion but stopped short of offering relief for farmers.

But, as one agricultural economist pointed out in 1931, formal collusion was hardly necessary.[88] Buyers knew the range of bids offered by their rivals. Because tobacco companies always had at least two or three years' supply as reserve in storage, buyers never purchased to satisfy immediate demand. They were not actually trying to obtain "the best" tobacco in order to improve their own product, or to deny it to their rivals. They were merely trying to secure their leaf requirement as cheaply as possible. Furthermore, manufacturers recognized their own influence on the price of tobacco leaf, and pursued nonaggressive bidding policies in order to maintain certain "rules of the game" by which all companies could buy leaf without actually engaging in a bidding war.[89] As the economist put it, "under these circumstances, actual collusion in fixing bidding limits is hardly necessary—a gentleman's agreement not to 'hog the market' would seem to be ample enough."[90]

Farmers could, of course, refuse to accept a bid—known colloquially as "turning the tag." But the pressures against doing this were so enormous as to render choice a farce. The opportunity costs faced by farmers tended to depress leaf prices by making it hard for farmers to say no to a bid. Regardless of whether the farmer accepted the bid price, he still had to pay auction fees and commissions; he had already sunk money into transportation and perhaps lodging, and he would not want to pay twice. Moreover, tobacco is a perishable crop—it needs to be re-dried after it is cured. Farmers could not simply hold the crop at home if they knew that prices had been low at nearby markets. They had to sell—and fast. Tobacco companies manipulated this uncertainty. "The big companies seem to have a double-barreled purpose," the Raleigh-based *Progressive Farmer* opined in 1920. "By paying nothing but low prices early in the season, they expect to . . . get a large part of their [tobacco] requirement ridiculously cheap." Having forced desperate farmers to sell their harvest early, tobacco buyers "expect to so increase prices to encourage tobacco farmers to plant enough to-bacco in 1921."[91] It's not as if farmers did not know what was happening: they just needed ready cash to pay down their debts. Tobacco companies could not only control prices in the present, but could also encourage overproduction so as to depress prices in the future. All farmers could do was produce—and overproduce, compounding their problems, reducing their payday.

Agriculture and Industry: Conflict and Cooperation in the 1920s

Tobacco farmers knew the auction system did not serve their interests. It thrived only because they needed the immediate cash to service the substantial debts they incurred over the previous year.[92] Just as government action during the First World War rehabilitated the cigarette during and after the war, so too did war expand the capacity of the government to act on behalf of the tobacco farmers. The First World War emboldened rural reformers to imagine greater coordination and planning for agriculture—the kind of coordination that could do away with the irrationality and chaos of the auction floor. The war made large-scale economic organization seem possible, while giving rise to a coterie of agricultural reformers, writers, and economists who pushed for ever-greater order in the marketing of agricultural commodities.[93]

Postwar economic nationalism hit farmers hard. American and British embrace of protectionist trade policies during the 1920s crippled tobacco growers, who relied heavily on sales for export.[94] After the war, overseas dollars dried up, and with them foreign tobacco markets. The United Kingdom was the tobacco farmer's most important overseas customer: British men smoked at higher rates than their American counterparts, and they had a particular taste for American flue-cured cigarettes. However, an interwar policy of "imperial preference" had special significance for tobacco as Canada, India, and Australia began competing in bright leaf production to satisfy British cigarette demand. At the same time, U.S. trade protectionism meant that American farmers had to buy more expensive finished goods from merchants. When farmers cursed the protective tariff for helping manufacturers at the expense of agriculture, they said more than they realized. During the 1920s, U.S. economic policy not only strained export markets for farmers. It also created new competitors in the global marketplace.

From postwar price highs, agriculture's descent into crisis was swift and spectacular. The prices that prevailed in late 1919 and early 1920 made the harvest of 1920 the most costly on record to produce. Slackened European demand and a postwar business recession created a panic just as farmers were bringing an expensive bumper harvest to market. Between July and December 1920, the average price of the ten leading farm crops fell by 57 percent; in May 1921, prices were just a third of what they were the previous June, and by November of 1921 prices had fallen below the 1913 level.[95] Farmers were worse off than city dwellers and wage earners as their purchasing power declined by 40 percent and commodity prices fell more rapidly than other costs and taxes.[96] Newspapers ran stories of crops left to rot in fields as labor and transportation costs exceeded returns from sales.[97]

Antagonism between industry and agriculture could be felt at the highest levels of government. Secretary of Agriculture Henry C. Wallace and Secretary of Commerce Herbert Hoover disagreed sharply, publicly, and personally over how best to organize the ailing agricultural economy. Wallace's directly interventionist vision, eventually embodied in the McNary-Haugen plan of 1927, achieved influence only after his death.[98] Meanwhile, Hoover's single-minded focus on developing commodity cooperatives, eschewing direct federal intervention in favor of the development of the associational state, had more widespread cachet among farmers than anything proposed by Wallace during his tenure.

Wallace and Hoover had more in common than either would admit. The pair of Iowans were administrative imperialists; they guarded, defended, and expanded their bureaucracies wherever possible. Wallace wanted his Department of Agriculture (USDA) to take a more activist role—to generate agricultural policy with the same gusto and reliability with which it produced agricultural censuses and scientific information about the composition of fertilizer or the best methods for controlling nematode infestation.[99]

The Bureau of Agricultural Economics (BAE), established in 1922, produced study after study proposing to remedy rural problems through the application of social science expertise.[100] The bureau served as kind of a postgraduate fellowship for recipients of advanced degrees from expanded Agricultural Economics and Rural Sociology programs, as Cornell and the

University of Wisconsin began to mint more Ph.Ds. in these fields. These social scientists pioneered market-forecasting and reporting techniques, issued reports to farmers about market conditions, and undertook an array of studies on nearly every step in the crop production process—from seed selection to product distribution. Perhaps most importantly, the BAE was a source of policy innovation: agricultural economists at the bureau helped to prepare the first McNary-Haugen bill in 1924.

Hoover, by contrast, envisioned a very limited role for the USDA in creating policy for the farm, much less contributing to discussions of national productivity. In a 1920 memo to the head of a congressional committee on administrative reorganization, Hoover explained his limited vision for the USDA: "the functions of the Department of Agriculture should end when production on the farm is complete and movement therefrom starts, and at that point the activities of the Department of Commerce should begin." Hoover wanted agricultural marketing work to be conducted in the Department of Commerce, believing that the USDA should merely "tell the farmer what he can best produce based on soil, climatic and other cultural conditions, and the Department of Commerce should tell him how best to dispose of it."[101] Agriculture should supply the brawn; Commerce, the brain.

Fundamentally, Hoover and Wallace differed on the question of whether the federal government should come to the direct aid of farmers whose crop prices were plummeting. In Wallace's corner were the Congressional Farm Bloc and the American Farm Bureau Federation (AFBF). These groups, predominantly representing Midwestern grain farmers, favored the establishment of a federal export corporation to purchase surplus agricultural commodities and sell them abroad. As proposed by the McNary-Haugen legislation, farmers would be paid a high, government determined domestic price, while the low export price would be set by the international market. Hoover, however, opposed such price fixing—despite (or because of) the fact that he oversaw price fixing during the war. Instead he advocated the cooperative as a tool for enabling farmers to bargain for better prices and eliminating market inefficiencies. Wallace was just as opposed to Hoover's zeal for cooperatives. Deriding the "over-enthusiastic persons who have held [cooperative marketing] up as a panacea for all the ills from which farmers are suffering," Wallace insisted that "the relationship of the government to cooperation should be one of service. It should help the farmers market their crops not by doing the work but by supplying the information which the farmers cannot get for themselves."[102] The agriculture secretary viewed co-operatives as one tool—and not even the most powerful one—for confronting farm problems.[103]

Southern farmers grew cotton and tobacco, two crops with large export markets. Their representatives in Congress were not part of the Farm Bloc, and the AFBF was, as yet, mostly absent from the region. Southerners were wary of proposals that might curtail foreign markets.[104] For most of the decade, southern farm leaders embraced Hoover's vision for the organization of agriculture. Subverting the auction system through cooperation was seen as a potential source of power, raising prices while also invigorating local democracy.[105] Unfortunately for southern farmers participating in cooperative ventures, higher commodity prices would require precisely the kind of direct government intervention that Hoover detested.

Cooperation—or "Fighting the Devil with Fire"[106]

Organization in the tobacco belt did not come from Washington. It came from lawyers and rural leadership. An active farm press, reformers based at land grant colleges, and the agricultural extension services collaborated with "practical," "business-minded," and "progressive" farmers, with whom the task of organization could be shared. Long-standing antipathy toward the Tobacco Trust, warehousemen, and speculators added rhetorical heat to calls for cooperation. Tobacco cooperatives had been tried before, and had failed before—most spectacularly in the Black Patch Tobacco Wars, which set fields ablaze in Kentucky and Tennessee as farmer vigilantes punished growers suspected of selling to the Trust rather than pledging their crop to the cooperative.[107] But at the beginning of the decade, farm leadership was hopeful.

In 1922, the Capper-Volstead Act was passed. This "Magna Carta of cooperation" exempted farm cooperatives from the Clayton and Sherman Anti-Trust Acts. The Act's supporters saw it as creating the legal architecture upon which farmers could organize and stand tall against industry, much as the labor movement had sought to do with industrial workers. As Arthur Capper, the Kansas senator and Farm Bloc member who co-sponsored the legislation, put it, the bill was intended "to give to the

farmer the same right to bargain collectively that is already enjoyed by corporations."[108] Even when they were busted into smaller parts, corporations
held the structural advantage: they spoke with one voice, possessed intri-
cate bureaucracies capable of long-range planning, and were under little
time pressure to buy tobacco at any given auction. Farmers, meanwhile,
were more unruly than capital. They had to be corralled and pledged to a
cooperative. And unlike corporations—whose nature and scope were
changing but whose reliability for aggregating capital was not in doubt—
cooperatives had to be created from the promises of debt-strapped farmers
living across vast geographic expanses. The cooperative movement, as
Robert Penn Warren's character Percy Munn observed, was first about getting names on pieces of paper.

Aaron Sapiro did not take down names, but he did draw up the papers.
The California lawyer was the decade's foremost evangelist for cooperative
marketing.[109] Versed in American and European agricultural reform
schemes, Sapiro spent the 1920s crisscrossing the United States, organizing
commodity growers into cooperative marketing associations.[110] His "California Plan" was based on the successful experience of Sunkist Fruit, a
grower-owned cooperative that had succeeded in increasing the price of
citrus. The cornerstone of his plan was the cooperative's monopoly control
of a single commodity. By controlling the product, specialty cooperatives
could dictate prices to buyers—not the other way around, as was so often
the case. "Iron-clad" contracts would bind growers to the cooperative.
Defectors—those who went behind the organization's back and sold to middlemen or processors—would be zealously pursued in courts. Only by concentrating their own power could farmers meet the concentrated power of
capital. It was "collective bargaining with a big stick," in the words of one
agricultural economist.[111]

Sapiro was a polarizing figure within farm circles. Many applauded the
"Sapiro method" as the application of scientific principles to agricultural
organization—a thoroughly modern and businesslike tactic. Others, in
comments with anti-Semitic undertones, criticized Sapiro as a meddlesome
outsider who peddled a one-size-fits-all approach to local marketing problems of which he was ignorant.[112] Whatever personal reservations North
Carolina reformers harbored about an individual so different from themselves dissipated in the exigency of material need.

Tobacco markets opened low in the late summer of 1920. The Extension Service, a new government agency founded six years earlier, saw opportunity in the crisis. Housed within the USDA, Extension's mission was to organize rural life through the dissemination of information conducted at the land grant colleges. Extension agents organized a meeting of tobacco farmers at North Carolina State College in Raleigh, hoping to explain and persuade the angry mass of the virtues of the California Plan.[113]

The South's leading farm publication, the Raleigh-based *Progressive Farmer*, had high hopes for a tobacco cooperative, conceiving of it as a coordinating, modernizing force for the region. The "farmers of the South" could learn the lessons of union labor, which had recently "demonstrated in a thousand ways . . . the power of effective organization." For rural reformers, organized agriculture was not so different from organized labor. Both had to coordinate their market efforts in organizations designed "not for talk but for business. They organize really for the specific purpose of *organized marketing*—'collective bargaining' on what they have for sale, which is their labor."[114] The *Progressive Farmer* argued on behalf of economic collectives without ever questioning that the basic orientation of the American economy should serve business. Organization could help farmers simply become better businessmen.[115]

Clarence Poe, the *Progressive Farmer*'s editor and publisher, was the most indefatigable booster of cooperation. Beginning in 1920, nearly every issue of his weekly paper devoted ink to the cooperative cause.[116] Poe's own enthusiasm for cooperative marketing was influenced by his travels in Europe. There, he was particularly impressed with Danish milk co-ops.[117] As an intellectual, Poe prided himself on his cosmopolitanism and his familiarity with the latest social science research conducted by rural sociologists and economists at North Carolina State and nearby Chapel Hill. Co-owned by Poe, a prominent member of the Populist Farmers' Alliance, would-be Democratic senator Josiah Bailey, and two professors at North Carolina State, the *Progressive Farmer* was an expression of southern progressivism: its faith in white supremacy born of the same commitment to science as its endorsement of diversified farming or cooperative marketing.

To set up a tobacco cooperative, Poe went directly to the source. He asked Sapiro to come to North Carolina to draw up incorporation papers, to which the lawyer enthusiastically assented.[118] Sapiro made good use of his time in the state. He helped establish the tobacco cooperative and also laid the groundwork for the passage of the statute that legalized cooperative marketing in North Carolina, freeing the organization from restraint of trade prosecution. "The only people in the United States who may and who have the power to organize without limitation are the farmers of the United States," Sapiro proclaimed. "Only the farmer can have a complete unlimited monopoly and still be in any measure within the law."[119] When Congress passed the Capper-Volstead Act in 1922, tobacco farmers were already organized and incorporated. As legal historian Victoria Saker Woeste writes, cooperative legislation in the 1920s "granted farmers a privilege that no other group of entrepreneurs received for more than a decade: recognition of the legality of collective action in the market."[120] Farmers may have been freed from antitrust restrictions, but farmer cooperatives were not allowed to require their members to restrict output—the very thing they would need to do to counter the monopoly on price that their antagonists in the Tobacco Trust wielded.[121]

In 1922, the Tri-State Tobacco Growers Cooperative Association (TGCA) was incorporated as a nonstock, nonprofit corporation in Raleigh. It was clear what it would need to do to succeed: subvert the auction system of marketing. After paying a $3.00 membership fee (frequently written as an IOU), farmers delivered their crop to Cooperative warehouses, where it was weighed and graded by organization officials. Growers received an advance payment, financed through credit extended to the Cooperative, for each grade they delivered. Farmers continued to receive payments throughout the rest of the marketing season in proportion to the amount of tobacco sold, regardless of how much buyers paid for it.[122]

The TGCA's goal was the destruction of the hated auction system. To achieve it required suasion and threat. Local leaders—politicians, professors, writers, businessmen—waged an incessant membership campaign, creating a sense of emergency and of possibility. Describing the sign-up campaign as a "crusade," Carl C. Taylor, a professor of agricultural economics at North Carolina State College, recalled that "all stores and other places of business were closed during the mass meetings" of the sign-up campaign. And at these mass meetings, all of the human reserves were tapped as well. "Agricultural extension officials, county agents, . . . teachers, college professors, publishers of agricultural journals, newspapermen,

lawyers, bankers and merchants were used as speakers" all over the state of
North Carolina. These meetings mostly took place in the "Old Belt"—the
hilly Piedmont towns of Virginia and North Carolina, where farmers were
more likely to be white.

Creating a culture of respectability around the Cooperative was not
enough for it to succeed. It needed control—control of output, and control
of members. This "orderly marketing" meant that farmers would not
have to accept a price dictated in the hurly-burly of the auction house as
other desperate farmers—market competitors, really—awaited their auction.[123] As Sapiro put it, "the one great aim of Co-operative marketing is to
abolish the individual dumping of farm products" and replace it with "the
merchandising of farm products." Control and order were keywords for
Sapiro: control of the harvest, control of members, and the controlled
"movement of crops into the markets of the world at such times and in such
quantities that these markets can absorb the crops at fair prices."[124] The
TGCA also embraced Sapiro's "iron-clad" contracts, which bound members
to the Co-op for five years. The TGCA pursued a vigorous policy of contract
enforcement, bringing lawsuits against hundreds of contract breakers. The
organization's newspaper, the *Tri-State Tobacco Grower*, frequently published
articles gloating over the Association's courtroom success against farmers.
A news release from 1922 is characteristic:

> It takes a long time to reach all contract breakers and court actions
> are slow, but after our association gets through with contract breakers
> they will hesitate a long time before breaking faith again with our
> 80,000 loyal members who have had enough of the auction gang, and
> are banded together for a square deal and fair prices *every year*.[125]

Members were instructed to police their local associations and to report
contract breakers to the Association's legal department. "You can do your
part in this collection work by helping the collection agent find every man
in his territory," members were told. "Loyal members can help by giving
information in detail concerning all violators."[126] While perhaps undermining the neighborly virtues of cooperation touted by idealists, the Co-
op's litigiousness meant nothing without the power of the state behind it.
The North Carolina Supreme Court rendered the broadest ruling in the

nation on the constitutionality of the Sapiro-made Marketing Act. In its 1923 decision, *Tobacco Growers Co-operative Association v. Jones,* members were deemed within their rights to vigorously pursue contract breakers because members assumed "all the risks" of the cooperative:

> They are asking no assistance from the public treasury. They are forcing no one to join, and they are exacting no inordinate prices for their product. They are associating themselves as authorized by the statute, like other persons, and they have signed mutual and fair agreements among themselves which will be futile unless those who have signed such agreements can be held to abide by the terms of their contracts.[127]

While many of the suits initiated by the TGCA against noncooperating members were settled out of court, the Association won nearly all of its legal battles.[128] It was a far cry from night riding, but the Cooperative sought to make sure that contract breakers knew they would be punished.

Farmer cooperatives were creations of the states in which they were incorporated.[129] But they also fit into Hoover's political vision of associationalism, which encouraged a close relationship between private industry and government. The War Finance Corporation (WFC) converted to peacetime operation by making loans to agricultural institutions. It loaned the TGCA $30 million, which the organization used to pay growers' advances before the first sale of the marketing season.[130] According to USDA records, during the peak of Association activity in 1921–1923, the WFC loaned more money to tobacco cooperatives than to any other commodity groups, save cotton and livestock organizations. The TGCA also secured credit from the National City Bank of New York, as well as local banks.[131] At least for a while, the Co-op seemed like a good credit risk.

Co-op officials were particularly solicitous of the support of area businessmen. Local commerce, Association officials reasoned, should be sympathetic to the cooperative movement because businesses "depend largely upon and are vitally interested in the success of the producer."[132] When the TGCA appointed a Richmond banker as its director, it seemed as if its respectability was assured. "Every real Big Man in the United States is in favor of Co-operative marketing," explained the *Tri-State Tobacco Grower.* "Only 'pinhookers' and men who make money out of the 'auction' system are against it. Any grower who does not sign up is helping the enemy of the farmers. Tell them to fight WITH you and not against you. Sign them up before it's too late."[133]

But the biggest men, the littlest men, and middlemen fought the organization. Despite the legal advantages endowed upon the cooperative form, the TGCA never came close to achieving monopoly control over the handling of the tobacco crop. And perhaps even more ominously, its first year was its best year: its control declined every year until its demise in 1926. Table 1.1 illustrates the declining percentage of deliveries that the Association handled.

Sapiroism worked well enough in California, where barriers to entry were high and production expansion by fruit and nut growers could only be achieved through considerable capital investment. Tobacco acreage, on the other hand, could be increased with little more than a promise of a share of the crop. Because the capital requirements of sharecropping tobacco were virtually nonexistent, pounds of tobacco produced by sharecroppers and tenants undermined the Cooperative's monopoly control of the harvest. Indeed, during the TGCA's operation, tobacco acreage was rapidly expanding in Georgia, which was not even organized under the cooperative plan.[134] Farmers in Georgia, like new entrants into the tobacco field across the rest of the South, frequently turned to tobacco because they were not making ends meet farming cotton. The idea of a commodity cooperative presupposed some stability in the number of farmers for any

Table 1.1 Percentage of Flue-Cured Tobacco Produced in North Carolina, South Carolina, and Virginia Controlled by the TGCA

Year	Percentage of Crop Controlled
1922	35
1923	28
1924	23
1925	15

Source: John Hanna, "Agricultural Cooperation in Tobacco," *Law and Contemporary Problems*, Vol. 1, No. 3 (1934): 317.

given commodity—a closed shop of agricultural production. But it was impossible to control the harvest of rapidly expanding commercial cultivation. Across much of the Southeast, it was common for farmers in all tenure categories, from landowners down to sharecroppers, to grow both cotton and tobacco. For this reason, it may have been impossible for the TGCA to even know if it was controlling the majority of tobacco produced.[135] Control of supply was elusive.

The law empowered the Association to sue for damages for pledged crops undelivered. But it could not force anybody to join the Association in the first place. In fact, tenants could frequently be coerced by their creditors into *not* joining the Association. Debt holders needed lump-sum payments, provided under the auction method, to pay their creditors; the smaller, multiple advances paid by the Association were not sufficient to free growers of debt, however temporarily. Indebted farmers who did pledge their crop to the Association were subject to lawsuits by their creditors. Landlords who were *themselves* members of the organization disputed the right of their tenants and debtors to pledge their crops, believing that they were owed payment in full. One merchant-landlord described his dissatisfaction at the "widow's mite" of an advance offered by the Co-op. "Please let me urge you to pay nothing if you cannot pay three to five times the original advance," the landlord, who was also a member of the Association, wrote officials. "Lots of people with whom I do business owe me. They need the money and I need the money."[136] Indebted men could not be controlled by the Association; they were already spoken for.

In accordance with the Sapiro method, the TGCA took a hard line against overextended tenants. It was up to tenants to fulfill their obligation to the Co-op and to "make the necessary arrangements with creditors and landlords to enable them to carry out this agreement." If creditors or tenants sold pledged tobacco at auction in an attempt to pay down debt, they would be found "in breach of the tenants' contracts" and subject to suit.[137] There was thus an incentive to prevent tenants from becoming members of the Cooperative in the first place: there was a good chance they would have to be pursued via litigation at a later date. As it was put in a 1921 letter to the Association's director, "Our greatest problems seem now to center around these six letters: T-E-N-A-N-T."[138] Unsurprisingly, the greatest amount of contract breaking occurred in areas where tenancy was the highest, namely, in North Carolina's tenant-heavy and heavily African-American Coastal Plain. This area also produced more tobacco than any other region of the state. Debt and tenancy posed insuperable obstacles to cooperation.

And the Co-op also faced outright sabotage. Warehouse owners, themselves sometimes creditors and always threatened by the Cooperative, campaigned for its demise. Auction house owners made contract breaking even more attractive by occasionally shading up the price for farmers that went around the Co-op. Warehousemen also fomented suspicion and gossip by alleging malfeasance on the part of TGCA officials. Detractors rarely missed an opportunity to comment on the Association's "California Jew" lawyer, its high-salaried employees, and the profits a few officials made on the re-drying of members' tobacco.[139] The allegation of mismanagement held some traction: the Association paid for the use of re-drying plants owned and operated by two of its directors. While the re-drying charges may have been standard, the two officials nevertheless made a hefty profit off the venture.[140] By 1925 Clarence Poe, that great cheerleader of the grower cooperation, could only muster whimpering, half-apologetic enthusiasm to demoralized and increasingly disloyal members. "Now to us the most encouraging thing about the . . . Association," Poe wrote, "is that while it does make some mistakes (who would expect a brand new sort of organization not to?), it does learn from its mistakes."[141]

But what was the point of offering the organization another chance? In many cases, cigarette manufacturers simply refused to buy from the Co-op. As a commodity, tobacco was fundamentally different than fruit and nuts, Sapiro's cooperative showpieces. Manufacturers kept several years' worth of tobacco in storage, an unspecified amount of leaf of unspecified grade—and the grades themselves were vague and unstable. For instance, the Imperial Tobacco Company and the American Tobacco Company simply did not patronize the Association. R. J. Reynolds and Liggett & Myers were notable among the big firms for making any large purchases from it.[142] The opacity and asymmetry of the tobacco market meant that virtually no amount of cooperation could force the companies to bargain.

———

The demise of the TGCA did not come as a shock. Without monopoly—or even majority—control over the tobacco harvest, commodity cooperatives posed a classic collective action problem. The Cooperative only worked if a majority of growers pledged to sell to it exclusively, thus empowering the organization to dictate a price to tobacco companies. But if the Cooperative succeeded in bargaining the price of tobacco upward, more and more farmers were tempted to defect by selling outside the cooperative at the auction market. The asymmetries within the tobacco trade—many scattered sellers, few concentrated buyers, Jim Crow, and a tenure system in which landlords and creditors controlled the tobacco of tenants—enabled the sabotage of the organizational effort. An alliance of manufacturers and middlemen was also able to undermine the monopolistic aspirations of the Cooperative by promising high prices to influential growers who defected themselves or instructed their tenants to do so.

But in failure, the TCGA left a legacy among Bright Leaf growers. In defeating the Cooperative, large landowners and warehousemen swung the political center of gravity toward the eastern part of the tobacco belt. Their support was crucial for the success of the supply reduction policies that were to come with the New Deal. The Cooperative's failure highlighted what was needed in order for agricultural reforms to succeed: wealthy landlords had to believe that allying with the government served them. As importantly, the process of organizing and administering the Co-op necessitated a crucial expansion of institutional capacity within the Extension Service and the Co-op's "locals"—the county-level clubs that evangelized the cooperative method.

As the cigarette became more central to American cultural life, the producers of cigarette tobacco were shunted even further to the margins. The year that the Tri-State went into receivership—1926—was the most profitable on record for the American Tobacco Company, a triumph over even its "banner year of 1925."[143] That same year, the FTC's investigation of the tobacco industry's efforts to destroy the TGCA yielded only a reproach of the Cooperative itself.[144] The turbulence of the 1920s taught that the cigarette's popularity was no guarantee of prosperity on the farm; neither was the enlightened goodwill of state officials in support of cooperative marketing. What farmers needed was not cooperation but compulsion.

2

Tobacco's New Deal

Living hand-to-mouth as most of our farmers live—both tenants and operating owners—the problems of farming as a business are well-nigh insolvable.
—Samuel Huntington Hobbs, 1930

"The sale of new and used automobiles to [tobacco] farmers in the Winston-Salem area has also registered a marked up-turn. One dealer in the low priced field reports sales of new cars to farmers at 150% above last year, while the sale of used cars has more than doubled."
—*Wall Street Journal*, December 1934

THE DAY AFTER he took the oath of office, Franklin Delano Roosevelt called a special session of Congress, an unusual measure commensurate with the unusual crisis the country faced. Bank failures, soaring unemployment, and commodity prices hovering around post–Civil War levels—nothing less than a national emergency in Roosevelt's framing—impelled the Congress to action, launching the flurry of legislation of the New Deal's first hundred days. The immediate purpose of the special session was the passage of banking legislation, the first of the New Deal measures to become law. But as lawmakers descended upon Washington, two men in Roosevelt's inner circle seized the chance to forge a New Deal for farmers.

Henry A. Wallace was perhaps the most utopian of the New Dealers. To the bemusement of his colleagues, the secretary of agriculture (and son of Harding and Coolidge's secretary of agriculture) dabbled in Theosophy and eastern religion. But the Iowa newspaper editor and statistician was also a pragmatist, and he saw opportunity in the special session. Wallace and Rex Tugwell, another economist who would have a hand in nearly every aspect of New Deal planning, approached Roosevelt with a proposition for agricultural legislation.[1] Within two days, representatives of more than fifty farm organizations had made their way to Washington, hopeful that the new administration might finally go far enough to strike at the root of what ailed agriculture: overproduction.

This "paradox of plenty" was intelligible only outside the economic orthodoxies that insisted that markets correct themselves over the long term. "When too much cotton and wheat and pork are forced into trade channels," Secretary of Agriculture Henry Wallace explained, "prices received by farmers dwindle to levels so low that they themselves cannot buy the goods which only workers manufacture." Wallace, who once proclaimed that "we need a 'heart trust' even more than we need a 'brain trust,'" saw a national pathology in the dislocation of agriculture.[2] The drying up of farmer and labor purchasing power continued a vicious cycle in which "factories close down and employees are thrown out of work," accelerating the spiral of "unemployment, falling prices, bank failures, bankruptcies, hunger, and suffering." Fundamentally, a surplus of labor and farm commodities had broken "the Nation's economic machine . . . just as surely as a human stomach gets acute indigestion if too much food is forced into it."[3]

Too much tobacco clogged the throat of commerce. Despite the political turbulence of the 1920s, prices of flue-cured tobacco never fell below 20¢/lb. during the decade. During the Depression, the prices of the chaotic Co-op years seemed positively lavish. Massive overproduction in 1931 sent prices tumbling to just 8.4¢/lb.[4] The only thing that saved farmers from an even worse fate the following year was their inability to finance a large crop—hardly a testament to the economy. As Roosevelt took office, flue-cured growers pocketed just under $35 million, compared to $93 four years earlier.[5]

The Depression demonstrated what the cooperative movement did not: the interrelatedness of the agricultural, financial, and business sectors. The Tri-State Tobacco Growers Cooperative Association (TGCA) failed because of the determined opposition of rich and large farmers, warehousemen, and bankers. The New Deal's tobacco program would succeed because those groups were invested in the stability that government-supported tobacco provided them. As the experience of the Co-op had shown, the participation of the largest growers in a tobacco program was essential to the success of any price-raising scheme. These elites were brought into the administration of the tobacco program from its earliest days. They did not "capture" the agricultural bureaucracy; rather, they helped to shape it.

Agriculture and Recovery

The National Industrial Recovery Act (NIRA) and the Agricultural Adjustment Act were the twin pillars of early New Deal recovery efforts. Both were passed as part of the flurry of legislation during Roosevelt's first hundred days. Both would be invalidated by the Supreme Court before Roosevelt's second-term reelection landslide. The NIRA and the Agricultural Adjustment Act were philosophically conjoined as well, reflecting a belief that "ruinous competition" was a root pathology of American capitalism. Too much competition for consumers caused senseless price wars and predatory business practices. It caused workers to compete with each other too vigorously in the sale of their labor, immiserating them in a race to the bottom of wages. It caused farmers to overproduce, driving down commodity prices. For drafters of New Deal recovery legislation, the problems faced by farmers and laborers, producers and consumers, were connected, a seamless whole of surplus in the face of want.[6]

The New Dealers hoped that what Wallace described as "economic indigestion" could be remedied through economic planning. The NIRA was the centerpiece of this centralizing effort for industry. Envisioning a collaborative relationship between business, government, and labor, the NIRA addressed cutthroat competitive practices through the establishment of sector-specific "codes of fair competition." These codes established maximum hours and minimum wages for workers by industry, and allowed unions to collectively bargain. Business, for its part, would enjoy a suspension of antitrust enforcement. While small and mid-sized businesses chafed especially under the constraints the law imposed, the industrial planning was not without recent example. The NIRA drew upon the precedent of the World War I–era War Industries Board (WIB). Hugh Johnson, the chief of the National Recovery Administration (NRA), the agency created by the NIRA to oversee industrial policy, had served on the WIB, working especially closely with that agency's chairman, Bernard Baruch.[7] For New Deal planners, the economic theory behind the NIRA was that it would facilitate national recovery by boosting workers' purchasing power, which would

Figure 2.1 The NRA's Blue Eagle, clutching the gears and volts of industry in its talons. (Graphic of NRA Blue Eagle, ca. 1933; Records of the National Recovery Administration [NRA], 1927–1937; Records Group 9 (NWDNS-9-X); National Archives Administration)

then redound to industry through an uptick in sales, trade, and production.[8]

The NRA has been characterized as the United States' closest brush with the kind of corporatism that animated nationalist experimentation in Italy and Germany.[9] Johnson was an avowed admirer of Mussolini, and possessed a flair for the iconography of the muscular state. In raising enthusiasm for the agency, Johnson celebrated the agency's signature Blue Eagle emblem with an extraordinary flurry of nationalist fanfare: parades, motorcades, mass meetings (see Figure 2.1).[10] "May God have mercy on the man or group of men who attempt to trifle with this bird," Johnson thundered at a St. Louis rally in 1933.[11]

Divine judgment is unknowable to historians, but in less than two years, a group of nine men hunted down the blue bird. In *Schechter Poultry Corp. v. United States,* the Supreme Court unanimously found the NIRA unconstitutional.[12] NRA codes ran afoul of the Constitution in two ways: by improperly constraining intrastate commerce, and through the improper delegation of Congress's powers to the executive. Despite Roosevelt's hopes for an extension of a modified industrial program, few in the ranks of business or labor were pained by the loss of a system seen as cumbersome, anticompetitive, and unfair.[13]

Yet another New Deal experiment in corporatist planning was to have a longer, more successful run. The Agricultural Adjustment Act was both longer lived and more beloved than the NRA (see Figure 2.2). The "Triple-A" was drafted with the same economic principles as the NIRA—indeed, it was drafted first. And some aspects of industrial recovery, such as the antitrust exemption, had been applicable to agriculture since the passage of the Capper-Volstead Act a decade earlier. Rex Tugwell had a hand in the drafting of both the Agricultural Adjustment Act and the NIRA. A broad-minded heterodox economist, having traveled to France to observe its system of agricultural production and to the Soviet Union to learn from its experiment in industrial planning,[14] Tugwell had long advocated wage and price controls set through coordination among government, business, agriculture, and labor.[15] The nature of the agricultural depression of the 1920s—as well as the decade's faltering, abortive attempts at cooperation—demonstrated that stronger measures were needed to restore balance to the relationship between industry and agriculture.

The remedy to overproduction in agriculture was supply control in the form of what was known as the "voluntary domestic allotment plan." Growers of "basic commodities"—wheat, cotton, corn, hogs, rice, tobacco, and milk—were to receive benefit payments on the condition of their taking acreage out of production. Just as minimum wages were a direct stimulant to workers' purchasing power, so too were the benefit payments for contracting farmers. Although it was part of national planning from the earliest days of the Roosevelt administration, the Agricultural Adjustment Act did not become law until May of 1933. The immediate goal of the legislation was to raise prices of farm commodities and the incomes of farmers. But the larger aim of the Act was to restore "balance" between industry and agriculture, a concept given technical definition as "parity."[16] Parity was a statistical formulation—a ratio of what a farmer received for his products versus what he paid for goods and services. It was devised as an explicit attempt to achieve "equality for agriculture" vis-à-vis industry. Because the years 1909–1914 were particularly good for farmers—the Golden Age of

Figure 2.2 The Agricultural Adjustment Administration toots its own horn, 1934. (*Agricultural Adjustment: A Report of Administration of the Agricultural Adjustment Act, May 1933 to February 1934* (Washington, D.C.: United States Government Printing Office, 1934), page 264)

agriculture, as that era was retrospectively called during the 1920s—it was selected as the basis for establishing the parity ratio.

The exception was tobacco. Had such a chronological range been applied to the crop, tobacco growers would have been locked into a parity price lower than what they received during 1932. And thus the base period of 1919-1929 was applied to tobacco alone, which allowed growers to realize the benefits of that decade's increased cigarette consumption, as well as the brief period of higher prices secured by the cooperative movement.[17] Use of the 1919-1929 period raised the base price level for tobacco farmers nearly 60 percent over the prewar base calculation.[18] Parity for farmers was to be achieved through direct payments to those who took part in acreage reduction programs. These payments were financed through a "processing tax" levied on the firms that first bought and processed covered commodities, including tobacco.

New Deal understandings of the organic connection between industry and agriculture were evident not only in the concept of parity, or the favored metaphors of Wallace and Tugwell. The first administrators of the Agricultural Adjustment Administration (AAA) and the NRA shared a long professional history and spent the 1920s as the nation's foremost evangelists of the parity concept. And both had served on the WIB, the agency comprised of businessmen that oversaw industrial production and distribution during the First World War.[19] George Peek was selected by Wallace to be the AAA's first administrator. Peek's counterpart at the NRA, Hugh Johnson, had succeeded him as president of the Moline Plow Company, an Illinois-based farm implement firm. As executives of a farm equipment company, Peek and Johnson were vitally concerned with whether farmers had the money necessary to make capital investments in plows and tractors.

During the agricultural depression that followed the First World War, the two men had become the foremost exponents of the concept of "fair exchange value"—synonymous with "parity." Peek and Johnson unveiled their plan at a 1922 national agricultural conference convened by Wallace's father, Henry Cantwell.[20] *Equality for Agriculture,* a pamphlet produced by the two men after the 1922 conference, was a call to arms. Farmers were instructed to urge their congressmen to "support legislative action" in favor of the parity principle.[21] The parity concept was central to the McNary-Haugen legislation, introduced every year from 1924 to 1928 and championed by the Farm Bureau.[22] The McNary-Haugen bill was the white whale of the Farm Bloc: passed by Congress only to be twice vetoed by Coolidge. It would have raised prices on farm goods by having the government buy surplus production at high prices and then dump the surplus on world markets. Peek and Johnson would leave the AAA and the NRA within a year of their appointment, both men apparently unwilling to compromise with their ideologically diverse colleagues. But the parity concept would stand as a testament to corporatist notions of national economic balance for nearly the rest of the twentieth century, guiding U.S. Department of Agriculture (USDA) assessments of farm welfare, quantifying where farmers belonged in the organic whole of the economy.[23]

Two Months in North Carolina

Achieving parity by controlling supply was a task of monumental proportions. It required the deployment of thousands of government officials spread over the expanse of the United States. And it required the consent of millions of farmers, who signed contracts in which they agreed to curtail production on the promise of payment from the government. This was no small feat: the concept of agricultural adjustment ran directly counter to the economic intuitions of producers, who had never before experienced the price-raising benefits of sustained collective action. Farmers, like the tobacco growers who had witnessed the previous decade's experiments in cooperative marketing, had made it a practice to produce to the hilt.

Farmers all over the nation were eager for help from Washington. At the time of FDR's inauguration, the fortunes of agriculture had slid further relative to industry, such that "the exchange value of farm products for industrial goods had fallen to 50 percent of the prewar average."[24] For tobacco farmers, the situation was acute. Receipt from the sale of tobacco had cratered during the first three years of the Depression, falling from $286 million in 1929 to $107 million in 1932. Adding fire to farmers' anger was the fact that during the same period, tobacco manufacturers saw profits rise to a combined $146 million in 1932, a significant increase compared with their $134 million profit in 1929.[25] Cigarettes, it would seem, were depression-proof. Tobacco was not.

The drive for production control had its dramatic moments: barnstorming rallies and the shutdown of tobacco auction houses. Cooling these tensions required the cooperation of agricultural officials and prominent growers—a mutual dependence that privileged elite control over broad-based democracy. Fewer farmers produced tobacco than wheat, corn, cotton, hogs, or milk. Nevertheless, tobacco was considered a basic crop by the agriculture law—more illustrative of the power that southern congressmen held in the New Deal coalition than of the crop's importance to the overall economy. But before working out a scheme for contracts with farmers, AAA officials met with the well-heeled representatives of the leading tobacco companies in July of 1933, attempting to persuade them to raise the prices they offered to farmers. The companies were noncommittal, expressing only a vague intention to "pay the farmer more for his tobacco" that year so long as "it could be done without causing overproduction in subsequent years."[26] Government officials were hoping to secure a concession from the companies as an incentive for farmers to sign contracts.

Production control was intended to be at least nominally democratic. Farmers would have an active role in the program's implementation, as the management of the program would rest with state and local farmer-committees. This decentralized planning scheme lent itself to control by local elites such as warehouse owners, farmer-lawyers, and large landowners. The nexus of influence binding growers and the agricultural bureaucracy was hardly new. It rested upon connections forged by the Extension Service in the early part of the twentieth century. Founded in 1914, the Extension Service operated through county agents dispatched all over the country to take the scientific innovations and management techniques of the USDA and the land grant colleges directly to farmers.[27] Most often, farmers that partnered with government agents were wealthy enough to implement such recommendations and influential enough to evangelize best practices to their neighbors. The Extension Service left an institutional legacy in the fields, establishing farmer organizations in many counties. These "farm bureaus" federated as the American Farm Bureau Federation in 1919, ensuring a conduit between federal policymakers and growers.[28]

Under the AAA, this web of local, state, and national policymakers grew. As agricultural economist M. L. Wilson explained, "a national administrative board would determine from price relationships" whether or not producers of a given commodity should be called upon to restrict production. With this information at hand, "state allotment committees of farm and business leaders would be necessary to divide each state's allotment among counties." At the more local level, "county and . . . community committees would finally apportion the allotments among individual growers with acreages and yields over a designated period as allotments." Farmers would be free not to participate, but those who did not would be ineligible for the benefit funds derived from the processing tax on manufacturers.[29]

Even as the adjustment plan seemed to be in place, farmers grew antsy. The legislation, after all, was introduced in the House nearly two months before it was signed into law. And tobacco farmers had to wait longer than others to see any relief. Wallace appointed John "Jack" Hutson as chief of the tobacco section shortly after the passage of the Act. More than any other person, Hutson defined the New Deal in tobacco, laying the foundation for subsequent program policy. Like the commodity he represented, Hutson had a knack for flying under the official radar. The Kentuckian moved noiselessly through the agricultural bureaucracy, barely making an appearance in the historical literature on the role of planners in the New Deal or the agricultural politics of the period.[30] But Hutson was an able administrator who got along equally well with liberal Alger Hiss and arch-conservative South Carolina senator James Byrnes. At an international sugar conference in London he even managed to become friendly with then-British prime minister Ramsay MacDonald. From his early career in farm management and Extension to his ascent through the Bureau of Agricultural Economics (BAE) and New Deal bureaucracy, and later as president of a tobacco export promotion association, Hutson represented the kind of associational hybridity that characterized agricultural policymaking during the twentieth century.[31]

Hutson's time at the BAE was cut short by a post to Europe with the Foreign Agriculture Service. What was supposed to be a one-year position appraising the "immediate market prospects" for American leaf in Europe turned into a three-year immersion in the European tobacco industry. Hutson was a public agent of private market expansion, witnessing—and facilitating—a shift in European preferences from "Oriental [Turkish] types of cigarettes to US cigarettes." Importantly, he made connections with "tobacco people" in the foreign departments of agriculture and manufacturing.[32] By the time he was appointed administrator of the tobacco section of the AAA in 1933, Hutson had discovered the two concepts that would become central to tobacco regulation for the remainder of the century: supply restriction and market expansion.

In the planning phase of tobacco's AAA, Hutson courted the participation of elite growers. Under the AAA, the six types of tobacco were covered under separate regulations. Hutson was forced to prioritize which would receive first attention. Although flue-cured growers were the most economically significant, Hutson considered them "comparatively favorably situated relative to other growers."[33] They would have to wait until after Burley and cigar-leaf producers were handled. But the AAA was not indifferent to the flue-cured regions. As Hutson told farmers in the summer of 1933: "Don't expect us to sit in Washington, devise a plan and say here it is."[34] This invitation presented an opportunity for local leaders to foment farmer sentiment for a program that they would also control.

These elites came through, providing AAA officials with huge audiences at mass meetings throughout the tobacco belt. At one such meeting, Hutson and AAA production chief Chester Davis opened the door for growers to rally around the agency and make their own demands while policymakers in Washington were crafting production contracts. Davis told the audience that "we think we are going to go further safely if we do not go too far in front of the army and get shot from behind."[35] And so AAA officials met privately with select growers in late July. The AAA wanted farmer–foot soldiers to lead the reduction drive but were also committed to ensuring that those foot soldiers did not get too far out in front of the generals and their logistical support.

Much as it had with the Co-op drive, the North Carolina Extension Service took the lead in spearheading AAA efforts. Ira Schaub, dean of agriculture at North Carolina State, commanded the shock troops of the AAA, leveraging the on-the-ground connections between his county agents and farmers.[36] Schaub was an entrepreneurial administrator who saw the New Deal as an opportunity to expand his bureaucracy.[37] Schaub instructed his agents to select growers to meet with AAA officials—a means of putting pressure on federal officials while responding to Hutson's invitation to devise their own plan.

Organization by the Best Citizens

The plan that farmers initially devised was not what Hutson had in mind. Talk of government help for farmers all over the country raised expectations in the flue-cured belt. When markets opened in the southernmost reaches of the tobacco belt in August, growers were disappointed. Prices had not budged, and, in fact, many had dipped a little for the highest grades of leaf. Dashed expectations coupled with the promise of government assistance proved galvanizing. Forty leading farmers and businessmen—the same men who had most ardently opposed the Tri-State Tobacco Growers Cooperative Association (TGCA)—arranged a mass meeting in Raleigh. On August 31, more than 2,000 angry growers got themselves to the Memorial Auditorium at North Carolina State—a demonstration of the awesome organizing power of tobacco leadership. They passed resolutions exhorting the governor and the AAA to swift and specific action. They wanted the AAA to ensure parity for the 1933 crop, and an immediate start to the acreage reduction sign-up campaign for 1934.[38]

Farmers wanted even bolder action from the governor. They urged him to "close every tobacco warehouse in North Carolina, under his exercise of martial law, and that [to] keep them closed until the Federal Government has put into effect measures that will raise the prices of tobacco."[39] Governor J. C. B. Ehringhaus was primed to respond to farmer demands—if only because his wealthy friends had been making similar requests all month. In a letter, merchant and landowner Lionel Weil drew Ehringhaus's attention to the "various price supporting movements that have recently been undertaken by the government." Surely, "no other commodity merits our immediate attention more than the proper price of tobacco this fall." Weil suggested coordinating some "interested people" for a visit with "Secretary Wallace and Mr. Davis" to secure "urgent and immediate action."[40] The governor proclaimed a "marketing holiday"—not unlike the banking holiday proclaimed by Roosevelt the previous March. The governor of South Carolina followed suit, bringing a halt to all flue-cured tobacco sales in the United States.[41] In his bid for the governorship, Ehringhaus had been seen as a tool of financial interests. Many farmers had voted for his opponent, a populist insurgent. After he shut down the tobacco markets, the governor became the most popular man in the state.[42]

The delegation of North Carolinians sent to confer with the AAA on the flue-cured program was originally meant to include only growers and warehousemen selected by Extension officials. But once North Carolina's senators and congressmen saw how popular Ehringhaus had become, they detected an opportunity to ride the wave of cresting populism and attended these sessions as well. In early September, tobacco leadership conferred in Washington to find a solution that would allow the markets to reopen as quickly as possible while still satisfying growers desperate for prices to increase. Two men from Greenville, in the state's Coastal Plain—Hutson's assistant J. Con Lanier and Congressman Lindsey Warren—spearheaded these efforts. They devised a makeshift plan for the season already under way: growers would sign a tentative contract whose details would be worked out later in further consultation with growers and AAA planners. A campaign to sign up growers for the tobacco program would begin immediately, and tobacco auctions would resume.[43]

Officials were now on the clock to get farmers to sign the contract with the AAA. Extension director Schaub handpicked growers to assist his organization with the campaign, utilizing the well-worn networks of agricultural associationalism. Claude Hall, a member of the Washington delegation, was named the president of the North Carolina Tobacco Growers Association—a descendant of an earlier state-appointed commission.[44] The assistant director of the Extension Service served as secretary. This public-private fusion was characteristic of tobacco section's administration. It was not a representative farmer democracy; it was a fusion of administrative oligarchy and economic populism.

The New Deal for tobacco relied on the interlocking coordination of private individuals and government officials to achieve public ends. Scholars attuned to the organizational and managerial aspects of the New Deal have argued that the exceptional bureaucratic capacity of the Department of Agriculture helped the AAA to succeed where the NRA had failed.[45] After all, administrators like Hutson, trained in the BAE, and officials like Ira Schaub, with decades in Extension, 4-H, and at North Carolina's land grant college, were crucial to the success of the AAA in tobacco. Still, the strong agricultural bureaucracy knew its limits. The structure of that bureaucracy, particularly the highly decentralized Extension Service, rested upon collaboration with the private sector.

During the frantic fall of 1933, the overworked Extension Service needed help in carrying out the sign-up. Pragmatic elitism ran the New Deal in North Carolina. Everybody wanted higher prices for tobacco; rich men—whether owners of warehouses, merchants, or landlords—were the most coordinated, organized, and easiest to enlist. "You would select an outstanding man from a community" to serve the AAA in an advisory capacity, Hutson recalled of those chaotic early days. "He might be an employee of a college of agriculture. He might be just a farmer. He might even be a farmer-lawyer." Whether the man was in a "public" position at a college or in the Extension Service, or in "private" life as a farmer, was not the salient point for policymakers. What mattered, simply, was that "he was a man that people respected in the area."[46] Crafting the program this way created a positive feedback loop, as handpicked local leaders' influence rose in tandem with the popularity of the tobacco program and with local communities' dependence upon it. The tobacco program depended neither solely upon the autonomous will of the AAA, nor on the desires of farmers. Instead, the government's power was legitimated, exercised, and augmented through the participation of private individuals and organizations.[47]

The AAA's reliance upon the "best citizens"—in Con Lanier's words—was evident in the geography of the contract sign-ups. Unlike the cotton plow-up campaign, where individuals were sought out individually to sign contracts, tobacco farmers went to designated centers to pledge their commitment to crop reduction. Merchants and warehousemen volunteered their businesses and staff to assist the sign-up drive.[48] Growers in the eastern Coastal Plain, home to many warehouses, signed up with remarkable speed. In Greenville, over 500 farmers signed the contract during the first hour alone. Farmers in the Piedmont were slower to sign, and their ambivalence over the administration of the tobacco program persisted throughout the decade. Nonetheless, the assurance of federal aid was overwhelmingly persuasive. Ninety-five percent of all tobacco growers—landlords and tenants—signed the contract in under two weeks.[49]

And yet, there was one crucial player yet to give assent to the New Deal for tobacco: the cigarette manufacturers.[50] In conferences that lasted "8–10 hours a day with the same group of people," Hutson and other AAA officials met with the "arrogant" tobacco executives. Meanwhile, in North Carolina, with the markets still closed and tobacco farmers still unpaid,

Ehringhaus grew impatient. The governor wired top officials at the AAA and the president himself, urging them toward speedy resolution with the manufacturers. Ehringhaus seemed genuinely surprised that Roosevelt did not respond to his frantic telegrams, informing the president that "if you could know the distress in our tobacco belt and the urgency of immediate and remedial action I feel surely you would see that it is forthcoming."[51] Roosevelt responded more than a week later, telling Ehringhaus to calm down while "conflicting interests" were being "harmonized."[52]

The president left a good deal unsaid. The negotiations grew rancorous and broke down over the issue of a licensing requirement for the manufacturers. The consumer division of the AAA, led by liberal lawyer Jerome Frank, wanted to protect the powers of the secretary of agriculture to inspect company books and forbid cigarette price increases. Frank was particularly concerned not to craft an agreement that would diminish Wallace's power in code negotiations with the NRA.[53] S. Clay Williams, the president of R. J. Reynolds, who represented the manufacturers at negotiations with the AAA, explained that the companies would simply never agree to any proposition that took business decisions out of the companies' hands.[54] Williams and AAA officials took their dispute to the White House. Despite Wallace and Frank's commitment to the licensing agreement, Roosevelt told his agriculture secretary to ease off for fear of antagonizing Williams and Peek, whose relationship with reformers within the AAA were already under strain.[55] Williams could not have felt too put off by those hard weeks of negotiations: less than a year later, the president prevailed upon the tobacco executive to succeed Johnson as the chief of the NRA. During the 1930s, tobacco was no rogue industry; the consent and participation of the tobacco companies were considered foundational to the success of the New Deal's experimentation in economic planning.

Ultimately manufacturers signed a marketing agreement, essentially dictating its terms. Buyers agreed to purchase the same quantity of flue-cured tobacco by March 31 of 1934 as they had used the previous year. They would pay an average price of 17¢/lb. The AAA would not inspect company books. The secretary of agriculture would not set cigarette prices. Williams later admitted that the price his buyers paid for tobacco really did not matter— as long as every other competitor had to pay the same price. Indeed, price

regulation redounded to the benefit of large firms like R. J. Reynolds as smaller players could not absorb any erosion of their already narrow profit margins.

Still, the autonomy granted to the companies did not matter much to farmers in the fall of 1933. As soon as the agreement was set in ink, prices soared. For 1933, growers received an average of 15.3¢/lb., compared with 11.6¢/lb. in 1932. By the end of 1933, farmers had pocketed a total of $85.6 million, more than two and a half times their cash total in 1932. This windfall reverberated through the local economy. Bank deposits doubled and taxes were paid more quickly.[56] The *Wall Street Journal* even turned its reportage toward the tobacco belt (though, admittedly, to Winston-Salem, R. J. Reynolds's corporate headquarters), noting brisk sales of used and new cars.[57] The lead headline of the December 1933 *Progressive Farmer* put it succinctly: "Tobacco Farmers Are Happy."[58] So too were other farmers across the country. By the end of 1933, cash income on farms had risen by an average of 30 percent.[59]

Coercing Economic Democracy

While farmers were feeling flush, officials in the AAA, the Extension Service, and the North Carolina Tobacco Growers Association worked on the details of the permanent contract. Participating farmers were to reduce their "base acreage"—the average of how many tobacco acres they cultivated between 1931 and 1933—by 30 percent. In exchange, they would receive a rental payment of $17.50 for each acre removed from production, and a benefit payment of 12 percent of the selling price of their tobacco at auction. In response to demands from the growers' group, North Carolina congressman John Kerr sponsored a bill imposing a hefty tax on nonsigning farmers.[60] The Kerr-Smith Tobacco Act punished those who did not sign production contracts and those who produced in excess of their allotment. Elite farmers relished the punitive aspect of the bill, viewing the overproduction penalty through the prism of their own disloyalty to the Cooperative. It was precisely in the parts of North Carolina where big landlords undermined the Co-op—the Coastal Plain of eastern North Carolina— that enthusiasm for the Kerr-Smith Act was highest. For large producers, the difference between the Cooperative and the Kerr-Smith Act was simple:

noncompliance, or "chiseling," could be punished.[61] At meetings across the tobacco belt, growers wired their representatives, in the words of one, "besieging" them with demands for control.[62]

While many farmers were squarely in favor of such coercive measures, Secretary of Agriculture Henry Wallace was less sold—or at least less comfortable outwardly expressing how essential coercion was to New Deal agriculture programs. The secretary opposed compulsory acreage reduction, reasoning that it was "an undemocratic approach to force a man to reduce whether he wanted to or not."[63] Insistent that any reduction program be voluntary, Wallace inserted a referendum provision in the legislation, which, at least, allowed for some communication between growers and the government.[64] As a result, when the Kerr-Smith Act passed in June 1934, it stipulated that two thirds of growers had to approve the program for it to go into effect. Two thirds was the figure required to turn acreage reduction into policy—and transform compulsory acreage reduction into "farmer democracy." The requirement that farmers approve the program endowed acreage restriction and price supports with moral significance. Farmers were not just paid to take their land out of production in exchange for a higher price of tobacco: they *asked for it,* and in asking for it, they transformed their economic need and desperation into something closer to stewardship. It was their program, though its administration was hardly shared equally.

Reviewing the operation of the tobacco program, the 1935 *Annual Report* of the state Extension Service explained that "the farmers had become firmly convinced that rigid control of production was the only way to guarantee a fair price for their leaf."[65] Though only a few growers refused tobacco contracts—certainly not enough to undermine the success of the tobacco program—participating growers still grumbled. Paradoxically, in what was the most popular of the AAA programs, compulsory control never went far enough at removing a phantom threat to satisfy some growers. As the Extension Service report put it, the growers "wanted a program with teeth in it, a program that would make it impossible for the non-signer to sell a pound of tobacco."[66] Reinforced by yearly referenda, the looming menace of disloyalty fostered defensiveness around the program. And through the practice of defense, and the necessity of campaigning constantly for the continuation of the program, elite growers consolidated interest and an economic identity in the federal regulation of tobacco.

Compulsory agricultural adjustment brought prosperity to tobacco producers. For the first three years of the AAA's operation, flue-cured farmers netted more cash with each year: $182 million in 1933–1934; $229 million in 1934–1935; $247 million in 1935–1936. Not surprisingly, farmers, on the whole, loved the program. More than 95 percent of those voting in the tobacco referendum in the summer of 1935 affirmed the program's continuation.[67] For flue-cured growers, the affirmation was even more striking, as 98 percent of growers—nearly 99 percent in North Carolina—voted yes to the question as it was posed on the referendum ballot in 1935: "Are you in favor of a tobacco production adjustment program to follow the present one . . . ?"[68] These figures indicate that the program was broadly popular, not merely a fig leaf for elite interests.

Because tobacco could be farmed profitably on a small scale, crop control for tobacco provided stability, if not prosperity, for many small-scale producers.[69] Those who farmed smaller acreages were able to pay off their debts and pocket a little extra.[70] A black farmer who had netted $11.30 for five acres of tobacco in 1932 earned $1,472 in 1934—despite a cut in his acreage. He explained that he planned to use the money to pay off family medical expenses, and "then have a little change after I buy Santa Claus."[71]

Still, small growers also knew that the prosperity brought by the AAA was unevenly distributed. The rules of the tobacco program benefited large growers at their expense. Small farmers often objected to the horizontal acreage reduction of the emergency 1933 contract. As a county agent explained in a letter to Governor Ehringhaus, small farmers felt "that the authorities should not require a 4-acre planter to reduce any until the man who is planting from 8 to 10 acres out of 15 is reduced to 4."[72] Clarence Poe, whose *Progressive Farmer* was animated by the dream of a yeoman's democracy for white, small-scale farmers of the Piedmont, captured the AAA's mixed record. While acknowledging that the AAA "has produced wonderful results for southern farmers" with a "program so magnificent that it should have the support of all friends of agriculture," Poe nonetheless suggested that not enough had been done for "the two or three-horse, one family farm." What was at stake in the New Deal tobacco policy was nothing less than "the right of the little man to live." For Poe, true farmer democracy had to redistribute power within the confines of Jim Crow, cutting more acreage from "wealthier landowners for whom farming is a commercialized business rather than a way of life."[73] Several months later, a sympathetic "little man" wrote to the paper and said it even more simply: "the small farmer has not been consulted or allowed a fair voice in the AAA program."[74]

As was true with many New Deal initiatives, racist elitism was built into the structure of the program. Extension agents selected growers to serve on the county and community committees that assisted in operating the program. These committees turned local elites into local officials. Their most important, visible, and controversial task was verifying the accuracy of "base acreages" after farmers submitted field measurements to the tobacco section. Fudging and favoritism were hardly concealed at this stage of policy. A Brookings Institution report commissioned by Wallace for each of the commodity programs concluded that many tobacco growers "deliberately padded their acreage and production figures to obtain financial benefits which would accrue from having a larger base."[75] The local committeemen charged with authenticating these figures frequently vouched for fabricated numbers submitted by kin, friends, and neighbors.[76] Once allotments were assigned—a fixed percentage of the base acreage—there was little dissatisfied farmers could do. Those who complained to their Extension agents or congressmen were referred back to the very committees that they believed had jilted them in the first place.

Black farmers bore the brunt of the AAA's discrimination. Whether sharecroppers, tenants, or landowners, black farmers sustained greater acreage cuts than white farmers. Black farmers, who already cultivated fewer acres than white farmers, saw their acreage cut by 50 percent, from an average of 6 acres to 3. White-owned tobacco allotments were cut by 30 percent, falling from an average 8 acres to 5.5. On the ground, the extreme administrative decentralization of the AAA farmer-committees amounted to extreme discrimination. One black farmer complained that he received an allotment of 2.3 acres from his local committee, while his white neighbor, who had never before grown tobacco, was given more than 7 acres.[77] These disparities would reverberate through future generations as allotments were capitalized into property values, perpetuating the initial discrimination.

Congressmen and administrators were also aware of the squeeze that crop reduction placed on small farmers, whom they imagined as white. The

Kerr-Smith Act attempted to ameliorate these inequalities by allowing counties additional acreage with the stipulation that a portion of the bonus must go to small growers. The problem was tenancy—or at least that was what officials claimed. Tobacco section chief Jack Hutson explained the AAA's unwillingness to broach any broad overhaul of the calculation of base acreages on the grounds that any attempt to help small farmers would come out of the allotment of large operators. This, in turn, would simply cause them to eliminate tenants—which is just what had happened under AAA cotton policy. "You would really hit the lowest people on the ladder," Hutson explained.[78] Given the administrative enormity of establishing, verifying, adjusting, and compensating tobacco allotments, Hutson and other officials did not want to add another layer to an already complex process, another opening wedge for complaints.

The AAA caused widespread displacement of tenants and sharecroppers throughout the South.[79] The human exodus from the land was, however, less pronounced in tobacco than in cotton production.[80] Tobacco contracts stipulated that tenants could not be removed because of acreage reduction, but, of course, it was not difficult for a landlord to contrive other reasons for letting a tenant go. The Extension Service was unwilling to become an arbiter of tenure disputes, as agents were overworked and reliant on friendly relations with the landlord class to do their jobs. Still, tenant-operated tobacco farms fell by just 10 percent in the 1930s, whereas according to one survey of the Delta belt in Arkansas, more than 30 percent of cotton tenants were displaced as a result of the New Deal.[81] And while the number of tenants in North Carolina fell during the 1930s, the number of small owner-operators actually grew, nearly offsetting the tenant loss.[82]

Tobacco looks better compared to cotton not because of any particular social imperative in its administration, but because of the crop's labor demands. Cotton landlords took government checks and bought machines that did the work of scores of tenants. No such labor-saving devices would be available to tobacco farmers for decades. When machines could replace mules and family labor, they did. Until then, tobacco farmers faced persistent labor shortages at harvest time.[83] This distinctive, labor-intensive cultivation pattern—and the regional economy just beginning to stir to life again—would be cast into doubt by the Supreme Court's invalidation of the Agricultural Adjustment Act.

Readjusting Agriculture

In the spring of 1935, the Supreme Court handed down its decision in *Schechter Poultry Corp. v. United States,* invalidating the National Industrial Recovery Act, the centerpiece of the New Deal's economic recovery scheme for industry. Although few mourned the demise of NIRA, which even many New Deal supporters had come to see as unwieldy and unfair, much of the New Deal's early regulatory efforts hung in the balance. Indeed, six months later, in *United States v. Butler,* the Court ruled the Agricultural Adjustment Act, NIRA's country cousin, unconstitutional. Both decisions cast a long shadow in tobacco country.

Schechter called into question the constitutionality of another key piece of tobacco regulation, the 1935 Tobacco Inspection Act. The Act was an attempt to control the chaotic auction place by regulating the inspection and grading of tobacco. Because of a scarcity of government graders to perform the service at every single tobacco warehouse, the Act allowed the secretary of agriculture to designate certain markets where the greatest number of growers could be served. Before requiring inspection at designated markets, the secretary had to conduct a referendum—a practice with which farmers were becoming increasingly familiar. All growers who sold tobacco at that particular market, regardless of race or tenure status, were eligible to participate. If at least two thirds of voters approved of the service, inspections would take effect. No farmer was required to sell tobacco at the designated market, even if he had voted for the service.

The inspection service was a way to raise tobacco prices and thus boost income. In the absence of a grading service, the average grower was disadvantaged by his ignorance and his insignificance in the rapid-fire auction market. Even though there were more than sixty official tobacco grades, most growers were only aware of five or six, which meant that they had no real idea of the value of what they were selling. It was easy for buyers to undervalue the farmer's lot of tobacco, especially in the helter-skelter atmosphere of the auction, in which a pile of tobacco was sold approximately every ten seconds. This information asymmetry sustained a brisk speculative trade performed by "pinhookers"—buyers who waited to "see some poor devil's tobacco going for a song and a dance." After purchasing tobacco on the cheap, the pinhooker would resell later that day on the very same warehouse floor. In the language of populist producerism that animated many southern Democrats who supported the New Deal farm agenda, Virginia Democrat John Flannagan, the author of the inspection act, condemned the auction system as generating "parasites" who siphoned off wealth that rightfully belonged to "the growers who have labored about 13 months in the year to produce the tobacco."[84] The Tobacco Inspection Act would remedy a farmer's ignorance by letting him know what he was selling—and what the same grade was bringing in other tobacco markets.

The Act also sought to level the playing field for farmers. The auction system favored large growers at the expense of small ones. Known derisively as warehouse "pets," these prominent growers who maintained a relationship with particular warehouses were rewarded for their patronage with higher prices. This kind of favoritism suggested a broad atmosphere of collusion between buyers, warehouse owners, auctioneers, and prominent growers—one that poor farmers were aware of but had no means to combat. "When the ordinary grower . . . offers his tobacco for sale the price is hammered down," Flannagan explained on the House floor. "The one-gallows fellow robbed in order to pay the 'pet' and maintain the average price level."[85] Because buyers were authorized to pay certain "average" prices for particular grades of tobacco, they had latitude in what prices they could offer favored growers, so long as they offered less to others. This system proved beneficial to the warehouse owners, who made money on volume of sales; to buyers, who absorbed excess prices offered to pets; and, most obviously, to prominent growers, whose loyalty to certain warehouses was cemented by the favoritism they were shown.[86]

Although questions were raised about its constitutionality during congressional debate, the Tobacco Inspection Act became law in August 1935. J. Bayard Clark, a North Carolina representative friendly to the tobacco and financial industries and a conservative opponent of many of Roosevelt's initiatives, invoked the specter of *Schechter* to justify his opposition to the Act. "There is no difference between picking chickens, slaughtering chickens, buying and reselling or transporting them after they have reached New York City . . . and going down to a pile of tobacco on a warehouse floor before it has gotten into the channels of interstate transportation."[87] In *Schechter*, the Court found that the NIRA exceeded the powers granted to congress under the Commerce Clause; and, at any rate, the code violations committed by the Schechter Poultry Corporation had occurred entirely in the state of New York. If interstate commerce ended at the Schechter slaughterhouses, why would it not also terminate at a tobacco warehouse? This question would remain unresolved for several more years.

More pressing was the Court's decision in *United States v. Butler,* which sent farmers across the country into a tailspin. "Back to Despair," read the headline of the Raleigh *News and Observer*'s editorial.[88] Speaking on the House floor a month after the decision, North Carolina congressman Harold Cooley noted the gulf between the wide popular support of the AAA and its invalidation by a handful of judges. "The Supreme Court voted against the Triple A by a vote of 6 to 3," Cooley lamented. "The farmers voted for the Triple A by a vote of 19 to 1, yet the Triple A is no more."[89] The congressman empathized with a worried constituent, confessing that many of his colleagues in Congress held the Court in great contempt. "You actually have no idea how many people would like to get a crack at at least six of the old boys," Cooley wrote.[90]

The Court held that the processing tax that financed the rental and benefit payments to farmers was an unconstitutional transfer of wealth from one sector to another, invading "the reserved powers of the States." Furthermore, the AAA was coercive: "at best" a "scheme for purchasing with federal funds submission to federal regulation of a subject reserved for the States."[91] While Congress acted within its rights when it taxed and redistributed wealth for the benefit of the general welfare, the Court did not consider the processing tax a tax in the strict sense. As Justice Owen Roberts wrote on behalf of the majority: "the word has never been thought to connote the expropriation of money from one group for the benefit of another."[92] But unlike the Court's decision in *Schechter Poultry Corp. v. United States,* which destroyed the regulatory scheme of the NIRA, *Butler* left the door open for alternative methods to manage agricultural supply.

Despite striking down the processing tax, *Butler* affirmed the right of Congress to achieve legislative aims that contributed to the "general welfare through its taxing and spending power."[93] Peeling away the unconstitutional parts of the 1933 Agricultural Adjustment Act from the parts that could be redeemed required some tweaking of the way the Act regulated commodity supply. Editors of the *Yale Law Journal* predicted that "sales made in interstate transactions, whether preceding or following shipment

across state lines, appear to constitute interstate commerce itself within all
the definitions thus far suggested by the Supreme Court."[94] Lawyers, agricultural officials, and legislators working on the replacement for the Act
would come to focus on the control of commodity sales rather than commodity production as the basis for adjusting agriculture. And the scheme
for redistributing wealth to farmers would be financed by taxpayers, not
by processors. Ultimately, these taxpayer costs were modest: between 1933
and 1941, losses on the tobacco program totaled just over $2 million.[95]

For tobacco farmers, control was still the essence of the farm program.
The 1938 Agricultural Adjustment Act, designed as a constitutionally acceptable replacement for the 1933 Act, authorized the secretary of agriculture to control supply by setting marketing quotas that dictated how much
a producer could sell. If the secretary expected a price-depressing surplus,
he could limit marketing for the following season. The 1938 Act contained
the same referendum proviso as the Kerr-Smith Act. Two thirds of producers
had to approve of quota restrictions in order for them to take effect. Farmers
who sold in excess of their assigned quota were subject to penalty with
fines even stiffer than under the old tobacco law. Indeed, the tobacco section of the 1938 Act punished overproducing tobacco farmers even more
harshly than producers of other commodities.[96]

Tobacco producers mobilized for strict production control. And they established a new organization to translate the desires of prominent growers
into government policy. During those uncertain months after the *Butler* decision, prominent growers and merchants in the eastern part of the state
realized that the legislative lacuna left by *Butler* meant that congressmen
would be unusually attentive to constituents as they sought to write a replacement farm bill. The American Farm Bureau Federation (AFBF), meanwhile, had claimed credit for New Deal farm policy from the start (an assertion that New Deal economists disputed).[97] While the organization had
grown in tandem with the popularity of the AAA, the AFBF had made frus-
tratingly little headway in the tobacco South. Growers' desire for crop control and the AFBF's desire to cultivate tobacco growers led to the formation of the North Carolina Farm Bureau (NCFB) in the spring of 1936.

The same individuals and institutions that had organized the market
shutdown in 1933 established the NCFB. Ira Schaub and the Extension
Service were particularly important in helping to establish the NCFB,

arranging meetings, encouraging membership, and even collecting dues. This relationship was in keeping with the twinned development of the farm bloc and the Extension concept. In its earliest incarnation, the Farm Bureau was institutionally indistinct from the Extension Service.[98] Particularly in the Midwest, county Extension agents were also Farm Bureau agents who organized local and state chapters of the pressure group. A historian of the Farm Bureau has characterized this cozy relationship as "one of informal reciprocity." Through networks and knowledge so tacit that they did not need to be spelled out, "the Farm Bureau gave political support" to the aims of the Extension Service, and the "Extension Service in turn gave whatever aid it could to the Farm Bureau."[99] The fledgling NCFB leeched off the Extension Service's name recognition and credibility; its letterhead announced that it was "Cooperating with the Extension Service for the Advancement of Agriculture."[100]

The class composition of the early NCFB provides a window into this business-oriented future. The NCFB's first chairman was J. E. Winslow, a prominent farmer from Pitt County, the state's most heavily producing tobacco district. Winslow was no stranger to local administration, having been an AAA committeeman in his home county and a member of state tobacco advisory committees. Winslow was a horse, mule, and livestock dealer and a tobacco farmer in Greenville. Today there is a hip gastropub in the town named after him.[101] Claude Hall, who had been handpicked by Schaub to go to Washington to help draft the 1933 Agricultural Adjustment Act, was also a founding director of the state Farm Bureau. So were six other initiators of the emergency meeting in Greenville demanding that Governor Ehringhaus close the markets back in 1933. It was clear upon its founding that the NCFB was a formidable organization representing the economic interests of merchants, bankers, larger farmers, and warehouse owners, primarily in the eastern Coastal Plain.[102] The rigid crop control achieved by the "Second" Agricultural Adjustment Act was a vindication of their vision. Indeed, the Kinston *Free Press* noted that farmers joined the NCFB because of the organization's promise to lobby for strict crop control.[103]

The close alignment of the Farm Bureau and Extension Service with the 1938 legislation carried a cost. In December of 1938, growers were subject to another referendum on whether or not supply-reducing marketing orders would be in force for 1939. This was the first referendum since the revised program was initiated. Keen observers of the dynamics of tobacco country could already tell that some farmers, particularly smaller-scale growers in the Piedmont, were angry at what they saw as the elitist orientation of the program. And the fact that the Extension Service was so closely tied to the referendum drive provided an easy target for antigovernment ire. One leaf dealer—a profession that was no friend to supply control efforts—described the Extension Service as employing "Hitler tactics" to "jam . . . this program down the farmers' throats."[104]

These grumblings turned into a full-throated roar—a "revolt of the little man," in the words of the *Progressive Farmer*.[105] Due to perceived inequalities in administration, growers rejected crop control for the following marketing season. Only 56.8 percent of flue-cured growers voted in favor of the program, well short of the 67 percent statutorily required to bring restrictions into effect. In light of the major legislative overhaul, many growers did not understand how their quota was determined, and procedures enacted to alleviate farmer discontent only caused more confusion. One North Carolina official charged with executing the math of the quota-determining equations as much as admitted the Act's bungled administration. He called the 1938 calculations his best technical achievement on paper, despite the fact that "some how the quotas never quite fitted."[106] And given the close association between the Farm Bureau and the 1938 revisions, many farmers were skeptical about the fairness of the allocation of acreage. According to the *Progressive Farmer*, votes against marketing orders "came almost exclusively from counties where small farms prevail."[107] After all, how could the program be fair if rich farmers were most enthusiastically for it? Small growers were not authors or administrators of the program, but they had an outsized influence at the ballot box. Agrarian democracy—the referendum—laid bare the networks of the elite associationism. The terms of a rigid social compact in which prominent men could make decisions on behalf of an entire sector were acceptable only when those decisions appeared to work to everyone's benefit—even if those benefits were not evenly distributed. Ironically, farmers rejected the regulatory scheme of the 1938 Agricultural Adjustment Act just as the Supreme Court affirmed its constitutionality.

Upholding Federal Tobacco Regulation

Tobacco figured so heavily in the Supreme Court's 1939 term that one suspects that the justices may have been able to join farmers for the transplanting of young tobacco, so versed were they in the nuances of the crop's production. Authored in the wake of the Court's volte-face acceptance of New Deal regulations, *Currin v. Wallace* and *Mulford v. Smith* upheld three features of agricultural regulation writ large: the acceptability of federal regulation of commodity sales as part of the stream of interstate commerce; the permissibility of federal marketing orders, as distinct from the production regulations invalidated by *Butler;* and the constitutionality of Congress's delegation of authority to the secretary of agriculture to allocate marketing quotas to individual farms, thus upholding the empowerment of farmer-committees to administer supply control.

J. Bayard Clark's invocation of *Schechter* in opposition to the Tobacco Inspection Act's passage presaged a legal challenge. In late 1936, D. T. Currin and a group of other warehouse owners in Oxford, North Carolina, a town in the "Old Belt" of the state's north-central Piedmont, challenged the constitutionality of the Act on several grounds: that, as with the president's establishment of fair codes under NIRA, the secretary's designation of tobacco markets was an unconstitutional delegation of legislative power; that the Act was discriminatory in giving the secretary leeway in selecting which markets to designate; and that the tobacco sold at auction was not part of interstate commerce.[108] These plaintiffs alleged that their warehouses, designated as inspection sites, were losing businesses to other warehouses where graders were not assigned.

As the congressional debates prior to its passage suggested, the Inspection Act pitted parts of the tobacco supply chain against each other, namely growers versus warehousemen. Indeed, Con Lanier, the second in command at the tobacco section of the AAA, served as counsel for the plaintiffs and had also testified against the Act before Congress. Lanier was a supporter of New Deal tobacco regulation. But he was also closely aligned with the interests of warehouse owners, having been "raised under the shadow of a warehouse" in Greenville, North Carolina. He had simultaneously served as the NRA's code administrator for tobacco warehouses while in service to the AAA.[109] His advocacy for the warehouse owners was less a principled opposition to federal regulation of commerce than it was a defense of his class.[110]

The Court was unmoved by Lanier's arguments, finding that the tobacco sales at the Oxford warehouse were "predominantly sales in interstate or foreign commerce" and thus rightfully subject to federal regulation. True, about 15 percent of tobacco sold at Currin's business was destined for cigarette manufacture within the state of North Carolina. But the leaves bound for intrastate, interstate, and foreign processing were "comingled," indistinct. "Whenever the interstate and intrastate transactions are so related so that control of one involves the control of the other," wrote Chief Justice Hughes for the majority, "it is Congress and not the state, that is entitled to prescribe the final and dominant rule."[111] As to the warehousemen's allegation that the Tobacco Inspection Act was discriminatory because not all facilities were subject to inspection, the Court found simply that "there is no uniformity in connection with the commerce power."[112] Under conditions of scarcity, Congress tried to serve the greatest number of farmers by allocating inspectors to the busiest markets.

The opinion devoted more attention to the question of Congress's delegation of power via the referendum provision. Had the Court accepted the argument that the referendum represented an impermissible delegation of power, it would have posed a serious challenge not only to tobacco inspection, but to the regulatory scheme for agriculture more generally, as marketing orders were triggered by the approval of two thirds of eligible producers voting in a referendum. But the Court framed the referendum not as producers drawing forth regulations from the state, but as "Congress . . . merely plac[ing] a restriction upon its own regulation."[113] Without acknowledging the ways that the referendum structure was the result of quiet negotiation between state agents and private citizens, the opinion in *Currin* framed the referendum as a check on Congress, rather than an expression of farmers' desire: "this is not a case where group of producers make the law and force it upon a minority."[114] And so the Court assimilated the vast administrative empowerment of a privileged sector, agriculture, into the language of restraint.

While most tobacco growers greeted the Court's approval of tobacco inspection with relief, some chafed under the constraints of the "second" Agricultural Adjustment Act.[115] Shortly after handing down its decision in

Currin, the Court issued another affirmation of federal agricultural regulation. In *Mulford v. Smith,* flue-cured farmers in Georgia and Florida who had been hit with penalties for marketing in excess of their assigned tobacco quota brought suit against the government. Unlike the "first" Agricultural Adjustment Act, the Agricultural Adjustment Act of 1938 did not regulate tobacco *production,* but instead "authorized the fixing of quotas for the amount of tobacco *to be sold.*"[116] From the perspective of the government, *Mulford v. Smith* was an excellent test of the constitutionality of the 1938 Act because nearly all of the tobacco purchased on the Georgia markets was destined for out-of-state or overseas processing. The decision in *Currin* provided a favorable context for the state's argument that *Butler* was not the relevant precedent by which to judge marketing orders. The Court accepted this argument, finding the 1938 Act "solely a regulation of interstate commerce, which it reaches and affects at the throat where tobacco enters the stream of commerce—the marketing warehouse."[117]

Disgruntled growers leveled another charge against the Act—one that would plague commodity programs for the remainder of the century: "the standard for setting farm quotas is so uncertain, vague, and indefinite that it amounts to a delegation of legislative power."[118] In response to this accusation, the government's brief included description of the farmer-committees empowered to apportion quotas to individual farms as within the overall regulatory scheme established by the 1938 Act. But the Court never took up the question of this extreme administrative decentralization—or the public reliance on private individuals to carry out economic regulation. Instead, its ruling focused narrowly on the delegation to the secretary of agriculture, finding that "Congress has indicated in detail the considerations which are to be held in view [by the secretary] in making these adjustments." With opportunity for "administrative and judicial review" of farmer complaints, the Court thus affirmed the pragmatic necessity of elite associationalism; the events of the next few months would enshrine it.

Tobacco Farmers at War

Despite the Court's affirmation of the legality of tobacco regulation, there was no control program in 1939—farmers had voted against it the previous

December. Responding to the same incentives that had governed tobacco before the New Deal, farmers greatly expanded their production in 1939. But the outbreak of war in Europe soon superseded the question of production controls. Now farmers had to worry about the loss of one of their most important export outlets, Great Britain. Tobaccomen faced what the *Progressive Farmer* called a "double barreled emergency": too much tobacco and too few buyers.[119]

As it had two decades earlier, war changed the course of tobacco's history. When Britain declared war on Germany in early September 1939, the stakes for tobacco farmers were high, but the consequences not obvious. In an attempt to conserve foreign exchange, the British government denied tobacco importers certificates required to purchase U.S. flue-cured. Less than a week after Britain declared war, Imperial Tobacco Company announced that it would withdraw from the U.S. markets. This was an emergency far graver than overproduction in the absence of the control program. Between 1934 and 1938, the United Kingdom consumed an average of 200 million pounds yearly of flue-cured tobacco. The next largest consumer of flue-cured tobacco was Canada, where factories churned out cigarettes made with only 27 million pounds of flue-cured yearly.[120] Britain consumed two thirds of total U.S. flue-cured exports. And because British buyers purchased the higher grades of flue-cured leaf, sales to England represented half of farmers' total income.[121]

At this moment of crisis, Jack Hutson's overseas experience was of unexpected value to farmers. While surveying the European tobacco scene earlier in the decade, Hutson had become friendly with the director of the Imperial Tobacco Company, Britain's largest buying concern. Well aware that the company's absence would spark panic in the tobacco belt, the director of Imperial contacted Hutson with advance warning of the news. This gave the AAA administrator time to meet with tobacco leadership in Raleigh to work out a quick response. Once again, the governors of tobacco-producing states closed the markets in September of 1939, grinding all tobacco sales to a halt, stopping buyers and auctioneers in their tracks as they rode the auction circuit. A few days later, Hutson, Treasury officials, and grower-representatives of the Tobacco Growers Association finalized the details of a rescue plan. The Commodity Credit Corporation (CCC), the government financing entity authorized to borrow money from the Treasury to administer agricultural programs, bought the entire British share of tobacco. This put money directly into growers' hands, while still offering British buyers the ability to purchase their share of tobacco at a later date. Until then, it would be held at taxpayer expense in government storage—a southern Lend-Lease.[122]

The British tobacco bailout was the best possible advertisement for corporatist control: the threat of ruin ameliorated by public-private collaboration. The swift action of elite growers and the sure hand of the federal government resulted in an emphatic affirmation of crop control when another referendum was held in December of 1939. Business owners, merchants, bankers, and chambers of commerce in eastern North Carolina joined Con Lanier, Farm Bureau officials, Extension agents, congressmen, the governor, and even Clarence Poe in urging farmers to vote "yes" on crop control. Full-page advertisements paid for by an eastern North Carolina bank made the appeal clearly: "Would you refuse to be rescued? Face Saving or Shirt Saving. Would you lose your shirt to save your face? Hoovercarts or Automobiles? You must decide."[123] Farmers did. Less than one year after rejecting production controls for 1939, greater than 90 percent of voters in North Carolina approved production control. They never voted against it again.

The North Carolina Farm Bureau seized the emergency to ensure farmers would have fewer opportunities to oppose crop control. That is, to make crop control more efficient, the NCFB needed to make it less democratic. J. E. Winslow proposed that farmers should only vote every five or ten years for crop control; Claude Hall proposed a compromise, of sorts, in suggesting a three-to-five year referendum cycle. Hutson agreed: from an administrative standpoint, a three-year control plan was easier to implement and would help stabilize prices. With support from tobacco state congressional delegations, the three-year crop control plan would be put to a grower referendum in July. Despite opposition from the Grange and other small-farmer advocates, 86 percent of growers voting approved three-year control. Less than a year and a half after rejecting crop control, tobacco farmers embraced its long-term continuation. Though it was given during a state of emergency, farmers' submission to control, their willing relinquishment of democratic checks on program administration, legitimated the elitist leadership of tobacco country.

War also reconfigured the relationships within the tobacco supply chain. Direct government intervention into the tobacco markets as part of the British bailout had cooled the heated antagonism between farmers and manufacturers. The cigarette's emblem as a wartime aid also gave the industry a patriotic glow. In war, cigarettes were not only the soldier's friend, they were his right: provided in his C-ration, and supplemented with gratis shipments from the manufacturers themselves. The war endowed cigarettes with special patriotism—one that the companies touted in advertisements. Lucky Strike famously commercialized the change of the brand's pack from dark green to white. "Lucky Strike green has gone to war!" the radio announcer declared, associating the brand with the bravery of the frontlines, and the sacrifice of the home front.

This was brilliant mythologizing. In reality, American Tobacco Company had already planned and paid for the package redesign as a way to enliven a flagging brand.[124] But the patriotic glow softened farmers to the tobacco companies far less than the simple fact of high prices. The price per pound of tobacco rose to new heights each year between 1940 and 1946, owing largely to huge domestic demand by the army.[125] Between 1941 and 1944, flue-cured farmers produced less tobacco than the trade desired.[126] Cigarette manufactures were forced to draw upon reserve stocks—and to pay premium prices for tobacco leaf. Quotas remained in place even as prices advanced against the wartime price ceilings imposed by the Office of Price Administration.[127] At long last, growers could finally behave like the manufacturers, like a cartel.

———

The end of the First New Deal did not spell the end of cartelization, at least not in the tobacco fields. Efforts to wrest control of the tobacco program from elites in the 1938 tobacco referendum—to put more emphasis on the "democracy" in Wallace's idealized "farmer democracy"—were abortive, and farmers were glad for it. In rejecting control and suffering the consequences, tobacco country entered the wartime economy more hierarchically organized than it had ever been before. This new stage of organization reduced the possibility that crop control would be defeated again. By the war's end, an elite crop of farmer-politicians could begin to imagine a global market for a cigarette harvest.

3

Cultivating the Grower

I am confident that the informed farmer can successfully oppose punitive
legislation at all levels—national, state, and local—if he has the facts.
—Carl T. Hicks, President of the Tobacco Growers Information Committee, President of
the Flue-Cured Tobacco Cooperative Stabilization Corporation, Tobacco Committee
Chairman of the North Carolina State Farm Bureau

PEACE POSED almost as many problems for tobacco farmers as war. The
memory of the disastrous price readjustments of World War I reminded
farmers and administrators alike that the smooth and mild taste of flue-
cured tobacco could not alone a market make.[1] But after the Second World
War, farmers had something they'd lacked decades earlier: proximity to
state power—power that had enabled them to wring a "golden stream of dollars" from the "golden crop."[2] On the ground in North Carolina, tobacco
farmers and their leaders were beginning to imagine their postwar world.
As the emergency of the late 1940s settled into the simmering competition
of the Cold War, tobacco was recast not as an aid to recovery but as a symbol
of capitalist consumption itself. The regulations that kept tobacco farms
small and acreage down were converted into tools of consumer expansion.
Through Tobacco Associates (TA), a grower-funded tobacco export organization, the federal tobacco program became a global smoking program. A
private vehicle of public policy, TA exemplified the associational state—a
state obscured through its mediation by the private sector and voluntary
organizations.[3]

Cigarettes were a product par excellence of the postwar consumers' republic.[4] The reorientation of the American political and economic life
around mass consumption refashioned how Americans thought of themselves and of the common good. But producers continued to exist within
the consumer society. And, in fact, they were producing more than ever.
In general, federal efforts to control agricultural production faltered as

farmers' productivity skyrocketed, juiced by the liberal application of fertilizers and pesticides.[5] But for farmers—and especially for partisans of high government supports for agriculture—surplus commodities did not reflect a problem of overproduction. They represented a problem of *underconsumption*. Throughout the 1950s, foreign markets were seen as a way to expand demand for U.S. agricultural products—tobacco foremost among them—while simultaneously maintaining the solvency of U.S. price support programs.

Tobacco embodied the slick, cellophane-wrapped ethos of the consumers' republic in yet another way. During the 1950s, tobacco farmers embraced public relations as a tool for combating detractors from within the halls of agriculture and from without. Conservative secretary of agriculture Ezra Taft Benson's attempts to claw back the expansive agricultural state were met with concerted attempts by tobacco growers—who produced under the kind of rigid rules that Benson detested—to tell "their side of the story." By the end of his tenure in office, Benson succeeded in ushering in a more "market-oriented" agriculture, reducing the level of price supports and production controls for every commodity except tobacco.[6]

Perhaps more significantly, tobacco farmers were drawn into the PR apparatus of Big Tobacco during the 1950s. The Tobacco Growers Information Committee (TGIC) was founded in 1958 as the farmer's wing of the Tobacco Industry Research Committee (TIRC), the infamous PR organization established to mislead the public on the scientific relationship between smoking and disease. Growers were willing participants in the industry's strategy of doubt-mongering; public agricultural institutions also benefited from Big Tobacco's deception, receiving grant funding to study and defend the beleaguered crop. After the Second World War, U.S. flue-cured tobacco was cultivated in meeting rooms as much as it was cultivated in the soils of North Carolina. And it was consumed by increasing numbers of foreign smokers not because of the deceptions of Big Tobacco, but through the legal endeavors of public and private agricultural officials.

Tobacco Associates: The Sir Walter Raleigh Hotel, 1947

Just weeks after V-J Day, the North Carolina Grange sponsored a meeting in the stately Sir Walter Raleigh Hotel near the capitol in downtown Raleigh.

Colloquially known as the "third house of government," the venue suggested that this would be no barnstorming meeting. Inside the hotel's banquet hall, the general topic of "safeguarding the future of tobacco" turned to the more specific question of how to enlarge foreign demand for flue-cured leaf. Memories of the price collapse after the First World War were still vivid; and the United Kingdom, still the largest importer of flue-cured tobacco, was economically fragile. To conserve currency and rely on imperial resources for its reconstruction, the British government had announced that it would encourage cultivation of flue-cured within its empire.[7] The *Progressive Farmer* warned that the high prices and brisk sales volume of 1945 were not likely to last. "History repeats itself," one agricultural official warned readers. "It looks at the present time as if conditions faced by growers following World War I are upon us again." By drawing an analogy between the 1920 and 1946 sales seasons, the *Progressive Farmer* warned farmers that the specter of depression loomed around the corner.[8]

Tobacco farmers were far from alone in fearing postwar readjustment. Even accounting for the pessimistic professional tendencies of the dismal science, economists predicted an eminent postwar depression unless the government did something to prevent it. Across the profession, memories of the previous world war lingered.[9] But the intervening decades had seen a fundamental reimagining of the capacity of the government to respond to economic disaster. Where in 1919, farmers and workers could only await layoffs and commodity surpluses, in 1945, organized labor and organized agriculture drew up more ambitious plans based on a fundamentally different understanding of the productive capacity of the American economy. The scarcity economics of the early New Deal—talk of the "mature economy" and "balance" between economic sectors—had been fully eclipsed by the doctrine of growth made possible by the awesome power of U.S. wartime production.[10]

The economics of abundance rested on high production, employment, and purchasing power.[11] Truman's Council of Economic Advisers articulated what Robert Collins has called "full-fledged growthsmanship," seeing growth as a balm for class, regulatory, and sectoral conflict.[12] Questions of distribution—which Americans get what—took a backseat to the sheer expansion of the size of the economy. "Government and business must work together consistently to achieve more and more jobs and more and more production," Truman explained in his 1949 State of the Union address. Such collaboration would "mean more and more prosperity for all the people."[13] The postwar growth paradigm augured a reorientation in labor-management relations as well, as unions embraced such bread-and-butter tactics as collective bargaining over wages and pensions. The New Deal–era language of industrial democracy and social solidarity began to sound quaint.[14] Mass consumption was conceived of as the antidote for postwar stagnation and recession. Affluence, marked by consumer spending, high wages, and an expanding public-private welfare state, animated the economic visions of tobacco farmers and labor leaders alike.[15]

The growers present at the Sir Walter Raleigh were there to harness and direct the ethos of growth. They met to stoke cigarette consumption. Between 1945 and 1947, tobacco leaders gathered frequently at the Sir Walter Raleigh to forestall impending disaster.[16] The biggest men in the small towns that depended upon tobacco production—representatives of the Grange and the Farm Bureau, warehouse owners, bankers, leaf exporters, government officials, and prominent tobacco farmers—vowed to set aside their economic differences in favor of the one issue that united all sectors of the trade: increasing the total volume of tobacco exports, thus solving the underconsumption problem.[17] By early 1947, these leaders—some employed by public money, some not—had settled upon a new organization to be the vehicle of postwar prosperity: Tobacco Associates.

Characteristic of associational governance, the relationship between growers and government—both state and federal—was obscured by the voluntary and private nature of farmer associations.[18] TA would not engage in the purchase or sales of tobacco directly. Rather, the organization would "promote, develop, and expand the export market for flue-cured tobacco" by maintaining contact with "public and private agencies in the United States and in foreign countries in which American flue-cured tobacco is being used or might be used." With this broad mandate to convince more people throughout the world to smoke flue-cured tobacco, TA envisioned an associational relationship with the state—to "cooperate with all Government departments and agencies charged with any responsibility for developing, handling or promoting the export trade of the United States." TA began as a flue-cured broker to the world, dedicated to cultivating cigarette smokers outside U.S. borders.[19]

TA promoted the virtues of American flue-cured tobacco—"mildness" and "inhalability"—two traits that, in fact, make flue-cured tobacco the most deadly form of the leaf.[20] In so doing, it yoked together several segments of the tobacco economy in an attempt to simply sell more. More sales meant more profits for leaf dealers, who could help facilitate such transactions; more for the warehouse owners, who received a commission for the use of their facilities; and, of course, more money for farmers, whose production quota could be raised on the basis of prospective demand. American cigarette manufacturers were the only segment of the tobacco economy left out of the equation. Well before the domestic tobacco manufacturers took aim at foreign markets to make up for decreased domestic smoking rates and increased taxation, an important segment of the tobacco economy was already staking its claim to prosperity by looking abroad.[21]

Manufacturers looked forward to surging domestic demand—growth estimated to have nearly no end in sight. Forecasts of continued population growth shaped the ambitions of manufacturers, who had every reason to expect that increasingly affluent Americans would smoke more and more. A 1944 survey by the Bureau of Labor Statistics showed that tobacco expenditures tended to rise with family income, with top earners (households earning over $5,000 a year) spending nearly twice as much as Americans who made half as much.[22] And, at any rate, foreign governments opposed the importation of manufactured cigarettes, as a threat to monopoly sales. At mid-century, only a slim proportion of U.S. manufactured cigarettes were destined abroad—mainly cheap brands.[23]

TA was a private nonprofit corporation endowed with public power. Inside the private sector, TA was safe from political meddling, budgetary austerity, wrangling over appointees, or even public scrutiny. The initial financing for the group reflected its support among "private" tobacco organizations. Its $100,000 budget was to be generated from donations from farmers, bankers, leaf dealers, and warehouse owners. Leaf dealers were to contribute $15,000; bankers, $5,000; merchants, $10,000; and farmers, $50,000. The hefty contribution from farmers was subdivided further, reflecting the size of tobacco production among the five tobacco-producing states.[24] Tar Heel growers would ultimately furnish the lion's share of the budget, with a $35,000 contribution. Virginia and South Carolina were to contribute $5,000 each, while Florida and Georgia were responsible for $5,000 together. This rough breakdown of contributions reflected tobacco production's firm gravitational center in eastern North

Carolina. Many of the farmers who funded TA in its first year of operation were members of the Farm Bureau, which conducted a vigorous fund-raising drive through local meetings and direct mailings, and drew most of its support in the eastern Coastal Plain.

There was only one man right for the job at the helm of the new organization: Jack Hutson. And it just so happened that Hutson needed a new appointment. His service in the New Deal had earned him a post at the United Nations, where he began as undersecretary of agriculture in 1946. However, his stint at the UN was cut short by a misstep in the delicate dance of Cold War diplomacy. In May 1946, Hutson was invited to speak at a luncheon honoring the Polish general Tadeusz Komorowski at New York's exclusive Metropolitan Club. Komorowski, known colloquially as General Bor, was a hero to Poles in exile for his role in staging the Warsaw Uprising against Soviet "liberation." Hutson was castigated in the press for welcoming a man whom Poland's communist-led government considered a war criminal. Delegations from both Poland and the USSR launched protests with UN secretary-general Trygve Lie. Less than a month later, Lie reorganized his cabinet, and Hutson was out of a job.[25]

The North Carolina Farm Bureau (NCFB) approached Hutson in early 1947 with the idea for a tobacco promotion organization. Hutson knew these men well. He had "discussed many things before about tobacco" with them during his time as chief of the tobacco section of the Agricultural Adjustment Administration (AAA) in the 1930s. The NCFB, meanwhile, built anticipation for TA among its own ranks by touting that it had begun negotiations to "obtain the services of perhaps the best qualified man in America to head this organization."[26] TA's legislative patron underscored the associational nature of the organization: the chairman of the North Carolina General Assembly's House Agricultural Committee—a man who also happened to be the Farm Bureau representative from a tobacco-producing county in the eastern Coastal Plain—secured the passage of a bill that secured the long-term financing of Tobacco Associates. The bill enabled tobacco farmers to tax themselves 10 cents per tobacco-producing acre in support of the nascent organization.[27]

The similarities between the TA vote and the federal tobacco referendum were striking. As with the tobacco program vote, campaigns to raise voter turnout were waged by various state agencies such as the North Carolina

Extension Service and the AAA.[28] The reason for such involvement was clear: grassroots support was essential for TA to function, for two-thirds of voters had to approve the TA assessment for any funds to be collected at all.[29] Again, the parallel with government was unmistakable: price supports and crop controls also went into effect once two thirds of quota holders approved the referendum. In some places, the federal quota referendum and the TA referendum occurred simultaneously, but farmers were instructed to deposit two separate ballots into two different ballot boxes.[30] At other polling locations, the ballot for the federally financed program and TA were one and the same.[31]

It is likely that many of the farmers voting for TA thought they were voting for a government program. After all, government officials encouraged farmers to vote, the balloting procedures were similar to those of the U.S. Department of Agriculture (USDA) referenda, and farmers voted to authorize TA assessments on the same three-year basis that quotas were authorized. From its origins to its leadership to its operation, TA epitomized the associational state linking the private sector with public power. Its president was known to farmers because of his leadership of the AAA. Its primary boosters, leaders of the NCFB, were closely aligned with the Extension Service and frequently served on the county committees responsible for the implementation of the tobacco program. TA's referendum structure mimicked the federal tobacco referendum, borrowing the confidence farmers placed in that program to legitimate itself.

Flue-cured tobacco reached TA through another institution that blurred the line between public and private. Beginning in 1946, the tobacco program was financed through a Raleigh-based cooperative called the Flue-Cured Tobacco Stabilization Cooperative Corporation. Known to most farmers simply as "Stabilization," this private farmer-run cooperative was responsible for the physical and financial management of the federal tobacco program. Stabilization bought, dried, stored, and later sold tobacco that failed to reach the support price on the auction market. It did so through nonrecourse loans provided by the government-owned Commodity Credit Corporation (CCC). Stabilization's personnel also embodied the hybridily of official affiliation in the governance of the tobacco economy: the organization's longtime president was a member of the Farm Bureau and the governor-appointed Tobacco Advisory Committee.

Many farmers understood Stabilization as the entity that bought the tobacco nobody else would; but the institution was more than that. If Stabilization accumulated too much tobacco, storage costs might overwhelm the
program. Surplus tobacco would also trigger an automatic reduction in
farmers' quota assignments. TA worked hand in glove with Stabilization:
the former sold the excess reserves held by the latter. By the end of its first
year in operation, TA rested on a stable base. Its mission—to "promote, develop, and expand the export market for flue-cured tobacco"—was a desir-
able goal in itself, and equally a tonic for the even more crucial tobacco
program. Firmly planted in the local soil, TA turned its attention to Washington and beyond.

European Reconstruction: 1424 K Street, N.W.

In the summer of 1947, Hutson registered as a lobbyist in Washington. With
an office on K Street, TA sought to secure the inclusion of flue-cured tobacco in the European reconstruction package being debated before Con
gress.[32] Hutson's goal was to solve the problem of postwar surpluses by
taking advantage of the American-initiated rebuilding of Europe. He was
far from alone in this ambition, and tobacco was but one commodity that
moved through new channels of postwar commerce. Although Western
European nations were rebuilt as mixed economies with social-democratic
welfare commitments, they were also to embrace a pro-market orientation.[33]
The United States presided over the remaking of the international order,
creating new institutions to ensure collective security (the United Nations)
and trade among states (the World Bank, the International Monetary Fund).
Domestically, the Import-Export Bank supplemented these institutions, ensuring a steady supply of credit to finance U.S. exports.

The idea that commerce would secure peace—one of liberalism's oldest
guiding notions—lay behind these institutions. But the institutions of Pax
Americana were also built upon quite modern understandings about the
planning capacities of nation-states. Keynesian macroeconomic management required that nations practice a mild form of economic nationalism,
restraining transnational capital flows in order to manage economic
growth. Thus, as Daniel Sargent has lucidly described, the postwar international economic order "was a regime that would permit economic statism

to coexist with international trade."[34] Statism and internationalism defined tobacco, too.

But what pragmatic arguments could be marshaled in favor of a commodity that was neither food nor fiber?[35] Hutson sought to join consumer desire in Europe—a "desire probably stronger than it has ever been before"— with dollars. The Marshall Plan would be the vehicle for joining supply and expanding demand. The threat of oversupply of leaf, a threat made visible by the greater volume held by Stabilization, compelled TA to seek market expansion. Hutson's twenty years in agricultural policymaking circles had resulted in a wide network of influential friends and colleagues. The most important of these was North Carolina Democrat Harold Dunbar Cooley, who would shortly go on to occupy the chairmanship of the House Committee on Agriculture, a position he would hold longer than any other representative.[36] Cooley was also a member of a House Select Committee on Foreign Aid—a nineteen-man contingent that spent part of the summer of 1947 studying the economic situation in postwar Europe.

Cooley was ready to do battle on behalf of the crop. His first opponent was formidable: General Lucius Clay, the military governor of the U.S.-zone of occupied West Germany. The four-star general was at the height of his prestige and popularity, waging peace in West Germany by encouraging industriousness among Germans. "He told the Germans to stop feeling sorry for themselves," the *New York Times* reported, "to cease grumbling and to get back to work."[37] Though Clay was himself a chain-smoker, he adamantly opposed the use of American taxpayer dollars to finance European tobacco purchases. "You are not going to get a damn cent for tobacco," Con Lanier recalled Clay telling Cooley and Hutson.[38] Fortunately for the crop's patrons, however, European officials had different ideas about their recovery needs.

Flue-cured tobacco held a special place in European visions of recovery.[39] The Committee of European Economic Cooperation (CEEC) made specific mention of leaf tobacco in its report to the U.S. State Department.[40] The CEEC, comprised of representatives of all aid-recipient nations, estimated that total tobacco imports would rise substantially over prewar averages during the years of the Marshall Plan's operation.[41] European officials' demand for flue-cured tobacco aided TA in lobbying for the crop's inclusion in Marshall Plan designs and later helped officials in engineering European-produced cigarettes made with American-grown leaf.[42]

Flue-cured tobacco had influential patrons stateside as well. Cooley, Hutson, and Lanier descended upon Dennis FitzGerald, the agricultural director of the Economic Cooperation Administration (ECA), with arguments about tobacco's value to Europeans.[43] With FitzGerald, they took the position that "if you give a man either a pipe full of tobacco or a chew of tobacco after a day's work, he will work better and produce more."[44] FitzGerald ultimately supported tobacco's inclusion within the Marshall Plan package. Perhaps the arguments of the tobacco interests had special sway with the administrator, who had occupied the same professional circles as Hutson both within the New Deal agricultural establishment and also at the Bureau of Agricultural Economics. FitzGerald shared the assumptions of the tobacco delegation: tobacco was a humble luxury, a small yet powerful reminder of what capitalism could offer by way of leisure, and what leisure could inspire by way of incentive.[45] Soon, Secretary of State George Marshall began to tout the virtues of tobacco as a "concession to human nature." As the secretary put it to the National Cotton Council meeting in Atlanta in January 1948: "As a practical matter, it has been found that the availability of tobacco is an effective stimulus to morale and productivity." Perhaps hoping to appear measured in his endorsement of cigarettes, the secretary subsequently noted that he was a reformed smoker.[46]

Tobacco also functioned at the level of the macroeconomy, supplying much-needed revenue to European governments. A tax on tobacco, generally thought of as a luxury tax, actually made the crop a necessity during an era in which European governments needed money. Congressman John Flannagan, a Virginia Democrat, cited the fact that the French, Austrian, and Italian governments realized more than 30 percent of total government revenues in 1946 from net profits from state tobacco monopolies.[47] This was why European nations were so keen to get their hands on American leaf and not manufactured American cigarettes. The "golden crop" helped to replenish state coffers during a time of hardship and desperation. At the same time, the postwar tobacco trade augured a definitive shift in European consumer preferences toward the taste of flue-cured tobacco.[48]

For its American boosters, tobacco's greatest value was not material but ideological. Neither man nor democracy could live by bread alone. "It is probably difficult for the people of any country to be truly thankful for aid supplied on the basis of austerity" when the bare necessities of life could be provided by "any form of autocracy," Flannagan argued. War-weary Europeans needed "something that will give a sense of satisfaction, that will add comfort, and will soothe strained nerves and tired bodies." Tobacco legitimated the American vision of capitalism and democracy. As Flannagan put it, "Tobacco is something they want, and it will instill a desire to strive for the better things in life which can be obtained under freedom of initiative provided by democratic governments."[49] The cigarette was an emblem of American abundance; its inclusion as a necessity of reconstruction demonstrated the friendly goodwill of the United States, rather like offering a smoke to a stranger who was down at the heels and in need.

On April 3, 1948, the Marshall Plan was passed. The dollar assistance provided to Europe through the Economic Cooperation Administration was used for the purchase of food, fuel, machinery, and tobacco. For the four years of the Marshall Plan's duration (1948–51), an estimated $13 billion in assistance was provided to sixteen countries. A staggering $1 billion went to the procurement of tobacco, a figure that represented a third of total food aid.[50]

In this scheme, TA played a dual role as administrator and advocate. The organization smoothed the channels of trade by physically linking Europeans who bought on behalf of national tobacco monopolies with North Carolina growers. TA was also a consistent advocate of aid packages that increased the total amount of dollars available to recipient nations. Hutson saw the availability of currency to purchase tobacco as a more sustainable basis for the flue-cured export economy than simply the temporary infusion of "governmental loans and grants" or dollars earmarked for tobacco purchases.[51] He feared that an impoverished Europe with a crippled manufacturing sector would be unable to generate enough currency through export to buy American agricultural products.[52] "A great deal more is involved [in reconstruction] than stopping the spread of communism or selling goods to Europe," Hutson told a crowd at the annual convention of the American Farm Bureau Federation (AFBF). "We have a direct economic interest in these areas for a much longer period than the next four years."[53]

As the largest prewar economy and the front line of the Cold War, Germany received special attention from Hutson. There, smokers clamored to get their hands on cigarettes after years of rationing, deprivation, and moral pressures against tobacco consumption. Smoking in occupied Germany was a politically potent act, symbolizing a backlash against the anti-tobacco policies of the Third Reich.[54] Smoking may well have been a sign of liberation for individual Germans, but that does not explain the marked shift toward cigarettes produced with American-grown tobacco. For that we turn to the forces that made the German tobacco market: American growers, the German government, and U.S. dollars.

At the same time as Marshall Plan aid provided dollars and credits for the purchase of American tobacco, the German cigarette trade association *(Verband der Zigarettenindustrie)* successfully lobbied for a reduction in the cigarette tax. Its goal was to boost cigarette consumption over cigar consumption.[55] German cigarette manufacturers did not succeed in the ambitious goal of creating a "cigarette that American occupation soldiers would prefer over their Lucky Strikes"—as they had set out to do.[56] But they did achieve a resounding success at engineering the smoking preferences of German civilians. By 1949, one informal survey conducted by a German cigarette manufacturer suggested that between 85 and 90 percent of West Germans preferred the taste of flue-cured over the "oriental" tobacco, largely procured from Greece and Turkey, they had long smoked.[57]

Some of these smokers may have enjoyed the $450 million worth of American tobacco shipped to the country under the auspices of the Marshall Plan. But not all Germans were equally grateful. The West German magazine *Der Spiegel* deemed American tobacco an "unnecessary thing" that Americans were "quite glad to get rid of"—a succinct synopsis of the U.S. congressional debates in 1947 and 1948 about the incentive value of surplus tobacco. *Der Spiegel*'s commentator also observed that the influx of flue-cured tobacco was changing what Germans had historically considered a good smoke. These new preferences could not be satisfied through the old trade routes that linked Germany to Greece and Turkey, where darker smoking tobaccos were grown.[58] Other critics objected that American flue-cured imports were undermining the very economies that the Marshall Plan was supposed to reconstruct. Should not Greece and Turkey, which were recipients of Marshall Plan aid, have been encouraged to redevelop tobacco as an important part of their agriculture sector?

French officials thought so. There, the national tobacco monopoly, *Société Nationale d'Exploitation Industrielle des Tabacs et Allumettes* (SEITA), practiced a kind of cigarette nationalism. SEITA simply refused to purchase large quantities of American flue-cured tobacco and instead focused its efforts on its most popular cigarette brand, Gauloises, which primarily contained an indigenously grown brown tobacco. Such was the dominance of Gauloises that, in the words of one historian, they "could be construed as a national symbol next to the beret and the baguette."[59] The recalcitrance of the French did not go unnoticed by growers in North Carolina, where TA had paid for a delegation of European aid recipients to visit and sample tobacco at warehouses. The French "sons of bitches wanted us to give them some more [tobacco samples]" without any intention to actually buy, Lanier insisted.[60] Yet even in France, where particular consumer tastes were guarded as symbols of the nation, brands made with flue-cured tobacco rose slowly but surely in popularity—from just 5.3 percent of market share in 1952 to 14.7 percent in 1976.[61]

The French example underscores a fact that Jack Hutson had identified twenty years earlier: taste was political, not natural. And it was always the result of negotiation. Europe's turn toward the American-style cigarette was the product of efforts by a handful of Americans and Europeans. As Lanier told a gathering of businessmen in a small town in eastern North Carolina, tobacco farmers' most pressing need was "to devise some means of supplying countries with some flue-cured tobacco in order to preserve the taste and the desire" for American-style cigarettes "until these nations will become self-supporting"—until, that is, they were no longer reliant on Marshall funds to purchase tobacco.[62]

The federal tobacco program was a treasure and foreign trade helped to secure its defense. The program had unleashed a "golden stream of dollars" from the "golden crop."[63] The program, which involved a frank redistribution of money from taxpayers to tobacco growers, was itself a political privilege—a fact that some of tobacco's stewards recognized in candid moments among friends. "Manufacturers of automobiles cannot, under existing law, come together and decide the quantity of automobiles to be built in any period," Lanier explained to his fellow tobacco leaders in 1948. "Nor can the auto group prevent a new plant from engaging in the manufacture of automobiles." But tobacco growers, by contrast, "are permitted to control the production of tobacco" and can "deny the right to engage in the production of tobacco [to others] except on a very limited scale."[64] Lanier realized he presided over a government-subsidized, grower-administered cartel.

Wise stewardship of the tobacco economy required the use of tobacco's remarkable political privilege—the benefit of government-assisted organization, the referendum financing of a private lobbying organization, close access to policymakers—to further safeguard farmers' monopoly production rights. TA both rested upon and secured the federal tobacco program. As Lanier framed it, TA maintained market equilibrium by stimulating demand, thereby safeguarding the tobacco farmers' ability to restrict supply.

Farmers' dreams of opening global markets for flue-cured were given considerable lift by the U.S. embrace of surplus commodity disposal as a Cold War foreign policy technique. The mandate of surplus disposal and the ideal of democratic humanitarianism justified the passage of the Agriculture Trade Development and Assistance Act of 1954, Public Law (PL) 480. Better known as the Food for Peace program, the act authorized export sales of surplus American commodities in exchange for foreign currencies, thus circumventing the dollar-shortage problem that had stifled purchases of tobacco in poorer countries. Supporters argued that American commodity assistance would alleviate hunger—and the dangerous ideological tendencies that supposedly festered in times of material deprivation. As a *surplus* disposal program, meanwhile, PL 480 also underscored the abundance that capitalism and democracy produced. The goal of PL 480 was not just temporary commodity disposal; it was the spread of capitalism secured by permanent market expansion—a goal that resonated with its Republican congressional sponsors, but did little to alienate farm state Democrats anxious about surpluses.[65]

Initially, nations eligible for such assistance were primarily in Western Europe and East Asia, but as the 1950s progressed, PL 480 became increasingly associated with Southeast Asia, Latin America, and the Middle East.[66] As European reconstruction had illustrated to tobacco farmers, aid could both prevent the buildup of dangerous surpluses, and also change long-term tastes. Food for Peace was especially suited to the task of shifting consumer preferences, enabling private organizations to use local currencies to engage in "market development activities." Ongoing promotional programs were only allowed to operate when private trade groups contributed substantially to their operation—hiding the guiding hand of government. Private grower and agribusiness groups cooperated with the Departments of Agriculture and Commerce and the United States Information Agency in two major types of marketing campaigns: international trade fairs and ongoing, embedded promotional campaigns.

Across Europe, Asia, Latin America and, eventually, the Soviet Bloc countries, TA developed markets by promoting flue-cured at trade shows and

directly assisting in the manufacture of new cigarette products.[67] At trade
shows, growers and U.S. officials staffed festively decorated booths inside
cavernous convention halls. These displays demonstrated how American
surplus commodities available through PL 480 offered an upgrade to national consumption traditions. Thus the Spanish were first introduced to
potato chips fried in soybean oil (soybeans were in massive surplus during
the early 1950s) rather than olive oil.[68] By the same token, at international
fairs in Thailand, Japan, Germany, and Spain, Jack Hutson handed out free
samples of locally made cigarettes that contained American leaf. As he put
it, these events were "excellent opportunit[ies] for us to further develop good
will for US tobacco in foreign countries and at the same time call . . . attention to its fine qualities and characteristics."[69]

These were just the first steps in securing a new market. Later, TA would
assist in the design of consumer surveys in foreign countries; or sponsor a
delegation of foreign tobacco officials to visit North Carolina, where they
could see firsthand the craftsmanship that went to making high-quality
Bright Leaf. In 1957, TA helped finance trips to the United States for Austrian, Finnish, French, and Korean officials.[70] Foreign technicians and engineers supplemented the efforts of the Americans. The Thai Tobacco
Monopoly worked particularly closely with TA throughout the 1950s. TA
arranged for Thai chemists and packaging experts to attend courses at
North Carolina State to learn the techniques that went into designing an
American cigarette. Between 1955 and 1957, Thailand's imports of flue-
cured rocketed from 8.6 to 13.4 million pounds per year. By 1968, that
figure stood at 24.1 million pounds—an increase of more than 274 percent
since the inauguration of the TA-USDA venture in that country, meaning
that a full 5 percent of total U.S. flue-cured exports went to Thailand.[71]

American officials attributed the great rise in Thai tobacco imports to
increased advertising (see Figure 3.1). Of the eleven Thai cigarette brands on
the Thai market in 1968, nine contained American flue-cured tobacco. TA
contributed to the advertising campaigns of those nine brands, whose sales
all grew between 1957 and 1968. Sales of unadvertised brands, by contrast,
languished.[72] The USDA interpreted this as clear evidence of "the relationship of the promotion program to the dollars received by . . . producers."
Without a brand promotion campaign, agriculture officials estimated that
the value of American flue-cured used in Thailand would have reached
about $8 million. In actuality, flue-cured tobacco sold to the Thai Tobacco

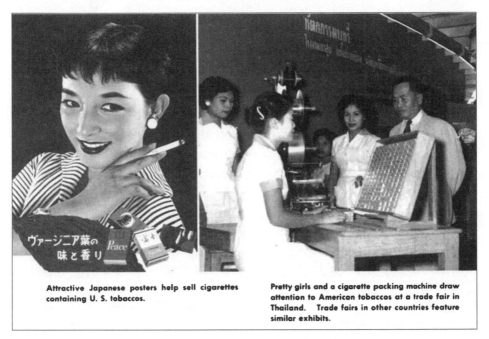

Attractive Japanese posters help sell cigarettes containing U. S. tobaccos.

Pretty girls and a cigarette packing machine draw attention to American tobaccos at a trade fair in Thailand. Trade fairs in other countries feature similar exhibits.

Figure 3.1 A 1958 U.S. Department of Agriculture circular touts the success of trade fairs in boosting Asian consumption of U.S. tobacco. (*New Markets for U.S. Agricultural Commodities: A Pictorial Report of Foreign Market Development,* Miscellaneous Publication No. 756 (Washington, D.C.: U.S. Department of Agriculture, 1958), page 14)

Monopoly was worth approximately $14 million—a fact that TA proudly touted in its 1968 annual report.[73]

TA also vindicated the aspirations of American officials who hoped that Food for Peace would fight communism. Under the program's auspices, flue-cured tobacco arrived in Poland in 1960—the first time American cigarette tobacco had reached that country since the 1930s.[74] Hutson died in 1964 en route to TA's newly opened office in Brussels. But his successor, John Palmer, continued to chip away at the Soviet Bloc, which he characterized as "one of the largest untapped markets in the world for our tobacco."[75] The Leipzig Trade Fair was an ideal venue for TA's efforts. During the interwar period, Leipzig had boasted Europe's largest trade fair, with thousands of exhibitors flocking to the twice-yearly event.[76]

Within the German Democratic Republic, the Leipzig Trade Fair was key to the development of a consumer market within the Soviet Bloc (see Figure 3.2).[77] In the spring and fall of 1966, TA staged a two-room exhibit at the fair. One room was replete with samples from the various flue-cured tobacco–producing belts of the United States—demonstrating the link between highly regional production and globally renowned quality. The next room boasted another talisman of eastern North Carolina: a cigar-store Indian that once stood outside an export warehouse in Wilson, North Carolina.[78] In 1966, two East German tobacconists visited North Carolina to see production firsthand. Maybe they were also treated to a football game at the University of North Carolina, a common extracurricular activity during TA-sponsored visits.[79] Subsequently, sales to East Germany expanded steadily, growing to 1,201,000 pounds in 1969, which was a large increase over the 135,000 pounds sold just four years earlier.[80]

TA achieved its most pronounced success in the 1950s and 1960s through its collaboration with the Japan Tobacco Monopoly (JTM). In 1956, the first

Figure 3.2 A view of the Leipzig Trade Fair, where Tobacco Associates brokered deals across the Iron Curtain, 1973. (Ulrich Hässler, photographer / German Federal Archives / 183-M0905-0134)

year of Japan's participation in Food for Peace, the nation imported 5.6 million pounds of American flue-cured tobacco. By 1968, that figure had jumped to 41.9 million pounds—an increase of more than 722 percent.[81] Over the next ten years, TA's work in Japan "evolved from a subordinate position in [the JTM's] advertising activities to one of major importance in its annual planning operations."[82] By working to develop not only specific Japanese brands but also American-style advertising practices within Japan, TA's efforts reached well beyond the surplus disposal mandates of PL 480. The goal was always to increase flue-cured use in Japanese brands, which, according to the trade journal *Tobacco Reporter,* "contained about two-thirds American flue-cured" by 1969.[83] By the late 1970s, after Japan had ceased participation in the program, it was importing more American flue-cured tobacco than any other country. The intervening years saw numerous trips by Hutson and his successor to Japan—as well as longer excursions taken in the other direction as the JTM established a permanent office in Raleigh.

Agriculture in the Mixed Economy

With demand surging at home and abroad, tobacco farmers did well in the 1950s. Friendly congressmen sat in control of key congressional committees, helping to ensure that the crop was supported at 90 percent of the parity ratio—significantly higher than the purchasing power ratio introduced during the 1930s.[84] It was higher, in fact, than the level at which every single other commodity was supported. Despite encountering a great amount of opposition, even within his own party, Secretary of Agriculture Benson prevailed upon a Republican-controlled Congress to lower price support levels in 1954. Among all commodities, only tobacco would continue to be supported at wartime levels of 90 percent.[85]

Tobacco diplomacy had resulted in rising foreign demand for U.S.-grown tobacco. And despite some fluctuation in the size of allotments and the quality of the crop, the average crop value for the whole decade exceeded previous all-time highs as demand hummed.[86] In 1958, leaf prices rose to new heights amid record cigarette consumption. That year, Americans smoked 424 billion cigarettes, signaling "public acceptance of an important product that 160,000 to 175,000 farm families depend on for food, clothing, and shelter," in the words of a *North Carolina Tobacco Report* issued by the

state.[87] The USDA observed matter-of-factly that "the recent sharper increase in number of teenagers [smoking] has contributed to greater cigarette consumption."[88] In short, all over the world, more people were smoking,
and the U.S. government signaled its deep commitment to the economic
security of producers in case that should cease to be the case.

But there was plenty of reason for industry concern—partly because of
domestic political debates over farm support prices, and partly due to the
emerging medical consensus that cigarettes were deadly. Although tobacco
had mostly avoided the surplus production problems that were plaguing
corn and wheat farmers of the 1950s, the rigid nature of the tobacco program was an appealing target for politicians who sought to restore "free enterprise" to agriculture. At the same time, epidemiologists and researchers
in the United States and Britain were intensively studying the relationship
between cigarette smoking and disease. Through significant methodological innovations in experimental design, data collection, and statistical evaluation, investigators began to circle around three "c" words:cigarettes
caused cancer.[89] Joined by Harold Cooley, the NCFB, and the cigarette manufacturers, tobacco growers embarked upon a defensive PR strategy to insulate themselves against indictments on medical or political grounds.
Their approach simultaneously rested upon and obscured farmers' cozy relationship with government.

Harold Cooley thought farmers were getting a bad rap. One did not need
to look further than the newsstand to see troubling portraits of American
farmers. In a 1955 article entitled "The Country Slickers Take Us Again,"
Harper's Magazine launched a stinging attack against "our pampered ty-
rant, the American farmer." The article told urban Americans to brace
themselves for the political pandering that would ensue in the year ahead.
The farmer, the article began, "is about to get his boots licked again by both
political parties." The crux of the case against the farmer centered on the
long-term taxpayer financing of "the dole." "When any hog keeps his jowls
in the trough long enough, he gets to thinking he owns the trough."[90]

Dark undertones of consumer resentment slipped out even in coverage
that should have been favorable to farmers. When twelve Soviet agricultural
officials toured hog and corn farms in Iowa, they were, at least by one account, in search of "the secret of how this combination works." The *New
York Times* reported a story of fellowship and goodwill between Iowans and
Soviets—most of whom hailed from the Ukraine, "Russia's closest approxi-

mation of Iowa." While Iowans' eyes may have been set on the "Soviet Russians" in their midst, the *Times* reporter was transfixed by the shiny tractors and new farm equipment. In the reporter's words, "the ordinary Iowa farmer . . . has a minimum of two new cars and they are usually brand-new Buicks or Oldsmobiles or Cadillacs." Iowa was the anti-Potemkin village. Urban newspapermen argued that farmer success was too good to be true, not because it was fake, but because it was real—and that taxpayers kept farmers "living in clover and Cadillacs."[91]

As fewer and fewer Americans were living on farms, the prospects for gaining the sympathies of the American people seemed to dwindle. Farm population continued its decline after World War II. In 1945, 18 percent of Americans lived on farms. By 1959, less than 12 percent did, and by 1964 that figure had fallen to less than 7 percent.[92] The vast majority of Americans experienced farms in two ways: as consumers of farm products, and as taxpayers underwriting farm subsidies. Gallup found Americans in 1952 sharply divided on the issue of farm aid. Those who opposed subsidies reasoned, along with one Utah housewife, that farm "incomes should not be kept up any more than others—it's unfair to consumers."[93] That year, the federal government spent $504 million on farm price support programs—more than it spent on housing, schools, and public health, but far less than it spent on natural resource development, or subsidies to private industry to expand production during the Korean War.[94]

Within the halls of agriculture a debate roiled over the extent to which the federal government should be supporting farm products, particularly those in extreme surplus. On one side stood tobacco, peanut, dairy, wool, and cotton producers—mostly Democrats but a few Republicans as well—who advocated high price supports and stringent supply control. Arrayed against the scheme for controlled production were Midwestern corn and hog farmers, most influentially represented by the AFBF, whose views were reflected in the agriculture planks of the Republican Party Platform throughout the decade. They sought "flexible" farm supports—that is, a lower level of automatic government support—in exchange for the right to produce larger quantities of their crop. Proponents of what was termed "market-oriented" agriculture argued that a freer market would end the problem of taxpayer-held surplus, and would hasten the development of a more efficient farm sector. Marginal farmers should simply seek their fortunes elsewhere.[95] For tobacco farmers, this was precisely the danger of the unfettered market: a return to the debilitating overproduction that had plagued them for the first three decades of the twentieth century.

Even within the world of subsidized, regulated agriculture, the tobacco program stood out for its rigid adherence to supply control. This, in turn, served to maintain the viability of small farm units. But for all of its unique features and repeated legislative carve-outs, tobacco was a clear byproduct of the mixed economy, in which the preference of well-organized producer groups shaped macroeconomic policy. During the 1950s and 1960s, tensions between business and government gave way, in many instances, to a well-regulated consensus.[96] Postwar affluence was achieved through the public subsidy of private firms, federal investment in research and development, macroeconomic planning, and industry-specific regulation.

Defense contractors—firms like Boeing, General Electric, Lockheed— were the most visible beneficiaries of the mixed economy, nurtured by the explosive demand for the technologically advanced weapons of the Cold War. While President Dwight Eisenhower left office warning of the "total influence—economic, political, even spiritual" of the military-industrial complex, other private-public complexes were flourishing. Regulated industries—airlines, communications, transportation, utilities—achieved steady growth, which in turn helped to undergird the growth of the rest of the economy.[97]

The expansion in the American economy was twinned with the expansion of government. It reflected the New Deal ethos of single-industry regulation as manifested in National Recovery Administration (NRA) codes, the Securities and Exchange Act, and the Agricultural Adjustment Act. But whatever suspicions some New Dealers harbored about the "old enemies of peace—business and financial monopoly"—had given way during the Second World War to a productive collaboration between business and government— productive in two senses of the term: the American economy had embarked upon a period of unparalleled growth, and the regulatory apparatus of the postwar decades tended to embrace the prerogatives of producers above all.[98]

Most postwar regulation of major industries was accommodating rather than adversarial. The government facilitated price stability and expansion of service while minimizing competition.[99] The mixed economy of the postwar decades had its roots in the economic philosophy and institutions

of the New Deal. Indeed, the agencies responsible for overseeing the key industries of the 1950s and 1960s were established during the 1930s. The
Federal Communications Commission (FCC), for example, was established
by the Communications Act of 1934. After the Second World War, the FCC
and state utility commissions oversaw the operation of the Bell System,
America's telephone monopoly. The Civil Aeronautics Board (CAB), set up
in 1938, shepherded the American airline industry into commercial success
in the years after the war. Rates, routes, mergers and the entry of new firms
into the air system were tightly controlled, which worked to the benefit of
established firms. By the 1960s, the CAB had helped to create an eleven-firm
cartel in the skies.[100] As the heterodox economist Karl Polanyi memorably
asserted, at the dawn of this new economic era, "laissez-faire was planned."[101]

What political scientists Jacob Hacker and Paul Pierson call "American
amnesia"—the refusal to understand that extraordinary postwar economic
growth required an extraordinary amount of government—was not a
straightforward political pathology. Because subsidies were routed through
private companies, economic planning was frequently seen as a result of the
dynamism of free enterprise and the superiority of the American Way, particularly at the height of the Cold War.[102] This was especially true in agriculture, which had received lavish state support since the passage of the
Homestead and Morill Land Grant College Acts in the 1860s. These agriculture colleges, in turn, pioneered research into farming techniques that
made American farmers unequaled in their productivity per acre—and in
their use of pesticides, as the biochemical industry was also nurtured in the
labs and experimental farms of agricultural colleges.[103] Since 1914, the Extension Service had ensured that research derived from experiments at the
"cow-colleges" quickly found its way to select farmers.

By the 1950s, government-funded research through the National Science
Foundation, the National Institutes of Health, and at universities created
private sector profits and enabled business development.[104] The developmental dimension of the postwar mixed economy remained hidden by the
ultimate receipt of federal grants by corporate and university-based research
teams, engineers, and laboratories.[105] Indeed, the commercial potential of
government-funded research was part of its appeal.[106] From birth, the
postwar mixed economy outwardly favored its private parent over its
public.[107] It was in this context that private sector voluntary associations

like TA and the NCFB worked hard to make sure the state stayed hidden, even as those organizations relied upon state power for their own operation.

Benson was an avid supporter of the developmental state: he approved of increased funding for research at land grant universities and had no compunction about wresting open new markets and disposing of U.S. surpluses abroad. He was, however, a stalwart foe of the price support and production control features of farm policy inaugurated by the New Deal. Benson was the most ideological and polarizing of Eisenhower's cabinet, prone to biblical condemnations of the New Deal farm program, and fundamentalist proclamations about free-enterprise farming.[108] For Benson, the high price support system was as unnatural as it was counterproductive. On the one hand, it encouraged farmers to produce more with little regard for the market for their products. As a result, huge surpluses of wheat, cotton, corn, and milk had accumulated in CCC warehouses.[109] For these programs, supply reduction had been a manifest failure and the public was footing the bill.

On the other hand, price supports were as enervating to the soul of the farmer as they were to the sanctity of the free-enterprise system. "Freedom is a God-given, eternal principle vouchsafed to us under the Constitution," announced Benson in one of his first statements as secretary. "It is doubtful if any man can be politically free who depends upon the state for sustenance." Too much state intervention into the marketplace "weakens initiative, discourages industry, destroys character, and demoralizes the people."[110]

In pursuit of a reduced role for government in agriculture, Benson was not above whipping up consumer resentment against farmers for "feeding at the public trough." "At what point will the 140 million Americans who do not live on farms rise up and demand outright the elimination of all aid to agriculture?" he asked amid a huge wheat surplus during the 1960 election year.[111] For the duration of his eight-year tenure as secretary of agriculture, Benson had insisted that if only the federal government stopped supporting commodity prices, surpluses would disappear as farmers yielded to the immutable law of supply and demand.[112] Benson's doctrinaire, righteous approach to farm subsidies alienated even farm state Republicans, and he was blamed for Republicans' disastrous returns in the 1958 midterm elections. Candidate Nixon cut him out of his 1960 presidential campaign.[113]

Harold Cooley relished making life difficult for Benson. As the chair of the House Committee on Agriculture for most of Benson's tenure, he had plenty of opportunities. The Democratic representative could not have disagreed more with Benson's notion of free-enterprise. "The farmers were free in 1932 and we had starvation prices."[114] The House Agricultural Committee chairman was a fierce defender of acreage controls and price supports—two pillars of the tobacco program that the secretary viewed as particularly unholy. "Mr. Benson proposes to scrap this program, and he offers nothing in its place but what he calls a 'free' market at lower and lower prices for farmers," Cooley proclaimed. "It has been evident virtually from the day he took office that it was his purpose to break down the support program for agriculture."[115] Tobacco farmers suspected Benson, an elder in the Mormon Church, of harboring religious biases against their crop. To protect supply management from attacks within and outside the house of agriculture, Cooley encouraged farmers to tell their side of the story.

Interest Group Ideas

Many political observers in the postwar decades thought that organized agriculture had a great deal of influence over policy and its own public image. Indeed, observations about the Farm Bureau's influence in Congress and in the fields were common to both liberalism's supporters and its critics. Intellectuals like Daniel Bell, Seymour Martin Lipset, and Arthur Schlesinger Jr. praised the postwar mania for joining civic organizations—striking even in a nation of joiners. Interest groups such as farm organizations were the political embodiment of this impulse—part of what Arthur Schlesinger Jr. described as the vital center of liberal democracy, buffering the extremes of fascism or communism.[116] This is also how the Farm Bureau portrayed its political role. The "great national organizations" such as the Farm Bureau, Chamber of Commerce, National Association of Manufacturers, or unions like the American Federation of Labor and Congress of Industrial Organizations (AFL-CIO) had "the high responsibility of studying the problems in its field, and helping us decide what is best," explained a 1958 primer on the organization. Such organizations were responsible not only for their "industry, profession, or trade, but also for this nation as a whole."[117]

In the postwar years, political theorists understood interest groups as essential for mass democratic society. Although few champions of pluralism went so far as to assert that interest groups always acted "for the nation as a whole," unions, farm groups, and professional associations were seen as crucial links between citizens and the state. Interest groups were understood as essentially representative organizations, conveying the sentiments of membership to elected officials.

In this rendering, both pressure groups and the state served as transparent vectors of popular will, devoid of autonomous powers.[118] "The groups exist for the individuals to whom they belong," wrote political scientist Earl Latham in *The Group Basis of Politics* in 1952. The state existed alongside private associations, serving to ensure the "consensus by which the groups exist in mutual relations."[119] In this harmonious scenario, "every statute tends to represent compromise because the process of accommodating conflicts of group interest is one of deliberation and consent."[120] For the pluralists, the dominant leitmotif of political life was dynamism and motion. They imagined politics as a self-correcting marketplace, constantly adjusting to new configurations of power to achieve new equilibrium, where "today's losers may be tomorrow's winners."[121]

Not all were sanguine about the self-regulating nature of interest groups. Where the pluralists saw the political process as a constant search for equilibrium, critics saw sclerosis and the hardened accretion of power around unrepresentative organizations. Faith in such platitudes as democratic representation, equality before the law, and impartiality of institutions were increasingly seen as naïve by the late 1950s. C. Wright Mills, the sociologist famous for his commentary on the stultifying conformity of mid-century life, argued that within American political culture, "public relations displace reasoned argument," and "manipulation and unabated decisions of power displace democratic authority."[122] For Mills and other left-wing commentators, the state looked less like a neutral arbiter of authentic competing interests and more like a crooked umpire picking winners and losers in advance. For other critics, the problem lay not only in the partiality of the state, but in the elitism of pressure groups themselves.[123] Interest groups did not so much represent the will of a broad membership base as they reflected the class position of their leadership.

Political scientist Grant McConnell was an early critic of the pluralist ideal within his discipline. In his 1954 *Decline of Agrarian Democracy,* McConnell dated agriculture's fall from Eden to the middle of the New Deal, when the conservatives in the AAA vanquished the reformist Farm Security Administration, affirming the power of an agricultural oligarchy. In McConnell's thesis, the Farm Bureau was the serpent in the grass, born powerful because of its long-standing connections to the agricultural Extension Service.[124] Specifically, the history and operation of the Farm Bureau contradicted the assumptions of pluralist theory on two counts: the neutrality of the state and the extent to which the organization represented the material interests of its mass membership. McConnell's subsequent classic, *Private Power and American Democracy,* expanded on the fundamental paradox that he observed in agriculture: the smaller the organized constituency, the more powerful the interest group. Far from the pluralists' law of mechanical equilibration of interest group power, McConnell invoked a darker law of political ecology: "the iron law of oligarchy," which observed that all private groups, increasingly invested with public power, drift toward rule by an elite few.[125]

Thus, in the eyes of left-wing critics of American political institutions, agricultural organizations served as a prime example of special interest corruption. Wesley McCune's *Who's Behind Our Farm Policy?* (1956) was a muckraking indictment of the "interlocking directorates" of the agricultural bureaucracy and farm and business pressure groups. McCune, who served as assistant to the secretary of agriculture in the Truman administration, wrote with an eye toward the growth and operation of farm pressure groups since the Second World War, with the Farm Bureau foremost in size and influence. Indeed, the very size of the Farm Bureau, which had since the 1940s aggressively solicited the membership of nonagricultural business interests, made it the least representative vehicle for pressing the interests of its "more than 1,600,000 farm families."[126] The Farm Bureau was also nurtured by its close relationship to state Extension Services. "The history ... of the Farm Bureau organization," read one Farm Bureau pamphlet, "is so interwoven with the history of the development of the Extension Service of the U.S. Department of Agriculture and the state colleges of agriculture" that "it is impossible to sketch the development of one without mention of the other."[127]

Who's Behind Our Farm Policy did not take aim at pluralism on a theoretical level, but its rhetoric and analysis reveal the distinctive imprint of McConnell and Mills. "Nowadays the chief function of these organizations is to deal with government agencies which were created by their earlier hell-raising."[128] In McCune's telling, since the Second World War, farmers had found themselves as the target of seemingly friendly outreach efforts by corporations and trade associations such as the Food Retailers Committee, Sears, Roebuck, or the Quaker Oats Company. Plied by well-funded PR campaigns, elite farmers and businessmen drew closer together. "What old-time farm leader would have expected a representative of the Association of American Railroads to attend regularly meetings of the Grange and Farm Bureau—and be invited to do so?"[129] Nonagricultural interests entered "the deliberations of farm organizations at high places," using "their farm connections as 'fronts,'" but always doing so by exuding "love and affection for the farmers."[130]

Tobacco producers did not come in for special scrutiny by either McCune or McConnell. But the patterns of flue-cured policymaking and power would not have surprised them. By the early 1950s, tobacco's agricultural stewards also were drawn into alliance with their erstwhile foes, the cigarette manufacturers. Farmers had traded angry opposition to the manufacturers for a businesslike alliance. Manufacturers, for their part, welcomed farmers into their smoke-filled chamber.

Public Relations for Agriculture

Tobacco farmers' foray into PR was animated by defensiveness—a spirit not unlike that which had animated the old Tri-State Tobacco Growers Cooperative Association (TGCA). PR was conceived of as a tool for farmers to obtain the privileges and advantages that were perceived to benefit other sectors at agriculture's expense. The NCFB, which had departed with the AFBF in its support of rigid and high price supports, worked closely with Cooley in developing a language of umbrage. The organization's newsletter contained information to help farmers "set the American public right" on common misperceptions about the parity system, commodity marketing, and the "actual cost of food as compared to previous years."[131]

Farm Bureau's recruitment and internal messaging was obsessively focused on Agriculture's fate relative to other sectors—especially organized labor.[132] For example, a pocket-sized pamphlet distributed to Tar Heel farmers was intended to supply ready answers to questions recruits might have about the organization. Why join the Farm Bureau? So that farmers could reclaim "their fair share of the Nation's income, their rightful portion of the consumer's dollar."[133] After all, "all other groups are organized," the NCFB observed in a resentful echo of cooperative agriculture's collective bargaining in the 1920s. "Farmers must be organized."[134] The Farm Bureau stoked a sense of beleaguerment by asserting that farmers were culturally devalued—"not fully recognized by other groups"—as they were working to "feed and clothe the world," through U.S. agriculture aid programs.

In this rendering, farmers' privileged relationship to the state—the existence of foreign aid programs for commodity sale and surplus disposal—was deliberately obscured. Instead, the Farm Bureau endowed farmers with a kind of martyrdom: toiling for the benefit of humanity and unrecognized for their efforts. In such a hostile environment, farmers could not leave politics to their enemies. "We farmers," the pamphlet announced, "can write our own Farm Program or let other groups write it for us." At stake was nothing less than the policies that had lifted North Carolina farmers out of the Great Depression. Tar Heel farmers were implored to "remember the 1930s" when considering whether or not they "know more about a Farm Program than those who don't farm."[135] Umbrage was a useful organizational strategy. Tobacco growers were simultaneously encouraged to advocate for "their" farm program and to view government largess as earned and natural.

For the NCFB, PR meant getting other Americans to see members as the responsible property owners they knew themselves to be. Beginning in 1953, the organization's resolutions contained an expanded plank on public relations in service of "better understanding and cooperation between the decreasing rural and increasing urban population of our country."[136] Its section on "Community Improvement" provides further clues about what kind of rural life Farm Bureau members wanted urban Americans to see. "An attractive and cooperative community adds to dignity and contentment in rural living," and so the Farm Bureau urged its members to "have attractive mail boxes with the owner's name in large letters either on the mail box or a sign under the mail box."[137]

Private upkeep of the "community" was of paramount importance. Members were instructed to voluntarily "participate in movements to beautify rural churches and cemeteries."[138] And, of course, Farm Bureau members always had to "actively promote and participate in county fairs," putting forth their own "individual farm exhibits" to be highlighted by state agricultural officials. Farmers were instructed to think of themselves as citizens, family patriarchs, church members, and community stewards, and not as recipients of government aid. And although the Farm Bureau encouraged members to consider the superiority of rural values, Farm Bureau members were not alone in assimilating government largess into a sense of earned property. Indeed, at the very same time, suburban Americans likewise began to understand single-family homes, purchased with federally subsidized mortgages, as the birthright of the middle class.[139]

Whiteness was central to the Farm Bureau's vision of farmer citizenship—not unlike other visions of nuclear families that circulated in the decade of *Ozzie and Harriet*.[140] The NCFB strenuously opposed social policies that could benefit black Americans, even if such policies were consistent with other planks in the NCFB platform. By supporting high price supports for tobacco growers, the organization supported a welfare state for rural white people even as it opposed the "steady expansion in welfare expenditures and the steady increase in the numbers of persons on relief rolls."[141]

The organization's racism was equally clear on questions of public education, where it remained steadfastly committed to Jim Crow. Earlier in the decade, the NCFB had decried the state's reputation for low educational attainment, and demanded more money for rural public schools.[142] By 1959, the language of the educational recommendations suggested a developing racial nuance. The Farm Bureau's educational platform asserted primacy of the family rather than the public schools, highlighting the "responsibility of parents for student guidance."[143] The following year, as integration with "all deliberate speed" finally reached North Carolina, the Charlotte-Mecklenburg School District consolidated. In response, the Farm Bureau affirmed a plank on "States' Rights" and educational localism: "the control, administration, and financing of our public school system must remain identified with the smallest unit of government capable of satisfactory performance."[144]

Explicit racial hierarchy was so characteristic of white agricultural politics that when it surfaced it barely received mention in the mainstream

press. In May 1951, Cooley gave a keynote address at an awards ceremony for USDA employees. The crowd was composed of 4,000 black and white agricultural officials—the USDA, and particularly the Extension Service, was still organized along Jim Crow lines. In his speech, the congressman joked repeatedly about "nigger preachers" and "nigger tenants," occasioning a walkout by hundreds of African Americans in attendance.[145] Citing his well-known "record of friendship to Negroes," Cooley later claimed that he meant no harm. "I don't care if I did say it, either inadvertently or intentionally," Cooley snapped. "Any Negro who took exception is hypersensitive."[146] The epithet received mention in the black press only. For the foremost congressional proponent of PR for agriculture, the "farmer's side of the story" began with white male entitlement to property and ended with white farmer entitlement to "write their own" farm program.

By encouraging members' investment in markers of private, virtuous citizenship, the NCFB deemphasized the extent to which tobacco growers' very property was a creation of the federal government. The central mechanism of supply control was the "quota," a state-created property right. It allowed owners of property to which quota had been assigned to participate in the tobacco auction market; and it entitled owners to price support and loan benefits, which were sculpted continuously by the dictates of the secretary of agriculture, and the administrative prerogatives of local agricultural committees. Like a New York City taxi medallion, the right to grow tobacco was valuable in itself—quite apart from the auction price of tobacco, or the price of cab fare, though both of these figures were artificially inflated by virtue of aggregate supply restrictions.

The quota was a regulatory device made into transferrable wealth.[147] Revisions to the tobacco program in 1961 made this point all the more obvious when Congress allowed up to five acres of a farmer's allotment to be leased and transferred within the same county. The quota, then, was fully a commodity in its own right—severable from production, fungible, and useful as collateral on loans. "The value of a farm today that produces tobacco is pretty well based on [its] tobacco allotment," Everett Jordan, the Democratic senator from North Carolina, observed in 1965.[148]

The quota paid political dividends as well. Many of the inactive quota owners who rented out their assigned poundage were elderly—sometimes retired farmers, sometimes widows. This rental money was a valuable

supplement to a fixed income. "This acreage represents their life investment," explained one lessee whose active farm operation was cobbled together by renting unused quota. "Due to this money these people are not on the welfare roles [sic]."[149] The grower came to think of the government-created value of the quota as natural ("*their* life investment"), drawing a racially inflected distinction between rental income and the welfare dole.

But a check to an elderly landlord did not fully free the quota from its origins on particular plots of land. The quota was only transferrable within the same county, which had the effect of forestalling the total consolidation of tobacco production in low-cost regions, tying areas that might have abandoned tobacco for industry or real estate development or higher education to the crop's political fate.[150] The federal tobacco program sealed in place a large and sympathetic constituency for pro-tobacco regulation. Masked as a form of private property, the federal tobacco program reinforced the notion that farmers deserved all that they had—and more.

It was precisely the bounty bestowed by the tobacco program—high price supports and value-inflating quotas—that required assiduous defense through PR and interest group representation. "We want nobody dictating a farm program to us," Cooley said in a 1955 radio address. "But as we work out our own problems and policies, we need the understanding of people in the cities where votes are cast in Congress."[151] Although they represented a diminishing proportion of Americans, farmers were not about to relinquish their claim on virtuous citizenship. Interest groups like the NCFB—influential precisely because New Deal political economy rested upon associational relationships between the state and civil society—concealed their debts to the state through the language of voluntarism, private property, community, and family.[152] The decentralized, committee-based nature of the farm program—which was always intended to be run with the support of farm organizations—facilitated the NCFB's power. The NCFB's relentless veneration of family and property created a sense that white tobacco producers, unlike other racial or professional segments of Americans, were entitled to government support. Tobacco farmers in North Carolina operated under a kind of ironic agrarianism: the federal tobacco program produced smallholder democracy, which was socially valuable and thus worthy of federal protection.

226 The York Building, Raleigh, N.C.:
The Tobacco Growers Information Committee

By 1953 it had become clear to the cigarette makers that even their own for-midable organizational capacities would be tested by the emerging evidence of the cigarette's harm. Advertising or ad hominem attacks were inadequate responses to the decade's new breed of anti-tobacco sentries. It had been easy enough to deride the morally strident proclamations of a Lucy Page Gaston; but to condemn the findings of well-credentialed medical men when scientific expertise was highly valued and increasingly subsidized by the federal government—and when some of those experts were former smokers themselves—was another thing entirely. Popular publications like *Reader's Digest* (the highest-circulation outlet of the time) and *Time* reported on the early scientific studies. And with titles like "Cancer by the Carton" and "Beyond Any Doubt," readers barely needed to get beyond the headlines to understand the direction in which smoking-and-health research pointed.[153]

Americans were learning, seemingly by the day, that lung cancer, once a medical rarity, was a rapidly rising cause of death in American and British men. Scientists in both countries were increasingly associating lung cancer with high national smoking rates. And the types of American men who smoked had changed as well. Cigarettes had once been a vice of immigrants and juvenile delinquents. But war, advertising, and Hollywood had helped to broaden, professionalize, and glamorize smoking's appeal. In 1955, more than half of all American men and nearly a quarter of all American women were active smokers.[154] Servicemen, issued cigarettes as part of their rations, smoked at even higher rates.[155] Humphrey Bogart, Marilyn Monroe, and James Dean invited men and women to consider the cigarette as a companion to sex; politicians like Lyndon Johnson and Everett Dirksen demonstrated that its enjoyment knew no political bounds; men of distinction like nuclear physicist turned antinuclear advocate Robert Oppenheimer and National Association for the Advancement of Colored People (NAACP) chief counsel Thurgood Marshall were chain smokers. Skillfully parleying the vaunted status and expertise of doctors, R. J. Reynolds launched an advertising campaign in 1946 that would inundate Americans for the next six years: "More Doctors Smoke Camels Than Any Other Cigarette."[156]

Regardless of one's professional class, educational attainment, looks, or political affiliation, to smoke was to be American.

While the brand preference of the medical establishment was unknown, the smoking habits of doctors *did* lay the groundwork for one of the most significant investigations into smoking and lung cancer. The British Doctors Study, which began in 1951, would ultimately track the mortality of doctors over five decades. By 1954, results of the study had already demonstrated significantly greater death rates among doctors who smoked versus those who did not.[157] By the end of 1954, fourteen statistical studies confirmed the association between lung cancer and cigarette use.[158] "The amount you have smoked daily and the number of years you have maintained the habit determine your chances of developing lung cancer," admonished Dr. Alton Ochsner, a renowned surgeon who had observed the association between smoking and lung cancer in 1939.[159]

Ochsner's warnings went unheeded, as per capita cigarette consumption rose throughout the 1950s.[160] The growing number of reports failed to bring about an immediate change in Americans' sense of the threat that cigarettes posed. Between 1954 and 1962, Gallup polling revealed that the percentage of Americans who believed that cigarettes were a cause of lung cancer and heart disease rose by only 5 percentage points—from 42 percent to 47 percent.[161]

Credit for this dubious accomplishment can be laid at the feet of the cigarette manufacturers. Paul Hahn, the president of the American Tobacco Company, believed the manufacturers needed to come together to formulate a plan of action—a plan to match the scientists' concern for health with the industry's own. At the New York City Plaza Hotel in December 1953, tobacco executives agreed to set aside the temptation to exploit the health issue against rival firms. Instead, they would embrace collective action. With the assistance of lawyers and PR men at Hill & Knowlton, they would develop a strategy that would guide the industry over the next four decades.

The manufacturers' doubt-mongering followed a rhetorical template. They would counter scientific findings about the cigarette with the industry's own research—and then cite their own studies as proof that the "science is not settled." Representatives of the companies would parrot the rhetoric of science—declaring the need for an impossibly high threshold of certainty and proof of the causal link between smoking and disease—in the service of obfuscating the truth. The Tobacco Industry Research Committee (TIRC) was their main vehicle for doing so. Between 1954 and 1997, TIRC spent nearly $300 million funding scientific projects on "tobacco and health" intended to find no relationship between smoking and cancer, or on projects that were never intended to answer the question.[162]

Agricultural interests were a part of the tobacco industry's conspiracy from its inception.[163] Tobacco's chief executive officers were not alone at the Plaza: Jack Hutson was there too, in his capacity as the president of TA. Meeting notes reveal that Hutson was also tasked as the conduit to other growers' associations—connections he had forged during the New Deal.[164] Whether small farmers were aware of it or not, the structure of TA's funding—a mandatory assessment on producers linked to the federal marketing referendum—tied all tobacco farmers into the machinations of Big Tobacco. Organization originally intended to help farmers overcome their marketing weakness vis-à-vis the cigarette manufacturers ultimately redounded to the manufacturers' benefit.

The result of the Plaza meeting was a canny bit of advertising. The "Frank Statement to Cigarette Smokers" appeared in hundreds of newspapers in January 1954 (see Figure 3.3). The advertisement evinced concern with public health while also laying the groundwork for a long-term project of scientific subterfuge. On the one hand, the statement reassured readers that the industry "accepted an interest in people's health as a basic responsibility" and promised to "cooperate closely with those whose task it is to safeguard the public health." To this end, it announced the formation of TIRC—an industry-funded research consortium that would aid research into "all phases of tobacco use and health." Its board would be filled with the ranks of "distinguished men from medicine, science, and education." Broader media coverage of the "Frank Statement" lauded the tobacco industry as responsible and enlightened.[165] In reality, TIRC trafficked in what Robert Proctor has called "red herring research" intended only to generate doubt about the causal connection between smoking and illness.[166]

At the bottom of the "Statement" was a list of the document's sponsors. Naturally, there were the presidents of cigarette manufacturers like American Tobacco, Brown & Williamson, R. J. Reynolds, Philip Morris, and P. Lorillard. But there was also "J. B. Hutson" of Tobacco Associates, Inc.

A Frank Statement

to Cigarette Smokers

RECENT REPORTS on experiments with mice have given wide publicity to a theory that cigarette smoking is in some way linked with lung cancer in human beings.

Although conducted by doctors of professional standing, these experiments are not regarded as conclusive in the field of cancer research. However, we do not believe that any serious medical research, even though its results are inconclusive should be disregarded or lightly dismissed.

At the same time, we feel it is in the public interest to call attention to the fact that eminent doctors and research scientists have publicly questioned the claimed significance of these experiments.

Distinguished authorities point out:

1. That medical research of recent years indicates many possible causes of lung cancer.

2. That there is no agreement among the authorities regarding what the cause is.

3. That there is no proof that cigarette smoking is one of the causes.

4. That statistics purporting to link cigarette smoking with the disease could apply with equal force to any one of many other aspects of modern life. Indeed the validity of the statistics themselves is questioned by numerous scientists.

We accept an interest in people's health as a basic responsibility, paramount to every other consideration in our business.

We believe the products we make are not injurious to health.

We always have and always will cooperate closely with those whose task it is to safeguard the public health.

For more than 300 years tobacco has given solace, relaxation, and enjoyment to mankind. At one time or another during those years critics have held it responsible for practically every disease of the human body. One by one these charges have been abandoned for lack of evidence.

Regardless of the record of the past, the fact that cigarette smoking today should even be suspected as a cause of a serious disease is a matter of deep concern to us.

Many people have asked us what we are doing to meet the public's concern aroused by the recent reports. Here is the answer:

1. We are pledging aid and assistance to the research effort into all phases of tobacco use and health. This joint financial aid will of course be in addition to what is already being contributed by individual companies.

2. For this purpose we are establishing a joint industry group consisting initially of the undersigned. This group will be known as TOBACCO INDUSTRY RESEARCH COMMITTEE.

3. In charge of the research activities of the Committee will be a scientist of unimpeachable integrity and national repute. In addition there will be an Advisory Board of scientists disinterested in the cigarette industry. A group of distinguished men from medicine, science, and education will be invited to serve on this Board. These scientists will advise the Committee on its research activities.

This statement is being issued because we believe the people are entitled to know where we stand on this matter and what we intend to do about it.

TOBACCO INDUSTRY RESEARCH COMMITTEE

5400 EMPIRE STATE BUILDING, NEW YORK 1, N. Y.

SPONSORS:

THE AMERICAN TOBACCO COMPANY, INC.
Paul M. Hahn, President

BENSON & HEDGES
Joseph F. Cullman, Jr., President

BRIGHT BELT WAREHOUSE ASSOCIATION
F. S. Royster, President

BROWN & WILLIAMSON TOBACCO CORPORATION
Timothy V. Hartnett, President

BURLEY AUCTION WAREHOUSE ASSOCIATION
Albert Clay, President

BURLEY TOBACCO GROWERS COOPERATIVE
ASSOCIATION
John W. Jones, President

LARUS & BROTHER COMPANY, INC.
W. T. Reed, Jr., President

P. LORILLARD COMPANY
Herbert A. Kent, Chairman

MARYLAND TOBACCO GROWERS ASSOCIATION
Samuel C. Linton, General Manager

PHILIP MORRIS & CO., LTD., INC.
O. Parker McComas, President

R. J. REYNOLDS TOBACCO COMPANY
E. A. Darr, President

STEPHANO BROTHERS, INC.
C. S. Stephano, D'Sc., Director of Research

TOBACCO ASSOCIATES, INC.
(An organization of flue-cured tobacco growers)
J. B. Hutson, President

UNITED STATES TOBACCO COMPANY
J. W. Peterson, President

Figure 3.3 The "Frank Statement" appeared in 448 newspapers across the United States in January 1954, reaching an approximate total circulation of 43,245,000. Circled portions show grower organizations that participated in the formation of the Tobacco Industry Research Committee. (Tobacco Industry Research Committee)

Hutson succeeded in his charge of reaching out to the agricultural trade, enlisting the sponsorship of the Burley Growers Cooperative, the Maryland Growers Association, and the representatives of several warehouse associations. The organizational activity that had brought stability to tobacco-growing regions during the New Deal also allowed growers to be politically, financially, and culturally enlisted into the project of obfuscation and deceit. Having stabilized the incomes of tobacco farmers, grower organizations turned their skills toward defending cigarettes themselves against the growing evidence that they were deadly.[167]

To preserve TIRC's appearance of scientific integrity, Hill & Knowlton advised the industry to form separate institutional units that could enter the fray of politics more directly.[168] In 1958, two new organizations were born under the umbrella of tobacco's PR efforts: the Tobacco Institute (TI) and the TGIC. The TI was a lobby. Its leaders during the 1960s and 1970s, Horace Kornegay and Earle Clements, had themselves served in high elected office representing tobacco-growing regions of tobacco-growing states. Kornegay spent four terms as the Democratic representative from North Carolina's Sixth Congressional District, sandwiched between the cigarette towns of Durham (American Tobacco and Liggett & Myers) and Winston-Salem (R. J. Reynolds). Clements was one of the highest-profile politicians of the time, a Democratic stalwart from the state of Kentucky, having served as a congressman, governor, and then senator. In the Senate, Clements whipped votes for his friend, majority leader Lyndon Johnson. His close personal and political ties to Johnson would later help shield the industry at a moment of vulnerability after the *Surgeon General's Report* of 1964.

Leadership aside, the TI was responsible for the industry's propaganda efforts. Until it was dissolved by the Master Settlement Agreement in 1998, it produced an endless stream of sound bites, press releases, white papers, ghost-authored articles, and camera-ready spokespeople purporting to debunk the scientific consensus that smoking caused disease. The TI quickly established itself as one of Washington's richest and most politically connected lobbies.

The TGIC translated this propaganda goal for an agricultural audience. The organization's goal was to combat "so-called health-scare talk and excessive taxation"—joining the farmer's long-standing fight against higher cigarette taxes to the contemporary issue of health. A blend of public and private

farm leadership incorporated the TGIC in Raleigh, North Carolina, in November 1958. The TGIC was comprised of larger farm organizations representing thousands of members. Grower cooperatives in all tobacco-producing
states—from Florida to Connecticut, Tennessee to Wisconsin—were early
members, as were all farm bureaus and granges from those same states.[169]

The leadership of the TGIC similarly reflected the long-standing associational ties between public and private organizations. The TGIC's
chairman was Carl Hicks. Hicks was also president of Stabilization and
chaired the NCFB's Tobacco Advisory Committee. He had been part of the
delegation sent to Washington to work out the provisions of tobacco policy
with New Deal tobacco policy planners in the 1930s.[170] Con Lanier, representing leaf dealers, signed the TGIC's articles of incorporation; Jack Hutson
was on the board of directors and was a frequent presence at TGIC meetings until his death. The TGIC drew upon even older organizing traditions
in the tobacco belt. W. T. Joyner, the son of a founder of the old Tri-State
Tobacco Growers Cooperative Association (TGCA), served as the organization's general counsel.[171] Representatives of public agencies also played
an important role. A member of the North Carolina Tobacco Advisory
Council, a policymaking body connected to the state Department of Agriculture, was a mainstay at meetings, while a member of the federal Farm
Credit Administration signed on to the board of directors.[172]

None of these men represented tobacco farmers in a racial, economic, or
social sense. They were wealthy and white, and spent less time farming and
more time running businesses. But politically and economically, they literally represented thousands of farmers, serving on elected boards and
running the organizations that made the rules for the tobacco belt.
According to the organization's proposed budget for 1960, Tobacco Associates, funded through growers' assessments on their tobacco acreage
and on the federal tobacco program referendum ballot, contributed as
much to the TGIC ($25,000) as did the manufacturer-funded TI.[173]

Funded by the Tobacco Institute, Tobacco Associates, and the membership contributions of participating organizations, the TGIC brought the
public relations apparatus of big business to the dense organizational networks of agriculture. The organization primarily operated through the
work of a full-time PR man who wrote the press releases, articles, and pam-
phlets that would be disseminated by the local press and farm organ-

izations and, of course, by the elected officials that the organization worked to cultivate. The PR officer also monitored the content of national and area newspapers, television stations, and radio shows, making sure that they were well supplied with pro-cigarette "facts" to counter the "opinions" of anti-cigarette "zealots."[174] The TGIC's first efforts at recruiting established the organization's tone—and suggested its corporate funding. A brochure entitled a "Call to Arms" was mailed to 350,000 "farmers and their friends." It was also distributed to farmers through the voluntary efforts of private businessmen—feed dealers, insurance agents, bankers—and public figures like Extension agents and county tobacco committeemen.[175] Through the TGIC, farm organizations developed a vocabulary of antigovernment umbrage that concealed the political privileges that had helped to constitute the organization in the first place.

Support from the agricultural media was crucial. At its founding, the TGIC received, by its own account, "strong support from the public-service media," including farm-focused publications like the *Progressive Farmer* and *Farm and Ranch Magazine,* and also regional newspapers with an urban reach such as the Richmond *Times-Dispatch* and the Raleigh *News and Observer.*[176] The TGIC also funneled information through the well-worn channels of farm meetings. It sent local granges, farm bureaus, warehouse associations, bankers, Extension agents, and county committees materials prepared by Hill & Knowlton via the TI.[177] Public relations for growers relied on the already existing, state-supported organizations, information channels, and personnel hierarchies. But as a private, corporate entity, the TGIC—founded with goals that were explicitly anti-tax and anti–public health—shrouded its own very statist mechanics in stridently antiregulatory language.

Just as the TIRC funded pro-tobacco studies that the TI then cited as proof positive of medical disagreement over the relationship between smoking and health, so too did the TGIC create a recursive loop of pro-tobacco knowledge. It received information from state and private sources, repackaged that information as grist for the pro-cigarette cause, and redistributed the knowledge back to those same feeder institutions—farm organizations, departments of agriculture, bankers, and tobacco trade organizations.

For instance, in one early publicity blitz, the organization published 80,000 brochures entitled "The First American Heritage," which were tailor-made for Georgia, Kentucky, North Carolina, Virginia, South Carolina, and Tennessee. For example, Virginia's "First American Heritage" brochure emphasized the historically and economically indispensable role that tobacco played in the state's development—from its cultivation in the colonial era through its contribution to state revenues derived from tobacco taxes. The very end of the accordion-style pocket pamphlet proudly proclaimed its sources as "the Richmond Chamber of Commerce, the Tobacco Tax Council, the Virginia Department of Agriculture and Commerce, Virginia Department of Labor, Virginia State Chamber of Commerce, Virginia State Ports Authority, United States Department of Agriculture, United States Department of Commerce, **Internal Revenue Service, U.S. Treasury Department**."[178] The TGIC relied on the authority and prestige of state statistics even as it sought to establish a parallel, trade-centered counterweight to the right of government to regulate tobacco.

The cigarette manufacturers were the main force behind the TGIC. But the organization cannot be written off as an attempt by industry to "farm the farmers." Hutson, after all, had been present at the founding of the TIRC. At one early TIRC meeting, Farm Bureau representatives and Burley tobacco growers sat shoulder to shoulder with industry lawyers, PR executives, and Clarence Cook Little, the infamous physician whose commitment to a genetic theory of cancer causation made him the industry's favorite doctor.[179] And, of course, three of the fourteen signatories to the infamous "Frank Statement to Cigarette Smokers" (1954) were representatives of farm groups.

Instead the TGIC represented a new chapter in the relationship between organized growers and manufacturers—a new chapter in the cigarette's history. Long gone were the days of night riding and thunderous denunciations of the Tobacco Trust. The federal farm program had empowered and organized elite tobacco growers to expand the market for cigarettes abroad, and to defend the smoky status quo at home. The TGIC vindicated Cooley's earlier calls for "a positive PR program for farmers."[180] With tobacco industry backing, farmers finally had their arsenal of "facts" and "truth" to supply to "the important writers, magazines, and newspapers, of the United States"; they finally had their "speakers bureau" and more than one "well qualified person" ready to present their side of the story.[181]

————

In collaboration with the industry, growers' rhetoric took on an antigovernment tone, even as flue-cured tobacco growers received a greater level of federal support than any other group of commodity growers. And the TGIC was enabled by government agencies themselves: its leadership and membership rested upon a small group of men who held power within and outside of the agricultural bureaucracy. The apparent hypocrisy of a highly subsidized industry decrying government regulation was no contradiction at all. One could choose to ignore the structuring hand of the state through participation in voluntary organizations like the NCFB and the TGIC. One could view Tobacco Associates' mandatory assessment as evidence of farmers' responsibility and ownership over a private program, rather than a compelled surplus disposal mechanism. And with enough help, one could even see the federal tobacco program itself not as a taxpayer-funded subsidy—because, after all, farmers did not receive direct payments from the government, only price supports that they received *in exchange* for reducing their acreage.

The associational nature of agricultural power—evident in the NCFB, the TA, and the TGIC—was not a simple story of private interest capture, as critics like Wesley McCune and Grant McConnell charged. Rather, the decentralized mechanisms for controlling tobacco established during the 1930s and expanded during the 1940s and 1950s were conceived of as joint ventures between select citizens and the state, shepherded by an elite coterie of men who were sometimes employed formally by government, and other times in the private sector. This allowed private organizations to disavow their political privileges, and even stoke antigovernment resentment against "political opportunists" trying to "legislate tobacco out of existence."[182] Guided by the postwar economic ideology of *more*—more cigarettes, more smokers, more exports, more quota—grower organizations and the industry drew close. When tobacco farmers finally embraced PR they did so in conjunction with the tobacco industry. At stake was not just a commodity or product. At stake was a way of doing government.

4

The Challenge of the Public Interest

The tobacco program might not mean much to those to chant, chant, chant nonsense, but it means something to those who remember 10 cent tobacco.
—Hubert Humphrey

We don't look for voluntary cooperation. We sue people—we sue the bastards.
—John Banzhaf III

IN 1964 it finally happened.[1] On Saturday, January 11, surgeon general Luther Terry stood behind a podium at the State Department Auditorium and announced the release of a much-anticipated report on smoking and health. A Saturday address was a departure from the normal order of official press conferences. But the Public Health Service (PHS) knew that the announcement would send tobacco stock prices tumbling, and so Terry's address was postponed until after the markets had closed. Nine "no smoking" signs had been hastily fastened to the walls of the auditorium where Terry spoke. A handful of the two hundred reporters, government workers, and industry spokesmen—including Terry's assistant for information—smoked in the hallways outside.[2] The surgeon general himself had recently switched from cigarettes to an occasional pipe or cigar.[3]

The *Report* announced in no uncertain terms that cigarette smoking was causally related to the American death rate. Smokers had, on average, a nine- to ten-fold greater risk of developing lung cancer compared to non-smokers; for heavy smokers, the risk was twenty-fold greater.[4] Smokers suffered from coronary heart disease, the leading cause of death at the time, at a rate 70 percent higher than nonsmokers.[5] Cigarettes were also judged to be the most important cause of chronic bronchitis, and were associated with an increased risk of dying from both chronic bronchitis and pulmonary emphysema.[6] Given the magnitude and gravity of the peril posed by cigarettes, the surgeon general confidently predicted that there would be no "foot dragging" by the government in tackling the problem.[7]

The *Surgeon General's Report* marked the high-water mark of the expert-driven, consensus-based policymaking characteristic of the U.S. government since the 1930s and intensified by the Cold War.[8] Terry had, after all, gone to great lengths to produce a report that was as politically unimpeachable as it was scientifically rigorous. The tobacco industry's recent innovations in organized denial highlighted the need for a document that would be understood as authoritative in the face of industry-generated controversy.[9] To compose the advisory panel responsible for reviewing the accumulated research on tobacco, Terry's staff compiled a list of 150 candidates recognized as experts in the fields of pulmonology, cardiology, epidemiology, and statistics. The list was then circulated to the American Medical Association, the American Heart Association, the American Cancer Society, the National Tuberculosis Association, and the Tobacco Institute. Each group could strike any name for any reason. The ten men ultimately appointed to the committee were thus chosen by a process of elimination and consensus (see Figure 4.1). Terry made sure that five committee members were smokers. Throughout 1963, the panel convened in a room at the National Library of Medicine. The air was thick with smoke and the table covered in papers and ashtrays.[10] Even the *Surgeon General's Report* was the product of a smoke-filled room.

The *Report* also augured the end of that era. The year 1964 marked the beginning of a wholesale reevaluation of the relationship between the machinery of government and the representation of the governed. Spurred by the civil rights movement and antiwar activism, a great many Americans had become increasingly skeptical of all manner of elite, expert-driven institutions—from doctors' offices to universities to the smoke-filled chambers of congressional committees. In many ways, Americans were becoming less tolerant of the everyday life of associational government itself.[11]

Over the course of the decade, scholars, lawyers, and activists would launch a powerful critique of the hermetically sealed corridors of power that ran between organized interest groups and the government. Critics advocated, instead, for a broader role for "the public"—not only as the target of

Figure 4.1 Luther Terry addresses reporters upon the release of the 1964 *Surgeon General's Report*. The Surgeon General's Advisory Committee on Smoking and Health is seated behind the podium. (Profiles in Science / U.S. National Library of Medicine / NNBDBV)

policy, but as participants in political decision making. Emerging just as the federal government pledged itself to "remedial action" on cigarettes, the public interest critique shaped the tactics and composition of the anti-tobacco movement. The elaboration of the public interest was a powerful condemnation of tobacco corporatism. It resonated with Americans who had already begun to suspect that modernity—found in suburban tract housing, in the agricultural chemicals that yielded supermarket abundance, in the cigarette—may well come to destroy itself.[12]

The Participatory Ideal

A few months after the 1964 *Surgeon General's Report* was issued, legal scholar Charles Reich published an essay examining what he called "the New Property." He observed that the growth of the administrative state at the federal and state levels had created not just new levels of wealth, but new categories of wealth.[13] "Increasingly, Americans live on government largess—allocated by government on its own terms, and held by recipients subject to conditions which express 'the public interest.'"[14] Agricultural subsidies, including subsidies for tobacco growers; franchises for motor carriers, airlines, oil and gas pipelines; broadcast and occupational licenses; direct government contracts; Aid to Families with Dependent Children; unemployment and Social Security insurance—these were but a few of the most obvious forms of property created by what Reich called the "public interest state."

But what the state created in the name of the public interest, it could also take away.[15] Indeed, the power of government largess—whether in the form of a broadcast license, admission to the state bar, an old age pension, or public welfare assistance—had legalized the abandonment of the Constitution: those in a position of dependence upon the government were, in many cases, found not to enjoy the protections of the First, Fourth, or Fifth Amendments.[16] Writing with a particular regard for the way loyalty oaths enforced an ideological conformity as a condition for the receipt of gratuities, Reich rather dramatically analogized modern American political economy to feudalism. "Just as the feudal system linked lord and vassal through a system of mutual dependence, obligation, and loyalty," Reich wrote, "so government largess binds man to the state."[17]

Tobacco growers were far from Reich's own consciousness, but they well understood the dynamics that he described. For the past three decades, the right to grow and sell tobacco had been an exemplary form of "new property." For Reich, some state-society interaction led to the diminution of rights for individuals or disfavored firms, and some facilitated partnership that allowed select private entities to act as branches of the government.[18] Undergirded by affluence and executed by layers of bureaucracy, associational governance was responsible for an "utterly joyless" political landscape that offered no refuge to "the spirit of man."[19]

Reich's romanticism was tempered by his faith that institutions could be reformed. To safeguard the freedom of the individual in collective society, Reich proposed transforming government largess into rights—claims that an individual could make upon the state. A right to government support would safeguard an individual's independence by establishing "a secure minimum basis for individual well-being and dignity in a society where each man cannot be wholly the master of his own destiny."[20] The only way to make man independent in a collective age would be to transform benefits into entitlements.

"The New Property" was hugely influential. It remains the most cited article ever to appear in the *Yale Law Journal,* its influence extending well beyond the echo chamber of academic citations. Justice William Brennan drew upon the essay in a 1970 decision that held that welfare benefits resembled property and not government grants, thereby establishing a higher bar for their termination.[21] Equally important, Reich's yearning for authenticity inspired a generation of young lawyers who also imagined that agencies and courts could be sites where the broad public interest could find affirmation.

Reich understood the value of state-created gratuities; he had seen first-hand what government could do for America's largest corporations. After graduating from Yale Law School in 1952, he clerked for Supreme Court Justice Hugo Black during the term in which the Court handed down *Brown v. Board of Education.* He then joined the prestigious firm of Arnold and Porter, a den of the District's indigenous political creature, the "Washington lawyer"—a consummate insider, offering his clients access and influence on Congress and administration officials while zealously advocating for their interests before administrative agencies or the D.C. Court of Appeals.[22] Five years at Arnold & Porter gave Reich "a ringside seat from which to observe the operation of private corporate power . . . intertwined with the exercise of the federal's government's regulatory authority."[23] Those five years also provided ample exposure to the nexus of the law and the economy—the "corporate state," as Reich and other critical observers would term it—and the young lawyer had his fill. Reich returned to Yale in 1960, and spent the rest of the decade teaching at a law school that grew frothy with student demands for institutional reform.[24]

The Greening of America (1970) solidified his reputation as a scholar-guru to the counterculture, but Reich was, above all, a liberal.[25] As "New Property" demonstrated, Reich viewed the federal government as the essential guarantor of economic security. But he saw a perversion of democracy in the cozy relationships that existed between some regulatory agencies and the industries they stewarded—relationships that effectively blocked the door to broader public participation in the administration of national resources. His 1962 essay "The Public and the Nation's Forests" was a critical appraisal of the government's stewardship of national forests. "The power to make fundamental policy for the publicly-owned forests has fallen to small professional groups," despite the fact that all Americans had "a major stake in forest policy."[26] The problem lay in the closed-door nature of agency decision making, which left little opportunity for public participation and even less for substantial judicial review of agency decisions. The problem lay in the circuitry of associationalism itself.

At Yale Law School, students formed the first environmental law organizations, explicitly citing Reich as a major inspiration.[27] By the end of the 1960s, this type of critique had inspired a new field of legal practice: public interest law. Public interest lawyers sought to represent people, ideas, and even objects (a famous 1972 essay by Christopher Stone inquired "Should Trees Have Standing?") that were left out of the normal channels of political power. This critique of federal agencies, particularly in connection with the environment and natural resource allocation, would become increasingly salient through the 1960s, giving rise to the modern environmental law movement.[28] Public interest law stood as a rebuke to a system in which corporations, well-funded interest groups, and politically favored constituencies held disproportionate power.

Scholars of government in the 1960s were increasingly characterizing interest groups and the agencies with which they interacted as two sides of an "iron triangle"—a metaphor for the unholy political geometry that existed between interest groups, regulatory agencies, and Congress, ensuring that policy was passed and implemented for the benefit of a small, organized cadre of moneyed elites. Condemnation of the business orientation of politics spanned the ideological and disciplinary spectrum. New Left critics of "corporate liberalism" and right-wing market-oriented critics of "regulatory capture" shared a deeply felt skepticism of the independence of government from vested interests.[29]

Whether one called it corporate liberalism, interest group pluralism or regulatory capture, such observations of public administration had a profound effect upon young public interest lawyers. Inspired by the example of the Legal Defense Fund of the National Association for the Advancement of Colored People (NAACP), public interest lawyers were particularly enthusiastic about the potential of the judiciary to force open bureaucracies "to the ordinary citizen." Courts in the 1960s inaugurated an era of wider participation in agency procedures. Their rulings expanded judicial scrutiny of agency decisions; intensified requirements that agencies open their meetings to the public and expand their notice and comment periods; and, perhaps most importantly, expanded notions of standing—who has the right to ask a court to review an agency decision. Under a narrow conception of standing, only a litigant who had suffered a direct economic injury by an agency could sue that agency. In the landmark decision *Scenic Hudson Preservation Conference v. Federal Power Commission* (1965), the Second Circuit ruled that an environmentalist citizens' group had standing to sue the Federal Power Commission because of its "special interest in aesthetic, conservational, and recreational" aspects of a New York mountain that the Commission had approved as the site of a power plant.[30] Agencies, in short, had to embrace a wider conception of the public interest, include a broader segment of the public in their decision making, and become more accountable to the public via a less deferential judiciary.[31]

This revolution in legal strategy was mirrored in the wider currents of culture. A growing number of Americans began to suspect that the policies that resulted from associational government were as poisonous to the body as they were to the body politic. Americans were sickened by milk contaminated by radioactive fallout from atomic testing, despite the fact that the Atomic Energy Commission had known of the risks since the early 1950s.[32] In suburbia, Americans were forced to confront the underside of affluence as synthetic detergents from septic tanks poisoned drinking water.[33] Rachel Carson's *Silent Spring* (1962) was, after all, not only an indictment of widespread pesticide use that destroyed ecological balance in pursuit of a hubristic desire for total control of nature; it was also a condemnation of the unaccountable decision making at the U.S. Department of Agriculture (USDA).[34] Concerns about the quality of American life were beginning to emerge as a powerful counterweight to unreflective pursuit of economic growth. By the time the *Surgeon General's Report* was published, more Americans than ever were willing to consider the terrifying idea that the same dynamics that had produced prosperity could also be poisonous.

In response, the outlines of a new political ecosystem were just coming into focus. Bureaucracies in thrall to organized interests would have to contend with lawyers speaking on behalf of consumers, the environment, women, and nonwhites.[35] Or better yet, public institutions would have to contend with the demands of unorganized Americans themselves. Beginning in the mid-1960s, institutions themselves began to yield to the participatory ideal. The 1964 Wilderness Act was the first piece of federal legislation to require participation by citizens' groups in proposals for wilderness designations.[36] And the mandate of "maximum feasible participation" of poor people in designing the War on Poverty's Community Action Programs suggested the potency of the participatory ideal.

Of course, neither tobacco interests nor their allies in Congress would cede ground to this broadened conception of the public when it was articulated in front of regulatory agencies and in the courts.

Regulating after the Report

The *Surgeon General's Report* triggered an equal and opposite reaction from Congress and the Federal Trade Commission (FTC). The *Report* called for "appropriate remedial action" to curb the emerging public-health crisis—a phrase as authoritative and vague as "all deliberate speed." In response, the FTC acted quickly to propose a strongly worded warning label. And Congress acted slowly and deliberately to obstruct agency regulation, ultimately preempting the FTC's warning label with a watered-down version of its own. The trajectory of cigarette regulation in the 1960s demonstrated just why advocates for the public interest saw more potential for democratic representation before agencies and the courts than they did in Congress.

Before 1964, the FTC seemed an unlikely threat to the tobacco industry. True, the agency had investigated the industry some twenty times over the past half-century for false and misleading advertising.[37] True, too, that the FTC itself was born of the trust busting that had broken Duke's American Tobacco Company into four smaller pieces in the early part of the twentieth century. And it was also true that since the early 1950s, the agency had doggedly cited misleading medical claims made by particular cigarette brands. However, agency scrutiny of false medical claims may have unintentionally spurred heavier cigarette advertising. A flurry of advertising promoted filtered cigarettes; Lorillard introduced Kent cigarettes in 1952, touting their "famous micronite filter."[38] Over the course of the decade, the branding strategy changed. Filters received less emphasis, but brands proclaiming "low tar" were ubiquitous. The term "tar derby" was coined among cigarette and advertising industry insiders to characterize the contestation among brands. Amid this intense competition, advertising for cigarettes skyrocketed, jumping from $55 million in 1952 to $150 million in 1959, as each brand vied to allay consumer concerns about safety.

This ramped-up advertising relied upon an implicit health claim: that filtered or "low tar" cigarettes were healthier than regular brands. Such a claim was demonstrably false. In 1960, the FTC negotiated a voluntary industry-wide agreement whereby such health claims were to be banned from cigarette advertising. "This is a landmark example of industry-Government cooperation in solving a pressing problem," FTC chairman Earl Kinter proudly announced in 1960.[39] The consensual nature of the FTC regulation was a hallmark of the agency's approach during the 1950s and 1960s, leading to allegations that it had abandoned its mandate to protect consumers in favor of stakeholders in business.[40] The moratorium on the tar derby may have helped industry more than it helped consumers, for in banning advertising references to tar and nicotine, the FTC helped to reduce the sense of foreboding implicit in advertisements for *less harmful* cigarette brands.[41] And, the tobacco companies welcomed an enforced reprieve from expensive, cutthroat competition that frequently pitted brands owned by the same corporation against each other.[42]

Paul Rand Dixon, the Kennedy-appointed chairman of the Commission, saw the surgeon general's mandate for "appropriate remedial action" as an opportunity for his agency to shake its reputation for lethargy.[43] The *Report* offered the kind of "competent, probative scientific evidence" that the FTC needed to issue regulations that could withstand judicial appeals.[44] Within days of the *Report*'s January release, the FTC gave notice of its proposed rules requiring strongly worded warning labels to appear both on cigarette packages and in television and radio advertisements.[45]

1. CAUTION—CIGARETTE SMOKING IS A HEALTH HAZARD.
The Surgeon General's Advisory Committee has found that "cigarette smoking contributes to mortality from specific disease and the overall death rate."
2. CAUTION: Cigarette smoking is dangerous to health. It may cause death from cancer and other diseases.

These statements were clear and unequivocal. They invoked "hazard" and "danger" directly and in the present tense. The specter of death loomed in the second sentence, as the logical conclusion to a life of smoking. The Commission held hearings on the proposed warning in the spring of 1964, in advance of a final rule to be issued a few months later. Congressmen, doctors, governors, businessmen, and even tobacco farmers were present to weigh in on the fate of the $8 billion industry.

Coordinated through the Tobacco Institute and the Tobacco Growers Information Committee (TGIC), tobacco's agricultural champions were unified in their opposition to FTC regulation. Secretary of Agriculture Orville Freeman testified against the proposed rules at the hearings on the grounds that labeling might be too effective—that it would harm farmers by reducing demand for tobacco. This was a point of view naked in its advocacy for a narrow interest over and above the public interest. Tobacco producers were perhaps even better spokesmen for this argument. Fred Royster, a rich and well-connected warehouseman-grower and TGIC board member, invoked the human cost of regulation in pleading his case. Royster's decades-long stewardship of the tobacco economy—that is to say, his persistent championing of the federal government's commitment to the tobacco program, elite white leadership of the program, and the continuation of the auction system for marketing tobacco—had earned him the nickname "Mr. Tobacco" in North Carolina. "We think . . . that if any administrative or regulatory agency of the government takes such a drastic step against tobacco as contained in the proposed rule, the federal agricultural program of tobacco support would be gravely endangered and mortally wounded," a Royster-led committee of North Carolina growers declared. Should consumer regulation undermine agricultural regulation, "the economy of the many tobacco-producing and tobacco manufacturing states would crumble . . . cast into a deep economic depression, seriously affecting the national economy."[46] Shepherded by the TGIC, tobacco producers advanced a core argument of the industry: quality of life regulations kill jobs. In contrast to the health *risks* posed by cigarettes—risks deduced from investigations derided as "merely statistical"—producers like Royster painted a picture of *certain* job loss.

Despite the welter of industry-organized opposition to its proposal, the FTC's final rule differed very little from the original when it was issued in

June.[47] While nobody would have accused the Commission of secret radicalism, the FTC's rule making resonated with cultural critiques circulating among the New Left of the time. Herbert Marcuse's *One Dimensional Man,* also published in 1964, argued that technology such as advertising achieved social domination by creating false needs and then satisfying them. The FTC did not go so far as to accuse cigarette advertisements of causing what Marcuse termed the "moronization" of the American public.[48] But it did assert its rule-making authority by arguing that cigarettes continued to be deceptively marketed. Thus the agency proposed an "affirmative disclosure" for packages and cigarette advertisements as an "antidote" to ads, "which, by design or otherwise, may tend to cloud or obscure public consciousness of the health perils of cigarette smoking."[49] The stringent warnings were set to take effect on July 1, 1965.

Before the FTC could flex its regulatory muscles, Congress intervened, as the tobacco companies knew it would. The Federal Cigarette Labeling and Advertising Act of 1965 watered down the FTC's version of the cigarette warning label and did not require a warning on advertisements. On its face, the Act sounded reasonable. It mandated, for the first time, a warning label on the side of all cigarette packages destined for domestic consumption. But the label itself was weaker than the FTC's proposals: "Caution: Cigarette Smoking May Be Hazardous to Your Health." The FTC's decisive "is" was softened to "may be," the certainty of death revised down to a mere hazard.

Beyond the warning label lay several additional layers of protection for the industry. The Act prevented the FTC from taking any action on cigarettes for four years. It preempted local and state action on labeling, preventing lower levels of government from exacting more stringent public-health measures, and defying southern congressmen's professed fealty to states' rights. And in the long run—by the design of industry lawyers—the warning label inoculated the industry from tort litigation. Americans could no longer claim they had not been warned about the risks concerning smoking.[50] Writing in the *Atlantic,* the political reporter Elizabeth Drew called it "an unabashed act to protect private industry from government regulation," memorably dubbing Congress the industry's "best filter yet."[51]

The Johnson administration stayed aloof from the contest between Congress and the FTC. And in doing so, it knowingly helped cigarette interests. When the *Report* was published, less than seven weeks had elapsed since Lyndon Johnson took the oath of office aboard *Air Force One*. Johnson was not about to begin his presidency—in an election year, no less—needlessly antagonizing southern congressmen of his own party as well as the tobacco industry. As Johnson adviser Joseph Califano recalled, "There was only so much we could take on in the south." Johnson needed the votes of southerners in Congress and did not want to run "the risk of driving all the tobacco money to the side of segregationists and against civil rights."[52]

Still, Johnson's silence was notable, especially as the president pushed an ambitious public-health agenda. Tobacco was not on the list of the public-health items the president sent to Congress for consideration in 1965—a list that included Medicare and Medicaid, enacted as part of the Social Security Amendments of 1965. The 1964 Economic Opportunity Act expanded community health clinics into underserved areas and requiring maximum feasible participation of the poor on clinic governance boards.[53] Even as Johnson embraced the democratization of health as part of the Great Society, his deliberate silence on tobacco reflected pragmatism above principle. This was a view shared by members of the FTC, who viewed Johnson's inaction with a jaundiced eye. "If Johnson had gone to the mat on the FTC cigarette rule it would have survived," according to Philip Elman, a commissioner who had helped to draft the agency's proposed rules.[54] Johnson stayed far from the fray, counting representatives of the tobacco industry among his intimates.

Regulating among Friends

Abe Fortas was a key conduit between the tobacco industry and the Johnson administration, reflecting the persistence of the associational order. Fortas was perhaps the preeminent example of the Washington lawyer. An old New Dealer, he had been part of the original legal team of the Agricultural Adjustment Administration. After the Second World War and Roosevelt's death, many New Dealers "moved into greener economic pastures."[55] Arnold, Fortas & Porter, the firm he founded with other New Deal veterans after the Second World War, specialized in helping corporate clients navigate the bureaucratic maze that the New Deal lawyers had created. Fortas's liberalism "demanded the preservation of capitalism" through "imaginative representation of corporations."[56] It was the liberalism of the mixed economy, reflecting a belief in the ability of big business and big government to produce affluence. With enlightened government policy—Keynesian tax, spending, and monetary policies—affluence could be shared in a world of low unemployment. The regulated industries were also part of this government toolkit as the promotion of orderly communications, banking, and transportation was deemed vital to the national economy.[57] As much as the Federal Trade Commission, the AFL-CIO, or General Motors, firms like Arnold, Fortas & Porter were important features on the landscape of the mixed economy. Specializing in the fields of corporate, antitrust, and regulatory law, the firm represented some of the largest corporations in the United States within just a few years of its founding: Lever Brothers, Federated Department Stores, ABC, Pan-American Airways, Coca-Cola.[58] And in 1963, the firm added another lucrative client to its stable: Philip Morris.

Through Fortas, the tobacco industry enjoyed a close relationship with the Johnson administration. Arnold, Fortas & Porter did not only offer legal expertise and aggressive advocacy. It also offered influence and access to key politicians, none more key than the president. Fortas was a close friend of Johnson, a confidant, a member of the president's "kitchen cabinet" of unofficial advisers. Johnson, never one to defer to formalities such as the separation of powers, wanted a friend and ally on the bench. Two weeks after the 1965 Cigarette Labeling Act was passed, Fortas was confirmed to the Supreme Court as associate justice. In the run-up to the 1965 Act, Fortas's influence on the president had perhaps never been higher. This relationship would eventually catch up with Fortas. When Johnson later nominated Fortas to replace Earl Warren as chief justice, Senate confirmation hearings revealed undue coziness between the sitting justice and the president. Fortas would regularly brief Johnson on the Court's secret deliberations—a fact that galvanized conservative opposition to his nomination. Further scrutiny uncovered financial improprieties Fortas committed while on the bench, leading to his resignation in 1969.

In making the case for the industry's preferred regulation, Fortas was joined by another longtime Johnson intimate—Earle Clements, the Democratic insider and genial president of the Tobacco Institute. While serving in the Senate, Clements briefly took over as majority leader in 1956, after Johnson's near-fatal heart attack—an event that scared Johnson into finally abandoning his own cigarette habit. Clements was a frequent guest at White House movie screenings, and his daughter was press secretary for First Lady Lady Bird Johnson. Together with Covington and Burling lawyer Tommy Austern, who orchestrated the cigarette companies' initial response to the FTC proposals, Clements and Fortas joined the private interests they represented to the levers of political power. Michael Pertschuk, who would later become FTC chairman under President Carter, was a staff lawyer on the Senate Commerce Committee as it debated the labeling bill. Its chairman, Warren Magnuson, had introduced the Senate version of the Labeling Act. Pertschuk recalled seeing a note on Magnuson's desk: "Abe Fortas called— he wants you to vote for the [weaker] House version of the cigarette labeling bill." Pertschuk and his boss interpreted this as indicating the wishes of the president himself.[59]

In the wake of the *Report*, industry lawyers like Fortas wanted self-regulation above all. For Fortas, the benefits of industry codes were obvious. With the blessing of the Justice Department, the cigarette manufacturers could preempt action by even a friendly Congress, which, after all, was not uniformly in thrall to the industry.[60] The FTC's initial rules included mandatory warnings on all advertising. In order to avoid the imposition of an auditory warning, the industry announced the formation of the "Cigarette Advertising Code."[61] The Code forbade cigarette advertising targeted at children: in comic books and school newspapers, and on children's TV and radio programs. But the millions of young eyeballs glued to *Bonanza, Gilligan's Island,* or *Hogan's Heroes* could still receive a dose of tobacco ads. By design, these popular shows fell outside the definition of the craftily worded prohibitions because their appeal was broader than simply the youth market.[62]

The Code's rules sounded strict. And the Code's administrator was vested with far-reaching authority to impose fines up to $100,000 for advertisements that ran afoul of rules. But in reality, the rules left ample room for advertisers to continue to promote the cigarette's glamor. It applied only to print media and required no disclosure that cigarettes were damaging to human health.[63] It was an open secret on Madison Avenue that the Code was a sham. In the words of one advertiser, "You can sit there dressed for tennis, looking like a champ, and as long as you don't play you can smoke." Cigarette commercials could show "attractive, healthy-looking models, provided that there is no suggestion that their attractive appearance or good health is due to cigarette smoking."[64] After Erwin Griswold, the long-standing dean of Harvard Law School, turned down the job offer of code administrator, the industry settled on Robert Meyner, a two-term Democratic governor of New Jersey. Meyner's salary was paid by the nine cigarette companies responsible for his selection.[65]

The Motion Picture Production Code, still in existence though tainted by its association with McCarthyite censorship, was one precedent for the Cigarette Advertising Code. In terms of sanctions, the Cigarette Advertising Code went well beyond the standards set by Hollywood. Even in the fervid heyday of Hollywood red baiting, the Motion Picture Code never required cash penalties.[66] But, then again, Meyner never did impose any fines either. Still, the threat of agency regulation of cigarette advertisements—a major source of profit for manufacturers, broadcasters, and Madison Avenue— mobilized constituencies that depended on tobacco money. In 1966, the National Association of Broadcasters (NAB) devised its own lax standards for cigarette advertising, subject to its Television Code.[67] Founded in 1952 in response to congressional scrutiny of liquor advertising on television, the NAB's TV code was the result of a similar quest for self-regulation.[68]

Before its implementation, the Cigarette Advertising Code had to meet the approval of the Justice Department. The Justice Department could have interpreted the voluntary scheme as a form of anticompetitive collusion, so it was crucial that that the industry frame the Code as serving the public. The Code was "a good job, an honest job, and nothing but what appears," according to Fortas, who represented the industry in a June 1964 meeting with the FTC and the Justice Department. There were "no agreements" between the companies "except what appears in the code." In the meeting, Fortas tried to build a confessional rapport with government lawyers. "For your own knowledge only," he told William Orrick Jr., an antitrust division lawyer at Justice, "we hope [labeling] legislation will come through in this session [of Congress]"—as indeed it did. Fortas took this admission a step further in explaining the industry's interest. The "requirement that packages be labeled would be helpful in civil litigation" brought by smokers or the families of dead smokers alleging that consumers were given implied assurances that cigarettes were safe.[69]

Fortas believed that the government should have the industry's interests—and not those of ailing or dead Americans—at heart. Regulation should not be destructive but constructive, offering stability and predictability in exchange for modest concessions. Some of his contemporaries interpreted Fortas's corporate turn as a betrayal of the liberal ideals of the New Deal. But such analysis misses the extent to which the New Deal operated in partnership with big business. This was especially true of the Agricultural Adjustment Administration (AAA), where Fortas began his career in government.[70]

The parallel between the Cigarette Advertising Code and the industrial codes of the New Deal were not lost on the government lawyers who met with industry counsel in 1964. In their meeting, Orrick posed a historical question to Fortas—one that suggested a continuity between the explicitly corporatist schemes of the early New Deal and the self-regulation of the tobacco oligopoly. "Abe, as an old New Dealer, doesn't this smack to you as a kind of NRA-type delegation?" Orrick queried, referring to the Supreme Court's rejection of the National Recovery Administration (NRA) for its impermissible delegation of power from the legislative to the executive branch in the form of code-making bodies.[71]

Fortas quickly brushed aside such a suggestion. The Code, Fortas insisted, would exist "only in this industry"—a response that spoke to the specific degree but not to the overall nature of this regulatory scheme. Another government lawyer asked Fortas why the industry just didn't "let legislation . . . give you effective immunity" from antitrust action.[72] Fortas's response also displayed the battle scars of the New Deal. "I doubt as a legal matter whether congressional authorization to Meyner would be upheld"—referring specifically to the Supreme Court's 1935 rejection of the NRA as an unconstitutional delegation of legislative power.[73] Regulation by industry code *had* to originate with industry, and not with government. This was a useful line for the tobacco industry to tow. The Cigarette Advertising Code was deeply indebted to New Deal-era ideas about governing arrangements between organized groups and government. These ideas persisted, despite the fact that the Code's intended beneficiaries—children—were unorganized, unrepresented at the bargaining table.

The Cigarette Advertising Code simultaneously acknowledged the existence of a public constituency in need of protection while supplanting public for private regulation. It was a canny strategy. The Department of Justice (DOJ) approved the industry's code. In a letter to Fortas's law partner, DOJ lawyer Orrick noted that even though the Justice Department would grant code adherents criminal antitrust immunity, his assurances "shouldn't be taken to represent a judgment that a code will in fact reduce the health hazards resulting from smoking or lessen the appeal of cigarette advertising to youth."[74] For those publics, there would be no recourse—yet.

Advertising the Public Interest

By the time the Cigarette Advertising Code went into effect in 1965, Ralph Nader had become a household name. More than any other individual, Nader was responsible for a powerful critique of private interest government as morally corrupt and physically dangerous. "A great problem of contemporary life," Nader wrote in the preface to *Unsafe at Any Speed,* the book that made him famous, "is how to control the power of economic interests which ignore the harmful effects of their applied science and technology." Inspired by Rachel Carson's *Silent Spring,* Nader's text was a muckraking indictment of the auto industry's resistance to installing safety features in cars—resistance that "has brought death, injury and the most inestimable sorrow and deprivation to millions of people."[75]

Unsafe at Any Speed may have attracted only a niche audience of insurance adjusters had it not been for a scandal that seemed to validate the author's assertions of villainy on the part of car makers. In March 1966, Nader claimed that he was investigated and harassed by agents working for General Motors. This allegation triggered a series of events that resulted in the president of GM apologizing to Nader and settling with the thirty-one-year-old for invasion of privacy.[76] *Unsafe at Any Speed* rocketed to the top of the bestseller lists. With money from the settlement, Nader founded the Center for the Study of Responsive Law, which produced a series of colorfully titled monographs in 1970 that hammered home the critique of agency capture: *The Interstate Commerce Omission, The Chemical Feast, The Vanishing Air.*[77]

Ralph Nader was far from the only young lawyer energized by the prospects of using litigation in service of environmental and consumer advocacy. In 1966, a twenty-nine-year-old lawyer named Victor Yannacone sued Suffolk County, Long Island, on behalf of his client—his wife. Yannacone charged that the county's use of DDT insecticide—"dumping," in the language of the environmentalists of the 1960s—posed an environmental danger and risk to human health, and advocated for its prohibition. The suit was ultimately thrown out, but not before garnering wide attention among environmentalists for its novel use of litigation.

New institutions emerged from these court battles. The Environmental Defense Fund (EDF) grew out of Yannacone's quest for a DDT ban, initiating lawsuits throughout the country to ban the use of organochloride pesticides. "Gentle conservationists" these were not. Instead, the EDF looked more like "litigation minded activists"—at least to the *New York Times* when it reported on the organization's formation.[78] While marchers at the inaugural Earth Day celebration in Washington were led in refrains of "Give Earth a Chance" by Pete Seeger, Yannacone addressed the crowd by hailing the necessity of litigation.[79] Repurposing Woodie Guthrie's populist hymn, Yannacone closed his address by commanding his audience to "sue somebody!"—preferably government. "This land does not belong to the ICC, FPC, FCC, AEC, TVA, FDA, USDA, BLM, Forest Service, Fish and Wildlife Service, or any other federal or state alphabet agency," Yannacone said. "This land belongs to you and this land belongs to me."[80]

The Environmental Defense Fund as well as a host of other new public interest environmental law firms achieved striking success in the late 1960s and early 1970s. They defeated and delayed plans for public and private construction projects, helped to eliminate the use of DDT in the United States, and sued and petitioned agencies to make good on the mandates of the major environmental laws of the 1970s, the Clean Air Act and the National Environmental Policy Act.[81] These lawyers occupied an uneasy place within liberalism: critical of the closed-door, unrepresentative decision making at agencies, disdainful of the corporate corruption of Congress, yet solicitous of government action.[82] In their hands, the lawsuit was a tool for the people, and the judiciary was reimagined as the most democratic branch of government for courts could review agency decisions.[83]

The legal arm of the modern anti-smoking movement emerged from the youthful iconoclasm of the public interest law movement. In 1967, John Banzhaf, a twenty-seven-year-old associate at a Manhattan law firm, penned a petition to the Federal Communications Commission (FCC). In it, he requested that equal airtime be given to anti-tobacco messaging to counteract the voluminous airtime devoted to selling cigarettes. His argument was creative and bold: the Fairness Doctrine—an eighteen-year-old policy that required broadcasters to present equal airtime to views of public importance—meant that anti-smoking messages be given free airtime on public airwaves in order to match the time spent on cigarette advertising. Smoking, as the *Surgeon General's Report* made clear, was a question of major public import. Cigarettes were the most intensely advertised products on television. Banzhaf's innovation was to argue that tobacco *advertisements* should trigger anti-tobacco counteradvertising.

His quest began far less ambitiously. In late 1966, the young lawyer wrote to his local TV station, WCBS-TV, New York, informing it that it was not discharging its duties under the Fairness Doctrine. He argued that that the station was required to make available free airtime to "responsible groups" who could counter the implicit message of TV commercials—that smoking was "socially acceptable, manly, and a necessary part of a rich, full life." Parent company CBS disagreed, arguing that it had given ample airtime to anti-smoking views. It had aired six reports on smoking and health in its evening news since May 1966, given major reports from its science editor since September, and aired five one-minute messages by courtesy for the American Cancer Society "in the last few months." Even more, the station proclaimed, it had devoted half an hour in 1962 and an hour in 1964 to the question of the smoking-cancer link. In light of the station's dutiful presentation of contrasting viewpoints in its programming, CBS contended that the government need not intervene to consider whether or not the doctrine applied to paid advertising.[84]

Banzhaf's next move was aimed not at CBS, but at the FCC. The station's sporadic efforts to provide the public-health perspective on tobacco were positively paltry when stacked against the 5–10 minutes *per day* of paid tobacco advertising. Far from absolving the station of its responsibility to provide public-health commercials, WCBS's smoking and health coverage only highlighted the extent to which it was outmatched by the tobacco industry. Banzhaf's letter made clear that commercials were his real object, as he wanted to "establish the applicability of the Fairness Doctrine to cigarette advertising." Congress may have exempted advertising from even weak labeling requirements, and it may have neutered the FTC's ability to regulate the truthfulness of tobacco's on-air claims. But neither Congress nor the industry nor even tobacco's foes in the public-health community foresaw the possibility that the Federal Communications Commission would intervene in cigarette advertising. Like many a lawyer before him, Banzhaf engaged in strategic venue shopping on behalf of his client. Only his client was the broad, unspecified notion of "the public."

In a 7-0 decision, the FCC ruled in Banzhaf's favor. "We hold that the fairness doctrine is applicable to advertisements," the Commission wrote. This was a dramatic ruling, one that vastly expanded the obligations of broadcast licensees, and multiplied the effects of the meager resources of public-health organizations. The FCC rejected the broadcasters' assertion that the Fairness Doctrine applied only to programming. The Commission instead reiterated that the privilege of a broadcast license implied a reciprocal duty by the licensee of "the right of the public to be informed."[85] The nature of the content did not diminish the broadcaster's duty to the public interest.

At the same time, the FCC signaled its openness to similar such suits in the future, highlighting the Commission's interest in programming and advertising that pertained to public health and safety.[86] The FCC's most serious concern about advertising and the public interest lay in rising rates of teenage smoking. The Commission extensively cited medical studies published after the 1964 *Surgeon General's Report* to establish that the question of cigarette advertising was a serious issue of public importance. Even under the guidance of the Cigarette Advertising Code, tobacco ads still portrayed smoking as attractive, youthful, and enjoyable. The public interest demanded a countervailing message.[87] The decision was, in the words of the plurality of commissioners, "a simple and practical one, required by the public interest."[88]

But commissioner Lee Lovinger did not see the issue quite so clearly. Lovinger, a Kennedy appointee who saw himself in the antitrust mold of New Dealer Thurman Arnold, registered his "great doubt and reluctance" about the Fairness ruling in a concurring opinion. Since his vote would not change the result of the Commission's ruling, Lovinger used his concurrence to summarize the "difficulties" he saw in the agency's action. For Lovinger, the ruling was riddled with procedural irregularities, legally dubious overreach, and represented "a subjugation of judgment to sentiment."

In a terse indictment of the new legal activism, he observed that the Commission's "repetitive reference to the 'public interest' as establishing whatever conclusion is contended for is no more than question-begging." Nevertheless, Lovinger's own sentimental definition of the public interest ultimately swayed his vote. He concurred, "albeit reluctantly because of a strong feeling that suggesting cigarette smoking to young people, in light of present knowledge, is something very close to wickedness."[89]

Banzhaf fell just shy of a perfect coup at the Commission, which rejected his demand for "equal airtime." Instead, it mandated that "significant airtime" be devoted to public-health spots—later defined as one health commercial for every three tobacco advertisements.[90] Because tobacco was so heavily advertised, even this ratio was a tremendous coup for anti-tobacco forces. Indeed, the mid-1960s were something of a golden age for cigarette commercials—when Americans' high levels of television consumption overlapped with tobacco's prodigious investment in television advertising. In 1967, seven of the top ten products advertised on television were cigarettes.[91] By one estimate, public health reaped approximately $80 million in free advertising a year.

These commercials were not as slickly produced as the Code-vetted Marlboro Man. But they packed their own emotional wallop—perhaps especially for Americans unused to encountering death amid their steady TV diet of Star Kist, Alka-Seltzer, and Tang. One ad featured Bill Talman, the actor who portrayed the district attorney who lost his case each week to Perry Mason in the popular series. When the advertisement was recorded, Talman was dying of lung cancer. The sixty-second spot, which Talman directed, was filmed in his California home. The camera lingered on domestic scenes of his wife and six children—playing in the pool, petting a dog—before stopping on Talman, who sat beside a picture of himself in character on the set of *Perry Mason*. Although his character was notable for being the losingest attorney on television, Talman assured viewers that his fictional record mattered much less than his real-life battles. "I'm in a battle right now I don't want to lose at all because if I lose it, it means losing my wife and those kids you just met," Talman said, looking directly into the camera. "I've got lung cancer." By the time the ad aired, Talman was dead at age fifty-three. His dying admonition to viewers was all the more haunting: "Take some advice about smoking and losing from someone who's been doing both for years. If you haven't smoked—don't start. If you do smoke—quit. Don't be a loser." A broadened conception of the public interest had disturbed the steady balance of tobacco's iron triangle. In politics as in engineering, four-legged structures wobble where three legs stand still.

The man behind the Fairness Doctrine petition had no idea his letter would open a new front in the quest for public health. This was not because of any aw-shucks humility. By the time of his encounter with the FCC, Banzhaf had already amassed an impressive array of accolades, and more than a bit of notoriety. After graduating from MIT with a degree in electrical engineering, Banzhaf enrolled at Columbia Law School in 1963. While researching copyright law, he realized that nobody had ever received copyright protection for computer code. After some "haggling back and forth" between Banzhaf and the U.S. Copyright office, Banzhaf was given the first copyrights ever for computer programs. Banzhaf was twenty-three and a second-year law student when the *New York Times* published his story and photo on its financial pages.[92] In 1965 he appeared before Congress to represent the "views and positions of the data processing community," advocating the inclusion of computers into a proposed revision of copyright law.[93]

Banzhaf's technical achievements reflected the diminishing power of rural districts—a fact that would eventually loosen tobacco's grip on Congress. Before graduating from law school, Banzhaf had also found time to develop a mathematical model of voting power. Now known as the Banzhaf Index, the model produced new apportionment plans that conformed to the Supreme Court's "one man, one vote" principle recently established by recent apportionment cases of *Baker v. Carr* (1962), *Wesberry v. Sanders (1964)*, and *Reynolds v. Sims* (1964).[94] Before Banzhaf reached age twenty-seven, the New York State Supreme Court had cited his analysis and adopted his index as a requirement for statewide apportionment.[95] Banzhaf needed no convincing as to his powers of persuasion.

Perhaps the only thing that surprised Banzhaf was how little effort his successful petition to the FCC took. No mathematical modeling was needed—not even a simple ratio of public-health to cigarette ads. There were no rounds of submission to law journals, just three typed pages to the commissioners. This gadfly approach was evident in all of Banzhaf's appeals.

Whether the subject was cigarette advertising or voting power, Banzhaf relished identifying short circuits in the system and crafting an alternative—an engineer's approach to the law. Banzhaf did not consider tobacco among the most pressing social issues of the day. "If I had to rank them on a scale I would certainly put smoking below such things as the war in Vietnam or the racial issue," he confessed in 1970.[96]

But the civil rights and antiwar movements already had their champions. Tobacco, on the other hand, was a corporate Goliath that stood more or less unchallenged by any crusading David. Banzhaf's was a procedural, almost mercenary, approach to advocacy. "We're surrounded by a large number of windmills. I don't look for the biggest or the most important one and make a frontal charge because to a large extent I wouldn't do any good," Banzhaf told a reporter in a major profile with the *Washington Post* in 1970. "I like to look around and find one with a crack down at the bottom and a little loose brick and find where I can yank that loose brick and send the whole thing tumbling down."[97]

Banzhaf could occasionally sound like a flamethrower, but in reality his approach to activism was guided by considerations of efficiency. He would pursue tactics within the existing system of law. Banzhaf and Yannacone shared a pugnacious and pithy mantra: "sue the bastards"—a motto as hopeful as it was harsh. It implied a faith in the judicial system to respond to the claims of injured citizens and the clever public interest lawyers who argued on their behalf. Advocates for the environment, consumer protection, and public health worked within the system to improve, not overturn it.[98] "What we have to do is show this generation that a great many problems can be solved within the system," Banzhaf told a *Washington Post* reporter, expressing a sentiment that belied his twenty-eight years. "There are a great many which are attackable through either the legal system, as we are doing, or through the political system, or sometimes simply through publicity."[99] In this respect, Banzhaf was several shades more conservative than Nader, whom he saw as trying to change the overall system itself. "He's more apt to try to get a bill through. I'm more apt to file a complaint with an agency."[100]

As Yannacone prepared his case against DDT and Nader advocated for the passage of a meat safety inspection act, Banzhaf was doing his best to ensure that the FCC ruling would stand. He faced ferocious opposition from both the tobacco industry and the National Association of Broadcasters, the latter objecting to the government's mandate that salable airtime be given for free. Such a ruling was a violation of the broadcasters' First Amendment rights, it argued, and put the United States one giant goosestep closer to a regimented police state.[101] Despite petition from the Tobacco Institute and the broadcasters, the FCC declined to review its ruling, deeming it "a simple and practical one required by the public interest."[102]

The final decision would rest with the courts. The National Association of Broadcasters filed an appeal at the U.S. Court of Appeals in Richmond—so chosen because of the hearing the industry could expect in a state that produced tobacco, manufactured cigarettes, and was home to Philip Morris. They were horrified to find themselves caught flat-footed once again. Anticipating the move by the broadcast industry, Banzhaf had beaten them to the punch: the young lawyer had flown early one Saturday morning from New York to Washington to file his appeal in person with a judge from the friendlier D.C. Circuit.[103] In 1968, the D.C. court upheld the FCC ruling, affirming the Commission's authority to regulate in the name of the public interest: "for whatever else it may mean, we think the public interest indisputably includes public health."[104]

The broadness of the ruling in favor of the Commission infuriated tobacco's congressional allies. Although the court was at pains to limit its ruling by distinguishing the dangers posed by cigarettes from other types of consumer goods, congressmen nevertheless invoked the specter of the slippery slope. In the House of Representatives, congressmen from the tobacco-growing states launched into an hour-long diatribe against the Commission's "arrogation of Congressional authority" and "usurpation over the news." The ruling "opens a Pandora's box of decisions by the FCC that any individual with a pet peeve is entitled to free time on radio and television," contended Walter Jones, a representative from North Carolina's Coastal Plain. "Logic will demand the unlimited extension of the 'fairness doctrine' to a virtually endless list of products."[105] In siding with Banzhaf's and the FCC's conception of the public interest, the D.C. Circuit threatened the associational order that had empowered congressmen like Jones.

In a sense, Jones was right. The environmental and consumer advocacy movements were highlighting the hidden dangers lurking within the marketplace of American abundance. Nor were those dangers episodic: just as cancer causing agents were built into the very cigarettes being marketed, the "negative externalities" of mass consumption, whether in the form of highway deaths or polluted rivers, were attracting more scrutiny and drawing a crowd. Ralph Nader's morally upright shadow threatened to extend the reach of the ruling. "Automakers may now expect the 'Ralph Nader Hour' devoted to scaring the bejabbers out of drivers," opined the *Indianapolis News*. "What of other 'hazardous' products?" asked the irreverent *Boston Herald*. "Congress has legislated far more stringently as to automobiles than it has legislated as to cigarettes," the paper observed in reference to the recent passage of the Nader-endorsed Motor Vehicle Safety Act of 1966.

Other commercial interests were alerted to their stake in the Fairness Doctrine ruling. *Advertising Age* speculated darkly that "other Mr. Banzhaf's [sic], concerned about the hazards of driving high powered motor vehicles, or eating high cholesterol foods, or vegetables grown with the assistance of pesticides and chemical fertilizers, are sure to test the commission's stamina."[106] The value of reciting this parade of horribles lay not in prediction—the Federal Communications Commission made clear that it was not interested in pursuing other products. It lay in alerting other industries of their shared stake in battling insurgent litigators, and cautioning that the government agencies that had been part and parcel of industry's success in a mixed economy might no longer be as reliable as once assumed.

Objectors to the Fairness Doctrine ruling needed no warnings about the fickle nature of state support. Suddenly astute students of history, they frequently invoked Prohibition to denounce government intervention in the name of public health. Newspapers across the United States opined that the same mentality that led to the passage of the Eighteenth Amendment was in evidence in the FCC ruling.[107] "A Nonsensical Ruling!" opined the *Pueblo Chieftain*.[108] The Women's Christian Temperance Union was bound to "demand equal airtime to exorcise the Demon Rum or any of his milder alcoholic permutations that toothsome models sip ecstatically for the continued good health of the brewing industry," predicted the *Hartford Times*.[109] The trade magazine *Broadcasting* interviewed a Mrs. Fred J. Tooze, the president of the Women's Christian Temperance Union—the organization that spearheaded the temperance movement in the early twentieth century. Tooze was a perfect caricature of a humorless scold. In an interview that was no doubt intended to bait Tooze by way of illustrating the slippery slope of the FCC ruling, *Broadcasting* ominously asked "How Far Can Fairness Go?"[110] Tooze was enthusiastic about the prospect of securing free airtime temperance messages as a result of the ruling—a strategy that never came to pass.

The slippery slope of bureaucratic meddling and judicial overreach was irresistible to conservatives, who viewed tobacco through the prism of civil rights. By referencing Prohibition, opponents of the ruling were able to suggest that such nanny state action challenged the manhood of the viewing public—their competence, individualism, and fitness for self-rule. James J. Kilpatrick, the Richmond native and nationally syndicated conservative columnist, described the FCC as "mamas and papas" who had reduced Americans to "erring children." Kilpatrick had spent the previous decade making the case against *Brown v. Board of Education,* urging Virginia's governors toward massive resistance to the ruling. What slaveholders in the nineteenth century would have called nullification, Kilpatrick renamed "interposition," arguing that the states possessed ultimate power under the Constitution, and arrogated the right to "interpose" their authority against the federal government whenever they believed their prerogatives usurped.[111] In denouncing the paternalism of the federal government's tobacco rulings, Kilpatrick aligned tobacco with other catalysts of white resentment: integration, busing, welfare, women's liberation.[112] The fact that tobacco production was fully regulated by the Department of Agriculture—indeed, the fact that the white American middle class had been weaned on federal government programs since the New Deal—was not much observed by patriarchal, culturally conservative critics of tobacco regulation.

"Those Zealots:" Action on Smoking and Health

By 1969, much had changed in Banzhaf's life.[113] He moved out of his parents' house and quit his job in New York to take up a position at George Washington University's National Law Center. The location and the flexibility of academic life allowed him to focus his energies on legal action against tobacco. The formal vehicle for those energies was Action on Smoking and Health (ASH), which he operated from his law school office.

ASH was initially organized to assist Banzhaf in the Fairness Doctrine fight, and he secured star sponsorship for the group, which lent it the legitimacy necessary to solicit money for the part-time legal battles of a twenty-eight-year-old. Dr. Donald Frederickson, chief of the Molecular Diseases unit at the National Institutes of Health, sent an early letter of solicitation on ASH letterhead in January of 1968. Describing the recent FCC ruling as "the result of the work of only one man" who was then "struggling to defend the decision in his spare time," Fredrickson implored readers to give their money or their name-recognition. "Our immediate need is for funds and the names of supporters. Even a nominal contribution will allow the organization to list you as a sponsor."[114]

ASH's earliest sponsors were impressive. They included legendary public relations (PR) man Edward Bernays—perhaps as penance for his role in fashioning cigarettes as feminist emblems in the 1920s in a bid to open up the women's market.[115] Alton Ochsner, the physician who pioneered research into the link between smoking and cancer, also lent his support. So too did senator Maurine Neuberger, the Oregon Democrat with a reputation as a dogged advocate for consumer issues; Edward Koch, who was then just a New York City councilman; and Louis Jaffe, the Harvard Law professor and preeminent expert in administrative law. The prestigious *New England Journal of Medicine* even broke with its own editorial tradition and encouraged readers to support ASH. "The medical profession has a rare opportunity to help the miniscule financial structure of A.S.H.," the *Journal* wrote in an editorial that praised the FCC ruling. "It can do this by direct contribution and by encouraging patients to do likewise."[116] In 1968, ASH raised $75,000.[117]

For all its star-powered sponsorship, ASH was essentially a one-man outfit. Calling himself the Ralph Nader of tobacco, Banzhaf sought to become the pole star of the anti-tobacco movement. And where Nader had his Raiders—student activists who volunteered to rake the muck of government agencies and big business for evidence of "collusion, corruption, incompetence, and sloth"—Banzhaf had his Bandits. Banzhaf's Bandits didn't so much volunteer as were conscripted. In 1970, Banzhaf developed a course in "Unfair Trade Practices" at George Washington University. In it, groups of students were instructed to select contemporary examples of commercial deception, devise a clever acronym for their cause, and pursue a public action—an agency petition, an expose, a protest, or a lawsuit.[118]

In its first year, "Unfair Trade Practices" resulted in the formation of PUMP (Protests Unfair Marketing Practices), a group that supported a proposed FTC rule that required gas stations to display octane settings, and CRASH (Citizens to Reduce Airline Smoking Hazards), which petitioned the Federal Aviation Administration in support of a Nader initiative to separate smoking and nonsmoking passengers on airlines. But the Bandit group that went furthest in the Banzhaf method was SOUP (Students Opposing Unfair Practices), which alleged that Campbell's Soup advertisements deceived the public into imagining a thicker, chunkier product because of the strategic use of marbles in soup photography.[119]

In a 3-2 decision, the FTC ruled against SOUP's bid to intervene on behalf of the consumer interest. But it did result in FTC intervention against Campbell's—and, more importantly, in an ample serving of bad publicity for the company.[120] These crusades were signature Banzhaf: a mixture of publicity seeking, irreverence, and, not infrequently, irrelevance. These were charges that Banzhaf embraced. Banzhaf's personal and philosophic mien was fundamentally more pragmatic than that of Ralph Nader, who was an ascetic idealist, total in his commitment to consumer causes. And Banzhaf's approach was decidedly more ad hoc than those of the environmental lawyers, who embedded their legal activism in a broader ecological critique of industrialization, consumption, and waste. In Banzhaf's hands—and with the muscle of his students—citizen participation provisions of new environmental laws were leveraged on behalf of the public interest.

At times Banzhaf undermined the potential for anti-smoking advocacy to coalesce as both a legal and a social movement. Some of the lawyer's early public statements in his capacity as ASH director seemed to deliberately antagonize the existing public-health establishment. Part of the tobacco industry's advantage in passing favorable legislation in the 1960s lay in the unity of its forces. Tobacco farmers, unionized tobacco workers, distributors, retailers, grocers, scientists-for-hire, advertisers, broadcasters, and industry executives marched in lockstep under the guidance of the Tobacco Institute, the Tobacco Growers Information Committee, and the Council for Tobacco Research.[121]

The Interagency Council on Smoking and Health, formed in 1964, was the closest thing that anti-tobacco forces had to a unified front.[122] The Council was not an aggressive organization. Unlike a true "peak organization" representing a collection of similar organizations within a sector, the interests of the Interagency Council's members were sometimes at cross-purposes. The major health voluntaries—the Heart Association, Lung Association, and the American Cancer Society—were tactically and culturally conservative. They relied on the goodwill of the broadcasters for free airtime during funding drives, and were large, consensus-based nonprofits, more comfortable with uplift, education, and suasion than with the realm of single-issue advocacy and litigation. Indeed, the Council declined to send the FCC a petition in support of the Fairness rule, perhaps out of an abundance concern for member organizations' tax-exempt status—since laws prohibited tax-exempt organizations from lobbying, though not from advocacy.[123] The Interagency Council was, to Banzhaf, the embodiment of the establishment: hulking, hidebound, and incapable of proactive movement against the tobacco industry.

The Council did, however, sponsor the first ever World Conference on Smoking and Health, which was held at the Waldorf in New York City in September 1967—just a few months after the FCC ruling. The event brought together 500 delegates from thirty-four countries, though the speakers were largely Anglo-American, as the United Kingdom and the United States were the only states that had yet released government reports on cigarettes. Physicians, epidemiologists, educators, clinic directors, and, of course, politicians were eager to take on tobacco outside of the narrow confines established by Congress. Robert Kennedy, burnishing his reputation as a Democratic standard-bearer for health issues, gave the opening address.[124] He hailed the FCC ruling as "one of the most promising developments that has yet occurred in the effort to acquaint Americans with the dangers of cigarette smoking."[125] He also urged the Americans in the audience "to organize groups to monitor radio and TV stations to check compliance and to demand it and to complain to the FCC if it is found wanting."[126] Frank Moss, the Democratic senator from Utah whose Mormon faith was cited by tobacco's supporters as evidence of latent Prohibitionism on the part of public-health forces, sat on one of the Conference's closing panels. He was also sanguine about the development at the FCC. "In the face of the mounting evidence that seems to me completely overwhelming, I believe we can move forward in this field of equal time [in broadcasting]," Moss said in support.

Even a don of Madison Avenue lavished praise upon the Fairness Doctrine ruling. Emerson Foote, the former Chairman of the Interagency Council, spoke about tobacco commercials and praised Banzhaf by name. Foote's endorsement was significant. The elder statesman of persuasion began his career in advertising in the 1930s under the tutelage of pioneer Albert Lasker. Foote would come to handle one of the industry's most coveted accounts: American Tobacco. In 1964, he became the talk of Madison Avenue when he resigned as chairman of McCann-Erikson, one of the largest and most prestigious advertising agencies in the United States. "I will not have anything to do with any advertising agency which promotes the sale of cigarettes," Foote explained.[127] At the World Conference, Foote relayed his initial reservations about the FCC's decision, believing that it was outside the authority of the agency to "compel broadcasters to run free health advertising against the cigarette advertising for which they were being paid."[128] But then, he said, a friend suggested that he meet "the young attorney whose complaint had brought about the FCC action."

After meeting Banzhaf, Foote's attitude changed. "We are faced with a remorseless foe . . . which clearly puts profits ahead of people, and which for years has attempted to distort the truth about the dangers of cigarette smoking." Why should not public health seize any tool at hand to deal with such a foe? "The imagination and initiative of a young attorney and the boldness of the FCC decision have given us a new tool—with which to combat the dreadful toll cigarette smoking takes."[129] To judge by the words of the keynote speakers at the Conference, Banzhaf was the belle of the ball.

That is not how Banzhaf understood his position in the world of anti-tobacco advocacy. He used his time at the podium to deliver a sneering address that excoriated the Interagency Council and the "charitable health organizations" for their cowardice in not supporting his petition. Calling the voluntaries' inaction "nothing short of outrageous, deplorable and reprehensible," Banzhaf highlighted his lonely, righteous agency in taking on the industry.[130] "I have carried this fight so far only on my back and at no small risk," Banzhaf pled. "I cannot carry it any further alone and I need your support!" In a press conference after Banzhaf's address, an official for a health voluntary organization denounced Banzhaf as a "publicity seeker."[131]

The young lawyer had already expressed this disaffection in an even more public forum, authoring a pointed letter in the *Washington Post* just weeks before the Conference. He singled out the hypocrisy of the American Cancer Society and the National Tuberculosis Association (later known as the American Lung Association), noting that their "spokesmen have stated publicly that they are reluctant to act for fear of losing the goodwill of broadcasters." Banzhaf made it hard to form coalitions. Implicitly suggesting that no other disease or social condition could legitimately supersede tobacco-related disease in a hierarchy of priorities, Banzhaf pulled hard on the levers of guilt and moral outrage. "Before it is too late the public should let these charitable organizations know that they will lose even more if they continue to put their pocketbooks ahead of the public interest."[132] For a man lacking in allies and resources, it was a remarkably impolitic statement—but it was not without strategy.

Banzhaf insisted that he wanted the material support of the voluntaries, but he did not want the kind of compromise and consensus-based planning that an alliance would have entailed. Although it branded itself as the legal arm of the anti-smoking movement, ASH stood apart from the major public-health organizations. This was a strength more than a liability. ASH was nimble: Banzhaf did not have to consult with a chain of command before issuing a press release or submitting a petition or filing a lawsuit. ASH was bold: Banzhaf did not have to consider any august reputation of his organization, nor did he have to think about the conflicting interests of the executive committee. And ASH was poor: outrageous public statements were valuable free publicity, and litigation against regulatory agencies was, relative to lobbying, a cheap way to affect social policy. Foote's conversion experience notwithstanding, Banzhaf's brash persona did not ingratiate him to many. "A saint he is not," a colleague told the *New York Times.*[133]

But his attitude was crucial to the strategy and the success of ASH. Whereas Fortas represented an establishment view of the relationship among government, the law, and business—where the reigning principles were stability and compromise—Banzhaf employed a confrontational style that sought to highlight the corrupt politesse that operators like Fortas took for granted. Banzhaf could be off-putting and immature—like the time he threatened to detonate a smoke bomb at a hearing on smoking on interstate busses.[134] But shock was a technique to draw attention to the cronyism of Washington.

While Banzhaf was abrasive, he was not a radical. For all of his criticism, his approach relied upon using—not resisting—the power of mainstream institutions.[135] Banzhaf had characterized the Fairness Doctrine petition as a "legal loophole that might allow me a large output for a small amount of input."[136] For Banzhaf, the system was not a hopelessly tainted, all-encompassing entity to be smashed. It was a flabby and aimless body that could be worked with and "prodded."[137] Indeed, in comparison to other legal activists of his generation, Banzhaf sounded downright conservative. In his view, public interest law should represent "a revolution within the system to avoid a revolution outside the system."[138]

The substance of Banzhaf's FCC petition was similarly restrained. For in the Fairness Doctrine, Banzhaf had found a glitch in a regulatory system philosophically wedded to the notion of consent and choice. The Fairness Doctrine ruling derived from the idea that citizens could make a more informed *choice* about smoking if they were exposed to *both sides of the issue*. Some categories of Americans—minors—could not consent to smoking. For this reason, anti-cigarette advertising was crucially important.[139] Effective public-health advertising could serve to inoculate youth from the seductions of the tobacco advertisers. It could preserve smoking as a truly adult *choice*—one made freely, with a full assessment of risk, by individuals old enough to do so.

During its early years, ASH's agency-focused actions reaffirmed this paradigm of consent. Banzhaf monitored television stations for compliance with the Fairness Doctrine ruling. If he found that a station was slack in complying with the three-to-one ratio, he would inform the FCC. The FCC never took punitive action against a station, but it did send a few strongly worded letters reminding stations of their obligations under the ruling.[140] Much as the Environmental Defense Fund or the National Resources Defense Council would later monitor the efficacy of the Environmental Protection Agency (EPA) in upholding regulations, so too did ASH monitor FCC compliance with its own rules. With what was becoming his trademark brashness, Banzhaf called the FCC "notoriously weak," "understaffed," and having the "second smallest budget of any agency in Washington." These insults were meant to prod the system.

FCC officials, who felt these deficits as sharply as Banzhaf described them, quietly welcomed ASH's unpaid enforcement efforts. At least a few FCC commissioners were already favorably disposed to Banzhaf's arguments in 1967. "The F.C.C. had within it an ovum," one public interest lawyer rather crassly explained, "and Banzhaf provided the sperm."[141] ASH also made sure that the networks discharged their Fairness Doctrine obligations in the spirit of fidelity to the principle of informational parity and informed consent. In response to an ASH complaint, the FCC ruled that networks could not air anti-tobacco commercials during quiet hours while reserving prime time for paid cigarette advertisements.[142] Networks were required to air primetime advertisements that showed the pleasures of the smoker's life and the horrors of a smoker's death. What an American did with that information would be his or her choice.

Americans were beginning to make different choices about smoking—just not as quickly as public-health officials hoped. After an initial drop-off in cigarette sales after the *Report*'s release, sales had not only rebounded but achieved new records in per capita consumption and industry profits in 1965. The Office of the Surgeon General possessed neither the resources nor the mandate to go beyond anti-smoking education, but it did mail 350,000 copies of the *Report* by the end of 1965. Every medical student in the country was sent one. By 1970, smoking rates had started to decline—down to 37 percent from a high of 42 percent five years earlier. Per capita consumption fell as well.[143] Attitude polling suggested that these numbers had fallen because more Americans believed smoking was dangerous. In fact, 71 percent of respondents to a 1968 Gallup poll believed that smoking caused cancer, up from 44 percent a decade earlier.[144] The FCC-mandated counteradvertising was not entirely responsible for this turnabout—though smoking rates fell during the Fairness Doctrine years.[145] The gritty messages seemed to stick, with nearly half of those surveyed "recalling at least one of the cautionary broadcast messages."[146] Meanwhile, various public health organizations also launched nationwide anti-tobacco campaigns. Despite John Banzhaf's accusations of indolence, the American Cancer Society launched a nationwide "I Quit" campaign, featuring the actor Tony Curtis, himself a former smoker who had lost a father to lung cancer.

The mail delivery trucks of the United States Postal Service were conscripted into the anti-tobacco brigade by the Department of Health, Education, and Welfare (HEW), which distributed stark posters to be affixed to the fleet. With white lettering against a black background, the posters read, "100,000 doctors have quit smoking. (Maybe they know something you don't)." Tobacco's supporters in Congress and the tobacco-growing states immediately registered their opposition to these mobile advertisements, raising a technicality that may have impressed Banzhaf himself: the placards failed to cite the source of their information.[147] On the floor of Congress, North Carolina senator Sam Ervin called it "Government propaganda" in an "attempt to dictate to and brainwash the American people."[148] The experiment in mobile counteradvertising was soon discontinued, but HEW had joined the FCC, the Public Health Service (PHS), and the FTC as agencies with a stake in cigarette regulation.

The preemption provisions of the 1965 Labeling Act expired in 1969. That year, the FTC called for ban on all television advertising of cigarettes. Although the United States would later lead in global tobacco control, several other countries had already enacted a broadcast ban by 1969. Britain banned cigarettes from television in 1965, and Czechoslovakia, Denmark, France, Italy, Norway, Sweden, and Switzerland had all banned tobacco from either the radio or TV or both. And there was domestic precedent as well. By voluntary agreement between manufacturers and broadcasters, liquor was not advertised on television.

Elizabeth Drew, the political journalist who had been scathing in her indictment of the 1965 bill, observed that by 1969 many senators had stiffened their resolve to take on tobacco. "A great deal has happened since 1965," she wrote. "Ralph Nader, for one, has happened, and a number of politicians have learned that defending the consumer is good politics."[149] That same year, New York City mayor John Lindsay appointed former Miss America Bess Myerson to head the newly created Commission on Consumer Affairs.[150] Even as Americans enjoyed better health and longer lives, the idea that production endangered consumers resonated across the political spectrum. Gaylord Nelson, the Democratic senator from Wisconsin who organized the first Earth Day protest, characterized the consumer as the modern-day "forgotten man," in need of protection through a "Cabinet-level Department of Consumer Affairs."[151] Infuriating activists with his initial choice for just a part-time post of consultant on consumer affairs, Nixon quickly appointed a full-time special assistant for consumer affairs and suggested that the position be made into a permanent office.[152]

It was in this climate that some of tobacco's defenders began to concede that the time had come to withdraw from the airwaves. The ubiquity of the anti-smoking commercials had lowered the opportunity cost of retreat. "It is inevitable that TV advertising is going to end, one way or another," explained one longtime attorney for the Lorillard Tobacco Company. "Right now they're getting hammered by the antismoking ads, which are better than their own, and by the anti-smoking people, who are increasingly effective."[153] In 1970, the tobacco companies acceded to legislation that banned television advertising beginning at the stroke of midnight on January 2, 1971—safely after the end of the New Year's Day college bowl games. In the era of the credibility gap, the tobacco companies wagered it was better not to remind Americans of the gulf between the exuberant promises of the cigarette and its deadly realities.

Closing Ranks: Tobacco Producers Respond to the Public Interest Challenge

As public interest lawyers tried to pry open the nexus linking producers and the producer-friendly bureaucracy, leaders in the tobacco belt drew their allies ever closer.[154] For tobacco farmers, it was clear that the federal tobacco program was the gem that needed safeguarding. For those on the manufacturing side of the industry, the federal tobacco program was essential for a different reason: the hundreds of thousands of farm families that grew tobacco were crucial as public relations, and the federal tobacco program was what maintained their numbers and ensured their economic dependence on tobacco. And the state's deep investment in tobacco production meant that consumer-centric regulations would face an uphill battle in finding a foothold both in Congress and in the bureaucracy, where the U.S. Department of Agriculture (USDA) oversaw tobacco production.

The Supreme Court had diminished the power of malapportioned rural districts in a series of decisions earlier in the decade. When combined with the passage of the Voting Rights Act, enfranchising millions of African Americans in the South, these reforms diminished the electoral hold of senior southern Democrats and reduced the power of committee chairs— like Harold Cooley of the House Committee on Agriculture.[155] Cooley, who lost to Republican James Gardner by a landslide thirteen points in 1966, was one of forty-seven Democrats defeated that year.[156] The federal government's economic and political commitments to producers were strained by systemic political change as well as an expanded notion of the public interest.

It did not take long for politicians to exploit tobacco's tenuous position. In March of 1964, the first attack on the federal tobacco program was launched in Congress. John Williams, a Republican senator from Delaware, introduced an amendment to a bill whose original purpose was to bestow upon cotton and wheat producers the kind of grower-funded promotion program that tobacco farmers were financing through Tobacco Associates. Williams's revision was straightforward. "The pending amendment proposes to repeal the price support program for tobacco." Given the surgeon general's "rather strong report condemning the use of tobacco on the basis that it was injurious to the health of American citizens," the government now faced a "contradictory" situation. "One agency of the Government has suggested the use of tobacco is injurious to health, while another agency of Government last year spent approximately $40 million to support and encourage the production of this same commodity."[157]

Williams's politics were those of purity rather than pragmatism—he cared less about passing legislation than he did exposing the sins that surrounded the political process.[158] He was a personally and politically abstemious man: he did not smoke, drink, or swear—a conscientious objector to the Washington cocktail circuit. He made his reputation in the Senate by being more ostentatiously upright than his colleagues—he once tried to give his $1,500 office stationery allowance back to the Treasury. More significantly, his frequent charges of fraud and corruption in government agencies occasionally yielded huge dividends, such as the convictions of 125 Internal Revenue Service (IRS) employees on charges of bribery and extortion in the early 1950s. He was therefore an ideal messenger to punctiliously point out the incongruity of the state's position. This refusal to admit the complexities of the sprawling, modern state—one with competing constituencies and goals—was attractive, if naïve. Prefiguring Wisconsin Democrat William Proxmire's "Golden Fleece Award" by a decade, Williams was the first in a long line of critics to express high-minded frustration at the state's investment in a product it simultaneously discouraged.

It was a good thing Williams already eschewed the congressional social scene. The response to his amendment was ferocious, inviting extensive comments from members of the tobacco state delegations about the virtues of the hard-working farm families and communities that relied on the price support program. It gave supporters the opportunity to tout the fact that tobacco was the cheapest of the federal commodity programs to administer—and an absolute bargain when "one considers that the crop has provided to the Federal Government more than $2 billion a year in revenue, and an additional $1.2 billion to the States."[159] Predictably, Williams's amendment, which was not even submitted to the Senate Committee on Agriculture and Forestry before it was introduced, went nowhere—at least not legislatively. But journalists and commentators picked up the now-familiar thread of government hypocrisy—a trope becoming recognizable in the wake of Silent Spring and animating the critiques of political scientists who decried regulatory capture. Even the Knoxville News-Sentinel, based in a tobacco-growing state, wondered "How nutty can we be" to "roll out more millions in price support loans to hold up the price of the 'weed'—which the Surgeon General says is injurious to health."[160]

Growers felt persecuted by attacks on their program, and sought to close any opening for their enemies to latch onto. There was no bigger opening wedge for criticism of growers than the increasingly shaky finances of the tobacco program itself. The machinery of supply control was beginning to groan under the weight of a few years of heavy yields as the government's techniques of supply control were increasingly outmatched by farmers' more intensive cultivation methods. In 1964, the tobacco program's unit of supply control was the acre: farmers could only market tobacco produced on their allotted acreage. The rise of chemical agriculture had made acreage allotments a very poor tool of supply restriction as farmers were able to realize with greater frequency the Swiftian dream of making two blades of grass grow where one grew before. Overproduction meant lower support prices the following year, increased overhead costs, and, worst of all, increased scrutiny of the program for its use of taxpayer dollars.

The Flue-Cured Tobacco Stabilization Cooperative Corporation was a fat sitting target for scrutiny—one of those quasi-public organizations that could ignite the ire of a crusading journalist or a politician who sought to make his or her name by sniffing out impropriety. Stabilization was the body that actually administered the tobacco price support system. If a farmer's tobacco failed to receive a penny over the price floor at auction, Stabilization would buy it, process it, pack it, and store it until it could be sold later—hopefully at a higher price.[161] The money the farmer received for his crop was financed through a nonrecourse loan from the Commodity Credit Corporation (CCC)—a government agency established in the earliest days of the New Deal, and a public, taxpayer-financed organization. The money received from the delayed sales of stored tobacco was then used to repay the loans from the CCC.

In 1964, tobacco ranked fourth behind the much more extensively cultivated crops of corn, wheat, and cotton for the undesirable distinction of stocks held under government loan.[162] In 1968, taxpayer transfers to cotton and sugar had swelled to such an extent—$935 million and $500 million respectively—that tobacco's slice of the subsidy pie appeared miniscule in comparison. By the end of Johnson's tenure, the amount of public funds spent on private industry had swelled to mammoth proportions. In fact, $6 billion of taxpayer money was spent yearly on all manner of subsidies and programs for farmers, shippers, railway concerns, electric co-ops, and transportation concerns.[163]

At the same time, tobacco interests had the weight of historical figures on their side when they claimed that their agricultural program cost taxpayers less than that of any other commodity. During the Roosevelt, Truman, and Eisenhower administrations, agricultural subsidies totaled a combined $18 billion—just $200 million of which went to tobacco. During the early 1960s, only 10 percent of total tobacco exports were financed through government programs, whereas all cotton and rice exports were subsidized. The mechanics of tobacco associationalism perpetuated the sense that growers were not actually subsidized at all: the federal government never physically took title to the leaf; instead it issued loans to grower cooperatives like Stabilization.[164] And because tobacco yielded tax revenues of $2 billion each year, even a modest subsidy program could be recast as an economic bargain. "The cost of the tobacco support program . . . since its initiation has been in the neighborhood of about $40 million, while the proceeds to the government in excise taxes have been approximately $50 billion," explained North Carolina Democrat Lawrence Fountain at a 1969 hearing on cigarette labeling. "Think about that."[165]

But when some Americans thought about it, neither the economics nor the politics of the tobacco subsidy seemed to make sense.[166] Between 1954 and 1958, yields on flue-cured tobacco stood at 1,500 pounds of leaf per acre. Through more intensive cultivation practices and the aggressive use of agrochemicals, by 1964 yields had increased nearly 50 percent to 2,200 pounds per acre. Local USDA committees reported instances of production in excess of 3,500 pounds per acre. The rest was a vicious spiral enabled by the peculiarly modern paradox of technology and planning: increases in yields by farmers required decreases in acreage-based marketing quotas, which in turn stimulated more intensive cultivation practices, thereby increasing yields.

"I can tell you what the problem is in three words—too much tobacco," Tubby Weeks, the general manager of Stabilization, told the *New York Times*, a publication whose interest in tobacco production was doubtless piqued by the crisis unfolding over tobacco consumption.[167] When the 1964 *Surgeon General's Report* was published, Stabilization took in 284 million pounds of tobacco that went unpurchased at auction, the third largest amount in the program's history. Because of accumulations from previous years, Stabilization held nearly a billion pounds of unwanted tobacco—a figure worth nearly $500 million.

And Stabilization was not selling this stored tobacco as briskly as in years past. Worse still, yields per acre in 1964 were setting new records. Such figures "bear far more forceful witness than words to the grave and vulnerable position of the support program," read a Tobacco Associates annual report. Tobacco's enemies would hardly need to raise the question of whether or not government subsidy of a deadly commodity was prudent. The program was proving *itself* imprudent. "A duplication in 1965 of what occurred in the past three crop years may cut us aloose [*sic*] from the safe, secure mooring to which we have been tied for a quarter of a century and set us adrift on the turbulent waters of uncontrolled, unsupported production," the report warned.[168]

The Stabilization situation was also causing divisions among tobacco interests. The intensive use of pesticides was affecting the vaunted quality of American flue-cured tobacco—or at least that's what cigarette manufacturers said as they increased their purchases of cheaper leaf cultivated in other parts of the world. Farmers, however, suspected that the cigarette companies' criticism was a disingenuous ploy to pay less for homegrown leaf. After all, the ingredients of a cigarette included material of considerably lower quality than pesticide-treated leaf: sawdust, floor sweepings, and even polonium were known additives.[169] Nevertheless, too much tobacco—and tobacco of supposedly poor quality—invalidated two long-standing justifications of the program: it worked, and it worked because farmers produced a first-class commodity that had no trouble finding a market.

When framed as a problem of quantity produced at the expense of quality, the oversupply of leaf threatened to sow division within the tobacco industry—a dangerous fissure at the precise moment when spokesmen for the crop saw the need for unity above all. If excess production continued unabated, the interlocking organizational apparatus responsible for the welfare of tobacco-dependent families and communities—the very essence of tobacco associationalism—would be on the line. Despite its dependence on the public purse, Stabilization served a specific, narrow constituency, and it did so in a manner that minimized outside scrutiny or public accountability. For example, Carl Hicks served as the organization's director and president for over 30 years—from 1946 to 1978. And during the 1960s he also served as president of the TGIC, of which Stabilization was a member. But if taxpayers were asked to foot more of the bill for the tobacco program, such fluidity between public and private organizing—organizing that blurred the distinction between regulating tobacco production and advocating tobacco consumption—might garner more unwanted attention. Tobacco was still relatively cheap to taxpayers, but if trends continued, costs could be expected to skyrocket. Flue-cured farmers needed to get their house in order.

One month after the *Report* was issued, Harold Cooley introduced a bill that aimed to tighten controls on tobacco production by subjecting farmers

to poundage rather than acreage restrictions.[170] Several months of study by
a committee of tobacco leaders—chaired by the recently appointed president
of Tobacco Associates—ensued before the bill was reintroduced before the
Senate by North Carolina's Everett Jordan and Sam Ervin in early 1965.
This idea was not new—a similar scheme had been proposed the previous
decade. But it took the double-barreled pressure brought on by the *Report*
and the mounting stocks to force political action. The process of re-
forming the tobacco program bore all the hallmarks of associational
governance: unelected, elite representatives of the agricultural tobacco
economy hashed out policy in private, maintaining the posture of consensus as their plan got a friendly hearing in Congress, securing the speedy
passage of legislation.

This posture of consensus was frequently touted as justification for
growers' receipt of government largess. The 1965 Hearings opened with
Allen Ellender, the segregationist Democrat from Louisiana who chaired
the Senate Committee on Agriculture, praising the unique degree of agreement evident among tobacco farmers. "I do not know of any segment of
our farming community that has been better able to resolve their problems
than the tobacco people"—a fact that made the Committee's job easier in
passing legislation "that will redound to the benefit of the growers of the
Nation."[171] The poundage-based revision to the tobacco program did garner
a high degree of consensus among various classes of tobacco farmers. The
North Carolina Farm Bureau, which drew its membership from commercial farmers and agribusinesses, and the National Farmers Union, a champion of the small farmer, endorsed the legislation. Twenty-five farmers
from rural Nash County even took the overnight train from North Carolina to Washington, D.C., to make sure their names were entered into
the record in support of the legislation. John Palmer, the new president
of Tobacco Associates, presented senators with numerous endorsements
of the acreage-poundage measure from European tobacco manufacturers. Reemtsma, the largest cigarette manufacturer in West Germany,
noted that it "strongly welcomes the new acreage-poundage bill recently
introduced to Congress." So too did the Imperial Tobacco Company,
which offered its "emphatic confirmation and endorsement" of the bill, as
did Gallaher, the world's second largest importer of American flue-cured;

the other major foreign concerns with whom Tobacco Associates did business also lent their support to the bill.[172]

Such displays of sectoral solidarity were an able demonstration of associational policymaking. The speedy passage of Public Law 89-12, signed in April of 1965—in time for the summer's harvest—underscored how effective the tobacco sector could be at securing protective regulation. For tobacco growers, the counterweight to consumer regulation was not "free enterprise." It was a different vision of control—a vision of the state as the protector and benefactor of organized producers whose welfare was secured by the government's creation of a property right, a piece of new property. Like any property manager, the state needed to adapt to changing times, to make sure the underlying asset of the tobacco program maintained its value. But this system of largess management was unprepared for the arrival of noisy, litigious, and increasingly organized neighbors.

———

By the end of the 1960s, two regimes of tobacco control were headed toward collision: one premised on specific economic entitlements that belonged to producing groups, the other on a legally nebulous but increasingly powerful sense of the broad public interest. These two constituencies rarely met in person—the closest they got was in warring testimony delivered before congressional committees. They represented two competing visions of what government was, and whose interests it should protect. The challenge to producerist regulation posed by public interest lawyers was existential. Lawyers advocating for environmental and consumer rights were devising new strategies for taking on entrenched business interests. The power of organized producer groups was no secret. But public interest lawyers sought to make it a scandal. A grassroots anti-tobacco movement was springing up to vindicate lawyers' calls for public participation, transparency, and local control of tobacco policy.

5

Inventing the Nonsmoker

We must make smoking difficult and socially unacceptable. . . . We must lobby to make smoking rough.

—Public testimony, American Cancer Society Regional Forum, Denver, Colo., May 15, 1977

FOR THREE DAYS in June 1975, hundreds of public-health experts, doctors, civil servants, and activists from around the world converged in New York City for the Third World Conference on Smoking and Health.[1] This conference was larger and more diverse than the previous two, in New York (1967) and London (1971). Most importantly, it included a new, decisive figure: the nonsmoker. During the 1970s, it was in his or her name that the most significant regulation of tobacco would occur. At a panel dedicated to the subject of "Non-Smokers' Rights," Glenn Goldberg, a lawyer for Action on Smoking and Health (ASH), placed the legal and social movement for non-smokers' rights in the context of the rights revolutions reshaping Americans' sense of self, citizenship, and the obligations of the state. "Black Americans, Spanish-surnamed Americans, American Indians, American women, American homosexuals have all utilized legal action and legal process to obtain and preserve their fair share of government protection and largess," he explained. "At long last, and most encouragingly, America's nonsmoking majority is using the law to protect their lungs, to preserve their health, to save their very lives, from the forced inhalation of other people's tobacco smoke."[2]

But rights-based liberalism of the 1970s was a tangle of paradoxes, and rights for nonsmokers were no exception. Once nonsmokers had laid claim to a set of inviolable rights, smokers insisted that their own rights were under threat.[3] Even as activists spoke movingly of their pain and discomfort in smoky situations, rights were a language open to nonsmokers and smokers alike as they jostled for control of public space. White middle-class activists had learned from the civil rights movement's democratization of public space. "Everyone has the right to attend to daily business, to partici- pate in public affairs, and to seek recreation and entertainment without being subjected to constant, unnecessary health hazards and discomfort," explained a 1976 pamphlet produced by the California Group Against Smoking Pollution (GASP) Legal Fund.[4]

Yet nonsmokers' rights activists rarely considered the ways in which public-smoking restrictions fell unevenly upon Americans who were more likely to find themselves reliant upon public facilities: racial minorities and the poor. Like other middle-class citizen movements of the decade, GASP argued from a position of victimhood without reckoning with the ways in which its advocacy reflected its members own racial and class privileges.[5] Despite its pretense toward universalism ("everyone has a right to breathe air unpolluted by tobacco smoke"), nonsmokers' rights talk reflected a thin vision of collective life.[6] Of course, tobacco interests represented an *even thinner* slice of America. Woman-led, aspirationally universalistic, and in- sistent upon the democratization of public space, the nonsmokers' rights movement was a foil to the patriarchal, particularistic, and opaque regime that had dominated tobacco politics.

The sharp-elbowed, zero-sum mentality of asserting entitlement dove- tailed with changes in the political economy that forced Americans to con- front the limits of the federal government's ability to respond to inflation and unemployment. Deregulation—as a set of pro-competitive policies that reshaped the airline, trucking, and telecommunications sectors, as well as a political ideology that decried "big government"—had profound conse- quences for the nonsmokers' rights movement. As anti-tobacco lawyers dis- covered, suing administrative agencies—a strategy born of skepticism that agencies could capably represent the public, rather than private interests— could only work when there were administrative agencies to sue. The public interest critique of agency capture helped to stoke enthusiasm for deregu- lation.[7] But the demise of key regulatory agencies foreclosed the possibility of using lawsuits to force agencies to protect nonsmokers by restricting smoking in public.

Faced with the tobacco industry's superior resources in Washington—its stranglehold over Congress, its ability to grind the gears of much regulatory action—activists took their cause to lower levels of government: they shopped for a better venue. Even as the nonsmoker movement drew inspiration from federal environmental law and legal strategies, rights for nonsmokers were ultimately vindicated at the state and local levels. In this too, nonsmokers' rights activists shared much with environmental and public-health activism.[8]

Two complimentary movements succeeded in portraying the nonsmoker as a figure in need of protection and endowed with rights: Banzhaf's ASH and GASP, which was a decentralized, chapter-based, citizen-led social movement. Although their strategies were not centrally coordinated, each picked up where the other left off. ASH extracted rights from administrative agencies; GASP empowered nonsmokers to assert their entitlement to clean air. ASH pursued an elite strategy of legal change; GASP called upon the grass roots to make their presence felt. ASH was premised upon the idea that government agencies were closed to the will of the people; GASP enacted that great unrepresented will. Born of the rights revolution, the environmental movement, and the mania for deregulation, the nonsmoker was marked by the contradictions of liberalism in the 1970s. Nonsmokers were a new force on the political scene. But they were far from alone in demanding that politicians attend to quality of life issues increasingly seen as a birthright for the middle class.[9]

Inventing Nonsmokers' Rights

John Banzhaf's tussle with the Federal Communications Commission taught him that there was a lot of upside to asking what administrative agencies could do for tobacco regulation. The trick lay in convincing agencies that such a move fell under their purview. For many, the phrase "administrative agencies" conjured up images of staid men in suits talking in federal code. But for Banzhaf, administrative agencies presented an opportunity for creative legal action. He was just one of many legal academics who used their positions to test theories of social change. Indeed, he was part of the academy's inauguration of "legal clinics" into legal education. At NYU Law School, for example, clinical education became a standing part of the curriculum in 1969, and by 1970 there were ten clinical courses offered by the school. Students worked with New York–area economic development programs, provided services in the juvenile court system, defended indigents "charged with minor crimes," and worked alongside lawyers in providing services to the poor.[10]

When he began teaching at George Washington University's law school in 1968, Banzhaf called his approach "Anti-Establishment law."[11] His Legal Activism course, known among students as "Sue the Bastards," described "law as a weapon against major social problems." Banzhaf's Legal Activism course reflected an adversarial approach embraced by environmental activists of the era. Much of the environmental lawyering of the 1970s was, in essence, a critique of the New Deal's administrative state and its pro-development biases.[12] Some of these environmental lawyers, like Joseph Sax, a professor at the University of Michigan Law School, advocated the zealous use of citizen suits, portraying litigation as a tool for democracy, a cudgel to smash the iron triangle that bound interest groups, Congress, and the bureaucracy. The courtroom was reimagined not as a place where property interests always prevailed, but as "a forum where the individual citizen or community group can obtain a hearing on equal terms" with the "entrenched interests" that had "skillfully learned to manipulate legislative and administrative hearings."[13] A citizen came to administrative agencies "essentially as a supplicant." In court, by contrast, "he stands as a claimant of rights to which he is entitled."[14] Sax's "cri-de-courtroom" was a bit optimistic. Litigation was a costly strategy, especially when facing an opposition as well-heeled as the tobacco lobby. Banzhaf and his bandits pursued an adversarial strategy toward regulatory agencies; he would bring suit only after the cheaper strategy of public pressure had been tried.

Two important innovations in environmental law heightened the influence of student clinics. The major environmental legislation of the era enabled citizen suits and required environmental impact statements of federal agencies proposing actions that might affect the environment. Environmental laws dominated the congressional docket in the late 1960s and early 1970s, but they were also of a piece with statutes enhancing workplace safety, consumer protection, and workplace antidiscrimination.[15] Law clinics were training grounds for this expanding realm of public interest law. During the 1970s, Banzhaf's students were a part of the ecology of D.C.'s courts, agencies, and legislative bodies. In 1971, LABEL (Law Students Association for Buyers' Education in Labeling) took on the FDA over warning labels on cola drinks.[16] INFANTS (Interested Future Attorneys Negotiating for Tot Safety) agitated for better marketing of car seat safety. DEAFWATCH (Demanding Equal Access to Facts and Warnings Aired on Television for Citizens who are Hearing-impaired) successfully petitioned the FCC to order closed captioning for emergency messages.[17] The acronym crusaders were routinely featured in the *Washington Post's* "Washington Merry-Go-Round" column. The playful irreverence of the students' actions matched the winking tone of columnist Jack Anderson's insider's account of Washington.

At the end of the fall term of 1969, a group of law students called CRASH (Citizens to Reduce Airline Smoking Hazards) fulfilled the requirements of Banzhaf's legal activism course: CRASH submitted a petition to the Federal Aviation Administration (FAA) and the Department of Transportation proposing the segregation of smokers and nonsmokers on flights.[18] This petition, which shared official cover with a Banzhaf-authored ASH petition, arrived at the FAA hot on the heels of a more stringent proposal by Ralph Nader. Citing concerns about fire safety and passenger health, Nader petitioned for an all-out ban on cigarettes, pipes, and cigars on or near aircraft—"a veritable tinder box of potentially burnable materials."[19]

By contrast, CRASH and ASH merely wanted the agency to require "all domestic air carriers to effectively separate smoking passengers from nonsmoking passengers." Asserting that the Federal Aviation Act of 1958 enabled the FAA to "give consideration to the public interest including the highest degree of safety for the passengers," Banzhaf and his bandits positioned their proposal as falling within the purview of already established agency authority, which allowed the administrator latitude to act in a "variety of circumstances, foreseeable and unforeseeable, that might arise." These petitions—and the publicity they garnered—created circumstances to which FAA had to respond. Banzhaf gave cover for the agency to avoid a bold and politically difficult ban. Nader's petition, unyielding and absolute, gave regulators the outer bounds from which to negotiate a softer, "reasonable" restriction.

The bulk of the Banzhaf petition suggested the myriad ways in which the health, safety, and comfort of nonsmoking passengers were imperiled by tobacco smoke. In 1969 there was not yet epidemiology demonstrating a causal link between lung and cardiovascular disease in nonsmokers and exposure to secondhand smoke. Such studies would not appear until the early 1980s and the issue of disease in nonsmokers would not receive sustained treatment in a *Surgeon General's Report* until 1986. Nor were there studies of nonsmokers' exposure to cigarettes within enclosed places like airplanes, nor studies of what the short- and long-term effects of those exposures might be.

Anti-tobacco activists worked with a limited—but growing—scientific toolkit in which Americans' pre-existing allergies and sensitivities played a leading role. The 1967 National Health Survey, the first major nationwide attempt to gauge Americans' incidence of illness and use of health care since the 1930s, had revealed that millions of Americans suffered from respiratory diseases, such as chronic bronchitis and sinusitis, emphysema, asthma, and hay fever. Citing excerpted comments of recent medical research in specialty journals, the petition asserted that any one of these common underlying conditions could be exacerbated by exposure to tobacco smoke. Following a time-honored pattern of framing children as the primary beneficiary of government protections, Banzhaf's petition also observed that large numbers of American children suffered from asthma, and that pediatric specialists had long accepted tobacco smoke as a "non-specific irritant in many children with respiratory allergy." The petition then veered into the realm of the downright speculative, observing that for many passengers, flying was an emotionally taxing experience. For a person "with a pre-established susceptibility" to emotional disturbances, the "threshold level" for tobacco smoke irritation might be even lower.[20] It was an invitation to imagine turbulent skies indeed: cardiac arrests, wheezing children, and emotional tantrums by frazzled passengers pushed over the edge by the smoker across the aisle.

Banzhaf's arguments may have been tenuous. But his case did not need to be airtight. He simply needed to convince FAA administrator John Shaffer that the issue of in-flight smoking could be considered under his purview, thereby triggering an agency notice and comment period before the FAA issued a final rule. Indeed, the petition asserted without elaboration that the agency's mandate—to encourage the development of air commerce— brought the smoking issue under its purview: after all, many nonsmokers, it insisted, wished to fly but could not for lack of smoke-free air. And wasn't it possible that many "courteous smokers" were also unable to enjoy their flights, their enjoyment of a cigarette muted by the sidelong, seething glances of nonsmokers? Banzhaf's proposal to segregate smokers and non-smokers was modest, and probably ineffectual given the recirculation of cabin air. But for this reason, he contended that his proposal did not re-quire the absolute prioritization of nonsmokers' health. The FAA need only strive for "balance" between the "needs and desires" of smokers and non-smokers. Under the segregated seating plan, smokers "will not be deprived of their privilege," but those bothered, sickened, or deterred from flying al-together could fly in greater comfort.[21]

A few weeks after the airline smoking petitions were filed, a letter to the nationally syndicated advice columnist Ann Landers suggested that on-board tensions indeed ran high. The letter's author was a smoker ques-tioning his behavior on a flight from Cincinnati to San Francisco. "Mind if I smoke?" the man asked his neighbor. He was stunned when she replied with a yes. "Her answer irritated me since I am a heavy smoker and felt she was interfering with my rights," he wrote. After all, the airlines practically expected people to smoke since they "have signs regulating smoking during takeoff and landing." He suggested that the woman find another seat, which she did. So, the writer wondered, who was in the right—himself or the "in-considerate female"? Maybe the smoker expected an affirmation of his cour-tesy in merely asking if his nonsmoking neighbor minded. If so, he was disappointed. Landers invoked an eminently quotable—if simplistic—conception of rights. "Your right to smoke ends where the other fellow's nose begins." Landers advised that the author "should have found a seat next to another nicotine addict. The two of you could then hack and cough all the way to San Francisco without offending anyone."[22] Landers' chiding response notwithstanding, the smoker's missive revealed something pro-found about a smoker's perception of the entitlement to smoke freely. That airlines prohibited smoking during takeoff and landing only served to high-light for some smokers that it was their right to smoke at all other times. Whether or not the petitions to the FAA succeeded—or what levels of pro-tections for nonsmokers a rule might ultimately provide—their existence recalibrated the social default away from smoking as a cruising-altitude right.

The quest for clear skies was given a big, unexpected assist from a well-placed legal observer. The same day that major newspapers reported on the airline smoking petitions, Chief Justice Warren Burger took up his pen to write a missive of his own to administrator Shaffer. On Supreme Court letterhead, Burger relayed a story that had taken place five years earlier. On a flight from Washington, D.C., to Minneapolis, the Chief Justice decided he could take no more of the smoky conditions. He explained that "37 passengers were smoking and the plane crew insisted that they could do nothing although the Stewardesses were as red-eyed as I was." Burger suffered no special tobacco allergy. He possessed "only an ordinary distaste for tobacco." But he was compelled to leave the plane at a stopover in Madison, hoping for clearer air on an outbound flight the next day. "I wrote the President of the airline and was not even accorded the courtesy of an answer," Burger wrote. Administrator Shaffer did offer such a courtesy, returning the chief justice's letter with personal assurances that "responsive action" was under way at the agency as the FAA announced it was initiating what it called "advanced notice and comment."[23] Burger's note was the primus inter pares among thousands that arrived at the agency as a result of the CRASH petition. The media attention the missive received may have spurred other Americans to send their own complaints to the FAA.

As the Federal Aviation Administration collected information and public comment, other agencies acted to segregate smokers from nonsmokers. In early 1970 Nader submitted a complaint to the ICC requesting a complete ban on smoking on interstate buses. The ICC rejected Nader's proposal, but announced in late 1971 that it would literally relegate smokers to the back of the bus—a seeming embrace of Banzhaf's quest for "balance" in segregating smokers. By January of 1972, bus companies making interstate trips were required to restrict smoking to the rear 20 percent of seats.[24] The rule was intended to "alleviate a substantial nuisance and a possible health hazard"—the lack of firm evidence on secondhand smoke preventing a Naderesque ban.[25] In a separate ruling, the agency also required the allocation of space for nonsmokers in coach class, parlor cars, dining cars, and sky-lit dome cars on the newly established Amtrak service.[26] In late 1972, Chief Justice Burger again penned a personal letter to an agency head to complain about smoke he encountered as he traveled in the first-class section of a Metroliner. "On the trip up the club car was polluted by three cigar smokers," Burger wrote to Transportation secretary John Volpe. "And on the return by four of them—all in addition to cigarettes." When he complained to the conductor, he was told to seek the cleaner, but less rarified, air of the coach class. Five days after receiving the chief justice's complaint, a ban on smoking in first class went into effect.[27]

Airlines preempted regulatory action, hoping that their own steps might obviate a need for formal regulation—a move that echoed that of the broadcast industry a few years before. In January of 1970, Pan Am announced it would designate twelve first-class seats and thirty-six economy-class seats on its new fleet of 747s as nonsmoking. American Airlines made a similar pledge a month later, highlighting the no-smoking section as one of the amenities offered on its new jumbo jets. Not to be outdone, TWA announced that it would offer no-smoking seats on all of its aircraft, from jumbo jets to propeller hoppers.[28] In just over three months and without formal legal changes, the social default in the skies had shifted. The smoking letter-writer to Ann Landers could no longer claim that the absence of an airline policy on smoking implied a "right" to smoke freely. The nonsmoking passenger had acquired more options at her disposal than a passive aggressive glance or a cough of resentment. But the airlines' voluntary rules did not quell the nonsmoking majority's discontent. Just over 30 percent of women and 44 percent of men smoked in 1970, yet Pan-Am reserved only 36 of 304 coach seats and 12 of 58 first-class seats for nonsmokers.[29] The airline's decision appeared more engineered for publicity than passenger safety.

Preemptive movement by the airlines coupled with the sluggishness of the Federal Aviation Administration during the "advanced" notice and comment period offered Banzhaf the perfect opportunity to generate publicity for the anti-smoking crusade. And in so doing, he worked to stake out his claim as the leading legal activist for the cause—a space still shared with the better-known Nader, who was more frequently referenced by name in newspaper accounts of the petitions. In March of 1970, Banzhaf held a press conference at the National Press Club to chide the FAA for not moving more quickly. He announced his plan: book trips on the airlines that had advertised no-smoking sections, request a no-smoking seat, and, if none were available, sue the airlines for "not protecting the rights of non-smokers."

Banzhaf highlighted the federal privileges bestowed upon tobacco to draw a contrast to the individual nonsmoker who was forced to initiate private action, lawsuits, in order to vindicate his rights. Banzhaf also called for the immediate end to all federal subsidy of tobacco—from the agricultural program to the discounted cigarettes sold to servicemen on military bases.

Such publicity-seeking proclamations did more than just feed Banzhaf's ego. A press conference was a cheap way of raising the profile of the non-smoking issue. And the young lawyer's brash tactics seemed appropriate given the contrast between nonsmokers' second-class status and the protections and privileges afforded tobacco's allies. Public outrage—and outrage in public—was part of Banzhaf's legal strategy. Anger was a dormant resource that could be mobilized to face the superior financial and political reserves of the tobacco companies and the airlines. "If you convince people that somebody is inflicting a health hazard on them," Banzhaf told the *Wall Street Journal* in 1970, "they'll get mad and do something about it."[30]

The federal government did not just rely on public comment to inform its airline smoking rule. It undertook its own study of the effects of cabin exposures to environmental tobacco smoke—a move that underscored the paucity of scientific research on a public-health issue that affected all air travelers. The study, carried out by the Department of Health, Education, and Welfare and a cluster of federal health agencies, was intended to "define the levels of certain combustion by products of tobacco produced by passengers' smoking; to determine passengers' subjective reaction to tobacco smoke; and to obtain passenger opinion on the need for regulatory change regarding control of smoking." Researchers began with the ambitious goal of measuring carbon monoxide (CO) levels in passengers exposed to cabin smoking, but this aspect of the study had to be scrapped because it proved difficult to obtain blood samples. Such a study would have been path breaking, and had it demonstrated elevated levels of CO in the bodies of passengers it would have offered the FAA a basis on which to regulate, or even ban, in-flight smoking in the name of safety. But the study only collected samples of environmental contaminants, and found "extremely low" concentrations of CO, "much lower than ambient concentrations in urban environments."[31]

To better understand how passengers experienced tobacco smoke on airplanes, a questionnaire was also distributed on twenty Military Aircraft

Command international flights and eight domestic flights. The vast majority of nonsmokers wanted "corrective action" taken to mitigate the annoyance of secondhand smoke—either in the form of segregation or a ban.[32] The study also noted a significant relationship between the prevalence of respiratory disease and the demand for smoking regulation. Given that "the incidence of respiratory symptomology among the American population is increasing," in-flight tensions between smokers and nonsmokers could only be expected to rise. Nevertheless, cabin smoke was judged "not to represent a hazard to nonsmoking passengers," though many passengers were bothered by it—especially those with underlying respiratory conditions.[33] By taking a closer look inside the cabin, officials found little scientific basis, but much social demand, for regulation.

The FAA and the Civil Aeronautics Board (CAB) received more comments from the public on the proposed smoking regulation than on any other issue in their history—perhaps unsurprising given the extended notice and comment period and the widespread ramifications of the rule for all air passengers. Newspapers, trade journals, and professional associations encouraged Americans to share their opinions with the aviation agencies. Banzhaf bought ads in national newspapers encouraging nonsmokers to write to the CAB in support of the proposed rule (Figure 5.1).[34] Years of pent-up grievance poured in to CAB offices—enough to fill five volumes in the Board's docket.[35]

The comments revealed deep resentment toward smokers' unquestioned dominance of public space. "There is no excuse for subjecting individuals in a closed environment to others' habits, regardless of how widespread," wrote Edwin Bierman, a professor of medicine at the University of Washington. On the letterhead of the Seattle Veterans Administration Hospital, Bierman condemned the "uncomfortable and irritating" smoke as an "infringement of the fundamental rights to breathe unpolluted air."[36] Another letter—written "from the point of view of a pilot, physician, and physiologist"—admitted that the "brief exposure" to the "noxious effluvia" of tobacco smoke might not be as dangerous to the nonsmoker as the habit was to the smoker himself, but "it can exacerbate pre-existing respiratory inflammations, allergies, and asthmatic problems."[37] Although their letters may have carried special weight, doctors were far from the only Americans to weigh in. "I consider it an infringement of my personal freedom and a

ATTENTION NONSMOKERS

The Civil Aeronautics Board has tentatively agreed to issue a rule, originally proposed by Action on Smoking and Health, to require all airlines to provide no-smoking sections for the health and convenience of nonsmoking passengers. The proposed rule provides that enough seats must be set aside to accommodate all persons who would prefer not to sit next to a smoker, and requires the airlines to enforce the restrictions.

The CAB has asked for public comments on the rule, and it appears likely that the rule will not be issued unless there is a substantial demonstration of support from nonsmokers. If you are bothered by cigarette smoke, or just sick and tired of being forced to breathe polluted air, we urge you to write IMMEDIATELY to express your strong support for this proposed rule.

If you send us a copy of your letter to the CAB, we will send you free of charge a copy of our petition requesting the rule, which outlines the health hazards presented by cigarette smoke to the nonsmoker; a copy of the Surgeon General's report reaching the same conclusion, and information about how ASH is fighting to protect the rights of nonsmokers. This advertisement is presented as a public service by Action on Smoking and Health (ASH), a national non-profit and tax-exempt organization serving as the legal action arm of the anti-smoking community.

Send Your Letter To:
Civil Aeronautics Board
Docket Section
Washington D.C. 20428
Re: Docket 21708-ASH

Please Send a Copy To:
Action on Smoking & Health
2000 H St., N.W.
Washington, D.C. 20006
Re: CAB RULE

Figure 5.1 Banzhaf's Action on Smoking and Health (ASH) encourages nonsmoking readers of the *Washington Post* to send their public comments to the Civil Aeronautics Board, 1972. (Action on Smoking & Health, Washington, D.C.)

detriment to my health to be a captive audience 40,000 feet up in the blue sky and have some inconsiderate bastard puffing and blowing around me," an angry passenger complained to the CAB.[38]

Tobacco companies recognized the groundswell against in-flight smoking and launched a counterattack—or at least they simulated one. In 1972, Lorillard, the makers of Kent, True, Newport, and Old Gold brand cigarettes, orchestrated a letter-writing campaign in response to Banzhaf's newspaper advertisement. A lawyer for Lorillard drafted five sample letters and urged the company's chief executive officer to "get some of the [advertising] agency people to write these—by hand—on noncompany letterheads, using home addresses, and ask each one to get one or two more, similar, but not exactly the same."[39] These letters, which had passed through the hands of lawyers, company officials, and admen, were intended to look as if they had come from everyday Americans. Each of the five letters conveyed a different personality type. The affronted civil libertarian asked, "Are all smokers, by virtue of this regulation, to be automatically declared second-class citizens who must be herded about like cattle?"[40] The resentful member of the silent majority argued, "Why should I have to sit anywhere except where I want—just because Mr. Nader tells you I should?"[41] The courteous smoker explained, "I was pleased when most of the airlines began to give smokers an opportunity sit in special 'smoking sections.' . . . Isn't the voluntary arrangement working?"[42] Counsel for Lorillard even ginned up a letter from an easygoing nonsmoker who wondered why such a regulation was necessary when "the ventilation systems on the planes appear to work fine."[43] The trick was quickly discovered by officials at the CAB—evidently the ad agencies had not taken counsel's advice to tweak the wording and sent a flurry of identical letters to the agency. Lorillard's lawyer protested that the industry's move was not prohibited by the CAB nor by the Codes of the American Bar Association.[44] Likewise, the rules of the CAB did not prevent regulators from considering the source of the comments it received.

In the spring of 1973, the CAB announced its new smoking rule: airlines had to provide separate sections for smokers and nonsmokers, and they had to accommodate any nonsmoking passenger who requested a seat in the nonsmoking section. Carriers were subject to a $1,000 fine for each violation of the rule. This victory did not mark the end of ASH's pursuit of the agency, for each rule promulgated by a regulatory agency offered the opportunity for a watchdog organization to monitor enforcement. There were hundreds if not thousands of instances in which passengers noted alleged violations of CAB regulations: from nonsmokers who could not be accommodated in the allocated nonsmoking sections to passengers who lit up in defiance of the rules. ASH filed scores of legal complaints against airlines throughout the 1970s on behalf of individuals denied no-smoking accommodations.[45] These complaints resulted in thousands of dollars in civil penalties, as well as settlements with two particularly egregious offenders in TransWorld Airlines and Eastern Airlines. In response to ASH prodding, the CAB tightened its smoking rules in 1976, requiring the segregation of pipe and cigar smokers, and prohibiting smoking when the in-flight ventilation system was not operational.

Smoking into the Sunset

The CAB's new smoking rules took hold as the political tide turned against regulation. New intellectual, demographic, and economic forces compelled a reassessment of Democratic liberalism. Liberalism's Keynesian underpinnings—that the government could stimulate growth though the judicious application of tax cuts and deficit spending, that vigorous regulation was essential for rationalizing the nation's core industrial sectors, that aggregate demand, and not individual choice, ought to be the focus of economic policy—were quivering under the twinned problems of inflation and unemployment. Left-leaning critics of corporate capture were joined by businesses and right-wing economists who detected "government failure" in public attempts to superintend industry.[46]

Deregulation was heralded as a panacea for the flagging American economy and welcomed by many as a tonic to a bloated political system. By the late 1970s, the American public was well-acquainted with the capture critiques that originated in the academy and were popularized by politicians and the press. According to a 1977 *U.S. News & World Report* poll, 81 percent of respondents agreed with the statement that "large companies have a major influence on the government agencies regulating them."[47] And the inconvenient intrusion of global competition into the decades-long idyll of American economic supremacy left businessmen and policymakers searching for new policies that could once again unleash American productivity. Boosters heralded deregulation as a cure-all for the malaise of the 1970s: for inflation, for consumer dissatisfaction, for America's fading industrial might. And as such, it was embraced by Democratic and Republican politicians alike.

Talk of loosening the strictures on regulated industries began well before the Reagan Revolution's full-throated denunciation of government. Initiated under a Democratic Congress, and shepherded by liberal lion Ted Kennedy, airline deregulation formed a centerpiece of Jimmy Carter's efforts to deregulate the transportation industry "as much as possible."[48] The Democratic "Watergate babies" elected in the wake of Nixon's resignation were less credulous of federal regulatory initiatives than senior colleagues who had come of age during the Depression. These new Democrats changed the priorities of their party, making it less economically populist but more liberal on social issues like civil and sexual rights, the environment, and consumer protection. Among this new cohort, the old, competition-stifling, giant-protecting CAB had few friends. The Airline Deregulation Act of 1978 passed easily in both chambers.

The CAB became the poster child for deregulation. It was an agency in which the corporatist DNA of the National Recovery Act was still visible in its alignment of "the public interest with the desires of the most powerful elements" of industry.[49] Ushering the agency out of existence was Alfred Kahn, the chair of the CAB. The Carter appointee and Cornell economist called himself a liberal Democrat, and it took some persuading by the President for Kahn to embrace his role as a deregulatory pioneer.[50] Before his appointment to the agency in 1977, Kahn sat at the helm of the powerful New York State Regulatory Commission, an experience that validated his academic observations about the tradeoffs between regulation and competition, between market stability and consumer price. Dubbed "The Father of Airline Deregulation," Kahn embraced a theory of marginal costs: that in the absence of price-distorting regulation, competition would cause prices to fall, opening the skies to more Americans. Airline deregulation became a general model for federal retrenchment from the trucking, bus transportation, railroads, telecommunications, oil, and finance sectors.[51]

In its lame duck years, the CAB relaxed some smoking rules as part of a commitment to "permit experimentation and encourage innovation by the airlines."[52] Airlines were much happier to advertise their new nonsmoking sections than they were to police disgruntled passengers. Under new rules promulgated in 1981, nonsmokers were no longer entitled to complain about being "unreasonably burdened" by nearby smoking, giving airlines more leeway to "sandwich" small nonsmoking sections between larger smoking sections. Under new rules, smoking would be permitted even when ventilation systems were not in use. And the new rules also allowed airlines to deny passengers nonsmoking seats if they did not meet the check-in requirements established by the airline—even if the customer's tardiness was due to a delayed connection. ASH soon initiated its final action against its longtime adversary, enabler, validator, and collaborator. In *ASH v. Civil Aeronautics Board* (1983), Banzhaf scored his last victory against the agency, which was ordered by the D.C. Circuit to reinstate the tighter rules.[53] But, as in many encounters between ASH and regulators, the victory was partial. Flooded with industry-sponsored letters opposing further restrictions, as well as political pressure from congressional allies, the CAB rejected ASH's proposal to ban smoking on short flights.[54] The agency limped into the sunset having raised nonsmokers' expectations without providing consistent relief.

Although Banzhaf's legal approach was rooted in a fundamental skepticism toward the ability of agencies to regulate in the public interest, it also depended upon a robust regulatory state.[55] The *ASH Newsletter* noted that the CAB's sunset at the end of 1984 posed "special problems," auguring poorly for " yet another suit, at least this time."[56] Banzhaf's brand of public interest law was highly technical, relying on the skills of an appellate lawyer rather than a broad critique of bureaucracy, industrial concentration, or consumer protection. Though he was frequently referred to as the "Ralph Nader of smoking," Banzhaf and his bandits did not establish a multipronged assault on tobacco's political power through muckraking investigations, think tanks, or citizen-lobby organizations. The technocratic nature of Banzhaf's legal activism was fundamentally at odds with the majority will on whose behalf he sued. ASH had unwittingly become a victim of the political process it had helped to set in motion. Born out of skepticism of the capacity of legacy agencies to regulate in the public interest, ASH had relied on legal tactics that sought to transfer authority outside of the agency itself—to the courts. But with fewer agencies to petition or sue, Banzhaf's leadership of the anti-tobacco movement was considerably weakened. Fortunately, another organization had long been organizing on behalf of the nonsmoker.

GASP: Vocal, Visual, and Vigilant

To invent the nonsmoker, ASH relied on the efforts of lawyers in specific legal forums. But GASP insisted nonsmokers were everywhere—they just needed to make themselves known.

Despite a shared penchant for irreverent acronyms, GASP and ASH embodied two different organizing traditions. Where ASH thrived in the courtroom, GASP came to life in library meeting rooms, church basements, and family rooms across the country. GASP was a grassroots effort led largely by women, not staffed by elite operators from the Washington legal scene.[57]

The single-issue anti-smoking organization was formed in Clara Gouin's living room in College Park, Maryland, in January 1971. Gouin was a housewife and the mother of two daughters, the youngest of whom had an allergy to smoke. The child's reaction to cigarettes was so severe that it prevented the family from going out to eat. Even worse than being restricted in public was the expectation that nonsmokers had to accommodate smoking guests in their own homes. Ashtrays in the homes of nonsmokers were monuments to smokers' supremacy. "What doormats we nonsmokers were!" Gouin recalled thinking as she lay awake one night contemplating nonsmokers' powerlessness. The friends with whom she commiserated—about the burn marks on furniture and carpets, the added chore of airing out one's coats and washing one's hair immediately after returning from a night out—agreed. And Gouin also knew the gravest costs of smoking. She was mourning the loss of her father, a longtime smoker, to lung cancer.[58]

The origins of the College Park GASP were humble. Using $50 of her allotted "grocery money," Gouin procured the first batch of buttons that would become a standard symbol in the national nonsmokers' movement: "GASP—Nonsmokers Have Rights Too." Six of Gouin's nonsmoking friends—"mostly mothers, and a few working secretaries"—met in her living room and launched their first action: banishing smoking from their own homes by removing ashtrays and putting up no-smoking signs. Several weeks later the first issue of GASP's newsletter, *The Ventilator*, was published thanks to the Prince George's Tuberculosis and Respiratory Disease Association (TB&RD), which allowed Gouin to use its mimeograph machine (see Figure 5.2). The Tuberculosis and Respiratory Disease Association (later known as the Lung Association) would prove instrumental in another crucial way: it mailed *The Ventilator* to members in surrounding counties and shared it with 200 state and local affiliates across the United States. Piggybacking on the association's national scope and reputation, Gouin's GASP quickly reached an enormous and diverse audience.[59]

Within days, inquiries poured in from individuals across the country for help in starting their own GASP chapters. Berkeley began its first GASP chapter when a board member of the TB&RD affiliate wrote to

Figure 5.2 Clara Gouin prepares the Group Against Smokers' Pollution (GASP) newsletter. (Courtesy of Clara Gouin)

Gouin for more information. Soon, other chapters formed in the Bay Area. There, GASPers immediately scored a victory after collecting over 650 signatures on a petition to ban smoking at a Berkeley grocery cooperative.[60] Outside of College Park, GASP chapters sprung up in the city of Greenbelt and in Howard and Montgomery Counties. By the spring of 1972, activists at the College Park GASP had assembled and mailed over 500 "New Chapter Kits"—literature that helped fledgling activists conceive of themselves as possessing both a legitimate grievance and the means to do something about it.[61] In Rochester, New York, a housewife like Gouin also spent $50 of her grocery money to purchase a newspaper ad announcing the establishment of the chapter. Within months, the chapter claimed 130 members and had convinced the city's mayor to declare a week in May of 1972 as "Be Kind to Non-Smokers" week. Newspapers around the country took note of the movement with headlines like, "New Militancy Gets Results," and "Where There's Smoke, There's Ire" and "GASP Tries to Clear Air of Smokers."[62]

Although GASP's earliest chapters thrived in college towns and liberal enclaves like College Park, Berkeley, and the Bay Area, nonsmoker activism was embraced beyond circles of bohemians, lefties, and university professors. GASP chapters were fully decentralized: there was no central institutional presence in College Park or Washington, D.C. GASP chapters thrived in Michigan, Georgia, Arizona, Kansas, and New York.[63] A GASP member in Flint, Michigan, threated to sue the Pontiac General Hospital for assigning her husband, who was recovering from a heart attack, to a hospital room shared with two smokers. Her husband was eventually given a private room—at "no extra $," the Berkeley *GASP News* happily relayed.[64] Newsletters kept nonsmoking activists abreast of innovative activities all over the country, inspiring activism closer to home. For example, in 1974, readers of *The Ventilator* learned that Willi's Wunderland Restaurant in Davenport, New York, and Harrah's Theater Restaurants in Lake Tahoe had begun offering nonsmoking sections to patrons. This was not a nonsmokers' version of the *Negro Motorist Green Book*. It was intended to inspire Maryland's nonsmokers to become more visible, to "voice their opinions" to local restaurant owners, to demand *more* nonsmoking accommodations. Adorned with hand-drawn cartoons (Gouin was a talented cartoonist), newsletters conveyed usable local information ("Smokefree Chinese Cuisine in Cambridge!"), a sense of the nonsmokers' national presence, and the righteousness and camaraderie of the cause.

Resentment was a defining emotion of the 1970s, and anti-smoking activists cultivated it, drawing forth political grievance where personal irritation and self-blame had existed before. Examples abounded for fashioning identities from historical oppression. The 1970s saw a rise in the voice and visibility of many groups of Americans—some a direct legacy of the civil rights movement, some formed in reaction to it. Identity-centric social movements were ascendant on college campuses, in print and popular culture, and in public spaces. Afrocentrist approaches to history and the arts reshaped textbooks and curricula for students of all ages; thanks to feminists, consciousness-raising became a widely used tool for describing and excavating the shared experience of private, otherwise unmentionable indignities. Even "unmeltable ethnics"—imagined as blue-collar white

Americans one or two generations removed from the old country—found a bard of resentments in the character of Archie Bunker.[65]

Legal and grassroots movements worked synergistically to produce a nonsmoker identity. Such symbiosis was evident in every rights movement that flourished during the late 1960s and early 1970s. Taking inspiration from the highly successful Legal Defense Fund of the National Association for the Advancement of Colored People, the Mexican American Legal Defense and Educational Fund, the Women's Legal Defense Fund, and Lambda Legal were established to expand the legal rights of Latinos, women, and gays and lesbians.[66] Banzhaf's petitions and letter-writing campaigns were fueled by the zeal of GASP; GASP newsletters kept members abreast of Banzhaf's activities in Washington.

What we might call identity politics was understood in the vocabulary of "liberation"—a term that at once suggested a history of oppression and the world-historical significance of group expression. GASP's 1973 *Nonsmokers' Liberation Guide*—"a manual of revolutionary tactics and strategies to secure the breathing rights of nonsmokers everywhere"—exemplified the tendency of the movement to deploy the rhetoric of revolution within the safe confines of suburban liberalism. In ten pages, the pamphlet elaborated the personal, community, and legal tactics available to nonsmokers, as well as the "grand strategy" of their cause. Nonsmokers were encouraged to make their presence known through signs at work, by making requests of private businesses and municipal buildings, and by lodging complaints when requests went unheeded. GASP suggested that individuals whose work or standing in the community required that they speak publicly—an indication of the professional backgrounds of many nonsmoking activists— "request no-smoking whenever you give a presentation," "propose a no-smoking policy or resolution," or pass around a "polite and reasonable request" to attendees (see Figure 5.3).

While these actions may have brought relief for nonsmokers, a middle-class professional announcing a code of conduct in a meeting was hardly the stuff of revolution. Suggestions for legal and community action, while focused on policy change, sprang from the fundamental belief that education, reflection, and the proper administration of pressure on political officials would yield smoking restrictions. The liberation guide possessed no analysis of power—no indictment of the political system that produced

A Polite and Reasonable Request
(Please pass it on)
SOME OF US here suffer discomfort and annoyance
from tobacco smoke. Won't you please refrain from
smoking while we share the same breathing space?
You will have our sincere thanks.

Group Against Smokers' Pollution

P.O. Box 632, College Park, Maryland 20740

...a gentle reminder

*perhaps you haven't noticed--
this is a "NO SMOKING" area*

THANK YOU for your compliance

Group Against Smokers' Pollution
P.O. Box 632, College Park, Maryland 20740

Figure 5.3 GASP produced courtesy cards to hand to
smokers, which encouraged nonsmokers to claim public space
while minimizing verbal confrontation. (Courtesy of Clara
Gouin)

and subsidized tobacco, no meditation on the cigarette as metaphor for
the poisons and pleasures of consumerism, no reflection on the possibility
that sanctions for indoor smoking might fall unevenly on the racially and
economically marginal. With buoyant middle-class entitlement, GASP
seized the sound and symbolism of liberation. The *Liberation Guide* was a
mirror image of the contemporaneous Virginia Slims "You've Come a Long
Way, Baby" advertisements (see Figure 5.4).[67] As Philip Morris conquered
cool, GASP liberated the bourgeoisie.

Many GASP activists were Democrats, but Nixon's metaphor of the
silent majority spoke to the sense of long-suffering resentment on the part
of respectable citizens. "Approximately two-thirds of adults are nonsmokers!" proclaimed a 1973 pamphlet produced by the College Park
GASP. "It is time for the silent majority to voice their objections to being

Figure 5.4 While playing on the Virginia Slims advertising slogan, GASP claimed contemporary emblems of liberation for nonsmokers. (Nonsmokers Liberation Guide (1973), Courtesy of Clara Gouin)

made the involuntary victims of tobacco smoke."[68] To overcome non-smokers' silence, GASP encouraged members to "become visual"—to adorn themselves, their property, and, if possible, other people's belongings. One of the first actions of Gouin's GASP chapter was a letter-writing campaign to 700 physicians in southern Maryland with a request to put up no-smoking signs in their waiting rooms. Most doctors did not reply, but fifty offices proclaimed themselves smoke-free. GASP chapters in places as distinct as Berkeley and Wichita sold buttons, bumper stickers, and posters with slogans like "Your Cigarette is Killing Me," "Yes, I Mind if You Smoke," and "Kissing a Smoker is Like Licking an Ashtray." These items were less valuable as a source of revenue (prices ranged from 25¢ to $1) than as a definitive declaration of nonsmokers' prerogative (see Figure 5.5).

Buttons and stickers were not just social identifiers: they were instruments of the movement. They changed the tenor of a room or an interaction even when their wearers were too timid to make their requests aloud. For the most silent members of the nonsmoking majority, GASP newsletters held "assertiveness training" workshops and some local chapters even maintained a support switchboard, in which GASPers offered "a sympathetic ear" to fellow nonsmokers suffering from "singed eyebrows and . . . bruised feelings" after a hostile confrontation with a smoker.[69] Like the

Figure 5.5 Buttons formed part of the visual vernacular of the movement for nonsmokers' rights. (Courtesy of Clara Gouin)

therapeutic session itself, GASP surfaced latent resentments and provided a setting and tools with which nonsmokers could understand their anger as a healthy response to a sick society. "If smoking is your monkey, keep it off my back," a Berkeley GASP pamphlet declared in the Blippo typeface that was a hallmark of the decade's printed aesthetic.

Consciousness-raising was another tool for increasing nonsmokers' sense of grievance. As powerfully expressed by contemporary feminists, consciousness-raising brought the hidden indignities of private experience out into the open, where they could be located in a structural critique of power and patriarchy. In the words of feminist historian Sarah Evans, the practice was premised on the belief that "people change . . . through a process of talking together, discovering common problems, and thereby understanding the need for collective action."[70] It was a tool admirably suited to the needs of the nonsmokers' movement—and not only because many of its earliest participants were women. "For a long time many nonsmokers have felt individually annoyed by smoking, but suffered in silence," Gouin explained in a 1972 profile. "People are more likely to speak out when they know others feel the same way."[71] The fact that nonsmokers comprised a majority of the population made speaking out a lower-risk proposition than other activism. But suffering itself ennobled the nonsmokers' cause, opening up avenues for analogy to the liberation struggles of other oppressed peoples.

GASP sought to catalyze a transformation in consciousness—to help nonsmokers see themselves as an oppressed category of people. For the middle-class whites who comprised GASP's ranks, there was surely a romance in understanding anti-tobacco activism as their own freedom struggle. At a freezing rally at the U.S. Capitol held on the occasion of Lincoln's birthday in February 1975, a tall, gangly nonsmoker dressed as the president proclaimed the event "a nonsmokers' liberation ceremony" (see Figure 5.6). "We are gathered here today to proclaim the emancipation of a large number of Americans who have been held in involuntary servitude," the ersatz Abe announced. "They are the millions of nonsmokers, persons who choose not to smoke, but who are, nevertheless, made slaves of the smoke of other people."[72] Presidential impersonation provided an unwittingly apt metaphor for the group's constituency. Though they perceived smoke as the yoke of slavery, activists for nonsmokers' rights also sought to occupy a special place of power reserved in American political culture for the organized, educated, and white.

Figure 5.6 "Mr. Lincoln" proclaims the liberation of nonsmokers in a 1975 ceremony on the steps of the U.S. Capitol on February 12—Lincoln's birthday. (Courtesy of Clara Gouin)

At times, activists spoke the heady language of civil rights and emancipation, drawing comparisons between the nonsmokers' rights movement and the African-American freedom struggle. Nonsmoking activists "reasoned from race," to borrow legal historian Serena Mayeri's evocative phrase, drawing analogies between civil rights for African Americans and civil rights for nonsmokers.[73] Though they were quick to hedge their comparisons, nonsmokers' rights activists' use of analogical reasoning frequently flattened the difference between the structural discrimination that African Americans faced and the crimped choices that nonsmokers contended with as consumers. "Although I would not suggest that nonsmokers' rights are trampled on to the same extent as have been the rights of minority groups," Peter Hanauer, the co-founder of Berkeley's GASP, told an audience of anti-smoking activists in 1976, "I would suggest certain parallels." After all, he wondered, "Is there any real difference . . . between saying to a person 'You can't eat at this lunch counter' and saying 'You can't eat at this lunch counter if you are concerned about your health or if you want to enjoy your lunch?'"[74] For Hanauer, nonsmokers—like African Americans denied public accommodation under Jim Crow—were victims of oppression.[75]

Quality of Life

All over the country, men and women like Gouin were forming little platoons to assert control over their environments—and to intervene in the political processes that drew the permissible limits of development, pollution, and noise.[76] An ethos of participatory democracy as well as the imperative to keep property values afloat spurred such suburban environmentalists to clean up rivers and green spaces, oppose aerial pesticide application, and insist on zoning standards to control development. In the suburbs, the environmentalism of the 1970s was frequently articulated in the language of "quality of life" and with reference to access to amenities such as parks and bike paths.[77] Nonsmoking activists were part of this quality of life constituency. After all, smoky environments prevented thousands of families from accessing the kinds of places considered the birthright of the middle class—restaurants, cafes, and movie theaters.[78] Suburban environmentalists and nonsmoking crusaders shared a consumerist approach to public space: it was theirs to enjoy.

The combination of middle-class entitlement and political theater was later captured by the acronym NIMBY ("Not In My Back Yard").[79] NIMBY originally referred to the ethos of neighborhood groups that opposed the nearby siting of landfills or prisons. But beneath this buoyant acronym lay a blinkered, acrimonious politics in which political action served class privilege: not in my backyard, but in someone else's. A hunkered-down mentality also pervaded the nonsmokers' rights movement. "I would not mind a smoker killing himself privately," wrote one peeved nonsmoker to the *Philadelphia Bulletin* in 1978. "I greatly object to his infecting my air."[80] This was the hard edge of the nonsmokers' civil libertarianism. At times, nonsmokers appeared to wear their contempt toward smokers on their sleeve.

GASP shared its acronym with a Pittsburgh-based grassroots environmental group: Group Against Smog and Pollution. Founded in 1969, the Pittsburgh GASP represented a broad, woman-led environmental coalition supported by a large institutional base of churches, community groups, and unions.[81] The two GASPs shared more than a memorable acronym and a female-led, demographic profile. The Pittsburgh GASP formed as a direct result of the Air Quality Act of 1967, which required public hearings to develop air quality standards at the state level.[82] GASP arose as concerned Pittsburghers sought to be a citizens' counterweight to the overwhelming influence of the steel and coal industry on air pollution control boards.[83]

The Group Against Smoking Pollution also conceived of itself as an environmental organization. Its *Liberation Guide* referred to tobacco smoke as "air pollution," a category that encompassed "contaminants which are likely to be injurious to public welfare, human health, plant or animal life, or to property, or which interfere with the enjoyment of life or property." Such language bore a striking resemblance to the congressional findings of the 1970 Clean Air Act, which decried pollution's "mounting dangers to public health and welfare, including injury to agricultural crops and livestock" and "damage to and deterioration of property."[84]

Federal environmental law undergirded activists' sense of entitlement. In the late 1960s, the state began to invite citizen participation in the formation and implementation of environmental legislation. For example, the 1967 Air Quality Act provided for citizen participation in public hearings, offering encouragement to neighborhood groups across the country. And the 1970 Clean Air Act encouraged grassroots involvement in policymaking, requiring that states hold public hearings on proposed environmental laws so that citizen groups could present testimony.[85] From the War on Poverty's Community Action Agencies to city-based experiments in community policing to the advisory committees of the Occupational Safety and Health Administration (OSHA), state regulations began to open to new constituencies in dramatic ways that reflected an expanding conception of the public. These experiments in openness were never as accessible as their architects intended. But they did stimulate the formation of countless citizen groups, and a rising sense of expectation among Americans who could see promise and peril in the new social legislation. The relationship among citizen, group, and law was dialectical: legal consciousness produced new social and legal realities on the ground, which, in turn, reshaped the expectations and outlooks of newly formed organizations.

The expansion of the legal doctrine of standing provided yet another bridge between elite legal movements and the quest for citizen participation in political decision making. The most significant acronym group formed in John Banzhaf's Unfair Trade Practices course was called SCRAP (Students Challenging Regulatory Agency Procedures). Even though a Sierra Club lawsuit that sought to block the development of a California ski resort was rejected by the Supreme Court in *Sierra Club v. Morton* (1972), the Court nevertheless affirmed that a loss of aesthetic rights provided a legitimate cause for action.[86] In *Sierra Club,* the Court found that because the group had not argued that *their use* of the area in question would be affected by the construction of the ski resort, the plaintiffs had not suffered an "injury in fact," required by the Administrative Procedure Act. At the same time, however, the Court expanded its definition of "injury in fact" to include "aesthetic and environmental well-being," which "like, economic well-being, are important ingredients of the quality of life in our society."[87] The door remained open for environmentalists to explicitly claim an aesthetic injury resulting from a regulatory decision.[88]

John Banzhaf's legal strategy consisted of throwing open doors left ajar. SCRAP began in the classroom and ended in the Supreme Court. SCRAP, joined by the Environmental Defense Fund, challenged a freight increase by the Interstate Commerce Commission (ICC) that would have raised the shipping rates for recycled materials. The National Environmental Policy

Act of 1970 (NEPA) provided an opening for the students to assert that the public was inappropriately excluded from the ICC's rate decision. NEPA required that agencies prepare an environmental impact statement, which included opportunity for public review and comment. By discouraging the use of recyclables, the ICC's rate hike would unintentionally increase "destruction of the natural environment from mining, foresting and other activity to obtain virgin materials" and "intensi[fy] the nation's waste disposal problem." The students asserted that they stood to suffer an injury in fact because of the "recreational and aesthetic harm directly as a result of the adverse environmental impact of railroad freight structure." Less recycling meant more garbage, which very well could be discarded in the D.C. neighborhoods in which the students resided, and where they enjoyed "camping, hiking, and fishing." The students also contended that the ICC's freight hike would increase the cost of transporting recycled goods, thereby resulting in more expensive recycled products at retail.

In a 6–2 decision, the Supreme Court held that the agency did not have to file an environmental impact statement; but in a separate 5–3 decision within the same ruling, the Court affirmed the students' right to challenge the ICC despite the "attenuated" nature of their injury. The Court agreed with the law students' assertion that as residents of Washington, D.C., they would be "adversely affected" by the ICC's rate increase. Litter around the "natural resources of the Washington Metropolitan area" caused the students to suffer "economic, recreational and aesthetic harm," Justice Potter Stewart wrote in an echo of the language of *Sierra Club*.[89]

U.S. v. SCRAP was the apogee in the Court's expansion of the standing doctrine, a landmark in the world of public interest law. And in granting standing to citizen-litigants, the judiciary also refashioned itself: open to a wider variety of Americans making a wider variety of claims. It became something closer to Joseph Sax's dream of a democratic branch in which citizen demands could ring out clearly, not muffled by the special interests that had captured the administrative and legislative branches. Even those who opposed the ruling understood its significance. In a law review article authored while he was a judge on the D.C. Circuit, Antonin Scalia would later deride the decision as an indication of the Court's wrongheaded "willingness to discern breathlessly broad Congressional grants of standing."[90] Indeed, just a few years after the *SCRAP* decision was handed down, the Court began to scrap this line of reasoning, tightening its criteria for standing.[91]

Through the mid-1970s, Banzhaf and the nonsmokers' rights movement rode a cresting wave of citizen participation in federal decision making. Their successes built upon those of environmental and consumer legal activists, widespread grassroots demand for political incorporation of social movements, and the federal government's own uneven acknowledgment of a role for everyday people in policy implementation.[92] *SCRAP*'s contribution to environmental law is well known.[93] But it was through fights over indoor smoking that Banzhaf developed the theory of citizen-regulation that gave rise to *SCRAP*. The fight for nonsmokers' rights shared institutional, legal, and intellectual air with the environmental movement, reflecting the law's incorporation of participatory ideals.[94] The same legal ecosystem nurtured the nonsmokers' rights movement and the environmental movement. The same concerns over quality of life issues—health, environmental protection, access to recreation—connected the social and legal identities of nonsmokers.

Defining Rights and Measuring Risk

A surprise declaration by Nixon's surgeon general gave an aura of authority to calls for nonsmokers' rights. In January 1971, just as Clara Gouin and her fellow activists were removing the ashtrays from their homes as first tentative steps toward confrontation, Jesse Steinfeld launched his own broadside against smoking. On the seventh anniversary of the landmark 1964 *Surgeon General's Report,* Steinfeld appeared before the Interagency Council on Smoking and Health, a bloated consortium of public and private health organizations. "It was as effective as the UN," Steinfeld recalled. "Meaning it was ineffective."[95] Most of his speech was focused on the effects of smoking on smokers themselves. But he changed tack at the end of his address, which had not been vetted by his bosses in the Department of Health, Education, and Welfare. Steinfeld made a bold declaration that managed to combine environmentalism and rights talk with a hefty dose of resentment. "Nonsmokers have as much a right to clean air and wholesome air as smokers have to their so-called right to smoke, which I would define as a 'right to pollute.'" Gaining steam before the friendly crowd, Steinfeld continued: "It is high time to ban smoking from all confined public places such as restaurants, theaters, airplanes, trains, and busses." This was a vision that would take more than three decades to fulfill—and one that went well beyond what Banzhaf, GASP, or even Nader called for at the time. "It is high time that we interpret the Bill of Rights for the Nonsmoker as well as the smoker."[96]

The metaphor of the "Nonsmoker's Bill of Rights" was consistent with the rhetorical shrouding of contemporary consumerist movements. Seizing the mantle of consumerism from zealous advocates like Nader, President Nixon proposed a "buyer's bill of rights" in a special message to Congress in 1969.[97] It was an attempt to coopt the consumer protection movement's critique of corporate fraud and deception into the Republican vision of market participation.[98] Meanwhile, the American Medical Association came in for special scorn when it rejected a proposal by its own committee to provide American patients with a "healthcare bill of rights," entitling them to certain expectations in their interactions with the American medical system. Steinfeld's exact language may have been borrowed from a New York state assemblyman who introduced an ill-fated bill limiting smoking on public transportation as a "Nonsmoker's Bill of Rights" in 1970.[99] None of these "bills of rights" went anywhere legislatively. But their simultaneous invocation revealed not just an intense identification of citizenship and consumption, but also a connection between citizenship and *skepticism* of institutions that structured the marketplace for goods and services. Whether for buyers, patients, or nonsmokers, the bill of rights discourse suggested a growing recognition of social and economic hazards that threatened Americans' quality of life expectations.

The rhetoric of rights helped Americans to consider where they belonged in an economy increasingly organized around the provision and consumption of services. Without explicit rights-based guarantees, the individual citizen-consumer was likely to get swamped by the superior organization of industry. As one influential 1974 law essay put it, law abetted and reinforced this skewed political-economic arena, making sure that the "haves" came out ahead. "Repeat players" like corporations and the organized professions helped to design the very rules that structured the legal order.[100] Even in the absence of legislation, calls for a bill of rights for patients, consumers, or nonsmokers created new paths to power by ennobling the struggle for the recognition of rights.

The bill of rights framing also invoked the elegant rhetoric of enlightenment liberalism, particularly the harm principle expounded by John Stuart Mill in *On Liberty*: "the only purpose for which power can be rightfully exercised over any member of a civilized community, against his will, is to prevent harm to others."[101] The tobacco industry portrayed nonsmoking activists as prohibitionists, the inheritors of Carrie Nation's hatchet. But activists represented themselves as coolly rational, demanding only that when smokers and nonsmokers conflict, nonsmokers receive priority in a hierarchy of rights. Nonsmokers insisted that they were not opposed to smoking itself. But, as with sex, they reasoned that it "should be confined to consenting adults in private."[102] Of course, middle-class nonsmoking activists also brought Great Society expectations to their nineteenth-century analysis: they hoped the state would step in to enhance the quality of their lives.[103]

The libertarian impulse—a tendency to frame nonsmokers' rights as paramount because they ensured freedom *from* another person's choice—was present from the earliest days of the movement. Indeed, construing nonsmokers' rights as a negative right helped otherwise left-leaning activists reconcile their support for an expansion of civil liberties—decriminalizing recreational drug use, repeal of vagrancy, obscenity, and sodomy laws—with their demand for the regulation of public smoking. Anthony Roisman, a young public interest lawyer who represented Ralph Nader in his fight against airline smoking, addressed the Interagency Council at a 1970 conference. Neither a scientist nor a member of a public-health organization, Roisman's speech differed from that of other presenters in that it did not dwell on the health risks posed by smoking. Instead, Roisman deconstructed the "unexamined hypothesis" that the "so-called right to smoke was equal if not superior to the right to be free from smoke." Channeling the rhetoric of the nation's founding generation, Roisman continued: "It is safe to state as a general maxim that any activity when it is no benefit to society and which is clearly harmful to the person who participates in it is an activity which can be confined to private places where innocent members of our society will not be forced to suffer from it." Steinfeld was at the conference and would have heard

Roisman's call for a nonsmoker's bill of rights, rooted in the Declaration of Independence, which assumed, in Roisman's words, "the right to be free from tobacco smoke."[104]

For ASH, GASP, and Steinfeld, rights rather than risk were the basis of indoor smoking restrictions. Even in his January 1971 speech before the Interagency Council, Steinfeld cited no new studies testifying to second-hand smoke's harms to the nonsmoker.[105] The 1972 *Surgeon General's Report* took up the question for the first time, with new chapters on allergy, "air pollution from tobacco smoke," and the harmful constituents in cigarette smoke. Even by the *Report*'s own admission, scant epidemiological studies had been undertaken that would have established a causal relationship between exposure to secondhand smoke and disease. For example, no studies had yet been designed to "determine the prevalence of tobacco allergy." This meant that the report could only state definitively that "tobacco smoke can contribute to the discomfort of many individuals," and could exacerbate "allergic symptoms in nonsmokers who are suffering from allergies of diverse causes."[106]

Nor was there yet a robust body of literature on the effects of exposures to the "atmospheric contaminants" of tobacco smoke, which contained high concentrations of known toxins like carbon monoxide, benzopyrene, and oxides of nitrogen. The hazardous effects of even low levels of CO were well established: "altered auditory discrimination, visual acuity and the ability to distinguish relative brightness." Longer exposures—such as those that might be encountered by individuals whose coworkers smoked nearby—reduced motor function and placed "physiological stress on patients with heart disease."[107] But researchers were yet unable to measure typical exposures for nonsmokers. So much depended on variables such as the size, structure, and ventilation patterns of a room; the number, proximity, and smoking style of smokers; and, of course, the underlying physical condition of the nonsmoker. Secondhand smoke might be irritating in a young, healthy person, but could be "particularly significant for people who are already suffering from chronic bronchopulmonary disease and coronary heart disease."[108]

However, federal environmental law also created standards to which nonsmokers' rights activists could appeal. In 1967, a brief article in *Science* titled "A Damaging Source of Air Pollution" pointed out that while "public concern about air pollution has grown rapidly during the past few years," very few people considered the contribution of cigarette smoke to the burden of pollution. The article reported that carbon monoxide and nitrogen dioxide (NO_2)—both toxins present in car exhaust—actually appeared in much greater concentrations in cigarette smoke. People who worked in garages and tunnels were routinely exposed to concentrations of CO at the rate of 100 parts per million (ppm). Exposures of 120 ppm for one hour were known to cause dizziness, headache, and lassitude. "However, in a poorly ventilated, smoke-filled room, concentrations of carbon monoxide can easily reach several hundred parts per million, thus exposing smokers and nonsmokers present to a toxic hazard." Nitrogen dioxide, a brown gas responsible for the signature ruddy look of Los Angeles smog, was considered dangerous at levels of 5 ppm. Without specifying a typical length of exposure or speculating as to the conditions under which such an exposure might occur, the article noted that cigarette smoke contained 250 ppm of NO_2. While not citing specific studies or hypothesizing routes of exposure, the article also listed other hazardous possibilities of cigarette smoke pollution, rattling off "toxic agents in cigarette smoke [that] do not have counterparts in ordinary air pollution." In raising more questions than he answered, the author's motivations were clear: to place the cigarette alongside "the automobile, the smokestack, or the trash burner" in public conversations about pollution—and its regulation.[109]

Framing tobacco smoke as part of the broader problem of pollution, nonsmokers' rights activists made their cause intelligible to Americans who supported environmental regulation. As Surgeon General, Steinfeld promoted this environmental framing. His controversial 1971 address indicted smoking as "the so-called right to pollute." The 1972 *Surgeon General's Report* devoted a chapter to "Public Exposure to Air Pollution from Tobacco Smoke." In reviewing the research on "smoke pollutants," the *Report* concluded that in many instances, the tar and nicotine levels in the secondhand smoker were higher than those inhaled by the smoker. Carbon monoxide, benzopyrene, and oxides of nitrogen had been measured by researchers under experimental conditions and found to cause visual and motor impairments.

In short, the 1972 *Report* provided validation for aggrieved nonsmokers— "not disagreeable malcontents," according to Steinfeld, but individuals with "a legitimate cause for their complaint." And by flagging the gaps in the epidemiological and experimental literature on secondhand smoke, the report established an agenda for future study, ensuring that secondhand smoke would be scrutinized as a risk factor for the development of cancer, cardiac, and pulmonary disease.[110] Steinfeld's report would set a research agenda for the next two decades.

Other research focused on the cigarette's violation of federal air quality standards. These provided a structure for scientific inquiry into the effects of tobacco exposure, as well as a rallying cry for nonsmokers' rights groups. The 1975 opening of Pontiac Stadium furnished an occasion for further scientific inquiry. Home to the Detroit Lions, the 82,000-seat domed structure was the largest NFL venue in the country at the time—a distinction it held for more than twenty years. But sheer square footage did not do enough to alleviate the air quality burden of thousands of smoking fans. At half-time, the CO level in the stadium set off an alarm in researchers' instruments, which registered a reading of 50 ppm, as compared to 5 ppm before and after the game. The U.S. government recommended that Americans not endure CO exposures of more than 35 ppm more than once per year. Nitrogen oxides measured at the stadium also exceeded federal standards.[111] And particulate levels during the game were high enough to "cause an air pollution alert in any major city in the U.S.," in the words of Dr. Wilbert Aronow, a cardiologist summarizing the research at a 1977 public hearing sponsored by the American Cancer Society.[112]

Such studies helped to shade over the fact that scientists did not yet have a definitive body of research on the long-term effects of "passive smoking." The medical director of McGraw-Hill framed this uncertainty in terms of probability: "It is probable that air pollution by smokers is harmful to nonsmokers because of CO, tars, and nicotines, introduced into the air breathed by all." Or as the director of the Illinois Department of Public Health explained: "People with certain heart, lung, and allergic conditions may have their disease symptoms intensified as a result of the exposure to the tobacco smoke of smokers." Even a 1977 report by the National Cancer Institute conceded that "the effects of CO absorbed by nonsmokers are not yet fully known," and that "while nicotine in the environment is of concern, attempts to measure the amount of nicotine absorbed by nonsmokers have not as yet proven it to be a major health hazard."[113] Federal Air Quality

Standards legitimated activists' demands for public smoking regulations even though harms to nonsmokers from typical exposures were far from definitive. It was enough to contend, as did the co-chairman of the organization Californians for Clean Indoor Air, that "tobacco pollution pervades the health of the American public."[114] Unlike emissions from cars or smokestacks, cigarette pollution would fail to elicit *federal* regulation. But that did not mean that smokers' pollution went unabated.

The impulse behind calls for nonsmokers' rights was civic, not scientific. It rested upon nonsmokers' assertion of virtuous citizenship, and was fueled by a resentment of smokers. "Sensible people who happen not to smoke will always be at the mercy of the most selfish, stupid, uncaring, weakest, filthiest slobs in the world: smokers," wrote one irate reader of the *Village Voice,* particularly incensed with a columnist's defense of the habit.[115] Recognition of nonsmokers as a category of people meant reckoning with the ways they had been harmed, irritated, or inconvenienced by smoke—and by smokers themselves. Although Steinfeld spoke with a great deal more sobriety than some of the *Village Voice*'s readership, he too courted confrontation. This was a departure from the practice of previous surgeons general, who tended to be cautious in making pronouncements about tobacco until amassing overwhelming—some might say superfluous—evidence of harm. At the press conference preceding the release of the 1972 *Surgeon General's Report on Smoking and Health,* Steinfeld admitted that "we cannot say with certainty that exposure to tobacco smoke is causing serious illness in nonsmokers"—only that "exposure can contribute to the discomfort of the nonsmoking individual."[116] Widespread discomfort was enough to trigger government action "to give the nonsmoker relief" from forced inhalation of smoke in public spaces. This logic was convincing, at least to the New York City commissioner of marine and aviation, who quickly banned smoking on the Staten Island Ferry, purportedly on the strength of Steinfeld's recommendation.[117]

Steinfeld's own career did not escape the tobacco industry's machinations. A Democrat and the son of Jewish immigrants, Steinfeld was never entirely at home in the Nixon administration. "I certainly wasn't on the same political page as Nixon," he later recalled.[118] And his independent streak did little to endear him to other political appointees within the Department of Health, Education, and Welfare.[119] When Steinfeld broke with precedent and banned tobacco industry lobbyists from his office, HEW secretary Elliott Richardson opened his doors to the industry instead, reminding Steinfeld that the Office of the Surgeon General possessed little clout.[120]

After Nixon won reelection in the landslide of 1972, he asked for the resignation of all HEW appointees. Steinfeld's was accepted. Until his death, Steinfeld insisted that he lost his position due to pressure applied directly by the president of R. J. Reynolds on the president of the United States.[121] In the absence of documentation of such a claim, it would seem equally possible that Steinfeld was simply seen as disloyal and politically out of step with the Nixon administration. The position of surgeon general would go unfilled for four years, until President Carter's appointment of Julius Richmond in 1977. Steinfeld would later lament that he "felt frustrated in seeing how much good I might have achieved, and how much actually was accomplished."[122] But he understated his significance. Having helped to create a new political figure—the nonsmoker—the surgeon general endowed her with rights, legitimating her grievance.

Cigarette Federalism

In 1975, John Banzhaf, Luther Terry, and Clara Gouin flanked Father Robert Drinan as the Massachusetts congressman, antiwar activist, and Jesuit priest announced his introduction of "'The Smoker and Non-Smoker Health Protection Act." The bill would have tightened the requirements for a warning label on imported cigarettes, imposed a tax on cigarettes to fund research into smoking-related disease, and restricted smoking in federal facilities in a vindication of the "rights of non-smokers." In response, the Tobacco Institute circulated a "factsheet" to members of Congress. Calling the bill a "thinly veiled subterfuge for the mandated prohibition of smoking and the forced segregation of smokers," the text argued that "it could take the nation a giant step backward to the days of Carrie Nation and Jim Crow."[123] The Institute need not have wasted the paper: Drinan's multiple efforts to pass nonsmoker protection legislation all failed in committee.

Yet by the mid-1970s, the nonsmokers' rights movement began to score legislative victories—the kind of victories that suggested that activists had drawn closer to their goal of undermining the social acceptability of smoking, and the kind of victories that would be harder for the tobacco industry to undo by pressuring Washington. Indeed, industry continued to flex its muscles, helping to orchestrate the ouster of President Carter's Health, Education, and Welfare secretary, Joseph Califano. But tobacco's clout had become something of a double-edged sword: it vindicated activists' assertions that only a grassroots drive could snuff out industry influence, and it made the industry less prepared to combat local regulation.

In 1973, after two years of dogged and contentious lobbying, Betty Carnes succeeded in her goal of persuading the Arizona state legislature to implement the nation's first statewide law restricting smoking in some public places. Like Gouin, Carnes was moved to anti-tobacco activism from the depths of personal anguish. Carnes became involved with ASH— eventually becoming the organization's fundraising chairwoman—after a close friend died of lung cancer, leaving two young children bereft of a mother.[124] ASH helped Carnes in the design of the Arizona statute, but Carnes herself did the politicking, studying the smoking history of the legislators she was trying to persuade. She was also aided by a prop of her own design: "Thank You for Not Smoking" signs, which she sent to lawmakers, and to Surgeon General Steinfeld, who displayed one proudly on his desk, until he was asked to clear out his things.[125]

Described by the Tobacco Institute as an "ornithologist of substantial means," Carnes had long been active in conservation circles—highlighting the overlapping concerns of the environmental and anti-smoking movement, particularly in Arizona, long a destination for those suffering from respiratory disease.[126] The Arizona law was modest: it banned smoking in elevators, theaters, libraries, and buses, and established smoking sections in government buildings and health-care facilities. It appropriated no money for compliance or policing. But even so, the Tobacco Institute understood that it had been caught flat-footed, and it announced that California, Massachusetts, Illinois, Arizona, Connecticut, Michigan, Texas, Florida, and New York would be deemed "priority states" for more intensive legislative monitoring. But as field officers in these populous states monitored the dockets in the capital cities, South Dakota and Nebraska passed statewide restrictions nearly identical to Arizona's. The Institute's vaunted defenses, which relied on a concentration of political and media power, were ill-equipped to play the state-by-state game of legislative whack-a-mole, though they did thwart the passage of statewide laws in Illinois and Maine.

Evading the industry's field officers, Minnesota became the first state to pass a comprehensive "Clean Indoor Air Act" in 1975. The Minnesota law went further to make nonsmoking the social default by prohibiting smoking in all confined public places unless specifically designated as a "smoking section." Perhaps the most important part of the Minnesota law was that it required nonsmoking sections in restaurants, the popularity of which muted the force of the industry's argument that such a restriction would lead to a decline in eating out. The industry lamented that in Minnesota "a majority of restauranteurs surveyed found compliance with the law 'easier than expected.'" It was an especially disappointing result for the industry as the survey's population, members of the Minnesota Restaurant and Food Service Association, "might reasonably be considered to be our allies in this issue."[127]

The primary force behind the bill was Phyllis Kahn. Kahn was a Yale-trained doctor of biophysics and state representative of the Minnesota Farmer-Labor Party, a legacy of the state's tradition of populist progressivism. Kahn presented the bill as a "non-controversial" extension of the "desire to protect our environment from industrial pollution." After all, "we're only seeking to establish the right to breathe clean air as a fundamental right." Supporting the state's nonsmokers was Jesse Steinfeld, whose ouster from federal office left him freer to advocate for state laws. "Future citizens will regard ours as a primitive, unhealthy, unintelligent era inexplicable except for the greed of those who manufacture cigarettes and to the governments which derive revenue from taxation thereof," Steinfeld predicted as he testified before the state House of Representatives at Kahn's invitation. "I couldn't say that when I was Surgeon General. But I wanted to."[128]

Upon questioning, Steinfeld admitted that scientists had not proven "harm to everyone" resulting from sharing a room with a smoker. But he pointed to the 1958 Delaney Amendment to the Food, Drugs, and Cosmetics Act, which stated that if a substance was found to cause cancer then it could not be used as a food additive, to reason that a precautionary approach to secondhand smoke was warranted as well. The state of Minnesota embraced Steinfeld's logic, even describing the law as a "bill of rights for the three out of four Minnesotans who do not smoke."[129]

Although the federal government had yet to regulate on behalf of the nonsmoker, it encouraged states and cities to act on their own. A 1977 report produced by the National Cancer Institute, housed within the Califano-led Department of Health, Education, and Welfare, lauded the passage of state anti-smoking legislation as crucial to the protection of the "rights and health of nonsmokers." It reproduced the Minnesota statute in its entirety, and included suggestions for drafting effective nonsmokers' rights legislation: define all terms, require plainly visible signs announcing smoking restrictions, clearly delegate authority for publicity and enforcement, and announce penalties for violators.[130] What is more, the report noted that local ordinances were easier to pass than efforts at the state or national level, and allowed municipalities to put more teeth into enforcement of state indoor air laws.[131]

In California, the most populous state in the nation and home to a large and well-organized nonsmokers' rights movement, activists learned firsthand the possibilities and limits of federalism. Inspired by the Minnesota example, a well-educated coterie of GASP activists in the Bay Area pursued a state law. Two members of the Berkeley GASP chapter—lawyers both—sought to take advantage of the state's referendum process to appeal directly to Californians in support of a clean indoor air law. After collecting enough signatures for the referendum to appear on the 1978 ballot, activists found themselves wildly outspent by the tobacco industry, which poured in more than $6 million to defeat the initiative. Part of the industry's strategy was the disingenuous allegation that a nonsmoking law would cost tens of millions of taxpayer dollars to implement—a deliberate attempt by the manufacturers to ride the cresting wave of taxpayer discontent that had led to the passage of Proposition 13 the previous summer. In the end, the clean air referendum went down in defeat with 54 percent of voters opposing the proposal. Two years later, a similar referendum met the same fate, with the same margin again voting "no." Chastened by their losses, California activists deliberately changed tactics, devoting their energies entirely to local ordinances.[132]

The Tobacco Institute took note of the flurry of smoking restrictions passed by cities. Only four states passed any clean indoor air laws in 1976; but 59 cities passed ordinances restricting smoking that same year—up from fifty-four in 1975, but fewer than the sixty-four that did so in the banner year of 1974.[133] At a 1974 Tobacco Institute meeting, Tobacco Institute president Harold Kornegay noted that the "relative calm of Washington" concealed "the stormy weather out in the states," where "a nation is shaken by the frenzy of protest."[134] And there was no bigger symbol of protest than Berkeley, which passed an ordinance banning smoking in elevators, many municipal facilities, public transportation, and public areas of private businesses, excluding restaurants and bars.

Berkeley had been the second city in the United States to establish a GASP chapter when a woman on the board of directors at a Bay Area Tuberculosis and Respiratory Disease Association took notice of Gouin's College Park chapter. By banning—and not just restricting—smoking in a wide range of facilities, the City of Berkeley passed a stringent law commensurate with its reputation as the vanguard of social protest. However, in keeping with the city's fractious spirit, not all residents fell in line. One bookstore owner on Telegraph Avenue, the heart of the city's bohemian street culture, defied the ordinance by refusing to snuff out his cigar in his shop. Describing the law as "an example of local government being influenced by a concealed puritanism," the proprietor's objections were met with nonchalance by city officials. "He's just begging to get arrested so there can be a constitutional test of the law."[135]

No arrest was made in Berkeley; the few people arrested for violating antismoking rules tended to be black or brown. Local ordinances were passed in the name of civil rights for nonsmokers and because of grassroots pressure for their implementation. Yet enforcement of nonsmokers' rights laws ran headlong into the racial and economic disparities of both policing and the use of public space. In Chicago, for example, a "smoker's court" was established to hear cases involving violations of the city's anti-smoking ordinance, which prohibited smoking on the subway, elevated train, and buses. One reporter who spent two days observing the court's operation noted that of the fifty cases before the judge, two involved white defendants and two involved Latino boys with limited English skills. The rest of the defendants— most of whom pled guilty—were African Americans, mostly young men. While very few anti-smoking ordinances carried jail time as a penalty for violation (and fewer still were actually enforced with arrest), poor violators of the law in Chicago sometimes served jail time when they could not make $25 bail.[136] Nonsmokers' rights laws testified to the power of localism, and the classed and racist nature of local policing.

————————

By the mid-1970s, the nonsmokers' rights movement had racked up a string of remarkable successes, subverting the tobacco industry's stranglehold in Congress. Activists had cleared the air on planes, trains, subways, and buses. They passed legislation across the country that prohibited or restricted smoking in a variety of public places—from elevators to concert halls to municipal buildings to restaurants. By becoming visible and vocal, they opened up space for private businesses to capitalize on their own smoking restrictions, providing that it paid to listen to nonsmokers. These victories were possible because of the invention of the nonsmoker as a political subject endowed with rights and entitled to legal protections. The nonsmokers' rights movement was carried aloft by broader legal, political, and cultural currents such as the environmental, women's, and public interest movements. Wrapping nonsmokers' rights in the rhetoric of the African-American civil rights movement, the ultimate American quest for justice and liberation, activists valorized the use of rights talk, and concealed the class-based nature of their claims. Though deeply felt, nonsmokers' attempts to reason from race were ultimately shallow. Neither the elite, technocratic legal movement as practiced by ASH nor the grassroots efforts of GASP reckoned with the ways in which the rhetoric, tactics, and even goals of their movement reflected white, middle-class prerogatives.

The string of nonsmokers' rights ordinances passed in the late 1970s demonstrated the power of a vision of public space as an amenity to be consumed. Many nonsmokers' rights activists experienced environmental tobacco smoke—ubiquitous at restaurants, theaters, college classrooms, public transportation, and even hospitals—as a physical assault that prevented them from partaking in daily life. At the same time, the argument that smoking was a public problem because it violated "nonsmokers' rights" had consequences for how tobacco, smoking, and smokers came to be understood and regulated.

6

From Rights to Cost

Annual Costs of Tobacco
  1. 360,000 deaths
  2. 77,000,000 man-days lost from work
  3. 88,000,000 man-days sick in bed
  4. 360,000,000 man-days of restricted activity
  5. Mean 45 to 64 years: 28% of disability days due to cigarette smoking
—Dr. Alton Ochsner, *Smoking: Your Choice between Life and Death*, 1970

Smoking appears to occur at times and in places that fit social and task patterns of the work environment, but increasing evidence suggests that this fit may be at company expense.
—*Public Health Reports*, 1985

ON OCTOBER 15, 1985, Pacific Northwest Bell (PNB) became the largest employer in the country to adopt a comprehensive no-smoking policy at all of its facilities in Oregon, Washington, and northern Idaho.[1] This meant that 15,000 employees at hundreds of facilities would have to exit company premises to have a smoke. PNB was on the leading edge of a nationwide trend. President Reagan's surgeon general, C. Everett Koop, expressed hope that it could be a model for other businesses in the United States—an industrial stepping-stone toward Koop's dream of a "smokefree society by the year 2000."[2]

By 1990, PNB's ban, once an outlier, had indeed become part of the corporate mainstream—not standard, but also not remarkable. That year, 38 percent of companies surveyed nationwide reported a total smoking ban, while 68 percent reported some official policy, compared with only 15 percent of businesses reporting any policies in surveys ten years earlier.[3] These policies were by and large voluntary, as most businesses were left untouched by local ordinances.[4] And even in places where a law was in place, businesses sometimes went further than the law required, a trend that built upon itself. As a 1989 management survey observed, "once restrictions are established, they tend to grow into a complete ban."[5] Workplace smoking restrictions became part of a positive feedback loop that expanded non-smoking as the social default. The more shared space was governed by regulation, the more nonsmokers came to expect that their preferences would predominate, and the easier it became for them to complain when these did not. Over the decade of the 1980s, nonsmokers would become fully visible, unpinning the buttons that had served as humorous substitutes for verbal confrontation with smokers.

Although nonsmoking policies were adopted with increasing speed throughout the 1980s, the route to smoke-free air was hardly direct. The ban at PNB began a decade earlier on the other side of the country, when another Bell employee sued the company for permitting smoking in her work area. In the case of *Shimp v. New Jersey Bell* (1976), a New Jersey Superior Court judge found that New Jersey Bell had violated its common-law duty to provide a "safe and healthy work environment" for Donna Shimp. Still, the court did not require that New Jersey Bell promulgate a company smoking policy, nor did this narrowly construed case set a precedent. Over the decade, other courts repeatedly failed to find that workplace smoking violated an employee's common-law right to a safe work environment. The legal fight for nonsmokers' rights began to look like a dead end. But another avenue emerged.

What began as a fight for rights of nonsmokers ended as an actuarial exercise in accounting for the costs of smokers. Nonsmoking activists pushed smoke-free workplaces onto the corporate agenda with all the persuasive resources at their disposal: legal, scientific, moral, and economic. Though certainly less morally resonant than civil rights- or gender-based struggles for equality, nonsmoker activism was part and parcel of the legal and bureaucratic transformation of the workplace in the last decades of the twentieth century.[6] Corporations in the 1970s and 1980s became more bureaucratized in response to federal antidiscrimination laws—laws that themselves expanded to cover a wider swath of the American population.[7] But uncertainty surrounding equal employment law, a byproduct of the decentralized nature of the American state, endowed human resources professionals with special power in firms that feared litigation or bad publicity.[8]

The proliferation of workplace smoking rules beginning in the late 1970s and accelerating during the 1980s also resulted, in part, from the uncertainties created by the law's uneven recognition of a right to smoke-free air. Many forces converged to restrict smoking at work in the 1980s: nonsmoker activism, mounting scientific studies of the hazards of environmental tobacco smoke, inconsistent legal rulings that spurred companies to consider workplace smoking a liability, and the growing salience of the business case against smoking. These currents reinforced each other. Scientific studies attesting to the hazards of secondhand smoke were fodder for activists' demands and nudges for businesses considering implementing their own smoking restrictions. Nonsmoking activists portrayed workplace-smoking restrictions as part of a sound business policy, affording corporations both liability protection amid legal uncertainty and benefits to the bottom line.

The nonsmokers' movement was aided by changes in the broader culture that gave the business case a special resonance. As Daniel Rodgers has observed, the 1970s saw the rise of an "abstract and idealized" idea of the market as "the dominant social metaphor of the age."[9] Economists began to assign discrete costs to individual behaviors, practices, and goods that had once been hard to sever from their original social and institutional contexts. Like air pollution or a neighbor's noisy fight that wakes the neighborhood, smoking was understood to carry a "social cost"—one activists learned to quantify.[10] Today we might call these costs "negative externalities," the idea that the individual deciding to smoke does not bear the full cost of his or her decision. This was especially true in the case of smoking, as emerging science surrounding the health dangers of secondhand smoke expanded the delta between the private and social cost of smoking. The nonsmokers' movement tallied these social costs and brought them to bear at the workplace—a site particularly open to bottom-line reasoning. With every "no-smoking" sign erected and smoking shelter installed in office-park parking lots, tobacco moved further and further from mainstream American life. Where tobacco's ubiquity was once assured by a permissive federal regulatory regime, it was increasingly snuffed out by local and private action.

Donna Shimp v. New Jersey Bell

In February 1976, Donna Shimp addressed a thank-you note to Luther Terry, the former surgeon general of the United States. Shimp was a white, forty-four-year-old customer service representative at the Millville offices of New Jersey Bell Telephone. She suffered from an "acute sensitivity" to tobacco smoke and was suing her longtime employer for failing to provide a safe work environment by not banning smoking in her presence. Terry had agreed to serve as an expert on Shimp's behalf. A New Jersey Superior Court judge, Phillip Gruccio, would begin hearing Shimp's case in the spring. Shimp informed Terry that her case would especially need his expert opinion that "the presence of tobacco smoke in the work place can be a health hazard to a significant number of workers as well as a source of minor irritation to an even greater number of workers."[11] Terry's statement, Shimp hoped, would carry great weight in what was the first lawsuit brought by an employee against an employer's smoking policies.

Smoking on the job was but one of many customs challenged by activists during the decade. Ideas about acceptable workplace behavior changed as civil rights law and the Equal Employment Opportunity Commission (EEOC) opened new avenues for women and minorities to demand changes to employment practices. AT&T, the parent company of the Bell network, was the nation's largest private employer and the largest employer of American women. It was no stranger to civil rights complaints lodged by employees. The company accounted for 6–7 percent of all of the EEOC's discrimination complaints.[12] Indeed, Shimp's grievance looked positively puny compared to the landmark discrimination suit brought by the EEOC on behalf of 15,000 women and minority Bell employees in 1970.

Donna Shimp had not been an activist in GASP. She was unaware of John Banzhaf's plans to "sue the bastards." She was, instead, pushed to confrontation by her body's reaction to the smoke in her office—and her employer's and union's reaction to her. In 1961, at age twenty-nine, Donna Shimp began her career at the New Jersey Bell Telephone Company at an office in Salem. The office was not far from her home in the rural southwestern portion of New Jersey, on the Delaware River. In 1975, the company's Salem office closed, and Shimp was transferred sixteen miles southeast to the company's new Bridgeton facility—a low-slung, solid-looking brick building with few windows. Shimp's coworkers at Bridgeton smoked heavily, and the smoky air made Shimp nauseous, caused rashes on her face, and resulted in several episodes of intense eye irritation, redness, tearing, and swelling. Because of her sensitivity to smoke, Shimp had a long-standing prescription for anti-emetic drugs, which she took daily to ward off the nausea that overtook her around tobacco. Shortly after arriving at Bridgeton, she began wearing a gas mask to work—the "Gasfoe" model manufactured by the Mine Safety Appliance Company of Pittsburgh, Pennsylvania.[13] She would lower but not remove it when she spoke with customers on the phone or in person. She later marveled that the company allowed her to wear a gas mask in front of these customers at all.

In the Bridgeton office, seven of the thirteen employees smoked on the job, and there was no prohibition on customer smoking in the offices. Relative to other Bell offices, Bridgeton was particularly smoky, as documents from the *Shimp* trial later revealed that only an estimated 30 percent of all company employees smoked. Office managers did not attempt to segregate smokers and nonsmokers spatially, since they thought it would interfere with Shimp's job as a service representative. The only way to make her working environment better, Shimp thought, would be to find a doctor able to certify the necessity of smoke abatement in *the office*—rather than one who would prescribe an individualized palliative. The office needed the prescription, not the individual. Shimp found somatic and psychic validation from an allergist who recommended that the office open its air-circulating vents. This seemingly basic remedy had not been attempted by Bell because it made the office drafty. The company honored the doctor's request for exactly one afternoon, but the experiment in industrial hygiene was aborted after coworkers complained about the cold. As if to put an exclamation point on the smokers' reconquest of space, Bridgeton's union steward closed the open window by Shimp's desk that same afternoon (see Figure 6.1).

In April of 1975, Shimp was finally examined by the company doctor, who told her that "it was a disgrace for any employee to have to work in such an atmosphere."[14] He ordered that she go home on paid leave until her supervisors could find a way to accommodate her need for a smoke-free work environment. Shimp believed that she would be at home for just a few days. But days turned into months. During this extended leave—the duration of

Figure 6.1 Donna Shimp in front of her New Jersey Bell office. (Shimp Papers and Environmental Improvement Associates Records, University of California, San Francisco Special Collections)

which must have signaled the depths of her employer's unwillingness to implement a nonsmoking policy—Shimp became an activist. She immersed herself in anti-tobacco research and politics. She established contact with ASH, which provided her with pro bono advice; she got in touch with the recently formed New Jersey GASP, a thread in a national web of locally focused anti-smoking advocacy.[15] And she began learning more about the state of the field of tobacco research.

In 1971, Jesse Steinfeld, Nixon's surgeon general, had made headlines by announcing that it was "time . . . [to] interpret the Bill of Rights for the nonsmoker as well as the smoker."[16] The following year's *Report on Smoking and Health* gave substance to this proclamation, becoming the first of the *Surgeon General's Reports* to examine the issue of passive smoking. Citing recent studies of people and animals exposed to tobacco smoke, the *Report* concluded that smoking affected nonsmokers in three major ways. The mechanism of exposure was the emission of dangerous compounds in "sidestream smoke"—smoke from the burning end of the cigarette. Sidestream smoke, it argued, contributed to nonsmokers' acute discomfort, producing a range of symptoms including migraine, respiratory illness, skin irritation, and gastrointestinal distress.[17]

By elaborating on the serious ways in which a term as fuzzy as "discomfort" presented itself clinically, the *Report* helped to legitimize the physical (rather than emotional) plight experienced by nonsmokers. For women, this sense of scientific validation may have been particularly important. Women's physical pain was still easy to dismiss as unreal—merely a result of feminine sensitivity, or a somaticizing of schoolmarmish moral judgments. The gendering of nonsmoking had a basis in empirical fact. In 1975, 39 percent of American men and 29 percent of American women smoked. There was also a class dimension to the practice. In government surveys, more than 50 percent of blue-collar men and 39 percent of blue-collar women smoked.[18] On the job, the Marlboro Man was more apt to look like a male worker, senior to and better paid than his female colleagues, resentful of the physical sensitivities of coworkers. Describing nonsmokers' rights activists as "modern day Carrie Nations," tobacco forces subtly tied femaleness to the worst of all social regulatory excesses: Prohibition.[19] After Nixon fired him, Steinfeld joined Luther Terry as a spokesman for the anti-tobacco movement. Their personal interventions were decisive in the absence of bureaucratic structures for making rules about workplace smoking—as Shimp would soon discover.

At home in Salem, Shimp wrote to the New Jersey Department of Health, the New Jersey Department of Labor, county health departments, the Public Health Service, the Environmental Protection Agency (EPA), the Action on Smoking and Health, and the health voluntaries. From each, she requested more information and assistance on how to bolster the case against workplace smoking. The responses she received suggested that she was in uncharted legal territory. ASH and the voluntaries contacted Bell on her behalf, offering advice to the company on how to implement a nonsmoking policy in the workplace. The Departments of Health and Labor told her that there were no laws covering tobacco smoke in work environments, unless it was a question of fire safety. The Clean Air Act and the Occupational Safety and Health Act sought to limit air pollution and assure "safe and healthful work conditions" for workers. But neither the EPA nor the Occupational

Safety and Health Administration (OSHA) had promulgated rules governing indoor smoking.[20]

In June 1975, more than five hundred physicians, government officials, economists, activists, and public health officials from more than fifty countries descended upon New York City's Waldorf Astoria hotel for the Third World Conference on Smoking and Health. Sponsored by the American Cancer Society and the National Cancer Institute, the Conference presented an opportunity for tobacco activists to learn and share technical medical research, educational initiatives, policy, and social action that could reduce the social and economic cost of tobacco. As an event, the Conference was a living encyclopedia of those engaged in anti-tobacco science and activism. For the first time, the Conference had a panel devoted to "non-smokers' rights" in addition to other panels on general research reviews, smoking and pregnancy, smoking and cardiovascular disease, anti-smoking education for children and adults, and cessation methods. A representative from nearly every agency Shimp had ever contacted attended the conference, and she pored over its voluminous proceedings.

Within a week, she had prepared a recommendation for the implementation of a nonsmoking policy at New Jersey Bell, which she delivered to AT&T chief executive John deButts and the Board of Directors. Her plan would "have smoking in the work areas of the business offices banned in the same manner that it is in the central offices, switchboards, and . . . public offices." She cited "data on passive inhalation" presented at the "Third World Council on Smoking and Health" [sic] to support the contention that "passive inhalation of smoke . . . is injurious to the health of everyone." Shimp also leaned hard upon the 1972 *Surgeon General's Report* in claiming nonsmokers' rights, while noting that OSHA did not have legislative authority to regulate smoke as an occupational safety hazard. The claim for "rights" mirrored the use of the term by past surgeons general, but also reflected the salience of rights as a discourse of empowerment. This term allowed nonsmokers—who were not, of course, a protected category under the Civil Rights Act of 1964—to borrow the moral authority of the civil rights and feminist struggle.[21]

No laws or regulations forced Bell to acknowledge the rights of nonsmokers, and so advocates like Shimp presented creative arguments to change corporate policy. Alongside the claim for rights, much of the analysis in Shimp's short proposal focused on the "cost-factors" of workplace smoking. A no-smoking policy would not cost money, and would save the company even more. The Lung Association had offered to provide cessation clinics and anti-smoking programming for free. And smoking employees were costly employees. Citing the Public Health Service, Shimp pointed out that smokers spent a third more time away "from their jobs because of illness than do persons who have never smoked cigarettes," and that smoking women spent 17 percent more days in bed than nonsmokers. If Bell would not act on behalf of nonsmokers, it could act on behalf of its bottom line—wringing greater productivity out of its smoking employees by encouraging them to quit.[22] Shimp's appeal blended the discourse of rights with a business case against smoking employees.[23]

The company's Legal Department responded to Shimp's proposal with the blunt and factual statement that "there is not now any specific law or regulation which could compel the Company to prohibit smoking in its Commercial business offices." Bell's general counsel cited fear of unrest that might follow a unilateral smoke policy change without prior bargaining with the Communications Workers of America (CWA). For Bell to single-handedly impose a smoking policy in the absence of a judicial mandate would violate the collective-bargaining agreement between the company and its largest union. Bell was unwilling to take such a risk. By inviting the court to require a smoke-free accommodation for Shimp, Bell exacerbated conflict between Shimp and her union, which jealously guarded the collective-bargaining agreement from court interference.[24]

In her proposal, Shimp insisted that "employees deserve the same protection afforded the machinery so vital to our communications network, as the human body cannot be duplicated." Bell, it seems, took at least this part of Shimp's proposal seriously. In early July Shimp's supervisor offered her a smoke-free job: a demotion to the nonsmoking position of switchboard operator. Had not Shimp herself pointed out that these employees, by virtue of their proximity to valuable equipment, enjoyed a smoke-free work environment? Fortunately for Shimp, another solution presented itself.

In late July of 1975, Donna Shimp was reassigned to a new office in Millville, New Jersey, forty-five minutes southeast of her home. She was optimistic about the transfer: only one employee in the office smoked, and her doctor's request to keep her as far as possible from the smoking employee was honored for a few months. After October, the manager at Millville stopped adhering to the medical request, and an air-circulating machine that Shimp had been using was turned off because coworkers complained of the chilly air as the temperatures fell. When Shimp turned the fan back on, she was threatened with suspension. In her fall performance review, her ratings had fallen. She suspected that the company and the union were conspiring to fire her.

It is not surprising that Shimp sued Bell Telephone. Multiple forces pointed toward the courtroom as the only place where her grievance could be resolved. Allies within the nonsmokers' rights movement viewed legal action as an important tool to change the regulation of space. ASH was quick to offer assistance in a legal battle. Regulatory agencies had told Shimp that workplace smoking fell outside of their purview; her company told her that it would reconsider its smoking policy only upon court order; the CWA made it clear that the union viewed workplace smoking as a right, and not a threat to workers.

These forces all pointed toward legal action, but contingency played an important part in the outcome of the *Shimp* case. As she was searching for more scientific information on smoking, a desperate phone call to a reference librarian at Rutgers connected Shimp with Alfred Blumrosen, a professor of employment and labor law. Blumrosen had returned to teaching at Rutgers after spending much of the 1960s in public service in the Johnson administration. Active in the creation of the EEOC and later counsel to the agency, Blumrosen was a consistent advocate of the federal government's power to intervene in workplaces to affirmatively address racial discrimination in employment.[25] Shimp had a real-world need for the legal theory developed in his employment law classes, and, luckily for her, Blumrosen prepared Shimp's case pro bono.

Nothing about the procedure of the Shimp case was routine. On the strength of Shimp's medical affidavits, the New Jersey Superior Court issued an injunction against smoking in the work area at the Millville office in the spring of 1976. When a return court date was set, Bell filed no response to Shimp's charges, suggesting that the company indeed wanted a court to force its hand to act. In lieu of oral testimony, attorneys submitted only written affidavits. There would be no courtroom showdown. But based on the judge's earlier injunction, it seemed likely that the expert testimony provided by Shimp would carry great weight.

Indeed, when Judge Philip Gruccio handed down his final opinion in December 1976, he cited not only the 1964 and 1972 *Surgeon General's Reports,* but also the affidavits of the surgeons general who issued them: Drs. Luther Terry and Jesse Steinfeld. "The evidence is clear and overwhelming," Gruccio wrote, drawing on Terry's opinion that "passive smoking in the workplace can be injurious to the health of a significant percentage of the population." But Gruccio was also moved by Bell's existing policies to prevent damage to machinery—the same observation that had occasioned the offer of demotion to the position of switchboard operator. "The company already has in effect a rule that cigarettes may not be smoked around the telephone equipment," Gruccio wrote. "A company which has demonstrated such concern for mechanical components should have at least as much concern for human beings."[26] New Jersey Bell had a common-law duty to provide its employees a safe and healthy work environment, which, for Donna Shimp, meant an environment free of tobacco smoke. And so by court order, Bell was required to banish smoking to the lunchroom in whichever offices Shimp worked. The order applied only to Donna Shimp; it did not change overall company policy. Bell did not appeal the decision.

Legal Ambiguities

Shimp was heralded as a victory for nonsmokers everywhere, but subsequent attempts to find a legal right to smoke-free air met with less success.[27] As Donna Shimp waited for an injunction in New Jersey, a group of nonsmokers in Louisiana brought a class-action suit against the state agency that oversaw the Superdome stadium. The plaintiffs alleged that the haze resulting from the unrestricted smoking at Superdome events violated their "right of self-preservation; to be let alone; to be free from injury; and to be free from exposure to and the involuntary inhalation and consumption of hazardous smoke, gases, fumes and particulates." These rights, they contended, were protected by the fifth, ninth, and fourteenth amendments—the constitutional amendments from which environmental lawyers tried, and failed, to extract a right to a clean environment.[28] In *Gasper v. Louisiana Stadium and Exposition District,* the Fifth Circuit Court of Appeals found no constitutional basis for "injecting the courts and their injunctive powers into this tobacco-smoke controversy."[29]

The following year, a group of employees at the Social Security Administration's sprawling Baltimore campus also tested the theory of a constitutional right to smoke-free air. That is to say, they sued the federal government. A group of employees that called themselves FENSR (Federal Employees for Non-Smokers' Rights) solicited the assistance of ASH, which submitted an amicus brief on the employees' behalf.[30] Citing the Superdome decision, the judge for the U.S. District Court for the District of Columbia found that the plaintiffs' claims, "though worthy of consideration in another forum, should not be elevated to a constitutional level."[31] Mindful of its reputation as the legal arm of the nonsmokers' movement, ASH distanced itself from the constitutional strategy employed by the government workers. ASH noted in its newsletter that its amicus brief had been filed in order to preserve the principle that OSHA may provide a basis for lawsuits brought under different circumstances.[32] The quest for a constitutional right to smoke-free air seemed to be at a dead end.[33]

Even *Shimp*'s value as a direct precedent for establishing a common-law rather than a constitutional right appeared to be limited. In 1980, Paul Smith, a technician at a Western Electric office outside of St. Louis, sued his employer for failing to provide a safe working environment. Paul Smith and Donna Shimp were connected by more than the telecommunications supply chain. They faced many of the same challenges at their worksites, fighting against the indifference of management and the resentment of their coworkers. In 1975, Smith began complaining that his smoke-filled worksite caused physical problems: nausea, lightheadedness, sore throat, and difficulty concentrating. Despite lateral moves within the company, Smith continued to find other office environments equally smoky. After being told to refrain from any further submissions to the company's anonymous complaint system, Smith was presented with two options for keeping his job: wear a respirator helmet, or apply for a job in the smoke-free computer room and take a pay cut of $500 per month. Smith chose to wear the respirator, which he described as "torture," and which made talking on the phone difficult.[34] The respirator helmet made a sound like a vacuum cleaner; in the era of the first *Star Wars* release, this garnered Smith the nickname of "Darth Vader" around the office.[35]

Smith finally retained counsel and sued. Using *Shimp* as precedent, Smith argued that Missouri common law required an employer to provide its employees with a safe and healthful work environment. But his case differed from Shimp's in one crucial regard: lawyers for the tobacco industry and for Western Electric worked together to mount an aggressive opposition.[36] The industry did not want *Shimp* to become a precedent. After his case was tossed out at the trial level, Smith received assistance from ASH in preparing his appeal. In 1982, an appellate court found that Smith did have a basis upon which to bring suit. As in the *Shimp* case, Smith's lawyers amassed a dazzling array of expert scientific opinion submitted as affidavits upon appeal. The Tobacco Institute took particular note of the testimony of James Repace, an air quality researcher with the EPA and a founding member of Clara Gouin's first GASP chapter.[37] A lawyer at Covington & Burling mused to the counsel at the Tobacco Institute that Smith appeared to be in contact with the "the ubiquitous Donna Shimp."[38]

Things took a dire turn for Paul Smith when the case was reasserted at the trial level. While the judge in the *Shimp* decision was quite willing to accept the one-sided testimony of Shimp's doctors and the affidavits from public health experts, the St. Louis County trial court judge was less credulous of the scientific evidence. The tobacco industry's strategy of calling into question the credibility of the plaintiff's expert witnesses paid off. Finding no "organic basis" for tobacco sensitivity, the judge rendered his own diagnosis: Smith suffered from "hypochondriasis"—a diagnosis substantiated by the fact that other nonsmokers in the office did not "suffer physical irritation and discomfort as a result of the conditions under which they work."[39] The comparison to Smith's less sensitive (or at least less vocal) coworkers suggested that the judge felt more comfortable dismissing the physical reaction of an otherwise healthy man as malingering. By 1985, Paul Smith's decade-long odyssey had ended in humiliation and penury.

But even as a common-law right to a smoke-free workplace proved elusive, suits brought by employees changed the calculus for business. Irene Parodi, an employee at the Defense Logistics Agency, a procurement agency housed within the Department of Defense, claimed that the presence of tobacco smoke at work had caused her *to become* disabled. In 1977, Parodi began work at a site in which she shared a room with sixty to seventy other employees, many of whom smoked. She soon began missing work because of pulmonary symptoms and was diagnosed with "asthmatic bronchitis with hyper-irritable airway" due to her exposure to cigarette smoke. Her doctor recommended that she take a leave from work, and at home her symptoms subsided. In fact, she was only disabled on the job. On doctor's recommendations, she took a leave of absence from her job and applied for disability benefits. However, the Merit Systems Protection Board, the government agency responsible for adjudicating complaints brought by federal employees, denied her application, finding that she was not disabled in the traditional sense of the term.

Parodi appealed the Board's decision and the Ninth Circuit ruled that Parodi was, in fact, entitled to $20,000 of disability pay. This ruling represented an expansion of the concept of disability beyond the claim of a physical or mental limitation that prevented an employee from performing her job. Parodi, the court ruled, "has an environmental limitation." She could "physically perform the assigned work in a proper environment" but could not "perform her job due to its location in a smoke-filled office."[40] The court concluded that Irene Parodi would be able to provide "useful and efficient service" in a different environment. Therefore, the burden lay on the shoulders of the employer to determine if an appropriate substitute position was available. If it was not, or if the employer did not cure the employee by way of transfer, then a sensitive nonsmoking employee like Irene Parodi was eligible for disability benefits. A San Francisco appeals court upheld a grant of $60,000 in back pay for Parodi.[41] Few plaintiffs were, perhaps, as creative as Parodi. But others successfully brought disability, unemployment, and workers' compensation claims.[42] "Employers are paying the price for inaction," an American Lung Association pamphlet warned.[43] Though her personal legal challenge had borne limited fruit, Donna Shimp would be instrumental in raising the cost to business of inaction, and in assisting businesses in their response.

Consulting for Clean Air

Where *Shimp* failed as precedent, Donna Shimp was determined to succeed by persuasion. Shimp began considering alternative employment options during her trial. After all, neither the company nor the union seemed particularly committed to her continuing tenure at Bell. Shimp realized that her expertise lay in the very thing that imperiled her job: suing her employer. In fighting New Jersey Bell, she had gained knowledge of employment law, developed contacts and relationships with some of the leading figures in public health, and even became a bit of a celebrity within that world as well. Through *Shimp,* her name was indelibly connected to the fight for smoke-free air at work. She was, she realized, a perfect consultant: a source of knowledge, strategy, and inspiration for other Americans suffering through smoke at work.

Donna Shimp founded Environmental Improvement Associates (EIA), the first organization of its kind in the United States—and likely in the world. Incorporated in New Jersey in May of 1978, EIA defined itself as dedicated to improving "the indoor work environment"—especially offices—through educational means. It would be a broker of information to workers, management, and lawyers, distributing "materials on smoking as they relate to the improvement of the indoor environment"; providing "materials and expert witnesses for public, private, and legal hearings concerned with tobacco smoke as an occupational health hazard"; and coordinating "national efforts directed toward elimination of all smoking in the work environment."[44]

Funding for EIA was nearly nonexistent. Tasty Baking Company, the Philadelphia-based bakery most famous for producing Tastykake snack foods, made a grant of $500 yearly for the first four years of the organization's operation.[45] Shimp did not take a salary, but $500 did not even cover lodging and a plane ticket for her to make a presentation at a regional Lung Association meeting. And so Shimp routinely requested donations in missives to the mailing list, sometimes corresponding directly with wealthier board members to beg them for funds directly.[46]

Because of the significance of the Shimp trial, EIA's estimable Board of Advisers masked the organization's shoe-string nature. Luther Terry was a member, as was Father Robert Drinan, the most outspoken champion of nonsmokers' rights on Capitol Hill. Other members of the Board, while less publicly recognizable, provide a glimpse into the organization's aims and political milieu. Banzhaf, of course, had a seat at the table, as did Betty Carnes, the Arizona activist principally responsible for that state's pioneering 1973 anti-smoking law, and credited with inventing the "thank you for not smoking" sign; Eleanor Demarest, head of New Jersey GASP and a patron of sorts to Shimp, was also a founding Board member. The presence of Dr. Susan Daum, a specialist in occupational health riding a wave of notoriety for her 1973 book *Work Is Dangerous to Your Health,* suggested that EIA saw itself as part of the field of occupational health—a view consistent with Banzhaf's agency-focused approach.

Shimp never called herself a feminist, but she was sensitive to the gender dynamics of smoking, office work, and advocacy. Shimp confessed concern that "there are not more women represented on the council."[47] It is striking that Shimp would be so straightforward in articulating her concerns about gender equity to a group of well-credentialed near-strangers, nearly all of whom were men. But Shimp's vision for representation was rooted in her experience as part of a labor union—at the very heart, in fact, of what Ruth Milkman has described as the "fourth wave" of union organizing in the pink- and white-collar telecommunications, secretarial, and airline sectors.[48] "The majority of employees trapped in the 'ghettoes' of the workforce (secretarial pools, clerical areas, etc.) are women," Shimp wrote.[49] "Ghetto" was a revealing choice of words. During the 1970s, feminist observers of the American workplace spoke increasingly of the "secretarial ghetto" or the "pink-collar ghetto"—the poorly paid, low-status, dead-end service and clerical jobs that were feminizing the labor force.[50] The right to breathe smoke-free air was, for Shimp, a question of workplace rights. And given the rising tide of female office workers—who smoked less relative to their male colleagues—Shimp conceived of women as a laboring group in need of specific protection from ambient tobacco smoke.

Shimp's insistence on female representation on EIA's advisory committee perhaps sprang from her own experience of workplace democracy—and its absence—within the union movement. Per the recommendation of other board members, Shimp added four more women to the advisory committee. Indeed, she viewed the plight of office workers through the prism of her own experience, even calling upon Luther Terry to intervene on behalf of individual workers who requested advice from EIA. "Are there any strings you can pull in Washington to help this gal?" Shimp queried Terry in one case. "The place she works is an old warehouse, apparently, and is dusty as well as full of smoke." The media was not aware of it, nor did Shimp report her involvement in the woman's case back to the EIA advisory board, as was her custom. Rather, Shimp's correspondence on the subject was marked by a deep and personal concern for an ailing middle-aged woman whose talents were being wasted, whose coworkers scorned her, and whose complaints disappeared into bureaucratic cul-de-sacs. Shimp eschewed the language of feminism, but her actions belied a sensitivity to the shared struggles of women workers.

Shimp's personal interventions notwithstanding, the day-to-day work of EIA consisted of creating demand for the services that the consultancy provided. That is, EIA leveraged the creation of legal liabilities into opportunities for consulting on workplace-smoking policies. Ultimately, the case for smoke-free workplaces converged on a single, clear, and persuasive argument: smoking—and, quite often, smokers—cost too much. Smokers were bad employees, destroying equipment, taking frequent breaks to feed their habit, and sidelined with sickness. Shimp had broached this argument in her unsolicited proposal to AT&T, but she would hone and tweak it for labor, corporate, and employee audiences. Nonsmoking activists did not so much convince employers to take steps to eliminate smoking in the name of nonsmokers' rights as they convinced them to eliminate smoking employees, and the liabilities they created, in the name of the corporate ledger.

Shimp's efforts were part of a swelling wave of management consulting that analyzed work life and work efficiency from an expanding range of perspectives.[51] "The world's youngest profession," consulting had its roots in Frederick Taylor's studies of scientific management. But during the 1980s, consulting took up more space in the business ecology—so much space, in fact, that *Forbes* condemned the growth of the consulting profession as a symptom of national malaise.[52] In an influential 1983 *Harvard Business Review* article, sociologist Robert Jackall observed that for all the corporate-speak about "quality of work life" and "feedback sessions," "the productive return is the only rationale that carries weight within the corporate hierarchy."[53] Donna Shimp grasped this intuitively, writing to Luther Terry in 1981, "is there any better way to interest management in restricting smoking than through the bottom line?"[54] But for Shimp and other public-health activists, appeals to the bottom line were not in pursuit of profit, but rather a means toward the end of extinguishing the social acceptability of smoking.

With the $500 grant from Tasty Baking Company, EIA launched its first campaign in 1978: corporate participation in a smoke-free day at work.

"Smokefree Day at Work" was billed as a voluntary program that could, in fact, obviate the need for regulation by law. "Restricted smoking in work areas is a goal with substantial benefits to the employees and to the bottom line," the EIA proposal read. EIA requested that participating businesses merely designate January 11, 1978, as the day that employees leave their lighters at home. In soliciting participation, EIA framed the initiative as a business decision. As if to preempt concerns about creeping government regulation of labor, EIA promotional materials highlighted the day as "a *voluntary* one-day program" that could reduce office tension by "enabling fellow workers to establish guidelines based on good health for all." Through the smoke-free program, corporations would "reap the full reward" of better employee health. They could also reap more material rewards, recognizable on any balance sheet: "decreased sick days," "declining disability and workers compensation liability," "lowered utility bills and housekeeping expense," "increased productivity," and "reduced legal fees." The inclusion of these legal liabilities was both carrot and stick. EIA encouraged non-smokers to threaten legal action if employers refused to accommodate their requests. Alluding to Shimp's own "precedent-setting case . . . de-fining tobacco smoke as an occupational health hazard," the invitation to participate closed on an ominous note illustrative of how litigation could raise the costs of inaction. "Under the common law," EIA grimly warned, "*you* are responsible."[55]

Given the minimal cost and the abbreviated timeline, "Smokefree Day at Work" was a success, particularly in terms of raising the profile of the organization and the nonsmokers' cause. The *Wall Street Journal* reported on the initiative, noting its purposeful coincidence with Department of Health, Education, and Welfare (HEW) secretary Joseph Califano's an-nouncement of a major federal anti-smoking drive. Naturally, Shimp of-fered to lead a workshop in honor of the event at her own employer, New Jersey Bell. Unsurprisingly, the company both declined her offer and par-ticipation in designating a smoke-free day. Other firms, though, were more receptive to EIA's advice. In 1978 Chase Manhattan Bank; Mobil Oil; Camp-bell Soup; the CWA; the International Brotherhood of Electrical Workers; the Pennsylvania, New Jersey, Florida, and Philadelphia Departments of Health; and the Washington, Florida, South Carolina, and Nebraska Lung Associations had purchased the "Smokefree Day" at Work kits that New

Jersey Bell had turned down. On top of that, individual employees at TransWorld Airlines, New York Telephone, Dupont, the *New York Times,* ABC-TV, the University of California–Los Angeles, MIT, and several branches of the mammoth Bell System contacted EIA for smoke-free literature, even though their workplaces did not participate in Smokefree Day.[56] Not all of these diverse organizations were equally receptive to company-wide cessation. But their interest suggests a growing awareness of the worksite as a battlefront in tobacco regulation.

The day before the January 11 event, Donna Shimp made her national television debut on *Good Morning America,* squaring off against Ernest van den Haag, the conservative social critic and *National Review* writer. Van den Haag was comfortable in the role of conservative gadfly: he had been a regular on the talk show circuit for his opposition to *Brown v. Board,* his eugenic defense of racial difference, and his enthusiasm for the death penalty.[57] John Banzhaf would later throw a glass of water in his face, extinguishing his lit cigar, on an episode of *Nightwatch* with Charlie Rose. Unbeknownst to *Good Morning America*'s viewers, van den Haag also enjoyed an especially close relationship to the tobacco industry, appearing several times at the "Philip Morris Roundtable"—a conference for industry and academic researchers focused on enhancing the credibility of industry-produced research.[58]

On *Good Morning America,* Shimp addressed van den Haag as "Doctor." He did not address her by name at all. Van den Haag argued that "Churchill smoked cigars. Sigmund Freud would never have invented psychoanalysis without cigars. Thomas Mann would never have written his novels without cigars."[59] Shimp, however, held her own. "Do you have the right to make anyone sick, bearing in mind that everyone agrees tobacco smoke is [a] harm, because the oxygen level in your blood is decreased?" Shimp asked. "If people wish to, they are entitled to," van den Haag parried. Seconds later the segment ended. For the fledgling organization, even adversarial public events were good publicity. Shimp described the event as a "great success in terms of consciousness-raising."[60]

By describing her efforts as "consciousness-raising," Shimp positioned nonsmokers as a historically oppressed group whose liberation could be hastened if nonsmokers embraced their identity as such. Through education and public events, nonsmokers could realize their shared position, emboldening them to demand a smokeless environment—or at least help them feel less awkward about bringing up the subject with their boss. With workplace-centered events, EIA hoped to affect voluntary regulation on behalf of nonsmokers, while demonstrating to corporate employers that the benefits of such regulation—measured in terms of dollars—outweighed the costs. In response to the media coverage of Smokefree Day, the Pennsylvania Department of Health decided to sponsor a monthly statewide smoke-free day. "If we did this much with $500 and lots of volunteer time," Shimp wrote to the EIA advisory board, "imagine the effectiveness of a full-scale effort."[61] By the early 1980s, the strategy for such an effort was discernible. EIA would disseminate information that quantified the cost of smoking so as to push businesses toward smoking restrictions, and to empower nonsmokers to make their own case to employers. With these combined efforts, EIA would continue to shift the default attitude about both public and work spaces toward a smoke-free norm.

Shimp's cost-centric arguments would have sounded familiar to early twentieth century managers. After her trial, Shimp published a how-to manual for workers suffering from ambient tobacco smoke, which contained all of the legal materials from her trial, as well as a directory of anti-smoking groups and physicians. Distributed through Lung Associations, Clearing the Air at Work helped to make visible the legal remedies available to workers, the network of authorities available to testify to the harms of environmental tobacco smoke, and the arguments that workers might arm themselves with to make the case to their companies. For example, Shimp applauded a time and motion study conducted by a pool equipment manufacturer in Clifton, NJ. The results of the study showed that smokers were between 2 and 10 percent less efficient than nonsmokers—reason enough for company stockholders to pay a 2 percent bonus to nonsmoking employees. In another example, Merle Norman Cosmetics went smoke free voluntarily in 1976, estimating that the company would save thousands in lower absenteeism and higher productivity.

The aggregate numbers provided by EIA were also impressive: 399 million work days were lost annually by American workers a result of smoking; smokers were involved in twice as many accidents as nonsmokers; smokers were at greater risk for industrial poisoning because of the synergistic effects of chemical compounds and cigarette smoke; smokers damaged equipment and upholstery; smokers cost more in housekeeping and utilities; and, should these rank-and-file concerns fail to persuade management, "smoking executives are more susceptible to coronary or other crippling disease in their most productive years, and the cost of replacement is very high."[62] The bottom line was that nonsmoking policies were good for the bottom line. And smokers, as a rule, were bad for it.

The Business of the Business Case

A raft of economists and management experts began to make their own case against tobacco and would soon have their arguments bolstered by scientific findings that raised the stakes of liability for business.[63] Their arguments flowed from a different source than the rights-based claims that had initially animated Donna Shimp and Clara Gouin. Publishing in outlets like the *Personnel Administrator, Management World,* and the *Personnel Journal,* these management gurus touted the business savings of a smoking ban. William Weis, a professor of business administration at Seattle University, was one of the most prominent spokesmen for the business case against workplace smoking. Weis was not connected to ASH, GASP, or Donna Shimp. Indeed, he had only recently defended a doctoral dissertation on collegiate financial-reporting practices in 1979 before assuming his professorship. The birth of his academic career coincided with the rising salience of cost arguments in the workplace specifically and of economizing arguments in the Reagan era generally. Weis and the nonsmokers' movement offered businesses a way to cut costs just as American businesses were straining to maintain competitiveness in an era of inflation and heightened global competition.[64]

Weis's profit analysis of workplace smoking included four dimensions: absenteeism, productivity, damage and depreciation to equipment, and insurance coverage. Along every dimension, smoking workers were found to be costlier than their nonsmoking peers. "Would you like to shave personnel costs by 20%, insurance premiums by 20%, maintenance charges by 50%, furniture replacement by 50%, and disability payments by 75%?" began one typical article from 1981, entitled "Profits Up in Smoke."[65] Personnel costs were a capacious category, encompassing everything from the lost productivity of the smoker who wasted company time on smoke breaks to the morale boost for nonsmokers working for a firm that took steps to protect their health.[66] "I watched a dry-wall man lose 30 minutes of every hour to his smoking habit before I fired him," one business owner reported with some satisfaction. "Working and smoking don't mix."[67] These management-focused articles were not peer reviewed, their sources were not always cited, and the studies presented as evidence were only vaguely described. But they provided reassurance for businesses flirting with the idea of introducing smoking restrictions. With smoking policies as with downsizing or restructuring, consultants gave cover for managers to make unpopular decisions. Weis routinely emphasized that other firms, varying in size and across a wide range of sectors, had already implemented smoke-free policies—to great success and with no employee backlash.

Relying frequently on testimonials from managers, articles with titles like "Improve Productivity Overnight" made the case for smoke-free policies in the whiz-bang register of a TV pitchman with an accounting degree. "Every time she struck a match, it was a signal that the time had arrived for another informal—and unauthorized—work break," one vice-president of a bank complained. "Four or five staff members would move, in unconscious reflex, toward her desk to begin another 10-minutes of chitchat. Every single cigarette she lit was costing me an hour of lost productivity."[68] That a smoking woman was perceived differently than a smoking man had more to do with women's place in the corporate hierarchy than it had to do with their rates of cigarette consumption. Men who smoked in the office environment were more likely to be able to do so alone in private offices, where their habit was less likely to be perceived as an impediment to work. In the secretarial pool of an open office, lighting up was a social act, subversive and frivolous. Based on his calculations of smoker waste, sickness, and inefficiency, Weis estimated that each smoking employee cost employers "$4611 more [yearly] than the nonsmoking employee" in 1981. By 1987 he had revised that estimate upward. "I would feel fairly comfortable guaranteeing the company a cost savings in excess of $5000 per year per smoker."[69] The origin of these figures, which did not account for regional health-care, wage, and insurance differentials, was less important than their wide distribution.

The same arguments had been made by industrial titans like Ford and Edison in the early twentieth century. The trend toward smoking restrictions at work was presented as a rational evolution toward more efficient, profitable, and productive workplaces. Weis's mission was to expose the gulf between typical practice and best practice, to expose the hidden costs of smoking employees. Any floor manager knew that cigarette burns on furniture and carpets required their occasional replacement, but he may not have considered that overall painting and cleaning needs could be reduced by eliminating smoking. After the implementation of a no-smoking policy, "cleaning costs were more than halved," the president of an electrical components company explained. In terms that would have been familiar to Frederick Winslow Taylor as he observed pig iron handlers, the president continued: "one man does what two and a half would be doing if we still allowed smoking."[70] Ambient tobacco smoke represented a silent drain on company resources—a metaphor, perhaps, for the hidden costs of smokers themselves.

The metaphor was made real by insurance companies that began to selectively sell some policies at reduced rates to nonsmokers. Anti-tobacco forces greeted what was a profit maximization strategy for insurance companies as if it were a revelation about the worth of smokers and nonsmokers. "The data show conclusively that nonsmokers pay more than their share for the smoking habits of others," Weis wrote in a 1985 how-to volume titled *The Smoke-Free Workplace*. "This amounts to grand larceny!"[71] Or, as the president of the Californians for Nonsmokers' Rights (formerly California GASP) explained, it represented an injustice for nonsmokers to "financially subsidize the illnesses that smokers develop."[72] Life insurance companies were the first to offer discounted rates to nonsmokers after the publication of the 1964 *Surgeon General's Report*. Later, one restaurant owner in Seattle negotiated a reduction in her fire insurance premiums after banning smoking in her restaurant.[73] Boosters like Weis lumped all forms of insurance together when touting the amazing savings that would accrue to workplaces that adopted an anti-smoking policy. But the markets for health, fire, accident, and workers' compensation differed in their responsiveness to a corporate smoking ban. Because most employers purchased group insurance for employees, the differential risk rating of smokers was a moot point—but one freighted with a lot of symbolism.

The push for risk rating based on smoking status represented the apex in the nonsmoking movement's push to drive smokers out of the actuarial—and actual—commons. The lead article of a 1984 ASH *Smoking and Health* issue unwittingly revealed the extent to which insurance rating operated as a symbolic rather than substantive issue. After several hundred words of explication of the ways in which "it is not fair to require the nonsmoker to absorb the significantly higher health care costs smokers voluntarily create for themselves," the article closed with a request for readers to submit "any information on the economics of this issue."[74] A cartoon that appeared in the same issue got closer to the heart of the matter. In it, two bespectacled men sit in the "Surgeon General's office" examining the warning label on an oversized pack of cigarettes. "YOU'RE THE SCUM OF THE EARTH," the label reads. The man in the foreground comments, "Too strong." In another context, such a cartoon may have registered as hyperbolic satire on the rotating warning labels that Congress had finally voted to adopt. In the context of a newsletter devoted to the quantification of smoking's social cost, it was a sketch of the movement's hard edges, and the easy slide from economic analysis to moral judgment.

For insurance companies, the virtues of risk rating for smoking were less obvious. One 1993 survey of private insurers in California revealed that risk rating for smoking was considered by 48 percent of insurers, and adopted by less than a quarter. Only 2 percent of the self-insured companies surveyed risk-rated employees by smoking status. Three times as many corporations that had considered risk rating rejected it as adopted it, citing difficulty of administration, uncertainty about the differential premiums charged, and questions surrounding cost-effectiveness.[75] Indeed, among health economists there was some ambiguity about who was subsidizing whom, especially in the context of employer-provided benefits. It was indisputable that smoking was responsible for a large percentage of health-care spending, but health economists also pointed out that early death among smokers meant that they subsidized the retirement benefits of their longer-lived co-workers.[76] Nonsmokers may have subsidized the sins of smokers, but smokers also subsidized the virtues of nonsmokers.

At the same time, scientific investigations of the health consequences of smoking on nonsmokers began to yield fruit. Indeed, the impulse to quantify social costs was a tool of the public-health case against the cigarette. Joseph Califano's introduction to the 1979 *Surgeon General's Report* argued that "stepped-up" federal action on cigarettes was necessary because an individual's smoking habits implicated "every taxpayer." Citing smoking's $5–8 billion contribution to the $205 billion spent annually on "the spiraling cost of health care," the *Report* observed that even such a figure hid smoking's full cost. "Lost productivity, wages, and absenteeism caused by smoking-related illness" put the tally closer to "$12 to 18 billion."[77] The extent to which these figures could be reliably measured was less important than their invocation at every level of the nonsmoking movement—from the grass roots to managerial mercenaries to the official publications of the federal government.

From Nonsmokers to Passive Smokers

Beginning in the late 1970s, researchers began suggesting that ambient tobacco smoke was not just annoying to nonsmokers or a hazard to hypersensitives like Shimp, Smith, and Parodi. In 1978, James Repace, a biophysicist at the Naval Research Laboratory (NRL), began an extracurricular project to measure pollution levels in indoor environments. Repace's path toward the indoor smoking issue originated in an environmental air quality battle at his own workplace. The NRL's offices were located next to a sewage treatment plant. In 1973, the plant announced a plan to begin construction on sludge-burning incinerators. Repace pored over the environmental impact statement required for the incinerators' construction and thought something was amiss. The plans misrepresented the air pollution effects of the incinerators. "Over my dead body will they burn that shit," Repace recalled thinking. To gird himself for battle with his superiors at the NRL—who supported the incinerator siting in the hopes that burning sewage would be less smelly than treating it—Repace immersed himself in air pollution research. He eventually produced his own counter–environmental impact study that quantified the toxins the incinerators could be anticipated to release. Soon, the *Washington Post* reported on the story, and, on the advice of a colleague, Repace sent his report to an attorney at the National Resources Defense Council who specialized in air pollution standards. The EPA eventually refused to approve the sewage incinerator on the banks of the Potomac.[78]

Repace's success in marshaling his professional expertise to thwart the incinerator siting made him an in-demand expert for citizens' groups

opposing incinerators across the D.C. area.[79] That is, Repace became a
NIMBY ("Not In My Back Yard") specialist. After a meeting with a Maryland citizens' group, an audience member encouraged Repace to turn his
technical skills to the question of indoor air pollution. By Repace's calculations, tobacco smoke in enclosed environments would exceed EPA-
permissible air quality standards. Fortuitously, Repace's attention to the
issue conceded with Jesse Steinfeld's political demise. Once out of office,
Steinfeld organized a conference on nonsmokers' rights at a Baltimore
community college. For the event, Repace designed a poster based on his
calculations, which attracted the attention of an engineer with the National Security Administration and a fellow Bowie resident (see Figure 6.2).
Together, they decided to form a new GASP chapter—enlisting the help of
Clara Gouin, with whom Repace also served on the Prince George's Environmental Coalition. Class, geography, and a shared commitment to environmental activism were crucial to nonsmoker activism.[80] But Repace's
technical abilities would also prove decisive.

At Bowie GASP, Repace was determined to convince the city council to
pass a law requiring smoking and nonsmoking sections at restaurants. To
do so, Repace put his professional skills to use. With Al Lowrey, a coworker

Figure 6.2 James Repace and his daughter tend a GASP booth at a mall in
Bowie, Maryland. (Courtesy of James Repace)

at the Naval Research Laboratory, he sought to measure indoor air pollution in typical settings. Using a machine called a piezobalance—essentially a Geiger counter for airborne particles—Repace measured respirable particulates at bars, bowling alleys, bingo halls, libraries, churches, restaurants, and private residences near his home. The results of the field study, which were supplemented by mathematical modeling of the interaction between sidestream smoke, standard room ventilation, and smoking prevalence and rate, were published in *Science* in May 1980. Repace and Lowrey found that the levels of air pollution at the smoky Maryland field sites exceeded the legal limits established for factories or on busy commuter highways. In contrast to the passage of legislation and standards governing outdoor air, "little legislative attention has been devoted to the quality of indoor air." But Americans spent upward of 90 percent of their time indoors. "Clearly, indoor air pollution from tobacco smoke presents a serious risk to the health of nonsmokers."[81]

Smokers, as Shimp put it, were "human smokestacks."[82] Sharing space with them was like living downwind of a polluting factory—only there were federal air quality standards in place to monitor outdoor pollution. Pollution levels "generated by smokers overwhelm the effects of ventilation and inflict significant air pollution burdens on the public," Repace and Lowrey concluded.[83] After publishing their study, the authors received some two hundred requests for reprints.[84] Such an investigation resonated with a white-collar workforce that increasingly worked in airtight office buildings—an architectural legacy of the previous decade's energy crisis. Nonsmokers, like the women who led the office workers' movement to acknowledge "sick building syndrome" in the early 1980s, sought to control the indoor environment in line with heightened expectations of comfort and safety.[85]

Before the publication of the article in *Science*, Repace took a position at the Environmental Protection Agency. This lent the nonsmokers' movement a greater degree of technical credibility, but also put a target on Repace's back as an employee of a federal agency already unpopular with tobacco's friends in Congress. John Banzhaf recalled Repace as his "go-to guy" on technical questions of ventilation and air quality. Repace's studies made their way into briefs submitted by nonsmokers seeking redress at work.[86] Repace himself frequently appeared as an expert witness in such cases, or before congressional committees considering ill-fated nonsmokers' rights legislation. And he was a spokesman for indoor air quality at EPA, spearheading the agency's report on environmental tobacco smoke.[87]

Repace's advocacy made him a persistent thorn in the side of the industry, which hired scientists to smear him on baseless scientific grounds while Tobacco Institute spokesmen antagonized him in the press.[88] The industry succeeded in making Repace's life difficult. Tennessee representative Don Sundquist called for an agency investigation into Repace's "apparently inappropriate outside activities."[89] Repace was eventually cleared of wrongdoing, perhaps in part because more research was published that vindicated his early analyses.

As economists and accountants quantified the economic burdens inflicted by smokers, those in public health sought to quantify the health burdens smokers imposed on others. The conclusions of Repace and Lowrey's study were limited to the degree of exposure of the public to sidestream particulates. It was not an epidemiological investigation. But shortly after publication, a raft of epidemiological studies provided evidence that environmental tobacco increased nonsmokers' risk of developing lung cancer.[90]

The most important such study, conducted by a Japanese epidemiologist at the Tokyo National Cancer Center, was published in the *British Medical Journal* in January 1981. In 1965, Takeshi Hirayama embarked upon a large-cohort longitudinal investigation of the relationship between lifestyle habits and disease outcomes (see Figure 6.3). Hirayama did not begin the 250,000-subject investigation focused solely on tobacco. Rather, he sought to study the relationship between health outcomes and "lifestyle factors," which included the consumption of cigarettes, alcohol, green vegetables, soy sauce, and dairy, in addition to social factors such as economic and marital status. The study's size and sensitivity enabled Hirayama to inquire into the disease patterns of nonsmokers routinely exposed to tobacco smoke.

His conclusions marked a turning point for the nonsmokers' movement. The data revealed a twofold increase in the mortality rate among the nonsmoking wives of smoking husbands. The relationship between a husband's smoking status and his wife's susceptibility to lung cancer followed a dose-response pattern—an important factor in establishing a causal relationship. The wives of the heaviest smokers had an even greater risk of lung cancer, while those married to partners who smoked less had less risk. The

Figure 6.3 Takeshi Hirayama, John Banzhaf, and Rita Addison, president of Massachusetts GASP, at a World Health Organization (WHO) meeting in Winnipeg, Canada, in 1983. (University of California, San Francisco Library)

study garnered instant attention in the American media.[91] The *New York Times, Los Angeles Times,* and *Chicago Tribune* all reported on the study within a day of its publication; the *New York Times* even ran a summary of the study on its front page. From there, reports were syndicated in newspapers all over the United States—from Daytona to Cape Girardeau. Headlines emphasizing the "high risk" of "mates' smoking" simplified the technical details of Hirayama's study. Americans did not need an advanced course in epidemiology to understand the study's message: other people's smoke poisoned them.[92]

The Hirayama study was itself an unintended testament to the tobacco regime of government price supports and subsidies. The cigarettes that Japanese husbands smoked were, by the time of the study's inception in 1965, increasingly filled with American flue-cured tobacco. The tobacco arrived in Japan by way of Tobacco Associates and the Food for Peace program, a vehicle for the disposal of American surplus commodities and the engineering of foreign consumption patterns. By the late 1970s, Japan was one of the most important export markets for American flue-cured leaf.[93]

The raw leaf that state-supported tobacco producers had sold to Japan—with the underwriting of the U.S. government—was reintroduced to the United States as epidemiological science.

At the 1987 World Conference on Smoking and Health held in Tokyo, Donna Shimp shared space on the program with Takeshi Hirayama and James Repace; William Weis was absent, though he had presented a paper on "The Smoke Free Workplace: Cost and Health Consequences" at the previous global gathering of anti-tobacco activists in Winnipeg. On a dais in Tokyo, Shimp confidently predicted that the "sheer economics" of the case against tobacco—in terms of the costs of smokers and the liability issues raised for employers—would ultimately eliminate the "pulmonary rape" of passive smoking. Nonsmoking activists had constructed a case against tobacco that was animated by the questions of efficiency as much as questions of rights and responsibilities.[94] "Pulmonary rape" was a violation of the nonsmoker, but it was also a theft from the employer, the risk-pool, and the taxpayer.

The Workingman's Friend

As the business case against tobacco hewed closely to cost and efficiency arguments, the case for tobacco's continued presence in the workplace initially came from sources that had always questioned the supremacy of the market's logic: labor unions. This must have been bittersweet for Donna Shimp, who retained a belief in the importance of organized labor as buffering the individual worker from the whims of her employer. As she wrote to a fellow employee as her trial was unfolding in 1975, "I feel the only way we are going to gain recognition of the real health hazard of 'second hand smoke' is through collective action."[95] But action to clear the air at work put the nonsmokers' movement on a collision course with the closest thing the postwar labor movement had to a sacred cow: collective bargaining. The nonsmokers' movement arrived at work just as a range of new forces—feminism, the Quality of Work Life movement, the rise of public sector unions, the occupational health movement—complicated labor's traditionally male-dominated, seniority-centered, bread-and-butter prerogatives.[96]

On procedural, political, and policy grounds, union leadership and non-smoker advocates were at odds. From the perspective of organized labor, *Shimp* established a dangerous precedent: it substituted a judge's decision for a provision of the collective-bargaining agreement. Indeed, Donna Shimp fought both her employer and her union, the CWA, when she sued New Jersey Bell. The managerial arguments proffered by tobacco's foes could hardly be expected to resonate with unions that sought to represent all workers, not just those that were cheapest for a company to employ.

Indeed, labor's initial hostility toward just workplace smoking restrictions encapsulated broader labor attitudes toward occupational health. Beginning with Samuel Gompers, labor leadership had worried that attempts to ameliorate—or at least catalog—occupational health would allow management to screen out sick, unacceptable workers. These concerns intensified in the 1970s with the passage of the Occupational Safety and Health Act—a result of union pressure, but also a tool of managerial control. For example, when OSHA issued standards on vinyl chloride in 1974, it mandated the removal of high-risk workers without guaranteeing status or seniority.[97] And, under the Nixon and Ford administrations, the agency's rulemaking denied workers access to their own medical records.[98] Complicating matters further was the fact that the workers and unions most invested in occupational health exposures—the Oil, Chemical and Atomic Workers International Union, representing plastic, rubber, and asbestos workers—faced special legal peril and personal surveillance should smoking become subject to managerial control.

Workplace smoking underscored worker autonomy and privacy, and the power of organized labor to control shop floor conditions. Smoking was valuable to employees precisely because it was not productive: the smoke break was a routine enjoyed either in solitude or in fellowship, affording absolutely no economic benefit to the company. The cigarette was, in a sense, a symbol of labor's postwar power.[99] The plants that symbolized America's industrial might were forced to abandon their prewar scruples about smoking on the job. "Smoke-ins" and strikes in protest of smoking bans at Chevrolet and Ford plants in Flint, Dearborn, and Detroit forced automakers and autoworkers to negotiate new smoking rules. After 1945, workers were increasingly able to smoke during break times and in a wide variety of locations—washrooms, lobbies, lunchrooms, and assembly lines.[100] With decades of advertising imagery connecting smoking to sweated, industrial production, the tobacco industry exploited the association between management and smoking restrictions. While R. J. Reynolds fought unionization at its own cigarette manufacturing facilities, the tobacco industry posed as a friend to the workingman. It mattered not that even most union members were no longer smokers, or that most workplaces no longer resembled the humming assembly line of a General Motors facility.

The workplace-smoking issue embodied the contradictions of organized labor within an increasingly diverse workplace. Majoritarianism was not pitted against the individual rights of nonsmokers, as was true in struggles for African-American or women's rights. Rather, unions sought to protect the prerogatives of *a minority* of their members as a way of asserting their own primacy in representation. Not all labor unions fought for smoking. Indeed, organized flight attendants spearheaded the passage of the first successful federal workplace-smoking law: a 1988 smoking ban on domestic flights of fewer than two hours duration.[101] But the position of union leaders and the Executive Council of the AFL-CIO was consistent: steadfast opposition to employer-imposed smoking restrictions without prior bargaining—regardless of the popularity of such a policy among workers.

This was not how Donna Shimp imagined the nonsmokers' movement would unfold. Labor was actually at the center of EIA's first proposed activities because she hoped recognition of tobacco smoke "as an occupational health hazard" would spur an accord between safety-concerned unions and cost-concerned management. Shimp routinely mentioned her membership in the CWA, proudly referring to her service as the steward of her local. Donna Shimp's relationship with the CWA illustrated the difficulties presented by the workplace-smoking issue. The steward at her office in Bridgeton refused to offer her assistance in initiating a grievance procedure. When Shimp turned to the sympathetic vice-president of her local to represent her in a grievance proceeding, the president of the local intervened to stop it. In July 1975, Shimp had a face-to-face meeting with the president, who, between puffs, informed her that her grievance would only be heard upon court order.

But the attitudes of union leadership eventually changed. After her trial, Shimp maintained a friendly correspondence with CWA president Glenn Watts, who wrote the foreword to a pamphlet on "smoke-free work areas" that EIA produced for labor unions. "Our union not only acts to protect the health of non-smoking members," Watts wrote. "We also seek to educate them about their right to a smoke-free environment."[102] But as battles over workplace smoking unfolded, unions avoided committing themselves on either side of the debate. "We have purposely tried not to develop union policies [on smoking]," the health and safety director of the CWA told the Bureau of National Affairs in 1986, distancing himself from Watts's comments of the previous decade.[103]

Within the nonsmokers' movement, Shimp functioned as a liaison to the world of organized labor—a world unfamiliar to the middle-class, white-collar constituency of GASP. She had a decades-long relationship with the American Lung Association and the National Safety Council, helping those organizations to target organized labor. Her advice to such groups was always the same: enlist the support of organized labor in crafting policy so that collective-bargaining agreements limit rather than permit smoking. She traversed the United States and spoke internationally on how unions could embrace smoking bans as part of a broader commitment to workplace "health rights."[104] EIA authored models for bargaining, policy suggestions, educational literature, and blueprints for cessation and addiction workshops.[105] Despite the praise Shimp heaped upon the union officials who represented nonsmoking workers at grievance hearings, it was impossible for nonsmoking advocates not to applaud management for initiating smoking bans even when they subverted collective-bargaining agreements. Nowhere was the tension between nonsmokers' rights and unionism on greater display than in EIA's support for Johns-Manville's smoking ban.

In 1976, Johns-Manville (J-M) adopted a strict smoking ban at several of its asbestos-processing facilities. It did so not out of concern for non-smokers but out of a desire to mitigate its liability exposure. The asbestos giant was facing an unprecedented number of tort claims brought by employees who had developed lung cancer, mesothelioma, and asbestosis as a result of their employment. This legal spectacle unfolded amid a popular fascination with the unseen hazards of work. Titles of cheap, mass market paperbacks attested to the popular preoccupation with hazards of the job: *Muscle and Blood, Expendable Americans, Work Is Dangerous to Your Health.*[106]

In what one legal scholar has termed "the heaviest onslaught of cases experienced in tort system," by the time J-M filed for bankruptcy in 1982, there were 16,500 lawsuits pending against it, and another 130,000 claims collected for filing. Lawyers for the asbestos plaintiffs would later apply the insights—and the hefty payouts—of toxic tort litigation to tobacco suits over the following decade.[107] But in the late 1970s, J-M was grappling with how to respond to research that demonstrated terrifying synergistic effects between asbestos inhalation and cigarette smoking. Asbestos workers who smoked had a ninety-fold greater risk of dying of lung cancer than people who neither smoked nor worked around asbestos.[108] To limit the corporation's liability for these excess deaths, J-M implemented a smoking ban.

Asbestos workers unions greeted the Johns-Manville policy with contempt. Not only did J-M subvert collective-bargaining procedures in unilaterally imposing the ban, but the ban itself implied that workers were themselves responsible for their own toxic exposures. The smoking ban, unions asserted, absolved employers from engaging in broader cleanup efforts, while also shielding them from fully compensating sickened workers who brought suit. While management gurus praised bans for limiting risk exposure, advocates for workers exposed to a variety of toxins condemned bans for the very same reasons. The International Association of Machinists, which represented asbestos workers at plants in Dallas and Boston, sued the company over its smoking ban. While the arbitrator in the Boston case upheld the company's decision, the Dallas ban was declared invalid. J-M then filed suit precisely on the grounds that nonsmokers' rights advocates like Shimp were trying to fortify: that common law supported an employer's efforts to eliminate threats to worker health. In 1980, the Fifth Circuit Court of Appeals affirmed the arbitrator's decision: the Dallas ban was invalid.[109] The integrity of the collective-bargaining process prevailed over management's overtures to workplace safety.

The victory was a sad index of labor's crimped power in an era of plant closures, liability management, and awareness of the latency period of disease.[110] The International Association of Machinists' defense of the integrity of collective bargaining was also a defense of a worker's prerogative to expose himself to risks—with the bleak prospect of the union's assistance in organizing a class action against offending corporations later on. However, courts were simultaneously holding smoking workers partially accountable for diseases they contracted on the job. In 1981, the North Carolina Supreme Court partially reversed a disability award to a worker at Burlington Industries, a textile plant in North Carolina. The court found that her debilitating byssinosis, a lung disease caused by the inhalation of cotton dust, was exacerbated by her smoking habit. Her disability compensation was therefore reduced by half.[111]

The reversals suffered by private sector industrial unions in the 1970s may have negatively predisposed them toward any policies that could divide workers or be perceived as capitulating to management. Blue-collar workers were both more likely to smoke than white-collar workers and more likely to suffer multiple toxic exposures while on the job.[112] "Our concern is that smoking is going to be used by employers to try to reduce just workers' compensation awards," said the director of the Chemical Workers Union's cancer control taskforce in 1986.[113] Workers in industrial and chemical sectors guarded the collective-bargaining agreement and rejected the insinuation that their cigarette consumption should detract one cent from the responsibility companies bore in exposing them to harmful substances at work. This latter concern was enough to drive Susan Daum, author of *Work Is Dangerous to Your Health*, to resign from EIA's board in protest of what she saw as the organization's management-centered focus.[114] "I believe that this strategy can only lead to disciplinary actions by companies against specific workers," Daum warned. "I remain available to help on specific projects which do not put extra weapons against the workers in the hands of the companies."[115]

The drive to maintain the appearance of solidarity and hold management accountable caused labor to shrink from the workplace-smoking issue. The AFL-CIO roundly rejected the 1985 *Surgeon General's Report on Cancer and Chronic Lung Disease in the Workplace,* which concluded that workplace smoking represented the greatest cause of death and disability for the vast majority of American workers. The health and safety director of the Service Employees International Union accused the report of blaming the victim and letting employers off the hook—an assertion that surgeon general C. Everett Koop regarded as a "misinterpretation."[116] Some of leadership's rejection of the workplace smoking issue was grounded in organized labor's mistrust of the Reagan administration, which it alleged placed "greater stress on the effects of smoking [relative to industrial hazards] than scientific evidence would permit."[117] Labor's well-founded hostility toward the Reagan administration colored its reading of occupational health science.

At its 1986 Executive Council meeting, the AFL-CIO expressed its opposition to both legislative and employer-imposed smoking restrictions. Its rationale was a familiar one: bargaining should be the vehicle for workplace policy, "worked out voluntarily in individual workplace between labor and management and in a manner that protects the interests and rights of all workers."[118] The last clause was also central to how unions conceived of workplace smoking. In an era in which unions were grappling with how best to protect worker health, they were loath to focus attention on smoking when it could distract from—and maybe even exonerate—industrial exposures while placing the blame for sickness on the shoulders of smokers themselves. "You're damned if you support it and damned if you oppose," said one official at the AFL-CIO's Public Employee Department.[119] In light of labor's economically and politically weakened status in the 1980s, it is not surprising that leadership did not embrace an issue that threatened to divide membership, weakened bargaining agreements, raised privacy concerns for workers, and undercut labor's attempts to hold business accountable for occupational exposures.

Tobacco workers led labor's fight against smoking restrictions. Structurally, the International Confectionery, Bakers, and Tobacco Workers Union (CBT) was well-positioned to reach the "grass tops" of the labor movement—the leadership of other unions, labor-aligned groups, and the Executive Council of the AFL-CIO. Tobacco workers, like tobacco farmers, had a clear economic interest in maintaining the ubiquity of the cigarette. Since the 1960s, the union had been outspoken against federal or state regulation of cigarettes, citing the loss of jobs that would result from the "zealotry" of tobacco "Prohibitionists." At the AFL-CIO's 1979 annual convention, CBT submitted a resolution to the AFL-CIO's Executive Council, which included the union's president. The resolution, calling for an end to the "ongoing demagogic, anti-smoking campaign," was formally adopted by the Executive Council in 1980.[120] The resolution passed only through the hands of leadership and was not put to a vote among the rank and file—who, though they smoked more than white-collar workers, were still majority nonsmoker. This ensured that the fissures that existed within local unions and among individual workers would be kept out of the spotlight. The duty to fairly represent all workers pushed union leadership into the position of ignoring the workplace smoking issue. On a grander scale, that commitment to solidarity (or silence) over nonsmoking majoritarianism helped to ensure that a resolution introduced by a member of the Executive Council would be adopted.

The cigarette manufacturers well understood the structural and political imperatives governing labor's position on smoking. And the industry also realized that the decentralized nature of local unions gave it grassroots credibility with city councils and state legislatures—venues where the industry was weaker relative to Congress. Not only could unions publicly oppose legislation that would adversely affect the industry, but they could also monitor legislative and worksite proposals that bubbled up far from the Tobacco Institute's offices on K Street. By forging an alliance with unions over workplace smoking, the tobacco companies put forth a positive, and not just obstructionist, message about air quality. The Tobacco Institute's vice-president explained that in framing the debate around "the broader issue of indoor air quality," the tobacco industry could "assume a role in the search for answers."[121] This strategic objective dovetailed with organized labor's concern that a singular focus on tobacco smoke as a workplace exposure would forestall employer commitment to broader worksite cleanup.

The waning political fortunes of labor made it an easy mark—receptive, in the words of a 1984 Tobacco Institute memo, to "direct union stimulus by the companies."[122] And so, despite the fact that R. J. Reynolds continued its vigorous, decades-long opposition to organizing workers at its manufacturing facilities (its products were on the AFL-CIO's "Don't Buy List"), labor and the tobacco industry worked together to oppose restrictions on indoor smoking.[123] When Senator Ted Stevens introduced The Non-Smokers Rights Act of 1985, a bill that would have restricted smoking in federal government buildings, the AFL-CIO submitted a statement that reflected the unanimous opposition of its member unions. According to the statement of the Public Employee Department, the legislation "infringes on the collective bargaining process," at "a time when many of the existing structures to protect worker rights have already been eroded."[124] The weakness of organized labor made it one of the strongest allies to the industry. Although the bill died after hearings, many unions continued to work with the Tobacco Institute to defeat workplace-smoking regulations in states and localities through the 1990s.[125]

The Confectionery, Bakery, and Tobacco Workers were the easiest mark of all, the shrillest in their opposition to workplace-smoking laws, and the most reliable friend to the Tobacco Institute. In 1984, the Tobacco Institute and five unions formed the Labor Management Committee (LMC). LMCs were vehicles for labor-management collaboration on issues of mutual concern that fell outside the bargaining agreement.[126] In addition to CBT, the other "third party allies" to the agreement were the Machinists and Aerospace Workers, the Brotherhood of Firemen and Oilers, the Sheet Metal Workers, and the Brotherhood of Carpenters and Joiners. With a racially diverse and disproportionately female membership, the tobacco workers fit uneasily next to these culturally conservative, and predominantly white, male craft unions. As the Tobacco Institute observed in internal memos, CBT was a small union with "limited resources." But these liabilities were, in the hands of industry advertising executives, political assets.

The Tobacco Institute announced the formation of the LMC with an advertisement that ran in the *New Republic,* the *Nation,* the *Progressive, In These Times,* and *Commentary* magazines. Targeting "the traditional allies of organized labor—individuals who have in the past supported a great many liberal positions," the advertisement was intended to highlight the fact that an attack on tobacco was also an "attack on many Americans [who] have jobs and careers they would not have otherwise": specifically, African Americans. The advertorial-style spread carried the headline: "We're the tobacco industry, too." Below was a photo of three members of CBT Local 203 who worked at the Philip Morris plant in Richmond. A black man, a white woman, and a white man stared directly into the camera, defiant and beseeching. The accompanying text narrated the union's recent actions in support of liberal causes—from marching on Washington on Martin Luther

King Jr. Day, to supporting social security, to fighting to save the Food
Stamp Program. "We want you to know that our industry is threatened—not
by foreign competition or old-fashioned technology, but"—in direct address
to liberal readers—"by well-meaning people who haven't stopped to consider
how their actions might affect others."[127] Arrayed in a triangle formation—
two men standing, the woman sitting in front—the tobacco workers evoked
the shape of a shield.

The cigarette manufacturers stood behind the human shield of the "livelihoods of thousands of working Americans who have marched, worked,
and struggled." Corporate power set the tone for cooperation with tobacco
workers. Tobacco executives lectured unionists on the jobs they would lose
if worksites continued to adopt smoking bans. "Smokers . . . said that they
smoke about one and one quarter fewer cigarettes each day as compared
with smokers who were not faced with workplace restrictions," the general
counsel for Brown & Williamson noted in a 1985 speech to an industry-
sponsored conference for union members. "In more personal terms, such
restrictions translate into a loss of about 5,000 jobs in our industry, 750 of
them in the manufacturing sector alone." Because of the expanse of the tobacco industry, worksite smoking bans put even more people out of a job
"in supplier industries, in the agricultural sector, at the wholesale and retail levels."[128]

The lawyer was not wrong. Workplace-smoking bans reduced tobacco
consumption and helped many smokers quit.[129] A 1996 study found that
such restrictions reduced both smoking prevalence and the level of cigarette
consumption for those who continued to smoke.[130] Drawn from National
Health Interview Data, the study found that workplace restrictions led to
a 5 percent decline in smoking prevalence and a 10 percent decline in cigarette consumption: or, at worksites with smoking rules, there were fewer
smokers who smoked fewer cigarettes. And the more complete the ban, the
stronger this association. Even as workplace restrictions reflected class dis-
tinctions, it also created new ones. By the mid-1990s, a chasm emerged
between smoking rates for those who worked and those who did not. Until
the mid-1980s, there had been no significant difference in the smoking
habits of the employed and unemployed. After 1985, when workplace restrictions became more common, smoking rates for workers fell significantly

faster than rates for nonworkers.[131] By the time workplace-smoking regulations touched the majority of American workers, smoking had become a fully classed phenomenon.

———————

By 1986, John Banzhaf could see a new society emerging from the clearing haze of tobacco smoke. It was a future that included smokers—just not in public. The outlines of this society were visible to many other observers as well. To Donna Shimp and activists at GASP, this society looked healthier and fairer to the vast majority of Americans who were nonsmokers. To those in public health, such a society represented an epidemic tamed. To management gurus, it looked productive, cost-effective, and legally prudent. For many in the labor movement, though, the prospect of smoke-free workplaces reflected the diminution of labor's power, and the elevation of the prerogatives of business. Such a society also raised the specter of diminishing employment opportunities for smokers. "Health spas have long recognized that their image and sales suffer significantly if they employ fat, flabby employees," Banzhaf analogized. "Major health organizations, hospitals, and . . . many others are now learning that the same is true if people smoke in their places of business."[132]

The success of the business case made this type of future imaginable—all without the heavy hand of the federal government. The lack of a uniform national rule for workplace smoking was the background against which the business case emerged. The legal ambiguities surrounding workplace smoking provided an opening for advocates to frame smoking restrictions as prudent and responsible, limiting legal liability and costs. Legal ambiguity as much as success in the courtroom cleared the air at work. With each workplace that restricted smoking, however, tobacco became more marginal, more out of step with a political culture that valued each employee, social practice, or government program not only by their positive contributions, but by the burdens imposed on others as well.

7

Shredding a Net to Build a Web

Now repeat after me: There is no tobacco subsidy.
—Jesse Helms, 1981

IN 1975, the Health Research Group of Ralph Nader's organization, Public Citizen, published a report titled, "Federal Support against the Public Health: The 60 Million Dollar Tobacco Subsidy." It laid out the case for terminating the federal tobacco program—a program it judged costly and corrupt. The "$60 million subsidy" was a tally of the program's yearly expenditures. True, the report conceded, "the loan support itself accounts for only 0.13 percent of the aggregate cost of all commodity price support programs of the past 44 years." But still the program was expensive and the bulk of its costs went to administrative expenses and to fund tobacco's participation in the Food for Peace program. And, at any rate, subsidies doled out in "the name of the small tobacco farmer" actually benefited "the well-to-do farmer." The report acknowledged "that small independent farmers would suffer from the elimination of tobacco subsidies." But was such a way of life even worth preserving? These small farmers "would benefit more from direct government aid unconnected with tobacco." The report faulted the program for retarding more *efficient* tobacco production—a position consistent with its prediction that in the absence of a tobacco program, tobacco leaf would get cheaper. However, "the price of cigarettes would be unaffected, since the value of tobacco accounts for only seven percent of the cost of cigarettes to consumers." Nader's indictment was not about tobacco consumption; it was about the economic distortions created by the supply control and licensure system. The report seemed to be saying that tobacco farms were terrible, the portions were too small—and that taxpayers shouldn't be footing the bill anyway.

For opponents of the subsidy regime, only the overwhelming and corrupting influence of tobacco-state congressmen could have produced such a contorted system. From the inception of the program, tobacco farmers had received "more than fair treatment by Congress," and had "consistently received special treatment" since. Tobacco state congressmen had a stranglehold on the congressional committee and subcommittee system. North Carolina congressman Harold Cooley was the longest-serving chairman of the House Agriculture Committee, a position he held with only a two-year interruption from 1949 until 1966. During the 1970s, Herman Talmadge (D-GA) chaired the Senate Agriculture and Forestry Committee.

And even once southern Democrats finally faded from outsized positions of seniority, tobacco still remained cossetted in political privilege because of the power of commodity-specific agricultural subcommittees.[1] When the Republicans took the Senate in the 1980 elections, Jesse Helms, North Carolina archconservative and Reagan ally, held the chairmanship of the Senate Agriculture Committee until 1987. And "all but two members of the tobacco subcommittee are from major tobacco-producing states," the *Public Citizen Report* observed without noting that this stakeholder dominance was entirely characteristic of all agriculture policy. "Decisions about the national program in the House are made almost exclusively by members whose states will receive tobacco subsidies."[2] In the tobacco program, Nader as well as ASH, GASP, and the American Medical Association saw a rare political vulnerability for tobacco. In the wake of Watergate, political tides were turning in Washington. A host of newly elected congressmen were less sympathetic to New Deal–style regulations—and the smoke-filled rooms that produced them.

"Sixty Million Dollar Subsidy" met with the media fanfare typical of Nader's *Public Citizen Reports*. The report appeared at the high tide of the consumer movement in the United States—and the pinnacle of Ralph Nader's political prominence as its prophet.[3] "Nader Group Says Tobacco Price Supports Spur Cancer Deaths," read the *New York Times* headline. The *Washington Post* announced: "Nader Calls for End to Tobacco Aid."[4] Within a decade, Nader and allies in the anti-tobacco movement were close to achieving their goal. Facing intensifying political scrutiny of the tobacco program, farmers accepted a dramatic revision to it in 1982—the beginning of a process that would unravel the fifty-year-old program. But contrary to the desire of anti-tobacco activists, the slaughter of the tobacco program enhanced the power of the tobacco companies. Manufacturers were not sorry to see it go.

The weakening of congressional support for tobacco and the fissures within the ranks of the "tobacco family" stood in contrast to the upsurge in nonsmoker legislation taking hold in cities across the country. While the federal safety net for farmers frayed, a web of smoking restrictions blanketed an increasing number of Americans. By the end of the 1980s, another reversal of sorts had occurred. As Congress became increasingly hostile to tobacco, the tobacco industry embraced federalism to combat the highly successful localistic strategy of the nonsmokers' rights movement. From the ashes of tobacco corporatism arose new, cost-centered conceptions of virtuous citizenship, in which Americans were judged by the scarcity of their footprint on the public ledger. In this new political terrain—where both farmers and smokers were understood as individually responsible for their health and economic success—the power of the tobacco industry was less traceable, but no less real.[5]

"We Think We Can Outvote the Tobacco Interests"

Tobacco producers had reason to hope that Jimmy Carter's election in 1976 would provide a reprieve from the political scrutiny of their crop.[6] Sure, candidate Carter had vowed in his campaign to appoint regulators "that would be acceptable to Ralph Nader."[7] And President Carter made good on this promise, appointing more than sixty consumer, health, and safety activists to important administrative posts—including elevating Michael Pertschuk to the chairmanship of the Federal Trade Commission (FTC). Under Pertschuk, who had helped to formulate cigarette labeling and advertising regulation as a staff lawyer for Warren Magnuson's Senate Commerce Committee, the FTC was known as the "largest public interest firm in Washington."[8]

But Carter was also a southerner, a farmer, and a beneficiary of federal agricultural largess through his participation in the peanut program—the commodity program most similar in structure to the tobacco program. Carter had shown his willingness to compromise with the conservative elements of his party in his support for Scoop Jackson instead of liberal

favorite George McGovern in the 1972 Democratic primary. These competing sides of Carter would eventually manifest as dysfunction in the cabinet and indecision on the president's part.

But in 1976, tobacco country was optimistic. In October of that year,
Carter assured North Carolina congressman Walter Jones that he would
continue to support the tobacco program as president, and praised the program in the terms its stewards used to describe it. "Nearly 600,000 farm
families receive a large portion of their income from tobacco sales," Carter
wrote in a mailgram that received wide dissemination as a news release. "I
personally see no need to do away with a program that costs the government next to nothing, while enabling so many hard-working farmers to
earn a living."[9] Carter won over 55 percent of the vote in North Carolina—
more than his 50 percent share of the national vote.

Carter's success among southern farmers was due in part to the antipathy they held for Earl Butz, the secretary of agriculture under Nixon and
Ford. Butz was the most polarizing figure to hold his position since Eisenhower's secretary of agriculture Ezra Taft Benson, under whom Butz served
as an assistant. Butz and Benson before him were fierce opponents of the
New Deal agriculture regime, particularly supply management. Butz was
bent on restoring "free enterprise" to American farming, reducing or eliminating farm supports, and freeing production from the strictures of supply
controls. He frankly embraced risk as an organizing principle of economic
policy and faulted the New Deal agriculture regime for insulating farmers,
particularly small, marginal farmers, from "market reality." By his own admission, Butz was against the political protection of the "inefficient family
farm," for it represented a perversion of market forces that compelled consolidation, efficiency, mechanization. American farmers needed to produce more—and more cheaply—for export. "Adapt or die; resist and perish,"
Butz told farmers in the 1950s, a decade that witnessed a mass exodus
from American farms.[10] Neither Butz's philosophy nor his abrasive style
had moderated in the intervening years.

Within the world of agriculture, Butz had many ardent supporters. He
was popular with the big grain and corn producers of the Midwest, with
processors and distributors, with the conservative American Farm Bureau
Federation, and with corporate agribusiness like Ralston Purina, which was
one of three corporations on whose board he sat before joining the Nixon

administration in 1972. He was also reviled by a crew of strange bedfellows: southern Democrats and farmers for whom commodity price supports were sacrosanct; advocates for smaller producers and defenders of the "family farm" like the Farmers Union; good government groups that questioned Butz's coziness with agribusiness; and health, safety, and environmental activists, whom the secretary described as responsible for condemning "hundreds of millions of people to a lingering death by malnutrition and starvation." He condescended to consumer activists and housewives frustrated over rising food costs, ignoring calls to investigate the role of middlemen like processors, packers, and retail chains in food price inflation. When confronted by "a housewife" angry at the price of fruit, Butz told her she was wrong that food prices were too high. "They're too low," the secretary snapped. "My wife sent me down here for strawberries, and they're all sold out."[11] Housewives possessed "a low level of economic intelligence" and did not understand that "you can't get more by paying less," Butz told a 1973 gathering of a farm credit association.[12]

Racism and not sexism ultimately forced the secretary's resignation just weeks before the 1976 election. On an airplane following the Republican National Convention, Butz described black Americans as "coloreds" whose aspirations were limited to, first, "a tight pussy; second, loose shoes; and third, a warm place to shit. That's all!"[13] John Dean, Nixon's former White House counsel, authored an article in *Rolling Stone* magazine that reported the remark, but did not name Butz. The irreverent *New Times* magazine eventually sourced the remark to the secretary.

The tobacco belt bid good riddance to Butz—not because of his racism or sexism, but because he wanted to weaken the allotment system. Butz proposed to dramatically increase the amount of tobacco farmers could market and decrease the level of price support they therefore received. He was trying to force farmers to produce more, to embrace the world market as the ultimate determinant of price. And if a producer could not get by without the high price supports that attended acreage reduction, then that farmer should get out of farming altogether. Predictably, supporters of the tobacco program scorned this plan. James Graham, a relentless Democratic partisan and North Carolina's commissioner of agriculture, described "Nixon-Ford-Butz" as pursuing feudal policies that only benefited "fat cats" and Midwestern farmers. "If the Washington boys had their way," Graham said on the stump for Carter in 1976, farming would be-come a "plant and pray proposition with everyone producing as much as they could or wanted."[14]

Carter's election was a reprieve, but not a solution to the problems faced by the federal tobacco program. Throughout his tenure, Carter repeatedly assured farmers that as long as he was president, the federal tobacco pro-gram would be safe.[15] But Health, Education, and Welfare (HEW) secretary Joseph Califano contradicted the president's assurances. On the fourteenth anniversary of the 1964 *Surgeon General's Report*, Califano announced a vig-orous anti-tobacco program. Califano, who had been a four-pack-a-day smoker during his days as a White House aide in the Johnson administra-tion, took on the industry with a convert's zeal. He declared tobacco "Public Enemy No. 1," and said that smokers were committing "slow motion sui-cide" in making a choice responsible for more than 300,000 preventable deaths a year. He proposed a ban on all smoking on commercial aircraft, a reinstatement of free airtime for anti-smoking commercials, and a ban on smoking in HEW buildings.[16]

Industry reaction was furious. In Kentucky, the legislature called for Cal-ifano's impeachment. North Carolina's popular Democratic governor James Hunt urged Carter to fire the HEW secretary. On the ground in to-bacco country, bumper stickers began appearing on the side of pickup trucks: "Califano Is Dangerous to Your Health." After the publication of the 1979 *Surgeon General's Report*, the industry dubbed him "Ayatollah Cal-ifano." House Speaker Tip O'Neill, a friend and confidant to Califano, urged him to resign, telling him that the industry might well put out a hit on him. In the end, the industry settled for Califano's job rather than his life. Carter fired the secretary in the summer of 1979 as part of a broad Cabinet shakeup that revealed the administration's concerns about the 1980 presidential campaign.[17]

In 1978, a survey by the *Flue-Cured Tobacco Farmer* magazine found both sympathy and skepticism for Carter's position: a mix of emotions that re-flected the administration's muddled messaging. "I think Carter's trying for the growers' and the nonsmokers' vote together," said one critical North Carolina farmer. "He bends over backwards to try to keep from being ac-cused of favoring the South," groused another—though the farmer did indicate that he approved of the president's performance. Carter, one to-bacco farmer observed, had performed "very well considering both sides and outside sentiment."[18]

Congress, once the unquestioned domain of the tobacco lobby, was even less predictable than the executive branch. Democrats newly elected in the wake of Watergate were publicly questioning the tobacco program. These "Watergate Babies" were less steeped in New Deal economic orthodoxies than their older Democratic colleagues, and more likely to embrace the public interest critique of regulated industries. Many of them won seats on promises to clean up government, and their arrival on Capitol Hill dimin-ished the power of committee chairmen—positions historically dominated by conservative southern Democrats. The crop of Democrats elected in 1974 heightened the rift in the party's coalition. "We are not a bunch of little Hu-bert Humphreys," announced freshman Colorado senator Gary Hart, who would fight tobacco alongside Ted Kennedy in the Senate Subcommittee on Health in the 1970s and 1980s.[19]

This new generation of Democrats represented the material interests of their suburban constituents: environmental protection, anti-inflation, def-icit reduction, civil liberties.[20] Their districts were places without ties to organized labor or agriculture, places where government-fostered economic organization was understood as a source of corruption and cause of pollu-tion. Henry Waxman was perhaps the most consequential of the Democrats elected to Congress in the wake of Watergate. By the late 1970s, the Los An-geles representative had already challenged—and bested—North Carolina Democrat L. Richardson Preyer for the chairmanship of the House Subcom-mittee on Health and the Environment. Leapfrogging over the more se-nior, moderate, and, most importantly, tobacco-representing Preyer, the lib-eral Waxman, whose affluent district included Beverley Hills, Santa Monica, Malibu, and parts of Hollywood, represented a changing of the party's guard.[21]

Preyer was a former federal judge whose decade of experience in Congress earned him the endorsement of the *Washington Post* for the chairmanship. But Waxman's contribution of surplus campaign money to the coffers of ten committee members who were to vote on the seat swung the chairman-ship to the Californian.[22] The seniority system that had helped ensure tobacco's privileged status in Washington was waning, even as Waxman's particularly transactional acquisition of the seat made his win less than a moral victory.[23] Waxman used his chairmanship as a bully pulpit, and by the early 1980s, he was recognized as the industry's most formidable foe on Capitol Hill—"something special," in the words of Ralph Nader, and "a very dangerous adversary," in those of a Philip Morris attorney.[24]

Republicans had traditionally posed more of a threat to the interests of tobacco growers than Democrats. With its general aversion to taxes, skepticism if not contempt for the new breed of public interest crusader, and an openness toward the prerogatives of big business, the Republican Party had been favored by cigarette manufacturers since the era of James Duke.[25] The tobacco program offered Republicans a new opportunity to opine against big government hypocrisy. But this time, they enjoyed the support of anti-tobacco Democrats. In the Senate, Orrin Hatch and Jake Garn—Utah's duo of Mormon Republicans—represented the anti-tobacco sentiments of their constituents. In 1977, Garn joined Democrats Ted Kennedy and Gary Hart to co-sponsor a major cigarette tax hike, while Hatch would enjoy a decades-long partnership with Henry Waxman focused on tobacco and drug regulation. Having jointly shepherded a 1984 bill requiring a stiffer warning label on the cigarette pack and, for the first time, the disclosure of cigarette additives, Waxman and Hatch garnered a reputation as "the capital's Odd Couple."[26]

Some Republicans seized upon tobacco exports under international aid programs. In 1977, Colorado representative James Johnson led the House effort to eliminate tobacco exports under the Food for Peace program. Mark Hatfield, an Oregon Republican who had introduced a Senate version of Father Robert Drinan's Nonsmoker Protection Act in 1975, spearheaded the Senate effort. The tobacco state delegations still had a few punches left, though. In one of his final legislative acts, Hubert Humphrey submitted a substitute amendment on behalf of tobacco state representatives. The "Humphrey Amendment" stipulated that food and fiber would be given priority over tobacco in PL-480 sales, which was how the program already worked in practice.[27] The tobacco program thus remained untouched. And when Johnson launched another attack on tobacco that year, threatening to introduce a bill to defund the tobacco program, he was met with a warning by North Carolina Democrat Charlie

Rose. If Johnson tried to take down tobacco, the House Committee on Agriculture would have to consider the cost and efficacy of subsidies to Colorado sugar beet growers. "We sweetened the pot," Rose told the *Washington Post*. "We wanted help on tobacco. We convinced him to modify his position."[28] As long as the agricultural committee held leverage through subsidies, the politics of government largess required moral compromise. This momentary battle won, tobacco's representatives were well aware that the program was out of step with the winds of Washington. Hubert Humphrey died of cancer in January 1978. The nationalist, pro-producer liberalism that he represented was also ailing in the face of bipartisan opposition.

In 1981, a duo of legislative attacks on the tobacco program forced tobacco farmers to rewrite their program. In June, Wisconsin Republican Thomas Petri introduced the "Tobacco Deregulation Act"—a framing its author hoped would resonate in Reagan's Washington. Meanwhile, Ohio Democrat Robert Shamansky introduced an amendment to the pending Farm Bill that would have abolished the tobacco program. By the time this amendment came for a floor vote, the House had already voted to dramatically restructure the sugar and peanut programs. Shamansky derided the tobacco program as a "monstrosity" out of step with the current vogue for "getting the Government out of the market economy." His plan to terminate the program was thwarted only with a promise written into the Farm Bill that, in accordance with "the intent of Congress," the program would be revised the following year, in a piece of stand-alone legislation.[29] This was a pyrrhic victory—a final cigarette before the execution: tobacco was the only commodity program in the 1981 Farm Bill not to come under the budgetary buzz saw. The following year, the No Net Cost Tobacco Act of 1982 was passed.

Tobacco Deregulation

Years of public debate from the time of Nader's indictment of the "tobacco subsidy" to the passage of the No Net Cost Tobacco Act revealed the economically and politically fraught nature of tobacco associationalism, and the inability of tobacco policymakers to shut out the demands of a public that extended beyond program beneficiaries. During the flush and smoky

1950s and 1960s, the farm press and tobacco industry urged the "tobacco family" to come together in defense of their shared investment in smoking. In 1981, the Tobacco Institute commissioned a study of the attitudes held by members of the tobacco family—company employees, growers, retailers, and wholesalers. Finding the "tobacco family . . . solidly behind the industry," the study recommended that the Tobacco Institute intensify outreach activities to tobacco farmers.[30]

Much as it did with unionized tobacco workers, the tobacco industry eagerly held up the family tobacco farmer as an emblem of the industry's virtues: hard-working, modest, patriotic.[31] But amid public hostility, a solid scientific consensus against smoking, and increasing intolerance of "big government" programs, the siege mentality exacerbated tensions within the tobacco supply chain. The bumper stickers that farmers affixed to their pickup trucks—"Thanks 4 Smoking," "Califano Is Dangerous to My Health"—did little to conceal the dissent within tobacco's ranks.[32] Spilling onto public display in congressional hearings, intramural fights bruised the image of the family tobacco farmer—a commodity that had been cultivated nearly as tenderly as the prized leaf itself. By the early 1980s, the tobacco family looked more like *All in the Family* than *Ozzie and Harriet*.

The twin pillars of the tobacco program itself rived the tobacco family asunder: production rights and the price of tobacco. These problems had both a local and a global dimension. Within tobacco-producing communities, active growers—frequently younger and managing larger, multifarm operations—resented inactive allotment holders, who lived off the rental income generated by leasing their allotment. Meanwhile, cigarette manufacturers began to import an increasing amount of cheaper, foreign leaf. The federal price support—a price floor for American growers, a ceiling for leaf produced in countries with low labor costs—had become an incubator for the development of foreign tobacco production. In agriculture as in auto manufacturing, the unforeseen consequences of postwar domestic welfare-state investments and foreign development aid were coming home to roost for American producers.[33] Japanese cars and Brazilian flue-cured eroded the paradigm of producer-centered supply management that had well served organized labor and agriculture in the postwar decades.

Growers had reason to suspect the motives of the cigarette manufacturers—the rich, overbearing patriarch of the tobacco family. Through an act of bureaucratic subterfuge, manufacturers had for years been importing increasing amounts of cheap, lower-quality tobacco, displacing American-grown leaf inside the cigarette. The authors of the Agricultural Adjustment Act understood that imports would wreck the entire price support scheme; price supports, after all, were by definition higher than prevailing world prices. For this reason, the Act contained a provision that authorized the president to impose import limitations on articles that "render or tend to render ineffective, or materially interfere with, certain agricultural programs."[34]

Domestic supply restriction could only be effective with a commitment to agricultural protectionism. This state-centric agriculture policy withstood early Cold War efforts to promote international trade. The 1947 General Agreement on Tariffs and Trade (GATT) not only exempted agriculture—the only economic sector so excluded—but also permitted export subsidies for American commodities, essentially giving farmers a leg up in world markets while making sure world prices did not interfere with domestic programs.[35]

Cigarette manufacturers subverted import limitations by altering their product—cheapening it and reducing the content of unadulterated tobacco leaf. Manufacturers increased their purchases of tobacco classified as "scrap," which was subject to lower import duties because it had not been considered a substitute and competitor for flue-cured leaf. Beginning in 1975, farm organizations sounded alarm bells to members of Congress and trade representatives, warning of the "strangulation of our tobacco farmers" by "'so-called' developing countries."[36] Between 1972 and 1979, scrap imports rose from 27,000 to 72,200 tons. On a percentage basis, scrap increased from 25 percent to 42 percent of total tobacco imports. "Imported tobacco continues to cost around one-half to two-thirds that of comparable domestic tobacco," noted a 1981 North Carolina Farm Bureau report on the problem. American tobacco constituted a decreasing share of American cigarettes—despite a supposed industry-wide reverence for the superior quality of American leaf. By 1981, scrap constituted 30 percent of American manufacturers' tobacco use in cigarettes.[37]

The impact of imports upon U.S. tobacco producers was the subject of several investigations under the Carter and Reagan administrations. That is to say, no investigation led to the passage of legislation that satisfied growers. Two days before leaving office, Carter ordered an International Trade Commission (ITC) investigation of the tobacco import situation—a political move intended to help North Carolina's Democratic governor Jim Hunt shore up farmer support against Jesse Helms, whom Hunt planned to challenge for the Senate in 1984.

What Carter viewed as an easy political favor turned into something altogether dangerous for the program. "Are you confident that public hearings would not result in legislative reaction that would be adverse to the interests of tobacco producers in your and other states?" Reagan's secretary of agriculture, John Block, asked Hunt.[38] After all, an attempt to defund the tobacco program had already garnered forty-two votes in the Senate. What might be the result of a full public airing of the program? The problem of cheap, imported tobacco was created by the price-raising features of the program itself. When the investigation concluded in the summer of 1981, the ITC found that tobacco imports did not, in fact, interfere with the domestic tobacco program, despite testimony to the contrary. And by a 3–1 vote, it recommended against import quotas.[39] Farmers would not be able to tariff their way back to solvency. The import issue reemerged a few years later. Facing what was considered to be a tough reelection race—polls in the spring of 1984 forecast a dead heat between Helms and Hunt—Helms loudly called for another ITC investigation into surging scrap imports, whose rise intensified with the strengthening of the dollar.

In 1984, Reagan was not particularly popular among farmers as a result of his administration's antipathy toward and mismanagement of farm programs. Office of Management and Budget director David Stockman—whom one agricultural economist described as possessed of a "tightfistedness" that was "penny-wise and not merely pound-foolish, but billion-dollars foolish"—was an object of special antipathy in tobacco-growing regions.[40] As an article in the 1984 *Progressive Farmer* proclaimed, "You may need a job if David Stockman gets his way."[41] In September of 1984, gearing up for a reelection campaign, the Reagan administration was thus particularly willing to inquire on the tobacco farmer's behalf, touting the North Carolina Farm Bureau's support for the request. Reagan and Helms both won reelection—the president by a landslide 62 percent in North Carolina, Helms by 4 points after what veteran political reporter Tom Wicker called "the ugliest and costliest race in the nation."[42] In February 1985, months after the campaign's tensions subsided, the ITC issued its recommendation: imports did not interfere with the domestic tobacco program. Restrictions on foreign leaf imports were once again rejected.[43] The inquiry had been election year theater.

Farmers felt these distant, global forces in their own backyards. For while the domestic price support system insulated them from global price fluctuations, it tethered them to the overall tobacco market via the quota system. As expensive American tobacco lost international market share, quota was slashed: in 1975 total quota for flue-cured tobacco stood at 1,491.4 million pounds. By 1981 that figure had fallen to 1,012.6 million pounds.[44]

By the late 1970s, not everybody who possessed production rights to tobacco was actively engaged in farming; in fact, most were not. A 1981 Government Accountability Office study found that 57 percent of flue-cured quota owners leased their rights to active growers.[45] Nonproducing quota holders were, essentially, rentiers who enjoyed high monthly rental payments for leasing their tobacco acreage and poundage. With less quota to go around overall, the cost of renting production rights went up. In the late 1970s, rental costs ate into more than a third of the profits from tobacco sales, at a time when input costs were already increasing due to inflation. Even the program's most stalwart champions conceded that "the cost of lease is a problem, a serious one," as Stabilization's longtime general manager put it to the *Flue Cured Tobacco Grower* in 1978.[46]

Don't Call It a Subsidy!

In response to the gathering storm over the tobacco program, the crop's defenders embraced a strategy of denial.[47] At every turn, politicians, farmers, and the industry-financed PR machine insisted that tobacco was not a recipient of government subsidy. Tobacco farmers simply received government-mandated *loans* on unwanted tobacco. Subsidies were handouts to the undeserving—the government deciding winners and losers. The tobacco loan program, by contrast, ensured a fair return for honest labor.

Jesse Helms, the Senate's most virulent critic of government support programs for the poor, put a fine point on the racialized entitlement of tobacco farmers. As the keynote speaker at the Tobacco Associates annual meeting in 1981, Helms lead a crowd in a kind of revival-style call-and-response.

"Now repeat after me," Helms thundered in his drawl. "There is no tobacco subsidy." The 500 farmers and warehousemen assembled at the Sheraton Hotel in Raleigh responded as one—an incantation they would find themselves repeating in the face of reports that put the cost of the tobacco program's losses at close to $50 million over its forty-seven-year history.[48] But the decade's revisions to the tobacco program revealed the hollowness of such denials. Tobacco farmers had indeed been granted a safety net. By the end of the decade, it was in tatters as different segments of the industry fought over what scraps remained.

These tensions between different classes of producers were fully on display at hearings on the program in Washington and in tobacco-producing districts. Growers who relied upon tobacco production for income favored the liberalization of the tobacco program. That is to say, they sought the relaxation of production controls and a reduction in the cost of renting allotments. They reasoned that if the price of tobacco fell in absence of a program, they would still be economically better off because they would no longer have to pay rent for the luxury of producing tobacco, and could thus expand their tobacco production. These businessmen-farmers welcomed the farm consolidation that was predicted to take place in the absence of the program.

Such commercial farmers were, however, a distinct minority. The vast majority of allotments were held by legacy owners of the new property created in the 1930s. Supporters of the price support system tended to portray this landlord class as comprised only of retired farmers and widows. In reality, old farmers and farm widows were just the most sympathetic allotment holders. "A very well-known poor tobacco farmer by the name of Mrs. Jesse Helms . . . is a beneficiary of this allotment," Shamansky observed in a floor debate over the fate of the program in 1981. Rich, nonfarming institutions like Duke University and Carolina Power and Light held allotments. Both institutions profited by renting to tobacco farmers.[49]

Held up to the light of public scrutiny, the federal tobacco program was, at best, puzzling to many Americans. With small farm size and high labor requirements, the dynamics of tobacco farming seemed to be of a different time and place. Depending on what aspect of the program one focused on, it could look either medieval or Rockwellian. The allotment system "preserved the small farms of the tobacco growing south, holding them in a state of suspended animation," read one sympathetic article in the *Washington Post*. The support system that priced American growers out of world markets also enabled tens of thousands of smaller farmers to remain in production. "There is absolutely nothing on this earth that can compete with tobacco money," a USDA economist told the newspaper—except, he added, "illegal smoking material." According to a 1980 USDA report, an acre of flue-cured tobacco netted farmers $2,700, as opposed to $150 for corn or $250 for soybeans.[50] In North Carolina, only 0.5 percent of the state's farmland was in tobacco production in 1980, yet the crop brought in more than a third of the state's farm income.[51]

Because the allotment system kept farm size relatively small, there were a great deal of tobacco farmers in the middle stratum of the farm income ladder, and relatively few at the top. According to a 1974 Census of Agriculture, only 15 percent of tobacco farms reported earnings over $40,000, as opposed to 26 percent of farms growing other staple commodities. As the general manager of Stabilization put it, the program "provided a better quality of life for families [than] could be achieved through the production of other crops."[52]

Indeed, the tobacco program sustained whole regional economies. Small farm size, heavy labor requirements, and a high-value crop meant that more people lived in tobacco-producing regions than in the sparsely populated wheat and corn belts. Tobacco was part of a productive supply chain with arteries that branched far beyond the cigarette manufacturers. Fertilizer producers and dealers, truckers, shippers, and warehouse workers were all invested in the continuation of the tobacco program. By assuring that all farmers got paid, the program also formed the basis for the consumer economies of regions where it was the number one money crop. Retailers, restaurants, car dealerships, department stores, and, most importantly, banks were fed by the reliable liquidity of farmers in late summer and early fall. This injection of capital into debt-ridden sleepy southern towns was, after all, precisely the goal of the New Deal's architects.[53]

Most importantly, the allotment system was capitalized into land values—the new property made real estate. Land with an allotment assigned to it carried double the value of similar property in the same county without an allotment. These production rights served as a source of collateral for their owners. Without the program, explained a North Carolina bank president, credit would "in many cases" dry up because the "bank's risk of loaning to tobacco producers would increase." "All banks," he explained at a 1977 hearing on the program, "would suffer earnings losses from lower interest income, lower deposit levels, trust accounts, and, just as important, the negative effect on retail trade."[54] The program did not just nourish the private sector; it enlarged the capacity of state and local governments to provide social services in rural places. Higher property values meant higher property taxes and greater revenues for state and local governments. This allowed "farm families to maintain their farms, educate their children, build schools, churches, hospitals, and contribute to the economic well-being of large areas of the state," according to an official at the Virginia Department of Agriculture and Commerce.[55]

By creating new forms of property and insulating tobacco producers from the fluctuations of the global market, the tobacco program enabled many Americans to possess the certainties of a middle-class life: a home, an occasional new car, decent schools, maybe college for the kids, and a secure retirement. And, in the process, it nurtured communities that, while certainly not posh, were at least populous enough to support schools, a main street, banks, churches, summer softball leagues, and movie theaters.[56] Agricultural economists affirmed these perceptions of tobacco communities. The director of the North Carolina Extension Service testified to Congress in 1978 that in the absence of the federal tobacco program, land values would drop, farms would consolidate, operations would mechanize, and rural communities would become hollowed out.[57]

Critics looked at tobacco dependent regions and did not see a quaint anachronism, or a testament to effective government intervention. They saw a program that was "archaic," even "feudal." In 1979, 120,000 of 193,500 flue-cured quota owners leased their production rights. In the media, stories circulated of quota owners, having inherited production rights from a father or grandfather, making thousands in rent, having never stepped onto "their" tobacco farm.[58] Even more damning were revelations that many nonfarm institutions were participants in the program, indirect beneficiaries of taxpayer transfers at the direct expense of those actually engaged in tobacco production. "What does Dorothy Helms, the wife of the U.S. Senator, have in common with Duke University, the North Carolina National Bank, the Roman Catholic diocese of Raleigh, Christ Unlimited of Apex, the Goodhope Baptist Church and the Southall Swim club?" the lead of a *Washington Post* story queried. "The answer is that they have a tobacco habit, of sorts."[59] Jesse Helms's unpopularity among his Democratic colleagues in Congress made the tobacco program an especially appealing target. As Senate Agriculture chairman after the Republican takeover of the chamber in 1980, Helms's support for tobacco—not a commodity, but a religion, Helms once explained—looked all the more hypocritical next to his vicious attacks on recipients of food stamps, school lunches, and foreign aid.[60]

Even program supporters began to openly question the operation of the allotment system. "I agree . . . that the leasing system has gotten out of hand," wrote one grower in the *Flue-Cured Tobacco Farmer.* "Why were the 1930s such magical years as to remain the basis for the tobacco allotments for 40 years more or less?"[61] Such disagreements began to divide even close relatives in the tobacco family. The editor of the *Flue-Cured Tobacco Farmer*—a Democrat, a Carter supporter, and a stalwart defender of federal price supports—warned as Reagan assumed office: "If tobacco growers don't keep their economic house in order, it may be done [in] from the outside."[62]

No Net (Cost)

Domestic politics and the global economy forced tobacco growers to get their house in order—or at least try to do so. The No Net Cost Tobacco Act was passed under the stewardship of tobacco congressmen in 1982. It required farmers to cover the full costs of the tobacco program, which taxpayers previously had to bear. Under No Net Cost, for each pound of tobacco that went into Stabilization, farmers had to pay a fee, initially 3 cents per pound of tobacco. This would be used to cover any losses in price support operations. The act also authorized the secretary of agriculture to revise price support levels downward for grades of tobacco for which there was excessive supply. Finally, the Act mandated a redistribution of allotments, putting more acreage into the hands of active growers and requiring nonfarm entities to sell their allotments by the end of 1983.

Even at its twilight, associationalism still guided program administration. The Act was originally proposed by a tobacco committee within the

North Carolina Farm Bureau Federation. Indeed, the "no net-cost assessment" was, essentially, a tax on tobacco entering Stabilization, harkening back to the processing tax of the First Agricultural Adjustment Act. Only this time growers themselves—and not cigarette manufacturers—were responsible for shouldering the program's financial burden. The financial risk of the program was cast back onto producers, a hallmark of emerging economizing approaches to social insurance.[63] Organized producers struggled to knit together a safety net from the frayed fabric of liberalism. What they came up with had holes big enough to fall straight through.

Growers grudgingly accepted the assessment as the price of the program's continuation.[64] Representative Charlie Rose, the Democratic chairman of the tobacco subcommittee and a voice for smaller-scale farmers in Washington, understood that any change to the program would represent "tampering with the farmer's safety net."[65] At first it seemed as though there might be political and economic benefits to the Act's passage. As longtime North Carolina representative L. H. Fountain put it, the revisions would make the tobacco program "strong enough to withstand the continued assaults of its severest critics in the years to come."[66] And, moreover, it ennobled the tobacco program as a sacrifice, not a benefit. Rose betrayed a note of pride in pointing out that with the passage of No Net Cost, "we are the first commodity to assume full responsibility" for program costs. Of course, Rose did not dwell on the fact that the 1981 farm bill took even more dramatic cuts to the sugar, peanut, and milk programs. Finally, by forcing tobacco farmers to assume a share of program costs, it was hoped that they would begin to produce more tobacco acceptable to buyers. In other words, farmers would be drawn closer to market dynamics.

In one sense this happened—except that the market for tobacco was still controlled by a cigarette oligopoly. No Net Cost laid a trap for program participants because it allowed cigarette companies to drown the program by refusing to buy—a restoration of the type of power possessed by the companies during the faltering days of the Tri-State Co-op. By 1983, the first full year of the revised program's implementation, the No Net Cost assessment had more than doubled to 7 cents per pound to cover the larger-than-projected intake of tobacco into Stabilization's pool. A quarter of all flue-cured tobacco produced in 1982 went into the loan pool.[67] Having destabilized the program, the companies agreed to "rescue" growers by buying their surplus tobacco from Stabilization at a deep discount. Tobacco farmers blamed cigarette manufacturers for their surplus tobacco problems.[68] After all, the cigarette companies were actively sponsoring the development of tobacco production in low labor cost countries like Brazil and Malawi—nations edging American growers out of the market. And how could growers believe that R. J. Reynolds and Philip Morris really supported the tobacco program when they chided growers for not remaining internationally competitive?

The companies were acutely aware of the rift within the tobacco family.[69] As they publicly touted their commitment to the tobacco program, tobacco executives privately wondered if they really needed tobacco farmers any longer. "The political base provided by the tobacco program in past years has deteriorated significantly," an R. J. Reynolds lobbyist wrote in a 1983 memo. "The political price being paid to maintain the program warrants a review of the political base which might be provided under a no program scenario."[70] In other words, was the tobacco program a greater political liability than the tobacco farmer was a political asset? R. J. Reynolds's "Pride in Tobacco" public relations campaign—newspaper ads, hats, license plates, t-shirts, and community festivals aimed at shoring up grower support for the industry's larger political battles—hid a cooling commitment to the farm program.

Growers were less important to manufacturers as each year passed. In 1982, Congress doubled the cigarette excise tax, which had been untouched since 1951. This move resulted in a predicted dip in cigarette sales, which declined 4 percent in 1983. But tobacco companies were swimming in profits even as they howled about tax hikes. They simply raised prices to more than offset the demand effect of the tax increase. Between 1980 and 1984, tobacco enjoyed a return on investment of more than 20 percent—more than double the return in the rest of the corporate world.[71]

As corporate profits swelled, farmers faced slimmer margins. During the 1980s, price supports were frozen and then lowered, and quota was slashed as imports continued unabated. The exodus of small tobacco producers from farming was a quiet chapter during a decade of farm crisis that saw the dramatic foreclosure of thousands of Midwestern farms. The nationwide trend of farm consolidation and capital-intensive production played out in the tobacco region in miniature.[72] Flue-curing, the very definition of American tobacco, was nearly gone. Instead, metal bulk-curing barns cured huge piles of unsorted, mechanically harvested leaves. The old, cube-shaped, wooden flue-curing barns stood empty and decaying in the fields—ghosts of an era only a decade past, an era in which the work was hard, but the returns were good.[73]

In 1986, surplus tobacco production required yet another rewrite of the tobacco program. By 1985, Stabilization was holding the equivalent of an entire year's worth of flue-cured tobacco in storage—storage that farmers were going bust trying to cover. Farm organizations and congressmen furiously scrambled to arrange a bailout of the program. The rescue package further tilted the balance of power toward the cigarette makers. Manufacturers agreed to buy the stored tobacco at fire sale prices—up to 90 percent off the loan price. In exchange, growers were required to accept lower price support levels—levels that insured that cigarette makers could continue to buy leaf from American and foreign growers at lower prices. Companies were also given more control in setting quota levels, an informal transfer of power from the Department of Agriculture to R. J. Reynolds and Philip Morris. Tobacco growers were, once again, at the industry's mercy. This was a kind of associationalism as well, only one that empowered organized capital at the expense of organized agriculture. In its twilight, the tobacco program revealed itself to have been a greater subsidy than most of its defenders even realized, redistributing political as well as economic power.

Dr. Unqualified, Dr. of Uncertainty

At the very same time that Congress began to unspool the safety net swaying unsteadily below farmers, smoking restrictions grew to cover an ever-larger expanse of public space. Retrenchment from federal tobacco regulation paralleled the expansion of tobacco regulation at the local and state level. This expansion was an expression of what legal scholar Heather Gerken has called progressive federalism—the idea that localism may protect minorities and dissenters from the marginalization they might experience at the national level.[74] In some localities, nonsmokers could rule public space because they not only outnumbered smokers (as they did nationally), but also because the tobacco industry possessed fewer resources outside of Washington. In cities and even in some state houses, the discourse of non-smokers' rights was transformed into the practice of nonsmoker rule—a legal reconfiguration accelerated and legitimated by the business case against smoking ascendant in many workplaces.

The local cause of nonsmokers' rights got a substantial boost from the encouragement and endorsement of Reagan's surgeon general, C. Everett Koop, highlighting the dynamic interaction between federal officials and local activists. In the case of smoking, the surgeon general had decidedly less power than local activists to make policy; but activists had decidedly less visibility than the surgeon general, perhaps Reagan's most popular appointee. Known as "Chick" to intimates (short for chicken coop), Koop cut a distinctive figure in Reagan-era Washington. With a bear-like body, a penchant for bow ties, and an Abe Lincoln–style beard, Koop understood that the power of his office lay in persuasion. "My strong point is to say things as honestly I can, in a strong and authoritative voice," Koop recalled in an interview with the *New York Times*. "People take what the Surgeon General says very seriously, and that makes a difference."[75] The military uniform he donned for all professional appearances, a nod to the Office of the Surgeon General's origins in the Marine Hospital Service, embodied Koop's unique blend of showmanship and gravitas (see Figure 7.1).

When his appointment was announced in the spring of 1981, few of the Democrats in the Senate responsible for Koop's confirmation were apt to take him seriously. The pediatric surgeon was seen as wildly unqualified in the realm of public health—his appointment a sop to the anti-abortion wing of Reagan's winning coalition.[76] Indeed, Koop's only previous statements bearing on public health were articulated from a position of his Christian faith. He authored a book announcing his faith-based opposition to abortion and euthanasia, and had appeared in a few films with Pastor Francis Schaeffer, a friend and fellow evangelical Presbyterian. As a board member of the National Right to Life Committee and Americans United for Life, Koop spoke of abortion in the strident tones of a man unused to compromise—unsurprising for a chief surgeon. He opposed amniocentesis as a "search and destroy" mission; condemned religious denominations that supported the right to an abortion as guilty of "depravity"; and argued that abortion itself was a slippery slope to euthanasia, "the very beginnings

Figure 7.1 Surgeon General C. Everett Koop, dressed in uniform, salutes the grave of Luther Terry at Arlington Cemetery in 1985. (National Library of Medicine)

of a political climate that led to Auschwitz, Dachau, and Belsen."[77] The nation's major newspapers roundly rejected Koop as unqualified, selected, in the words of the *New York Times* editorial page, "not for his medical skills, but for his political compatibility."[78] Koop ultimately placated Senate Democrats, who had held up his nomination for months, by promising not to "use any government post as a pulpit for ideology," and retiring from the "pro-life circuit."[79] Jesse Helms was ecstatic.[80] But only at first.

Koop turned out to be the most effective surgeon general of the twentieth century on the anti-smoking issue. Henry Waxman, chairman of the House Subcommittee on Health and the Environment, had opposed Koop's nomination. "Dr. Koop frightens me," Waxman said in 1981. But Koop quickly allayed the anxieties of Waxman and his allies within the anti-tobacco movement. The surgeon general, who had never previously been associated with anti-tobacco statements and even copped to enjoying an occasional pipe break, began to speak the language of the nonsmokers' rights movement early in his tenure. A few months after his confirmation, he released the 1982 *Surgeon General's Report on Smoking and Health,* a document Koop had done little to oversee, but insisted on reading and thoroughly marking-up before final revisions.[81]

The 1982 *Report* did not tell Americans much that they had not heard before: cigarette smoking was "the chief preventable cause of death in our society." But it did quash any residual hopes held by the tobacco industry that Reagan's antiregulatory crusade might insulate them from sweeping government pronouncements. Candidate Reagan had, after all, promised North Carolinians that "my own Cabinet members will be far too busy with substantive matters to waste their time proselytizing against the dangers of cigarette smoking"—a veiled reference to the hated Califano's anti-smoking crusade.[82] And the administration had crippled the Office of Smoking and Health, cutting its budget and staff significantly.[83] Koop overcame these constraints by leveraging the work of nongovernmental health groups, and encouraging policy change at the local level.[84]

The 1982 *Report* did signal one important new direction for research and policy: the health risk posed by "involuntary tobacco smoke." This framing of the nonsmoker issue was catnip to anti-smoking activists. "Involuntary smoking" drew attention to smoking as an assault on the unwilling, the physicality of forced inhalation.[85] While noting the technical difficulty of quantifying nonsmokers' exposures to tobacco smoke, the *Report* raised the possibility that "some [harmful chemical] constituents occur in markedly higher concentrations in sidestream than in mainstream smoke." How these chemicals actually affected involuntary smokers was less clear and depended upon a multitude of variables, but the report did note an animal study and one suggestive human study that pointed toward human absorption of toxic compounds.[86]

The most compelling evidence of the risks of passive smoking came from three major prospective cohort studies published in 1981 that examined the health outcomes of nonsmoking wives of smoking husbands: the Hirayama study from Japan, and two similar studies—one from Greece and one from the United States. Although the Greek and Japanese studies differed in methodology, both found a statistically significant elevation in lung cancer risk among the nonsmoking wives of smoking husbands.[87] And they also found that nonsmoking wives faced a greater likelihood of lung cancer if they were married to heavier smokers. A third study cited in the *Report* was more equivocal. An analysis of data collected by the American Cancer Society between 1960 and 1970 showed an elevated risk to the nonsmoking wives of smokers, but the risk did not rise to the level of statistical significance. Taken together, the three studies "raise concerns about a possible serious public health problem" resulting from involuntary smoking, the *Report* concluded.[88] Even so, Koop conceded that the link between passive smoking and lung cancer was not, as it were, airtight—that "the limitations in the data and study design do not allow a judgment on causality at this time."[89] However, "prudence dictates that nonsmokers' exposure to second-hand tobacco smoke be minimized to the greatest extent possible."[90] By noting the absence of abundant "available evidence" on the relationship between passive smoking and disease, the *Report* staked out a research agenda for scientists. Ten epidemiological studies published in the next five years demonstrated an increased risk of lung cancer for nonsmokers who lived with smokers.[91]

Despite having virtually zero statutory authority, something less than a scientific mandate, and certainly no political directive from the Reagan administration, Koop leveraged his own considerable popularity to pressure others to act where the federal government would not. In May of 1984, Koop wrote a speech that he planned to give at the American Lung Association Annual Meeting in Miami Beach. Fearing reprisals from the administration, he did not solicit input from his colleagues, let alone show his draft around the office. "Looking resplendent in his whites," one Tobacco Institute attendee sarcastically observed, Koop issued a call for a "Smoke-free society by the year 2000." Taking stock of the strides made against smoking during the 1980s, Koop attributed declines in cigarette consumption to education and the mounting cost of smoking to smokers.

But, above all, Koop attributed the shift in smoking culture to the "new *militancy of the non-smoking consumer, voter, and taxpayer.*"[92] Smoking was "becoming socially unacceptable," he crowed, borrowing the language of the nonsmokers' rights movement. "Many hostesses would like to ban smoking by guests in their homes, but are concerned with the social amenities," Koop observed, unwittingly recalling Clara Gouin's early nonsmoking coffee klatches with friends. "Now, the 140 million non-smokers have an acceptable way to notify guests that they are entering a nonsmoking household. An octagon brass plaque with the now familiar 'thank you for not smoking' can be screwed to the door [jamb] just above your door bell button." Here, too, Koop evoked, perhaps unconsciously, the pioneering work of Betty Carnes, the force behind the nation's first statewide anti-smoking law and the designer of the "thank you for not smoking" sign.

Koop's address drew upon the legal and cultural successes of the nonsmokers' rights movement. Perhaps seeking to blunt criticism from the Reagan administration, Koop insisted that the goal of a "smoke-free society by the year 2000" ought to be *the triumph primarily of private citizens and of the private sector, and not of the government."*[93] It was clear, however, that when Koop said government, he meant the *federal* government. His march through the public-health successes of the 1970s and 1980s dwelled on Arizona's smoking ban, Maryland's ban on smoking in health-care facilities, San Francisco's workplace smoking law, and the "more than 30 states and hundreds of local communities [that] have followed suit."[94] Koop especially applauded the business case against smoking, singling out Virginia's Alexandria, Arlington, and Fairfax counties for requiring police officers not to smoke in order to avoid costly compensation and pension claims. The key to ushering in the smoke-free utopia lay in aggressive nonsmoking citizenship, "demand[ing] smoke-free hotels, taxis, rental cars, waiting rooms, offices, schools and restaurants."[95] The speech demonstrated Koop's genius for spinning the dross of federal lassitude into the gold of vigorous state, local, and private activity. It was hard for even pro-tobacco forces within the administration to argue with Koop as he stood in his white, starched navy uniform, disavowing the heavy hand of the federal government while praising the thousands of cost-conscious decisions made by the private sector.

Passive Smoking, Active Government

There was a synergy to the words of federal officials and the deeds of local activists. Local nonsmokers' rights organizations heard the call for a "smoke-free society" as a catalyst to further action. In California, Stanton

Glantz, a biostatistician, professor at the University of California–San Francisco and the president of Californians for Non-Smokers' Rights, the successor organization to California GASP, took notice of Koop's widely publicized address. Glantz saw a model for ushering in a smoke-free society. "Activities at the state and local level are particularly effective because campaign contributions [are] less important and constituent pressure is more effective," Glantz wrote to Matthew Myers, the general counsel for the Coalition on Smoking OR Health, a Washington-based organization composed of the American Cancer Society, American Lung Association, and American Heart Association. "With the exception of the tobacco-producing states, the constituent power is strongly with us."[96] Sometimes the relationship between federal officials and activists occurred behind the scenes. Before departing as an FTC commissioner, Michael Pertschuk quietly met with Glantz to instruct him in "how to do nonsmokers' rights legislation."[97] Pertschuk, who had chaired the FTC under Carter but was increasingly out of step with the pro-corporate views of his Reagan-appointed colleagues, counseled Glantz to focus on "the organization of indigenous local groups made up of concerned local leaders and citizens."[98]

The arrows of influence led from the federal government to the states and to cities—and back again. For example, in response to a request by the president of the Michigan chapter of the American Lung Association, Koop penned a letter warning of the risks posed by passive smoking. The Lung Association president then read from the letter as part of his testimony in favor of a clean indoor air act. And the organization also distributed a copy of the letter to the entire Michigan legislature, which ultimately passed a Clean Indoor Air Act in 1986.[99] Koop's words were also distributed to the city council of Lansing, Michigan, as it deliberated the passage of a local ordinance. With Koop's implied endorsement, the Lung Association president vowed to drive the tobacco industry's lobbyist crazy with the introduction of local ordinances around the state. It was a promise that the industry's lobbyist in Michigan identified as a "major problem," as he could not be "trooping all over the State week after week on the series of local issues."[100] At all levels of government, tobacco's friends and foes well understood that, in Pertschuk's words, "those governments . . . which are closest to the citizens they serve, tend to be the least susceptible to external influence."[101]

The passage of smoking restrictions at the local level shaped the debate at the federal level too. In 1985, Alaska Republican Ted Stevens introduced a Non-Smokers' Rights Act in the Senate, which would have restricted smoking in all U.S. government buildings, mirroring statewide laws in Minnesota, Utah, Nebraska, Connecticut, Maine, and New Jersey, as well as in hundreds of cities. In his opening remarks to several days of testimony, Stevens cited the success of nonsmoking laws, the strict San Francisco municipal code, and the policies voluntarily adopted at Boeing and Pacific Bell. Joseph Califano was the first witness to testify—a symbolic repudiation of his ouster as HEW Secretary. Koop testified that "protection of nonsmokers' rights" was "adequately justified in the scientific literature."[102] Reciting a blizzard of scientific studies pointing to the elevated risk posed by smoky environments, Koop's statement previewed the forthcoming *Surgeon General's Report* from 1986—the first devoted entirely to the "health consequences of involuntary smoking."[103]

To no one's surprise, Stevens's bill died of legislative asphyxiation, smothered on the Senate's calendar. But Stevens's efforts were not futile. Nonsmoker protections in federal workplaces were ultimately realized through administrative means. General Services Administration (GSA) administrator Terence Golden suggested as much during his time in front of the Senate subcommittee, vowing to use his authority "whether or not" the Non-Smokers' Rights Act was enacted.[104] By late 1986, Golden announced that government buildings would prohibit smoking except in designated spaces. It was the largest workplace-smoking policy ever enacted, shaping the routines, interactions, and bodies of more than 800,000 Americans in 7,000 government buildings across the country. As significantly, Stevens used the bill's introduction to request information on the health and economic consequences of passive smoking from the Office of Technology Assessment (OTA), a bureau charged with providing scientific analyses to Congress.

The sixty-page OTA report provided a summation of research into the health effect of passive smoking, the implementation of workplace smoking laws around the United States, and the cost-benefit estimates of workplace-smoking restrictions. Finding "the data sufficient to warrant serious concern," the OTA portrayed workplace-smoking restrictions as offering tremendous upside and little downside to employers. When the GSA issued its rules in late 1986, Constance Horner, the director of the Office of Personnel Management, called the decision "a matter of health and productivity," citing cost estimates by the Heart Association, the OTA, and William Weis, the management professor and anti-smoking consultant.[105] Savvy to the possibilities his endorsement held, Koop squeezed further mileage out of the OTA report. The surgeon general sent letters to governors and big-city mayors outlining the GSA regulations and model legislation for Clean Indoor Air Acts—legislation attributed to Americans for Non-Smokers' Rights, the successor to Berkeley GASP, but actually developed by FTC commissioner Pertschuk.[106] What began as a seemingly futile legislative exercise ultimately resulted in millions of Americans being subject to stronger smoking rules at work—all without any action from Congress itself.

The OTA report was just the tip of the iceberg. By the end of the year, two more major assessments warned of the dangers of second hand smoke. The National Academy of Sciences (NAS) was tasked by the EPA and the Department of Health and Human Services with studying the uncertainties involved in estimating nonsmoker exposures. The formulation of this request was consistent with the Reagan-era attitude toward health hazards. "We must assume that life takes place in a mine field of risks from hundreds, perhaps thousands of substances," EPA administrator William Ruckelshaus said in a speech to the NAS. In a world filled with myriad risks—each subject to methodological uncertainty in its quantification and ultimate effects—the government could hardly be expected to protect everyone from the chance of an untoward outcome. Outcomes were uncertain but the cost of regulation could be illustrated with the brutal certainty of the ledger.

The political embrace of epistemological uncertainty dovetailed with the tobacco industry's longstanding strategy of cultivating doubt. But Koop did not perceive exposure to someone else's cigarette as an unavoidable consequence of modern life. By 1986, Koop was exceedingly popular, having burnished a reputation as a man of scientific integrity, unafraid, when evidence dictated, to take positions that ran contrary to the political and moral preferences of the Reagan administration. He spoke frankly and pragmatically about safe sex while the Christian flank of the Reagan coalition evangelized abstinence. He described AIDS as a preventable sexually transmitted disease that claimed too many as its victims, not as a punishment for a sinful life. And despite his own moral commitments—the reason why he was appointed surgeon general in the first place—Koop resisted administration pressure to assert that abortion caused breast cancer.

More than scientific rigor, Koop's pragmatism was on display as he rolled out the 1986 *Surgeon General's Report* on involuntary smoking. Calling the data in the *Report* abundant and cohesive, and therefore plausibly allowing "a judgment that involuntary smoking can cause lung cancer in nonsmokers," Koop further asserted that it was "certain that a substantial proportion of the lung cancers in nonsmokers are due to ETS [environmental tobacco smoke] exposure."[107] But the surgeon general's prefatory remarks gave way in the subsequent 300 pages to much more hedged and nuanced interpretations of scientific studies.[108] The tobacco industry's technique of doubt mongering was already well-known. Big Tobacco had cried wolf too many times: its lack of credibility provided cover for Koop's rather sweeping statements, as did the fact that "an overwhelming majority of both smokers and nonsmokers" supported smoking restrictions. At the press conference unveiling the *Report*, Koop called it a turning point on par with the initial landmark 1964 report on smoking. "Most of the action starts at the bottom and goes to the top," he said, reiterating his preference for local action.[109] He was partially right: 1986 did mark a turning point, but the path from bottom to top did not run in a straight line.

"In Deep Shit"

Ironically, it was on the issue of secondhand smoke—an issue where actual uncertainty existed, where scientists of good faith disagreed on the magnitude of risk if not on the existence of risk itself—that the tobacco industry was unable to stem the regulatory tide.[110] The industry could not keep up with the legislation at the local and state level—though it tried by astroturfing communities with pro-smoking organizations, especially with so-called "smokers' rights" groups.[111] And from the earliest days of the quest for smoke-free air, validated risks had taken a backseat to nonsmokers' demands for recognition. Whether environmental tobacco smoke was responsible for 500 or 8,400 excess deaths per year was beside the point. Nonsmokers outnumbered smokers. They possessed more economic, social, and educational capital. Why did they have to accept any environmental tobacco smoke—especially if it came with a price tag?

The tobacco industry was aware of the political peril posed by the passive smoking issue. In 1987, lawyers and executives for Philip Morris (PM) met at Hilton Head, South Carolina, to devise strategies to combat the ETS problem. With a flair for the dramatic and a touch of militarism, Philip Morris called its plan "Operation Down Under." John Rupp, a lawyer at Covington and Burling, set the tone of the retreat: "We are in deep shit," he announced.[112] A few of the 116 recommendations to emerge from the meeting included familiar tactics like "create our own expert," "more research," and "challenge publicly the scientific community."[113] Others were more ambitious, almost outlandish: "presidential primary initiative," "reestablish seniority system in Congress," "create a bigger political monster (AIDS)," and "get best-selling novel with subtle connection to evils of anti industry [forces]." But the overall tenor of the meeting and recommendations revealed an industry knocked back on its heels by the decentralized tactics of its adversaries in the anti-smoking movement. The PM execs parroted the language of the nonsmokers' rights movement, cribbing from Banzhaf's signature phrase to "Sue the Bastards!" and looking toward the development of a "Nader-like group to examine anti [tobacco] funding."[114]

The industry increasingly pinned its hopes on developing a broad, decentralized network to counter the force of the anti-tobacco movement at the local level. Notes from the meeting suggest that Philip Morris felt the Tobacco Institute to be ineffective and lacking credibility. To "chill" the heat of the passive-smoking issue, PM, then the nation's largest cigarette manufacturer, needed to shore up its traditional allies and make some new ones. It needed to tend to its "large family" of "consumers, leaf community, distributors, and vendors"—the diminished emphasis on farmers demonstrating the liability of the tobacco program. But what the industry really needed was a state-level strategy to "repeal smoking restrictions in target states." Until the 1970s, the industry's political clout had come from the disproportionate power of congressmen from tobacco-growing areas. But as the battle over tobacco shifted to states and cities, Philip Morris, at least, saw a need to cultivate further relationships with "libertarian and conservative groups," and adopt "the NRA strategy" to really "make it hurt"—to "take on vulnerable candidates, beat him/her, and let people know we did it."[115] In the dialectic between the nonsmokers' rights movement and Big To-bacco, the industry countered through emulation—and a whole lot of money.

The industry realized that, on some level, the battle over public space would be waged on civic, not scientific grounds. To be sure, the Tobacco Institute's instinctive reflex to manufacture doubt about ETS was still intact. Much as it financed the Center for Tobacco Research, a foundation that gave out grants to scientists to dispute smoking-and-health research, the industry also bankrolled the Center for Indoor Air Research (CIAR).[116] Recipients of CIAR's grants found that a broad array of toxins—dust in ventilation systems, decomposing animals in air conditioning ducts, hazardous fumes from carpets, toxic textile threads—were more responsible than ETS for causing widespread irritation and discomfort inside of buildings.

There was also a symmetry in the types of arguments made to discredit research on passive smoking. Beginning in the 1950s, the industry disputed that cigarettes were the primary cause of lung cancers and cardiovascular disease, and funded scholarships that advanced wider approaches to cancer causation like genetics, personality, and environment. With environmental tobacco smoke, the industry likewise sought to inflate the number of culprits responsible for nonsmoker discomfort and disease. As the Tobacco Institute's proposal for the development of CIAR put it, the new organization's goal was "to expand interest beyond the misplaced emphasis solely on environmental smoke."[117] Gray Robertson, the owner of an air-quality research firm, was the industry's favorite spokesman for this position. Robertson called himself "the Building Doctor," a reference to Sick Building Syndrome, a description of office environments that generated unexplainable symptoms in workers, mostly women.[118] In front of microphones, cameras, Congress, city councils, and state legislatures from Boise to Boston, Robertson testified that tobacco was wrongly scapegoated for the hazards of the modern office.[119] "Environmental tobacco smoke often is blamed for symptoms associated with Sick Building Syndrome," Robertson told *Choice*, an R. J. Reynolds publication. "The reason is obvious: the other pollutants in the air are invisible. Tobacco smoke is often the first visible sign of a far more serious problem."[120]

In the crucible of fighting anti-tobacco forces, the tobacco industry helped to forge a new model of business activism.[121] The groundwork had been laid a decade prior. Before he penned his famous 1971 memorandum laying out a strategy for business to press vigorously into the political fray, Lewis Powell watched John Banzhaf's activism with growing disbelief.[122] Powell, then a prominent Richmond lawyer, had served on the board of Philip Morris since 1964—a fateful year in the history of the cigarette business. In 1969, he consulted with Philip Morris executives as they sought to understand the growing "anti-cigarette environment" created by lawyers like Banzhaf. In one meeting, Powell articulated a strategy for the company that prefigured his advice for business generally.[123] Enabled by "sheep-like politicians" and the "attitudes of the intellectual class," the anti-smoking movement "now has the aspects of a national crusade." In response to a situation that looked worse by the day, the future Supreme Court Justice recommended "*confrontation* by industry" to make the case for smoking.[124] In reality, the industry had long embraced the strategy suggested by Powell—and then some. It is likely that Powell's intimate familiarity with the cigarette's rapid fall in social standing—and his observation of the industry's attempts to thwart the trend—shaped his recommendation for American businesses writ large.

By the late 1970s, Powell's vision of corporate activism had inspired new forms of lobbying. The Tobacco Institute and some individual cigarette manufacturers became important contributors to the American Legislative Exchange Council (ALEC), the conservative nonprofit responsible for drafting and disseminating model legislation on a range of issues. In 1979, the executive director of ALEC wrote to the president of the Tobacco Institute to solicit financial support.[125] The $10,000 yearly dues paid by member organizations were a good investment for an industry plagued with credibility problems. ALEC laundered the tobacco industry's influence, providing tobacco officials access to a network of legislators who may have been wary of cozying up to Big Tobacco in public, but were willing to do so under the cover of the anti-regulatory network. For example, in 1981 ALEC hosted a White House cabinet briefing with members of Congress, Reagan Cabinet officials, and the president himself. TI president Samuel Chilcote accepted the invitation to the exclusive meeting in the Pettigrew briefing room of the august Old Executive Office Building.[126]

Aside from providing the tobacco industry access to potentially wary legislators, ALEC propagated the industry's take on passive smoking. Through the 1980s, the organization proved "very helpful to us in getting solid evidence into the hands of its members on issues," in the words of an R. J. Reynolds official.[127] "Public Smoking Laws: Who Needs Them, Who Wants Them?" asked a headline in ALEC's publication *Legislative Policy,* mailed to receptive legislators around the country. What followed was a recitation of industry talking points on the unreliability of ETS research, authored by a South Carolina state senator, who also served as the chairman of his state's Tobacco Advisory Committee. ALEC's doctrinaire antiregulatory position also helped to transform the stakes of the argument over public smoking from the material and bodily to the abstract question of "yet another government fiat." The article proclaimed that "Smoking laws are an unwanted government intrusion that cannot be countenanced in a free society"—essentially disseminating tobacco industry ideas through a right-wing lobbying machine.[128]

The relationship between ALEC and the tobacco industry attracted little attention at the time. Founded in 1973, ALEC was still a young organization, with less clout in state legislatures than it possesses in the early 21st century.[129] Even industry watchdogs like ASH appeared to be unaware of the depth of connections between Big Tobacco and ALEC. In 1986, ASH general counsel Athena Mueller penned an expression of "concern and dismay" to ALEC director Constance Heckman. Mueller took Heckman to task for an issue of ALEC's *The State Factor* devoted entirely to passive smoking that reproduced the tobacco industry's one-sided approach. Mueller suggested that ALEC prepare an "updated report" supplemented with facts derived from the consensus of health professionals. "Your organization, which has done so much in other areas, can contribute successfully to this effort," Mueller implored. "ASH would be delighted to assist in any way possible."[130] Such a letter was tantamount to PETA asking the Cattlemen's Association to rethink its relationship to bovines. Not only did Heckman decline ASH's offer, she passed along the correspondence to a Tobacco Institute (TI) official. Industry counsel John Rupp was dispatched to "prepare a response [that] ALEC can use in such cases."[131]

ALEC's strategy centered on state capitols, which is where the tobacco industry's response to nonsmokers' rights legislation would be created.[132] Pro-tobacco forces brandished the legal doctrine of preemption to undermine local ordinances. According to the doctrine, when federal and state law conflict, federal law displaces state authority. Likewise, when state and local law conflict, state law rules. Many health and safety laws have been written so as to set a floor, and not a ceiling, for consumer protection. States and localities are free to regulate more stringently than Congress. For example, the 1972 Consumer Protection and Safety Act established safety standards for nearly all consumer products (excluding tobacco), but also permitted local and state regulation to establish a greater degree of protection.

But laws can also be written so as to set a ceiling, not a floor, on subsequent regulation. As the industry's efforts to create believable grassroots groups floundered—it was hard to fabricate a pro-smoking movement when many smokers themselves wished they were rid of the habit—cigarette makers sought a statutory end run around grassroots organizing altogether. Preemption was not an entirely new strategy for the tobacco industry. The 1969 Public Health Cigarette Smoking Act prevented states and cities from regulating cigarette advertising or promotion. Summarizing the lessons learned from the onslaught of local ordinances passed in California and Massachusetts at the end of the 1980s, the Tobacco Institute's senior vice-president of state activities observed: "state laws which preempt local anti-tobacco ordinances are the most effective means to counter local challenges."[133] And statehouses were more receptive to organized power and money than local councils. "Obviously," the Tobacco Institute lobbyist Walker Merryman explained, our job is "made a lot easier if you have a lobbyist who's been in the state capitol and knows the executive director of the state hospitality association and the state chamber of commerce and the state AFL-CIO and all the other groups that might help."[134] With lobbyists in all state legislatures, Merryman predicted that preemption could prevent "about 90 percent of legislation at the state level affecting our industry" from being enacted. By 1994, twenty-six states had passed laws prohibiting employers from refusing to hire smokers. Today, many in public health consider preemption laws "the biggest challenge to tobacco control."[135]

From the perspective of the cigarette manufacturers, these laws also had the added bonus of sowing division within the ranks of public health. The industry sought to include the poison pill of preemption in bills that had been earnestly originated by a public-health advocate, thus forcing the anti-tobacco coalition to decide between a flawed piece of legislation and none at all. In 1987, city councils in Pittsburgh, Philadelphia, Harrisburg, Erie, and little Radnor Township proposed measures to regulate smoking in restaurants, public places, and workplaces. Quickly, legislators in Harrisburg passed a weak clean air act that prevented stronger action by the cities.[136] Belatedly, the tobacco industry had alighted on a winning strategy to combat local nonsmoker activism. Between 1992 and 1998, thirty-one states enacted preemptive tobacco control laws, according to the Centers for Disease Control (CDC). Most of these prevented stronger smoke-free laws, but by the mid-1990s, the preemption of youth access laws and marketing restrictions also accelerated.[137] Having recognized a weakness in its own defenses, the industry changed its tactics, accelerating a transformation in American business lobbying.

Yet it is not fair to call the battle between the tobacco industry and the anti-tobacco movement a stalemate. For in 1987, the nonsmokers' rights movement finally achieved a victory in Congress. The NAS report on in-flight air quality opened the door for congressional action. Anti-smoking forces possessed just the slightest margin of support for a ban on all airline smoking for short flights under two hours. Illinois Democrat Dick Durbin introduced the ban as an amendment to a transportation bill. The "Durbin Amendment" was supported by a broad public-health coalition that included ASH, numerous GASP chapters, Americans for Non-Smokers' Rights, the American Medical Association, the Heart Association, the Lung Association, Surgeon General Koop, and, in an example of a labor-health alliance, the two flight attendant unions.[138] The measure barely passed the House—198 to 193—but sailed through the Senate. In the name of protecting tobacco farmers, Jesse Helms threatened to filibuster the measure.[139] But his threat did little to cow eighty-four of his Senate colleagues. As supporters predicted, smoke-free flights were popular.[140] In 1990, Congress banned smoking on all domestic flights.

With the airline smoking ban, the nonsmokers' rights movement had come full circle. Debates about public smoking began on airplanes, when John Banzhaf and Ralph Nader both proposed in-flight smoking regulations. During the 1970s, ASH was largely devoted to ensuring that the Civil Aeronautics Board was enforcing the smoking restrictions that the organization had wrested from the agency. Until the Durbin Amendment passed, tobacco's friends and foes saw administrative action as the likeliest route to smoke-free skies, and Congress, by contrast, as the greatest impediment.

That calculus changed during the Reagan era, when administrative agencies became more sensitive to the cost of implementing regulations. In the wake of the NAS study, Department of Transportation (DoT) secretary Elizabeth Dole, a North Carolina native, recommended to Congress that her agency take no action, citing a need for further research.[141] The combination of the NAS recommendation and the DoT's intransigence spurred Durbin to introduce what even supporters considered a long-shot amendment. First and foremost, the amendment transformed the travel experience of millions of American passengers—and the worksites of thousands of pilots and flight attendants. But federal regulation of airline smoking also marked a sea change in tobacco politics. Tobacco's strength in Congress had waned, leaving a tattered tobacco program in its wake, and thousands of farmers struggling to compete in a market controlled, once again, by the industry. And its strength gathered in statehouses, leaving the nonsmokers' rights movement scrambling to reassert its claim to public space, and to the levers of democracy.

————————

By the end of the 1980s, much in American life had been transformed in the debate over public smoking. American smoking rates were at pre-Second World War levels. And, unsurprisingly, this nation of nonsmokers and former smokers did not want to be around tobacco smoke. A major CDC survey revealed that in 1986, 88 percent of respondents—including 79 percent of current smokers—believed environmental tobacco smoke was harmful to health. These attitudes were markedly different from those held by Americans less than a decade prior, when a 1978 Roper Organization poll had found 58 percent of respondents—and just 40 percent of current smokers—believed passive smoking posed a harm to nonsmokers. When given the chance, the majority of nonsmokers—and even a sizable percentage of smokers—opted for a nonsmoking section. These changes in attitudes reflected and accelerated changes in Americans' physical experience of the world around them—the clear sight of a Department of Motor Vehicles lobby, the smell of an airline cabin, the taste of a special dinner consumed, for the first time, in a nonsmoking section of a restaurant.

Americans liked these changes. Even many smokers reconciled themselves to staying behind a smoky cordon sanitaire. For a shrinking mi-

nority of smoking Americans—28 percent at the end of the 1980s, poorer
and less educated than nonsmokers—a no-smoking sign could also be a relief: at least they knew where they should stand to avoid conflict. By 1988,
forty-two states and the District of Columbia restricted smoking in public
places; and at least an additional 969 ordinances were on the books as
well.[142] As more evidence emerged that suggested that smoking caused discomfort, disease, and even death in nonsmokers, the social estrangement
of smokers took on the cast of inevitability. Surgeon General Koop's call
for a "smoke-free society by the year 2000" sounded not just like a goal, but
a prediction.

As much as the nonsmokers' rights movement changed Americans
bodies, environments, and expectations, it was equally important in reflecting changes in American politics and political economy. Indicting the
federal government's weak response to the assault of tobacco smoke, nonsmokers' rights activists—and a growing number of allies in Congress—
attacked the government's New Deal-era commitment to tobacco farmers.
These bipartisan attacks began the process of unspooling the farmers'
safety net—deregulating the rigid tobacco control program, remedying, at
least partially, the federal government's "schizophrenic" stance toward tobacco. Weakened by reforms to the congressional seniority system, tobacco
state congressmen were no longer the force they had been in the 1950s and
1960s. They realized that if they did not act quickly to change the tobacco
program, it would be terminated—just another casualty of the Reagan budgets that had eliminated several other commodity programs.

The No Net Cost Tobacco Act of 1982 was a disaster for farmers. In
asking them to shoulder more of the cost of the tobacco program, the law
enabled cigarette manufacturers' control over all aspects of the tobacco
economy. Domestic manufacturers bought more and more imported leaf,
and domestic tobacco growers were left to drown in their own surplus production as the cigarette manufacturers held their heads underwater. These
renewed antagonisms within the tobacco family were also reflected in manufacturers' secret judgments that tobacco farmers—rapidly dwindling in
number during the 1980s—no longer held symbolic or political cachet.
While the manufacturers continued to hold the tobacco farmer up as the
noble face of the industry, privately they wrote of their desire for a more
"efficient" tobacco program, a euphemism for lower support prices and

greater leaf production. The industry ultimately succeeded in turning the political vulnerability of the price support program into a strategy to drive down the price of tobacco leaf.

The industry's response to the local ordinance movement also demonstrated a genius for spinning an apparent defeat into strategic victory. Tobacco's lawyers, executives, and public relations strategists could clearly see that by operating at a local level, the nonsmokers' rights movement was more agile and mobile than the wheezing and Washington-bound Big Tobacco. In trying to neuter the power of local anti-smoking ordinances, the tobacco industry was part of a broad transformation in conservative business lobbying. By embracing state-level preemption of local ordinances, businessmen, think tanks, and lawmakers appeared to uphold the political ideal of decentralization, while at the same time thwarting adverse local regulation. Preemption did not stop the anti-tobacco movement, but it heralded an end to the grassroots phase as larger sums of money were brought to bear upon smoking battles.

There was a kind of sad symmetry to the disintegration of the tobacco program and the waning influence of the rough-hewn, grassroots nonsmokers' rights movement. Citing the cost of smoking and the growing antipathy toward New Deal–era regulatory schemes, the nonsmokers' rights movement called for the destruction of the tobacco program and got it. In dismantling the program, the tobacco companies moved closer to the position of power that they had occupied in the early part of the twentieth century. And nonsmokers' rights activists also found that there were political limits to the strategy of progressive federalism they had so successfully employed. In transforming public space, nonsmokers' rights advocates from C. Everett Koop to the innumerable masses that insisted on their right to sit in a nonsmoking section changed American bodies. As importantly, nonsmokers also changed the body politic. By relying upon cost-centered analyses of private behavior and unraveling decades-old collectivist programs, the nonsmokers' rights movement refashioned what Americans believed the government owed to citizens, and what citizens owed to the government. And in their remarkable successes, nonsmokers unwittingly catalyzed a conservative political strategy whose far-reaching effects are scarcely fathomable, and all too real.

Conclusion

"Weeds Are Hard to Kill": The Future of Tobacco Politics

CIGARS ASIDE, Bill Clinton's presidency was marked by tobacco as much as it was by scandal or centrism.[1] Clinton's failed 1993 push for universal health care was to be funded by a federal cigarette excise tax. His Food and Drug Administration (FDA) commissioner broke with his predecessors and asserted jurisdiction over tobacco. With the enthusiastic support of First Lady Hillary Clinton, Vice President Al Gore, and Clinton guru-pollster Dick Morris, FDA commissioner David Kessler secured the president's blessing for the FDA's proposed regulations.[2] On the heels of the landmark settlement reached between state attorneys general and the tobacco companies, Clinton's Department of Justice sued the industry. "Taxpayers shouldn't pay the costs of lung cancer, emphysema, and other smoking-related illnesses," Clinton explained in his State of the Union address in 1999. "The tobacco companies should."[3] It seemed, at long last, that tobacco would be subject to a new regulatory regime in the courts, in the states, by the Congress, and by the executive branch.

The cultural cachet of tobacco had ebbed as well, as the industry increasingly appeared to be a refuge of scoundrels—or worse. A network news investigation in 1994 showed that cigarette companies had spiked their product with additional nicotine—a charge that companies did not deny but explained as a technique to enhance flavor. The duplicity of industry executives was on theatrical display a few weeks later before the House Energy and Commerce Subcommittee on Health and the Environment, chaired by California Democrat Henry Waxman. When pressed by Oregon Democrat Ron Wyden on whether or not they believed the judgment of the

1989 *Surgeon General's Report* that cigarettes were addictive, all six executives answered no. The footage aired live on CNN.[4] It was in this context that Jeffrey Wigand, a Brown & Williamson exec-turned-whistleblower, became an object of cultural fascination as the subject of multiple high-profile interviews and a Hollywood film. In *The Insider,* Russell Crowe portrayed the beleaguered Wigand—an angry David to the industry's Goliath.

But one political era does not give way easily to the next. Institutions, individuals, and arguments stick around. People resist change, loudly and emphatically, marshaling all of the assets at their disposal—history, race, nostalgia, money. And American federalism has encouraged multiple, contradictory, and overlapping regulatory regimes for just about every important political question of the twentieth century—from civil rights to wetlands management to welfare distribution. Moreover, even once an era passes, its hallmarks may linger as backlash or as inspiration for a new generation of political activists.

For all of the turmoil of the 1990s, in many ways the decade ended much as it began: with federal acknowledgment that secondhand smoke killed tens of thousands of Americans each year, but without federal regulation of indoor smoking; with a meager but intact federal price support program; with fewer smokers, who possessed fewer resources and fewer years of education than nonsmokers; and with a cigarette industry chastened, but firmly cartelized by regulation. The FDA's regulatory gambit was thwarted by the Supreme Court in *FDA v. Brown & Williamson Tobacco Corp.* (2000), a landmark decision in administrative law. It was not until the 2009 passage of the Family Smoking Prevention and Tobacco Control Act that the FDA would be granted the authority to regulate tobacco products. Meanwhile, states and localities continued to restrict indoor smoking; and Congress continued to thwart tougher measures on taxes, advertising, industry liability, and youth smoking.

Agencies Step In . . . and Out

By the early 1990s, many believed that the time had come for federal rulemaking on indoor smoking. After all, workplace-smoking restrictions had proliferated across the United States—largely to the satisfaction of workers and managers alike. And scientific consensus continued to build around James Repace and Alfred Lowrey's groundbreaking 1980 *Science* study of the harms of secondhand smoke, which showed that this was responsible for 5,000 lung cancer deaths per year in nonsmokers.[5] Repace, by then at the Environmental Protection Agency (EPA), spearheaded a years-long risk assessment study for the agency. Revising the consensus position downward somewhat, the EPA concluded that secondhand smoke was responsible for 3,800 lung cancer deaths in nonsmokers annually. Researchers pointed out at the time that this estimate wildly underestimated the harm of secondhand smoke because the vast majority of cases of debility and death—in both smokers and nonsmokers—was due to heart disease rather than cancer. One study put the death toll of cardiovascular disease at ten times that of lung cancer.[6] Nevertheless, the EPA's report was significant as it was the first time a federal agency had applied a concrete body count to secondhand smoke.

The EPA classified secondhand smoke as a known human carcinogen, but that was the extent of its authority. Federal regulation of indoor workplaces would have to come from the Occupational Safety and Health Administration (OSHA). John Banzhaf was delighted, having twice sued OSHA over its failure to regulate smoking as a workplace hazard. The EPA assessment, he hoped, would give him ammunition should he take OSHA to court again.[7] This time, however, OSHA moved first, proposing a rule requiring employers to restrict smoking to designated areas that were either outdoors or separate and ventilated directly out of the building. "OSHA has taken this action to prevent deaths," explained Clinton labor secretary Robert Reich. The rules were far-reaching, estimated to affect 92 million workers at more than 6 million workplaces—from factories to offices to sports arenas to bars and restaurants.[8] An agency cost-benefit analysis suggested that the restrictions would cost $8 billion in compliance costs annually, but save $15 billion in the form of worker "efficiency and productivity improvements, cost reductions in operations and maintenance, and reduced incidence of property damage."[9] Nearly twenty years after Donna Shimp's *How to Protect Your Health at Work* was published, her pragmatic appeals to management were echoed by a Democratic Department of Labor.

Industry response was furious. It submitted doubt-mongering science to OSHA's docket and ran full-page ads in newspapers denouncing OSHA's overreach (see Figure C.1). It orchestrated a massive letter-writing campaign, and coordinated the testimony of pro-industry speakers at the hearings.[10]

The Government is proposing to make it illegal for you to smoke in your own home anytime a workman or repairman visits. It's part of a massive effort to prohibit smoking that will allow the Government to make decisions for individual citizens that have always been matters of personal choice.

"COME OUT SLOWLY SIR, WITH YOUR CIGARETTE ABOVE YOUR HEAD."

The situation above may seem implausible at first. But right now, the Government is trying to compare cigarettes to heroin and cocaine. They are also proposing to entirely prohibit smoking in public places, company cars, trucks and any place of business entered by ten or more people a week. These same proposals could also affect your private home as you could be forbidden to smoke anytime a workman or repairman visits. In addition, a cigarette tax increase of 300% is being considered.*

This is nothing less than an attempt at tobacco prohibition, something that will have serious implications for Americans.

Earlier this year, the Canadian Government was forced to rollback the exorbitant cigarette tax they introduced just two years ago. Organized criminal gangs controlled a huge smuggling market, creating a climate of fear and violence throughout the country. "Smuggling is threatening the safety of our communities... and the very fabric of Canadian society", the Canadian Prime Minister said when he announced the tax reductions. In 1993, up to two-thirds of the cigarettes smoked in Quebec were purchased illegally.**

California, which raised its cigarette taxes to fund health education, reports that 7% of the entire tobacco market consists of illegal cigarettes.*** Higher taxes will only make things worse.

Despite the Government's denials, the proposed tax increases and the avalanche of other anti-tobacco legislation are all simply forms of backdoor prohibition. The end result, should this legislation pass, could be disastrous. How will they enforce the law? Will the homes of 'known' smokers be raided? Will we be encouraged to inform upon our neighbors? Has the Government given any thought to the consequences?

This opinion is brought to you in the interest of an informed debate by the R.J. Reynolds Tobacco Company. We believe that the answer to most smoking issues lies in accommodation, in finding ways in which smokers and non-smokers can co-exist peacefully. We encourage dialogue and discussion that will solve the issues without resorting to Government intervention.

For further information please call toll-free 1-800-366-8441.

Figure C.1 In a 1994 advertisement in the *Washington Post*, R. J. Reynolds denounced tobacco regulation as "nothing less than an attempt at tobacco prohibition." (Reproduced from Harvard Library Special Collections and Archives)

OSHA received 110,000 comments on the rule—the greatest volume of comments the agency ever received, and also the most vituperative. Agency officials fielded ashtrays full of cigarette butts, missives laced with swastikas and expletives, and even death threats in a campaign orchestrated by the tobacco manufacturers.[11] Even so, supporters of the rule saw no cause for alarm in the response. After all, OSHA had a clear mandate to protect workers from dangers on the job, and environmental tobacco smoke was now recognized by the federal government as a carcinogen on par with asbestos and vinyl chloride.

What is more, the FDA joined the fray against the industry. In 1994, FDA commissioner David Kessler announced that his agency would seek to regulate cigarettes as drugs. Whistleblower revelations that the companies had manipulated nicotine levels for years in order to maintain addiction gave fodder to this claim. Kessler's gambit represented a stark break with the decisions of past commissioners, who had not interpreted the 1938 Food, Drug, and Cosmetic Act (FDCA) as endowing them with the authority to regulate tobacco. But by August 1995, President Clinton had announced his support of proposed FDA rules with a televised press conference.[12] The FDA issued its final rule in the summer of 1996.

As OSHA and FDA would come to find out, the investments the industry had made in Congress, mercenary scientists, and third-party front groups continued to pay dividends, even after the industry's own credibility seemed shot. It took less than 24 hours for the five largest cigarette manufacturers to sue to block FDA action. Filing in federal district court in Greensboro—a city tucked between Winston-Salem and Durham—industry spokesmen argued that the FDA had exceeded its statutory authority. The industry responded to the OSHA rule with the "16 Cities Study," designed by the Center for Indoor Air Research and scientists from R. J. Reynolds. The study soft-pedaled workplace exposures to secondhand smoke by deliberately selecting workplaces where smoking restrictions existed and reporting exposure data as if the sites were completely unregulated. When the study was cited at OSHA hearings, the involvement of the industry in its funding and design went undisclosed.[13]

By the end of 1996, the OSHA rule and the FDA action had stalled. With the Republican takeover of Congress, Henry Waxman was no longer chair of the House Subcommittee on Energy and Commerce—a venue that had given commissioner Kessler an opportunity to expound on the addictive nature of nicotine. Instead, Virginia Republican Thomas Bliley—known colloquially as the "Representative from Philip Morris"—held the chairmanship. Facing industry opposition and fearful that Congress would cut the agency's funding and curtail its enforcement powers, OSHA shelved the workplace-smoking proposal. "The hostile environment we've been working in for the last two years isn't one in which a sane official would lead with his chin," a chastened Reich told the *Washington Post* in 1996.

FDA action also was met with judicial resistance. Although the Greensboro district judge initially ruled in favor of the FDA, the Fourth Circuit overturned this ruling on appeal. "The FDA has exceeded the authority granted to it by Congress," the Richmond-based court concluded. "Its rulemaking action cannot stand." In late 1999, the U.S. solicitor general faced a skeptical Supreme Court as he defended the FDA's extension of its authority. Although the agency's case rested on a newfound understanding of nicotine as an addictive drug, a bare majority of justices found that tobacco products "simply do not fit" into the scheme established by the 1938 Food, Drug, and Cosmetic Act (FDCA). For the five conservative justices in the majority, the Court's decision hinged on the question of congressional intent: did the FDA's rule reflect the express intent of Congress? The majority opinion, written by Justice Sandra Day O'Connor, did not dwell on the scientific evidence carefully amassed by FDA.[14] Rather, the FDA's previous decades-long disavowal of its own authority was crucial. So too was a deadly loophole of the FDCA itself. The FDCA required the FDA to prevent the marketing of deadly drugs with no therapeutic effect—a category that, by the FDA's own standards, cigarettes fell into. But Congress had, on multiple occasions, foreclosed the possibility of banning tobacco products. In short, Congress had deemed tobacco too dangerous and too useless to be a drug. "If they cannot be used safely for any therapeutic purpose, and yet they cannot be banned, they simply do not fit," O'Connor wrote for the majority.[15] The era of tobacco's power on Capitol Hill had waned. But its influence lingered secondhand, as judges looked backward toward history to determine the limits of agency authority.

Food and Drug Administration v. Brown & Williamson Tobacco Corp. is well known to students of administrative law—not for what it said about tobacco but for what it said about how courts evaluate agency decision making.

Since the 1984 case of *Chevron v. Natural Resources Defense Council,* courts have applied a two-step test for determining whether or not an agency's interpretation of a rule is legal: has Congress directly spoken to the precise question at issue? If so, then the agency must follow the express intent of Congress. If not, then as long as the agency's interpretation was neither "arbitrary, capricious, or manifestly contrary to the statute," then courts must defer to the agency. O'Connor's opinion expanded the first step of this test. Instead of addressing whether Congress had spoken directly to the ability of the FDA to regulate tobacco under the FDCA (which made no mention of tobacco), the justice took into consideration the "context" of the regulatory scheme established by law—specifically, repeated congressional inaction on tobacco. That is, the Court expanded its own interpretive powers at the expense of agency authority.

Insofar as the EPA under Democratic administrations has been more willing to expand its regulatory powers in response to climate science, *FDA v. Brown & Williamson* now poses a problem for environmentalists. It inhibited agencies from ever regulating outside their traditional areas of influence—even when science suggested the prudence of such a move.[16] Ironically, the confidence of the modern anti-tobacco movement worked to undermine environmental protections—the very laws that had once legitimated nonsmokers' conception of tobacco smoke as an environmental pollutant. As the judiciary that the public interest movement had once put so much faith in has grown more conservative, the plain letter of statutes issued from smoke-filled chambers of Congress grows more relevant.

The Promise and Perils of Local Authority

And yet, even as dramatic action by the federal government faltered during the 1990s, smoking restrictions continued to proliferate at the local level. Indeed, when OSHA withdrew its proposed workplace-smoking rules in 2001, many in the nonsmokers' rights movement breathed a sigh of relief, calculating that rules passed at the local level would be stronger than whatever the agency promulgated. John Banzhaf even described OSHA's retreat as a win for nonsmokers. "We might now be even more successful in persuading states and localities to finally ban smoking on their own once they no longer have the OSHA workplace smoking rulemaking to hide behind."[17]

While it was true that localities continued to pass ordinances that restricted or banned smoking in public places or at many worksites, few went as far as the OSHA proposal.

Some businesses were spurred by liability concerns to ban smoking on their own initiative when the EPA declared secondhand smoke a Class A carcinogen. Twenty-four hours after the EPA announcement, managers at Raytheon headquarters in Lexington, Massachusetts, planned to sit down with union representatives to work on a smoking ban. Of particular concern were workers' compensation suits brought by nonsmoking employees as lawyers for plaintiffs anticipated using the EPA report to buttress claims that secondhand exposures at work caused their illness. "There are clearly new liability issues," a spokesman for Raytheon explained of the EPA classification.[18] What had once been a novel expansion of workplace liability in the 1970s and 1980s was now inside the circuitry of corporate risk analysis.

Meanwhile, sickened workers fought the industry itself—in some cases dying as they waited for recognition of the harms posed by secondhand smoke. In 1991, a Miami attorney filed suit against the cigarette companies on behalf of Norma Broin, a flight attendant with American Airlines. Broin was a devout Mormon and a nonsmoker. Despite the demographic improbability, she had received a lung cancer diagnosis. The suit later became a class action on behalf of 60,000 nonsmoking flight attendants sickened by workplace exposure to secondhand smoke. After going to trial, the plaintiffs and the cigarette companies announced a settlement. Instead of paying damages directly to the flight attendants, the companies paid $300 million to establish a research foundation dedicated to the study of secondhand smoke. The Flight Attendant Medical Research Institute (FAMRI) was established in 2001.[19]

Norma R. Broin v. Philip Morris was the first time the tobacco industry had ever settled a case. It punctured the cigarette company's hefty legal armature in two ways: the large number of plaintiffs meant that the industry's doubt-mongering over the causality of disease in a *specific* individual dissolved in the face of overwhelming numbers. And, just as importantly, manufacturers' traditional "assumption of risk" defense—that smokers knew the hazards of smoking and should have stopped—did not apply to nonsmokers who got sick in the course of their work.[20] The approach to smoking regulation developed in the 1960s and 1970s—that airplanes were shared spaces uniquely subject to regulation, and that secondhand smoke constituted an unsafe workplace exposure—laid the groundwork for *Broin*. And since the terms of the settlement included a research fund, producing research that would later be mobilized in subsequent suits against the tobacco industry, the nonsmokers' rights movement had its own secondhand influence.

But for restaurant and bar workers in particular, relief from smoking workplaces was still years away. With much fanfare but little lost in the way of revenue, New York City banned smoking in bars in 2003. It would be more than a decade before New Orleans, another city famed for its gastronomic delights and hedonistic excesses, did likewise. In Las Vegas, hotel, casino, and restaurant workers still contend with secondhand smoke. The American Nonsmokers' Rights Foundation, which had its origins in the Berkeley Group Against Smoking Pollution, estimates that as of 2018, 41 percent of U.S. workers are still exposed to secondhand smoke at work.[21] These rates are even higher for African Americans, who are more likely to encounter secondhand smoke at work and at home than non-Hispanic whites or Mexican Americans.[22]

The power of local control in reshaping the social geography of smoking is underscored by a countermovement led by the tobacco industry. Since the 1980s, most of the industry's efforts at combating smoking restrictions have focused on the enactment of state laws that preempt local ordinances, placing a ceiling on the stringency of tobacco regulations. Between 1982 and 1998, thirty-one states enacted such preemption laws.[23] Not only do these laws serve the industry's economic goals, they also degrade the character of local government. Despite its tenuous analogies to the civil rights movement or its blinkered approach to class, the nonsmokers' rights movement succeeded in invigorating the character of local democracies. Activists educated their fellow citizens on the harms posed by other people's smoke. In letters to the editor, on local access TV, and in homespun newsletters, they persuaded their fellow citizens to understand themselves as nonsmokers. And their fellow citizens believed them. Preemption laws like those pursued by the tobacco industry curtail such democratic engagement on a variety of issues—from indoor-smoking restrictions to minimum wage laws to the removal of Confederate monuments.

An Uneasy Settlement

It was not action on tobacco by state legislatures that garnered the most attention in the 1990s, however. It was action taken by state attorneys general. Beginning with Mississippi in 1994, state attorneys general sued to recoup the Medicaid costs of smoking-related diseases from the tobacco companies. In Mississippi, attorneys estimated that the Medicaid costs of those suffering from smoking-related diseases amounted to $70–$100 million annually.[24] These suits were premised on the idea that taxpayers bore the economic burdens of smoking-related illness, but, as one Mississippi attorney explained, "the State of Mississippi never has smoked a cigarette."[25] In this rendering, states themselves were the innocent third parties—the nonsmokers choking on cigarette smoke. Attorneys general in Minnesota, West Virginia, Florida, and Massachusetts filed their own suits within the year. By the spring of 1997, thirty-one states had filed suit.[26] They were aided by an army of trial attorneys, eager to share in the spoils against the industry.

Facing division within its own ranks as well as the prospect of simultaneous, costly litigation, the industry assented to a negotiated settlement. Essentially, cigarette manufacturers agreed to FDA regulation of advertising and marketing, the financing of anti-tobacco advertising campaigns, fines if teenage-smoking rates did not fall, and payment to the states of hundreds of billions of dollars in health-care costs over a twenty-five-year period. In exchange, the industry got something it wanted more than money or even freedom from regulatory oversight: an end to class-action lawsuits and a cap on punitive judgments for individual suits. Although the settlement was negotiated by lawyers, some of its provisions could only become law if it were passed as legislation before Congress.

In contrast to the closed doors of congressional deal-making decades earlier, the tobacco proposal garnered intense public scrutiny. Many public-health activists derided the agreement as a sellout to the tobacco companies.[27] Henry Waxman, David Kessler, and Everett Koop thought it was a bad deal. "You can do better than the settlement," Kessler told the Senate.[28] Particularly galling to anti-tobacco activists were the settlement's immunity provisions—the provisions that made the industry willing to deal in the first place.

Surprising many in party leadership, Arizona Republican John McCain sponsored an aggressive bill that eliminated protection against future suits, raised the cap on industry liability, increased the federal cigarette excise tax, imposed further restrictions on tobacco advertising, and established provisions for fines if these measures failed to reduce youth smoking. When the bill was brought to the Senate floor, hundreds of amendments were proposed and voted upon—some of which were intended as sabotage.[29] In a measure of just how marginal they had become as a political constituency, tobacco farmers were totally absent from consideration in these negotiations; this fact enabled tobacco-state legislators to oppose the deal without having to remind the public that the companies had spent $40 million in advertising to thwart it.[30] The bill was dead by the summer of 1998. Once again, the cigarette manufacturers prevailed in Congress. Only now their arguments were couched in a broad, antigovernment message that had propelled Republicans to majorities in the House and Senate. "This is a massive tax on low-income Americans," explained Missouri Republican John Ashcroft, one of the Senate's most outspoken opponents of the tobacco settlement. "And it is used to proliferate the bureaucracy of this government."[31]

The flexibility of American federalism—the very quality that enabled a forceful nonsmoker movement to succeed at the local level and inspire regulatory action in the states and in Congress—stymied an aggressive tobacco settlement. Attorneys general and trial attorneys responded to their own financial and political incentives in pursuit of the settlement. Members of Congress, jealous of their prerogative to originate legislation and sensitive to the objections of business and farmers, faced a separate set of incentives—ones that Republican legislators could recast as stewardship over small government.

The agreement finally reached by the states and the companies disappointed public health advocates. Gone were the provisions that required congressional approval: FDA regulation, public and workplace-smoking bans, stronger package warnings, mandatory youth-smoking reductions. Instead, the 1998 Master Settlement Agreement (MSA) required the companies to pay $206 billion to the states for the next twenty-five years—a figure that did not even cover the cost of smoking-related diseases. There were no restrictions placed on how states spent the money, and today less

than 3 percent of MSA funds are used toward smoking cessation and prevention. Companies also agreed to a range of marketing restrictions: Joe
Camel was retired; free product samples were banned; sports sponsorships
were outlawed; product placement was forbidden. The MSA established a
foundation that would fund the gritty anti-tobacco advertising of the Truth
Campaign. And the MSA disbanded the industry's most notorious lobbying
and front groups. The Tobacco Institute, the Center for Indoor Air Research,
and the Tobacco Growers Information Committee were all shuttered.[32]

In a novel form of regulation that sought to disinfect the industry's mis-
information with sunshine, secret industry documents disclosed during
the discovery phase of civil, state, or federal litigation are now freely accessible online. There are currently more than 14 million industry documents
archived online relating to lobbying, advertising, and scientific research,
providing an unparalleled look inside the operations of one of the largest
businesses in America. These documents are a trove for historians and have
been used as evidence in subsequent litigation and regulatory proceedings.
In exchange for these modest concessions (all of which had appeared in
stronger form in previous proposals), the manufacturers were relieved of all
future litigation brought by the states. Individual and class-action suits,
however, were not preempted. In 2006, U.S. District Court judge Gladys
Kessler ruled that in hiding the health risks of smoking, tobacco companies were in violation of the federal Racketeer Influenced and Corrupt
Organizations Act (RICO).[33] As part of her ruling, Kessler ordered further
disclosure of industry documents produced for litigation through 2021.

Public-health advocates regarded the MSA as an utter failure for public
health and a coup for the companies. Wall Street shared that assessment:
tobacco stocks rallied upon the deal's announcement.[34] In many ways, it
turned public-health victories of the past decades upside down. If the nonsmoker movement had made the social cost of smoking an Achilles' heel of
the industry, the MSA set a ceiling on just how high that cost could rise.
The comparisons between the post-MSA Truth Campaign and the free airtime secured under the Fairness Doctrine are less flattering once we remember that modern anti-tobacco advertising is not freely given: it has to
be purchased with MSA funds. And if the states had once incubated a regulatory drive that did not exist in Congress, the 1998 Master Settlement
reversed the momentum. Because they were dependent upon the settlement

for revenues, which were largely used to balance state budgets, states were increasingly concerned with litigation against the companies. "There's no doubt that the largest financial stakeholder in the industry is our state governments," an R. J. Reynolds vice president noted in 2003—with what must have been a fair degree of satisfaction.[35]

Smokers and Farmers

By the beginning of the twenty-first century, tobacco smokers and farmers were out of step with a regulatory regime centered around the prerogatives of nonsmokers. The emaciated federal tobacco program had long been described as a Depression-era relic. Indeed, younger tobacco farmers had begun to see their livelihood this way too. A 1995 study conducted by the Bowman Gray School of Medicine at Wake Forest University—named after an R. J. Reynolds president—found younger farmers substantially more dubious than their parents and grandparents about the viability of the tobacco business. One of the study's authors agreed with the younger farmers. Older farmers "are living in the past, and the floor is going to drop out beneath them."[36]

The future that farmers faced was even bleaker than the present. The MSA made no provisions for tobacco producers. But a subsequent agreement established a $5 billion trust fund, paid for by the companies to compensate growers for loss of income due to declining cigarette sales. This represented a continuation of the precedent set by the 1980s "bailout" of tobacco growers. But this time, the bailout was less about leverage over a junior partner in tobacco production and more like a severance package. On the eve of the MSA, the U.S. Department of Agriculture (USDA) recorded the highest-ever share of imported tobacco: 41.6 percent of tobacco used in U.S. manufacturing came from overseas, up 10 percent from 1990.[37] A 1999 report issued by a consortium of anti-tobacco groups highlighted the industry's disproportionate embrace of foreign tobacco: between 1997 and 1999, domestic manufacturers bought 35 percent less U.S.-grown tobacco, even though domestic smoking declined just 4–5 percent over that same time period.[38] Exports of flue-cured tobacco fell as well, as U.S. cigarette firms established operations in the former Soviet Bloc and Asia. By the turn of the twenty-first century, 90 percent of the world's flue-cured and

Burley tobacco—the types that define an "American-style" cigarette—was grown by farmers outside of the United States. And, between 1980 and 1998, the American farmer's share of every dollar a smoker spent on cigarettes fell from 7¢ to less than 2¢, while the share captured by manufacturers increased from 36¢ to 49¢.[39] With the industry's characteristic ability to draw profit from crisis, the manufacturers consolidated their own power at the expense of domestic farmers, diversifying their portfolio of leaf producers while claiming to champion American farmers and touting the qualities of American flue-cured.

As manufacturers bought less tobacco, producers made less money: quota fell and price support levels were reduced. The tobacco program, popular precisely because it buffered tobacco producers from market forces and constrained the power of manufacturers to dictate prices, had finally failed. Active producers and owners of quota began to support an end to the seventy-year-old tobacco program. Congress considered legislation linking the program's termination to FDA regulation of cigarettes. Lobbying by the companies, particularly by R. J. Reynolds, eventually led to the removal of the FDA provision. Even without the Tobacco Growers Information Committee, the companies organized growers in opposition to bills that contained FDA provisions—even though such proposals would have meant more total dollars for farmers. Rumors circulated in tobacco country about FDA regulators swarming farms to inspect tobacco leaves. "Keep FDA off the farm" was the rallying cry at farm meetings.[40] Proposals that would have maintained some degree of economic regulation were also scuttled—an excise tax on crops to maintain domestic leaf prices, a licensing program to help smaller farmers.

The Fair and Equitable Tobacco Reform Act was passed in 2004, ending price supports and marketing restrictions on all tobacco growing in the United States. The act also contained a "buyout" of tobacco quotas: quota holders and active producers who leased quota were eligible to receive compensation funded through assessments on the cigarette manufacturers. It was the processing tax of the old Agricultural Adjustment Act in reverse: a final transfer of money from manufacturers to farmers, only this time farmers were ushered into the free market, not shielded from its vagaries.

Changes in tobacco country were swift and predictable: the price of tobacco dropped 25 percent. Using their buyout funds, older and marginal producers exited tobacco production altogether, while highly capitalized growers expanded production and mechanized their operations. Of the 500,000 tobacco producers who received buyout money, 80 percent received about $5,000 each—hardly a sum to finance a retirement. Some 500—mostly living in eastern North Carolina—received more than $1 million each.[41] The buyout reflected the elitist and racist system of land distribution enshrined by the tobacco program. It never attempted to compensate those whose livelihoods revolved around tobacco—day laborers, warehouse workers, warehouse owners, auctioneers—but who were not quota owners or lessees.

Although the media heralded the $10 billion buyout as a windfall for the North Carolina economy, the elimination of the program had an immediate effect on the local tax base. In the Wilson County, the largest producer of flue-cured, property values fell by $25 million countywide, resulting in a loss of annual tax revenue—a shortfall that would have to be remedied through a service cut. But Wilson was comparatively fortunate. Since the buyout, farms in marginal tobacco-growing regions have seen an acceleration of farm loss and population decline.[42]

Two contradictory truths about the federal tobacco program became evident in its absence: it was elitist and it was also populist, holding communities together that would have disappeared under the crush of global competition. For those who remained in tobacco production, the global dimension of their endeavor was unmistakable: tobacco prices were set by world markets; tobacco was sold to multinational tobacco companies that increasingly looked abroad for untapped markets;[43] and U.S. tobacco was cultivated by Latino migrant laborers—frequently undocumented workers (and their children) who would work for less than the minimum wage.[44]

The end of the tobacco program witnessed the shuttering of auction warehouses, which ceased functioning entirely by 2004.[45] The auctioneer's chant was heard only at state fairs—audible nostalgia between whiffs of funnel cake and glimpses of prize-winning livestock. Tobacco is now grown exclusively on one-year contracts between individual growers and the companies. Without collective bargaining power for farmers, corporations are once again in the position to dictate prices. But contracts also enable manufacturers to determine the conditions under which tobacco is grown—what fertilizer is applied, what type of curing barns are used—as a precondition to the awarding of a contract. And contracting also subjects farmers to a web of global surveillance. Each bale of tobacco contracted to Philip Morris or R. J. Reynolds is assigned a barcode as it moves through the global supply chain—a web much vaster than anything contemplated by the FDA. Ironically, for all of the ways that sophisticated, computerized farmers embody the cutting edge of agriculture, their position relative to the cigarette manufactures harkens back to the days of the Tobacco Trust, when growers were offered contracts to thwart their collective efforts.

The precariousness that lurks within each contract—the fear that it might be negotiated downward the following year, or cut altogether—also defines the end of the commodity chain. Smokers too inhabit a shaky social and economic position. U.S. smoking rates are at their lowest levels since the early twentieth century. In 2016, only 15 percent of Americans smoked—down from 21 percent a decade earlier, and just a fraction of the 46 percent that smoked at mid-century.[46] These numbers are a testament to the efforts of anti-tobacco activists. An estimated 8 million lives have been saved over the past fifty years due to their efforts.[47] Today, as electronic cigarettes surge in popularity—especially among teenagers—even these successes are cast into some doubt. E-cigarettes do not contain tobacco, but do contain nicotine and an array of other chemicals whose long-term effects on the body are unknown; and their secondhand effects are murkier still. Although they have been touted as effective smoking cessation devices, new studies indicate that teenagers who vape are significantly more likely to become established smokers.[48] Those in public health fear that smoking will inch its way back to social acceptability with every glowing cylinder that a teen brings to his or her lips.

Still, American adults are much more likely to light a conventional cigarette than an electronic one. The socioeconomic disparities that hide within the figures describing combustible cigarette use are also a testament to the shortcomings of the anti-smoking movement and the predations of the industry. Smokers are poorer and less educated than nonsmokers, and they are more likely to live in rural and impoverished communities, where lung cancer rates are 20 percent higher than in urban areas. Poor nonsmokers are also more likely to suffer from poor health due to higher secondhand smoke exposures.[49] The tobacco industry is responsible for these health inequities: manufacturers directly target people of low socioeconomic status through discounts and coupons, and there are simply more places to buy cigarettes in poor neighborhoods.[50] But some of the discrepancy between the smoking habits of rich and poor Americans may well be due to the strategies pursued by the nonsmoker activists of the past five decades. Fewer blue-collar than white-collar workers are protected by workplace-smoking restrictions—in part, perhaps, a consequence of non-smoker activists' management-centered approach. And poor Americans are less likely to succeed in quitting smoking than wealthier Americans—an unsurprising fact since quit attempts are more likely to succeed when supplemented with medications that are available only with prescription drug coverage.[51]

From seed to smoke, the responsibility for tobacco production and consumption has been privatized and individualized. Nonsmokers' rights activists achieved their goal of making smoking socially unacceptable—an achievement that has caused further declines in tobacco use.[52] Smoking was once a ubiquitous public practice; it is now a shameful private vice. While disparities in smoking prevalence by race and socioeconomic status suggest a broad failing in public health, smoking is experienced and understood as an individual failure of judgment and will.[53] By a two-to-one margin, smokers and nonsmokers alike blame smokers rather than the tobacco companies for smoking-related diseases.[54] And just as the tobacco companies have increased the amount of control they exert over farmers, workplaces too possess tremendous power over the private lives of employees. In many places, it is legal for employers to fire or refuse to hire an employee because he or she smokes—a logical consequence of the cost-centric framing of the nonsmokers' rights movement. Citing health-care costs, some employers have even gone so far as to refuse employment to candidates with a smoking spouse.[55] Smoke-free workplaces are increasingly imagined as smoker-free workplaces.

For the past hundred years, the political economy of tobacco has been a thicket of contradictions, fitting perhaps for a deadly substance that both stimulates and relaxes. The early years provided economic stability for the few at the expense of the broad public health; the new system saves lives even as it stigmatizes. The perils and promises of both regimes invite our empathy, our imagination, and the confidence to believe in a different future.

Notes

Introduction

1. "Smoking Banned at News Parley," *New York Times*, January 12, 1964.
2. "Only a Temporary Decline in Sales Expected," *Washington Post*, January 12, 1964; "Britons' Smoking Up after Report," *New York Times*, January 13, 1964.
3. "Wall Streeters Recommending Tobacco Stocks," *Los Angeles Times*, January 10, 1964.
4. Allan M. Brandt, *The Cigarette Century: The Rise, Fall, and Deadly Persistence of the Product that Defined America* (New York: Basic Books, 2007), 237.
5. Centers for Disease Control and Prevention, "Trends in Current Cigarette Smoking among High School Students and Adults, 1964-2014," accessed September 4, 2018, https://www.cdc.gov/tobacco/data_statistics/tables /trends/cig_smoking/index.htm.
6. Danielle Flood, "School for Smoking," *New York Times*, March 20, 1977.
7. Centers for Disease Control and Prevention, "Trends in Current Cigarette Smoking."
8. Elizabeth Drew, "The Quiet Victory of the Cigarette Lobby: How It Found the Best Filter Yet—Congress," *Atlantic*, September 1965, 76.
9. For a thorough examination of the tobacco industry's power in Congress during the 1950s and 1960s, see A. Lee Fritschler, *Smoking and Politics: Bureaucracy Centered Policymaking* (Englewood Cliffs, NJ: Prentice Hall, 1975). Legal scholars call this dynamic "compensatory federalism": the expansion of policies at the subnational level precisely *because of* inaction at the federal level. See Brent Cebul, Karen Tani, and Mason Williams, "Clio and the Compound Republic," *Publius: The Journal of Federalism* 47, No. 2 (April 2017): 235-259; Sara Mayeux and Karen Tani, "Federalism Anew," *American Journal of Legal History* 56 (2016): 128-138. For an in-depth examination of "uncooperative federalism," see Jessica Bulman-Pozen and Heather Gerken, "Uncooperative Federalism," *Yale Law Journal* 118 (2009): 1256-1310. For the possibilities of progressive federalism, see Richard Schragger, *City Power:*

Urban Governance in a Global Age (New York: Oxford University Press, 2016). In attending to tobacco federalism, this book cuts against the tendency to view policy made at the local and state levels as reactionary—as was so often the case when many of these same white southerners invoked "states' rights" in opposition to demands for national civil rights legislation by African Americans. See Mayeux and Tani, "Federalism Anew," 130.

10. Glenn A. Goldberg, "Legal Aspects of Non-Smokers' Rights or 'If We Are Not For Ourselves, Then Who Will Be For Us'" in *Smoking and Health: Proceedings of the Third World Conference On Smoking and Health* (Washington D.C.: United States Department of Health, Education and Welfare, National Institutes of Health, National Cancer Institute, 1976), 366.

11. For the "family farm" mythology that helped to sustain producerism, see Shane Hamilton, "Agribusiness, the Family Farm, and the Politics of Technological Determinism in the Post–World War II United States," *Technology and Culture* 55, No. 3 (2014): 560–590. See also Shane Hamilton, *Supermarket USA: Food and Power in the Cold War Farms Race* (New Haven: Yale University Press, 2018), 144–150.

12. Indeed, agriculture has been a source of much scholarship on the development of the American state. See Gabriel Rosenberg, *The 4-H Harvest: Sexuality and the State in Rural America* (Philadelphia: University of Pennsylvania Press, 2015); Ariel Ron, "Developing the Countryside: Scientific Agriculture and the Roots of the Republican Party" (PhD diss.; University of California, Berkeley, 2012); Bill Winders, *The Politics of Food Supply: U.S. Agriculture Policy and the World Economy* (New Haven: Yale University Press, 2010); Adam Sheingate, *The Rise of the Agricultural Welfare State: Institutions and Interest Group Power in the United States, France, and Japan* (Princeton: Princeton University Press, 2002); Daniel Carpenter, *Forging of Bureaucratic Autonomy: Reputations, Networks and Policy Innovations in Executive Agencies, 1862–1928* (Princeton: Princeton University Press, 2001); Victoria Saker Woeste, *The Farmer's Benevolent Trust: Law and Agricultural Cooperation in Industrial America, 1865–1945* (Chapel Hill: UNC Press, 1998); David Hamilton, *From New Day to New Deal: American Farm Policy from Hoover to Roosevelt* (Chapel Hill: UNC Press, 1991); Kenneth Finegold and Theda Skocpol, *State and Party in America's New Deal* (Madison: University of Wisconsin Press, 1991); John Mark Hansen, *Gaining Access: Congress and the Farm Lobby* (Chicago: University of Chicago Press, 1991). However, among modern American political historians, the New Deal's long-lasting agricultural legacy has largely been overshadowed by the New Deal's legacy on labor, business, and the welfare state. The seminal volume *The Rise and Fall of the New Deal Order*, for example, does not devote a single essay to agricultural regulation. See *The Rise and Fall of the New Deal Order, 1930–1980*, Steve Fraser and Gary Gerstle, eds. (Princeton: Princeton University Press, 1989). Indeed, farm regulations barely make an appearance in synthetic assessments of the New Deal's legacy on business or political realignment.

13. Beginning in 1933, the government began directly shaping the price and supply of most types of tobacco grown in the United States. The most widely produced types of tobacco were those that went into the manufacture of cigarettes: Burley and flue-cured. The latter was mostly grown in Kentucky and Tennessee, whereas flue-cured accounted for the bulk of all U.S. tobacco production and was grown in Virginia, North Carolina, South Carolina, Georgia, and Florida. Together, North Carolina and Kentucky produced 66 percent of the total U.S. tobacco crop. Because flue-cured tobacco is the primary tobacco ingredient in an American-style cigarette and because the majority of flue-cured tobacco was grown in North Carolina, this study focuses upon the federal flue-cured tobacco program, and primarily utilizes sources from North Carolina. For a technological history that demonstrates the legal construction of the flue-cured variety, see Barbara Hahn, *Making Tobacco Bright: Creating an American Commodity, 1617–1937* (Baltimore: Johns Hopkins University Press, 2011). For an ethnographic account of recent transformations in Burley tobacco, see Ann K. Ferrell, *Burley: Kentucky in a New Century* (Lexington: University Press of Kentucky, 2013).

14. The most comprehensive study to date about the operation of the tobacco program during the New Deal continues to be Anthony Badger, *Prosperity Road: The New Deal, Tobacco, and North Carolina* (Chapel Hill: University of North Carolina Press, 1980). For the persistence of multiracial landowner-ship despite U.S. Department of Agriculture (USDA) discrimination, see Adrienne Petty, *Standing Their Ground: Small Farmers in North Carolina since the Civil War* (New York: Oxford University Press, 2013). For a social history of tobacco production in the historic flue-cured areas of Virginia and North Carolina, see Evan Bennett, *When Tobacco Was King: Families, Farm Labor, and Federal Policy in the Piedmont* (Gainesville: University Press of Florida, 2014). For an environmental history of tobacco in the Old Belt region of flue-cured production, see Drew Swanson, *A Golden Weed: Tobacco and the Environment in the Piedmont South* (New Haven: Yale University Press, 2014). For the New Deal's transformation of southern agriculture generally, see Jack Temple Kirby, *Rural Worlds Lost: The American South, 1920–1960* (Baton Rouge: LSU Press, 1987); Pete Daniel, *Breaking the Land: The Transformation of Cotton, Tobacco, and Rice Cultures since 1880* (Champaign: University of Illinois Press, 1986); Gilbert Fite, *Cotton Fields No More: Southern Agriculture, 1865–1980* (Lexington: University Press of Kentucky, 1984). For more on the USDA during the New Deal, see Jess Gilbert, *Planning Democracy: Agrarian Intellectuals and the Intended New Deal* (New Haven: Yale University Press, 2015); Sarah Phillips, *This Land, This Nation: Conservation, Rural America, and the New Deal* (New York: Cambridge University Press, 2007); Richard S. Kirkendall, *Social Scientists and Farm Politics in the Age of Roosevelt* (Aimes: Iowa State University Press, 1966).

15. This book joins other recent reassessments of the rise-and-fall framework for understanding twentieth-century political life. See *Shaped by the State*, Cebul, Geismer, and Williams, eds. See Brent Cebul, Lily Geismer, and

Mason B. Williams, eds., *Shaped by the State: Toward a New Political History of the Twentieth Century*, (Chicago: University of Chicago Press, 2018).

16. This approach draws upon the "organizational synthesis" framework, which highlights the interconnections between elites and experts in private and public sector bureaucracies. See Louis Galambos, "The Emerging Organizational Synthesis in Modern American History," *Business History Review* 44, No. 3 (Autumn 1970): 279–290; Brian Balogh, "Reorganizing the Organizational Synthesis: Federal-Professional Relations in Modern America," *Studies in American Political Development* 5, No. 1 (Spring 1991): 119–172.

17. For more on the associational model of state-building, wherein formal public capacity is enhanced and legitimated by reliance on civic, voluntary, and private sector organizations, see Brian Balogh, *The Associational State: American Governance in the Twentieth Century* (Philadelphia: University of Pennsylvania Press, 2015); William J. Novak, "The Myth of the 'Weak' American State," *American Historical Review* 113, No. 3 (June 2008): 752–772. The associational approach bears many similarities to European studies of corporatism in the 1970s and 1980s. Animating questions centered on the structure of interest groups—whether unions, agriculture organizations, or trade and peak associations—and their relation to political bargaining and the allocation of resources and entitlements. Neo-corporatist scholarship rejected as "insufficiently complex" the oppositional binary between state and market implicit in many pluralist accounts between the state and market/community. As transnational scholarship on corporatism developed, scholars of American institutions played only a limited role, even as foundational works in American political development began to interrogate some of the same questions—namely, those about the state itself as an organizational structure. To a large extent, the siloed development of the "neo-corporatist" European school, on the one hand, and the "state-centered" American school, on the other, represented both American and European assumptions about U.S. exceptionalism. As one neo-corporatist theorist wrote, "It is illuminating to remember . . . that while pluralism was an American creation, neo-corporatism was primarily a European one. [It was] originally inspired by reflection upon the different relationship between the state and subgroups which distinguished the European world from the USA." See Noel O'Sullivan, "The Political Theory of Neo-Corporatism," in *The Corporate State: Corporatism and the State Tradition in Western Europe*, Andrew Cox and Noel O'Sullivan, eds. (Aldershot, UK: Elgar, 1988), 5; Philippe Schmitter, "Still the Century of Corporatism?" *Review of Politics* 36, No. 1 (1974): 85–131. See also *Trends towards Corporatist Intermediation*, Schmitter and Gerald Lembruch, eds. (New York and London: Sage, 1979); Alan Cawson, *Corporatism and Political Theory* (Oxford: Blackwell, 1986). One notable exception to the Eurocentric focus of most studies in corporatism is Donald Brand, *Corporatism and the Rule of*

Law: A Study of the National Recovery Administration (Ithaca: Cornell University Press, 1988). More recently, some scholars of the American state have begun to use the vocabulary of corporatism. See Laura Phillips Sawyer, *American Fair Trade: Proprietary Capitalism, Corporatism, and the "New Competition," 1890–1940* (New York: Cambridge University Press, 2018).

18. Indeed, scholars of U.S. foreign policy have long attended to the ways in which private business and interest groups expand the formal capacities of U.S. diplomatic and economic power. Michael Hogan is the exemplar of this paradigm. See Michael J. Hogan, *The Marshall Plan: America, Britain and the Reconstruction of Western Europe, 1947–1952* (Cambridge: Cambridge University Press, 1987); Hogan, "Corporatism: A Positive Appraisal," *Diplomatic History* 10, No. 4 (October 1986): 363–372.

19. Balogh, *The Associational State,* 3. For accounts of the ways in which the U.S. state frequently operates "out of sight" of most citizens, see Suzanne Mettler, *The Submerged State: How Invisible Government Policies Undermine American Democracy* (Chicago: Chicago University Press, 2011); Jacob Hacker, *The Divided Welfare State: The Battle over Public and Private Social Benefits in the United States* (New York: Cambridge University Press, 2002); Jennifer Klein, *For All These Rights: Business, Labor, and the Shaping of America's Public-Private Welfare State* (Princeton: Princeton University Press, 2003).

20. Mark Tushnet, "An Essay on Rights," *Texas Law Review* 62 (1984): 1371.

21. Ira Katznelson, *Fear Itself: The New Deal and the Origins of Our Time* (New York: Liveright, 2013), 14–16. See also Katznelson, *When Affirmative Action Was White* (New York: Norton, 2005). Historians of southern agriculture have been particularly attentive to the discriminatory elements of USDA policy. See Pete Daniel, *Dispossession: Discrimination against African American Farmers in the Age of Civil Rights* (Chapel Hill: UNC Press, 2013). A class-action discrimination suit was brought by African-American farmers against the USDA for the agency's discrimination against them between 1983 and 1997. See Timothy Pigford, et al., v. Dan Glickman, Secretary, United States Department of Agriculture, U.S. District Court for the District of Columbia, Civil Action No. 97-1978.

22. For the left-wing version of the critique, see C. Wright Mills, *The Power Elite* (New York: Oxford, 1956); Gabriel Kolko, *The Triumph of Conservatism: A Reinterpretation of American History, 1900–1916* (New York: Free Press, 1963); Grant McConnell, *Private Power and American Democracy* (New York: Knopf, 1966). McConnell especially discusses the way in which agricultural interest groups and the USDA maintained a high-level integration. Marver Bernstein's thesis of the "life cycle" of regulatory agencies was particularly influential to economists' understanding of "captive agencies" as promoting economic inefficiencies through the rent-seeking behavior of regulated industries. See Marver Bernstein, *Regulating Business by Independent Commission* (Princeton: Princeton University Press, 1955). For the right-wing version of the capture thesis, see George J. Stigler, "The Theory of Economic Regulation,"

Bell Journal of Economics and Management Science 2, No. 1 (1971): 3–21; Richard A. Posner, "Theories of Economic Regulation," *Bell Journal of Economics and Management Science* 5, No. 2 (1974): 335–358. For an overview of the history of the capture thesis, see William J. Novak, "A Revisionist History of Regulatory Capture," in *Preventing Regulatory Capture,* Daniel Carpenter and David Moss, eds. (New York: Cambridge, 2013).

23. For a discussion of the way in which young activist lawyers reimagined the judiciary as a site of democratic participation, see Reuel Schiller, "Enlarging the Administrative Polity: Administrative Law and the Changing Definition of Pluralism, 1945–1970," *Vanderbilt Law Review* 53, No. 5 (2000): 1389–1453; Schiller, *Forging Rivals: Race, Class, Law and the Collapse of Postwar Liberalism* (New York: Cambridge University Press, 2015), especially 143–146; Sean Farhang, *Litigation State: Public Regulation and Private Lawsuits in the United States* (Princeton: Princeton University Press, 2010). In what political theorist Michael McCann calls the "judicialization of public institutions," reformers reimagined the courts as a respite from and check on the elite-dominated legislative and administrative branches. See Michael W. McCann, *Taking Reform Seriously: Perspectives on Public Interest Liberalism* (Ithaca: Cornell University Press, 1986), 104.

24. Robert L. Rabin, "Federal Regulation in Historical Perspective," *Stanford Law Review* 38, No. 5 (1986), 1304. For an examination of the United States' early leading role in the passage of stringently precautionary laws, see David Vogel, *The Politics of Precaution: Regulating Health, Safety, and Environmental Risks in Europe and the United States* (Princeton: Princeton University Press, 2012). For an engaging study of the Reagan-era rollback of EPA and the Federal Trade Commission (FTC), see Richard Harris and Sidney Milkis, *The Politics of Regulatory Change: A Tale of Two Agencies* (New York: Oxford University Press, 1989); David Vogel, "The New Social Regulation in Historical and Comparative Perspective," in *Regulation in Perspective: Historical Essays,* Thomas McCraw, ed. (Boston: Graduate School of Business Administration, Harvard University, 1981).

25. The only sustained treatment of the history of smoking as an aspect of the history of organized labor is Gregory Wood, *Clearing the Air: The Rise and Fall of Smoking in the Workplace* (Ithaca: Cornell University Press, 2016).

26. U.S. Public Health Service, Office of the Surgeon General, *The Health Consequences of Smoking: A Report of the Surgeon General, 1972* (Washington, DC: Government Printing Office, 1972); Takeshi Hirayama, "Non Smoking Wives of Heavy Smokers Have a Higher Risk of Lung Cancer," *British Medical Journal* 283 (1981): 183–185; D. Trichopoulos et al., "Lung Cancer and Passive Smoking," *International Journal of Cancer* 27 (1981): 1–4; L. Garfinkel, "Time Trends in Lung Cancer Mortality among Non-Smokers and a Note on Passive Smoking," *Journal of the National Cancer Institute,* 66 (1981): 1061–1066.

27. U.S. Department of Health and Human Services, *The Health Consequences of Involuntary Smoking: A Report of the Surgeon General* (Washington, D.C.: Gov-

ernment Printing Office, 1986); National Research Council Committee on Passive Smoking, *Environmental Tobacco Smoke: Measuring Exposures and Assessing Health Effects* (Washington, DC: National Academy Press, 1986).

28. See Brandt, "Blow Some My Way: Passive Smoking, Risk and American Culture," in *Ashes to Ashes: The History of Smoking and Health*, Stephen Lock, Lois Reynolds, and E. M. Tansey, eds. (Amsterdam: Rodopi, 1998), 167. See also Constance Nathanson, *Disease Prevention as Social Change: The State, Society, and Public Health in the United States, France, Great Britain, and Canada* (New York: Russell Sage, 2007).

29. C. B. Barad, "Smoking on the Job: The Controversy Heats Up," *Occupational Health and Safety* 48 (1979): 21.

30. Bureau of National Affairs, *Where There's Smoke: Problems and Policies Concerning Smoking in the Workplace, a BNA Special Report,* 2nd ed., 1987; Tobacco Institute Records, n.d., University of California at San Francisco (UCSF) Library, https://www.industrydocumentslibrary.ucsf.edu/tobacco/docs/yzhv0060.

31. The argument that civil rights claims accelerated the demise of the collective-bargaining paradigm has been advanced by a number of labor historians. See especially Nelson Lichtenstein, *State of the Union: A Century of American Labor* (Princeton: Princeton University Press, 2002); Reuel Schiller, *Forging Rivals: Race, Class, Law, and the Collapse of Postwar Liberalism* (New York: Cambridge University Press, 2015); Paul Frymer, *Black and Blue: African Americans, the Labor Movement, and the Decline of the Democratic Party* (Princeton: Princeton University Press, 2009). For a cultural account of the role of "identity politics" in dissolving the class solidarism of labor, see Jefferson Cowie and Nick Salvatore, "The Long Exception: Rethinking the Place of the New Deal in American History," *International Labor and Working-Class History* 74, No. 1 (2008): 3–32. Historians of race and gender have highlighted how African Americans, women, and ethnic minorities reconstituted the meaning of citizenship at worksites, expanding upon the institutional mechanisms established during the New Deal. See Nancy MacLean, *Freedom Is Not Enough: The Opening of the American Workplace* (Cambridge, MA: Harvard University Press, 2006); MacLean, "Getting New Deal History Wrong," *International Labor and Working-Class History* 74 (2008): 49–55; Alice Kessler-Harris, *In Pursuit of Equity: Women, Men, and the Pursuit of Economic Citizenship in 20th-Century America* (New York: Oxford University Press, 2003). Legal historians have focused in particular on the role of Title VII of the Civil Rights Act of 1964 in expanding the fabric of economic inclusion while at the same time drawing new battle lines over the meaning of "equal opportunity." See Katherine Turk, *Equality on Trial: Gender and Rights in the Modern American Workplace* (Philadelphia: University of Pennsylvania Press, 2016); Sophia Z. Lee, *The Workplace Constitution: From the New Deal to the New Right* (New York: Cambridge University Press, 2014); Serena Mayeri, *Reasoning from Race: Feminism, Law, and the Civil Rights Revolution* (Cambridge, MA: Harvard University Press,

2011); John Skrentny, *Minority Rights Revolution* (Cambridge, MA: Harvard University Press, 2002).

32. Lily Geismer, *Don't Blame Us: Suburban Liberals and the Transformation of the Democratic Party* (Princeton: Princeton University Press, 2015). Geismer provides a compelling account of the ways that suburban quality of life concerns helped to reshape the Democratic Party.

33. Wendy Brown, "The End of Liberal Democracy," in *Edgework: Critical Essays on Knowledge and Politics* (Princeton: Princeton University Press, 2005), 43. For an engaging case study of the multiple dimensions of the economy of cheap, see Bryant Simon, *The Hamlet Fire: A Tragic Story of Cheap Food, Cheap Government, and Cheap Lives* (New York: New Press, 2017).

34. Some scholars use the term *neoliberalism* to describe the ascent of free-market orthodoxy. For a historical account of neoliberal ideas, see Angus Burgin, *The Great Persuasion: Reinventing Free Markets since the Great Depression* (Cambridge, MA: Harvard University Press, 2012); Daniel Stedman Jones, *Masters of the Universe: Hayek, Friedman, and the Birth of Neoliberal Politics* (Princeton: Princeton University Press, 2012); Philip Mirowski and Dieter Plehwe, eds., *The Road from Mont Pelerin: The Making of the Neoliberal Thought Collective* (Cambridge, MA: Harvard University Press, 2009). For a theoretical account of neoliberalism as a political project, see David Harvey, *A Brief History of Neoliberalism* (New York: Oxford University Press, 2005); Wendy Brown, *Undoing the Demos: Neoliberalism's Stealth Revolution* (New York: Zone, 2015). My understanding of modern political economy has been greatly enriched by these texts. However, this study does not use the term *neoliberalism* to describe the political economy of the last decades of the twentieth century because of the multiple meanings that it carries, a point highlighted by Daniel Rodgers. See Rodgers, "The Uses and Abuses of 'Neoliberalism,'" *Dissent* 65, No. 1 (Winter, 2018): 78–87. For example, the political economy reflected in the rise of the nonsmoker was far from deregulatory.

35. In 2005, 63 percent of flue-cured producers and 56 percent of Burley producers who had farmed the previous year quit farming tobacco. See Linda Foreman and William McBride, "Policy Reform in the Tobacco Industry: Producers Adapt to a Changing Market," *Economic Information Bulletin* 77 (May 2011), https://www.ers.usda.gov/webdocs/publications/44553/7423 _eib77.pdf?v=41055; Erik Dohlman, Linda Foreman, and Michelle Da Pra, "The Post-Buyout Experience: Peanut and Tobacco Sectors Adapt to Policy Reform," EIB-60, U.S. Department of Agriculture, Economic Research Service, November 2009.

36. Ariel Ramchandani, "The Overlooked Children Working America's Tobacco Fields," *Atlantic*, June 21, 2018, accessed September 12, 2018, https://www .theatlantic.com/family/archive/2018/06/child-labor-tobacco/562964/; Oxfam America and the Farm Labor Organizing Committee, *A State of Fear: Human Rights Abuses in North Carolina's Tobacco Industry* (2011), accessed September 12, 2018, https://www.oxfamamerica.org/static/media/files/a-state -of-fear.pdf.

37. Peter Benson, *Tobacco Capitalism: Growers, Migrant Workers, and the Changing Face of a Global Industry* (Princeton: Princeton University Press, 2012).

38. Kristin Collins, "Tobacco Buyout Shows Shift to Giant Farms," *Raleigh News and Observer*, October 17, 2004.

39. Allen Ginsberg, *Howl and Other Poems* (San Francisco: City Lights Pocket Bookshop, 1956).

40. Allan Brandt's *Cigarette Century*, Richard Kluger's *Ashes to Ashes*, and Robert Proctor's *Golden Holocaust* are models of meticulous, ethical scholarship. And in the case of Proctor and Brandt, their scholarship has also served to regulate the industry, compelling further disclosure of once-secret documents that have provided the basis for subsequent research and litigation. Both historians testified against the companies in United States v. Philip Morris *USA, Inc.* (2006), which found that the companies had engaged in a "massive 50-year scheme to defraud the public, including consumers of cigarettes" and had violated the Racketeer Influenced and Corrupt Organizations Act. See especially Robert Proctor, *Golden Holocaust: Origins of the Cigarette Catastrophe and the Case for Abolition* (Berkeley: University of California Press, 2011); Brandt, *Cigarette Century*; Richard Kluger, *Ashes to Ashes: America's Hundred Year Cigarette War, the Public Health, and the Unabashed Triumph of Philip Morris* (New York: Knopf, 1996); Philip Hilts, *Smokescreen: The Truth behind the Tobacco Industry Cover-Up* (Boston: Addison-Wesley, 1996); Stanton A. Glantz, John Slade, Lisa Bero, Peter Hanauer, and Deborah Barnes, *The Cigarette Papers* (Berkeley: University of California Press, 1996). For an insider's account, see David Kessler, *A Question of Intent: A Great American Battle with a Deadly Industry* (New York: Public Affairs, 2001); Louis M. Kyriakoudes, "Historians' Testimony on 'Common Knowledge' of the Risks of Tobacco Use: A Review and Analysis of Experts Testifying on Behalf of Cigarette Manufacturers in Civil Litigation," *Tobacco Control* 15, Suppl. 4 (2006): iv107–iv116; Jon Wiener, "Big Tobacco and the Historians," *The Nation*, February 25, 2010. For a journalistic account that emphasizes the relationship between the tobacco industry and the modern Tea Party, see Jeff Nesbit, *Poison Tea: How Big Oil and Big Tobacco Invented the Tea Party and Captured the GOP* (New York: Thomas Dunne Books, 2016).

41. Proctor, *Golden Holocaust*, 261–262.

42. Naomi Oreskes and Erik M. Conway, *Merchants of Doubt: How a Handful of Scientists Obscured the Truth on Issues from Tobacco Smoke to Global Warming* (New York: Bloomsbury Press, 2010); *Golden Holocaust*; *Agnotology: The Making and Unmaking of Ignorance*, eds. Robert N. Proctor and Londa Schiebinger, (Palo Alto: Stanford University Press, 2008).

43. "Smoking and Health Proposal," 1969, Brown & Williamson Records, https://www.industrydocumentslibrary.ucsf.edu/tobacco/docs/psdw0147.

44. As Naomi Oreskes and Erik Conway have demonstrated, these techniques proved inspirational to a variety of other industries, especially the fossil fuel industry in its denial of global warming. Against the backdrop of

today's climate crisis, a deeper understanding of the cigarette's history promises insights beyond smoking. Oreskes and Conway, *Merchants of Doubt*, 169–215.

45. In looking beyond Big Tobacco, my approach is consistent with one recently called for by historian Nan Enstad, whose *Cigarettes, Inc.* situates the rise of the multinational tobacco corporation within broad cultural currents running from the Jim Crow south to China. In this rendering, the cigarette functions less as an object lesson in corporate villainy than as an emblem of particular forms of political power. Nan Enstad, *Cigarettes, Inc.: An Intimate History of Corporate Imperialism* (Chicago: University of Chicago Press, 2018), x–xii.

46. Brandt, "Blow Some My Way," 165. Historians of foreign relations have thus far been the most attentive to the relationship between American systems of production and international consumption patterns. See Nick Cullather, *Hungry World: America's Cold War Battle with Poverty in Asia* (Cambridge, MA: Harvard University Press, 2010); Winders, *The Politics of Food Supply*.

47. The nexus between agricultural producer associations and state policy regarding consumption can provide a model for future research into the nexus between producer associations and the federal government that has shaped global consumer capitalism since World War II. See Sarah Milov, "Promoting Agriculture: Farmers, the State, and Checkoff Marketing, 1935–2005," *Business History Review* 90, No. 3 (2016): 505–536; Hamilton, *Supermarket USA*, 4, for a similar approach to the "intertwined politics of food production and consumption." The historiography of consumption and consumerism in modern America is vast. See Lizabeth Cohen, *A Consumers' Republic: The Politics of Mass Consumption in Postwar America* (New York: Vintage, 2003); Meg Jacobs, *Pocketbook Politics: Economic Citizenship in Twentieth Century America* (Princeton: Princeton University Press, 2007); Robert Collins, *More: The Politics of Growth in Postwar America* (New York: Oxford University Press, 2000); Gary Cross, *An All Consuming Century: Why Commercialism Won in Modern America* (New York: Columbia University Press, 2002). Louis Hyman powerfully highlights the role that credit and debt played in the construction of the consumer economy. See Hyman, *Debtor Nation: The History of America in Red Ink* (Princeton: Princeton University Press, 2011). For analyses of rural America as a staging ground for a consumerist, market-oriented ethos, see Shane Hamilton, *Trucking Country: The Road to America's Wal-Mart Economy* (Princeton: Princeton University Press, 2008); Bethany Moreton, *To Serve God and Wal-Mart: The Making of Christian Free Enterprise* (Cambridge, MA: Harvard University Press, 2009).

48. The movement for nonsmokers' rights grew out of a broader suburban environmental ethos, frequently woman-led, and focused on quality of life issues. For more on suburban environmentalism, see Christopher Sellers, *Crabgrass Crucible: Suburban Nature and the Rise of Environmentalism in the Twentieth Century* (Chapel Hill: UNC Press, 2012); Adam Rome, *The Bulldozer in the Countryside: Suburban Sprawl and the Rise of American Environmentalism*

(New York: Cambridge University Press, 2001); Geismer, *Don't Blame Us: Suburban Liberals and the Transformation of the Democratic Party* (Princeton: Princeton University Press, 2015), especially chapters 4 and 7.

49. The history of the cigarette complicates the historiography of modern conservatism that emphasizes business's dismantling of New Deal economic commitments. For histories of the political mobilization of business, see Benjamin Waterhouse, *Lobbying America: The Politics of Business from Nixon to Nafta* (Princeton: Princeton University Press, 2014); Kim Philips-Fein, *Invisible Hands: The Businessman's Crusade against the New Deal* (New York: Norton, 2009); Elizabeth Fones-Wolf, *Selling Free Enterprise: The Business Assault on Labor and Liberalism, 1945–1960* (Urbana: University of Illinois Press, 1995).

50. Campaign for Tobacco-Free Kids, "The Toll of Tobacco in the United States," updated October 6, 2017, https://www.tobaccofreekids.org/problem/toll -us/.

51. Wendy Brown, "Suffering the Paradoxes of Rights," in *Left Legalism / Left Critique,* Janet Halley and Wendy Brown, eds. (Durham: Duke University Press, 2002), 421.

52. Brandt, "Blow Some My Way." For a provocative exploration of the way in which modern notions of health are tools of censure that serve economic and political interests, see Jonathan Metzl and Anna Kirkland, eds., *Against Health: How Health Became the New Morality* (New York: NYU Press, 2010).

53. J. J. Prochaska, A. K. Michalek, and C. Brown-Johnson, "Likelihood of Unemployed Smokers vs Nonsmokers Attaining Reemployment in a One-Year Observational Study," *JAMA Internal Medicine* 176, No. 5 (2016): 662–670.

54. Frank Newport, "Impact of Smoking, Being Overweight on a Person's Image," *Gallup Poll Briefing,* 2008, 1; *Business Source Complete,* EBSCOhost, accessed October 12, 2017, https://www.ebsco.com/products/research -databases/business-source-complete.

55. Wendy Brown, *Undoing the Demos: Neoliberalism's Stealth Revolution* (New York: Zone, 2015); Daniel Rodgers, *Age of Fracture* (Cambridge, MA: Harvard University Press, 2011), 3.

56. Ganna Sheremenko and James E. Epperson, "The United States Tobacco Industry after the Buyout," Selected Paper prepared for presentation at the Southern Agricultural Economics Association Annual Meeting, Corpus Christi, TX, February 5–8, 2011, http://ageconsearch.umn.edu/bitstream /98630/2/The%20U.S.%20Tobacco%20Industry%20after%20the%20 Buyout-1.pdf.

1. Tobacco in Industrializing America

1. Robert Penn Warren, *Night Rider,* reprint ed. (Nashville and Lanham, MD: J. S. Sanders Books, 1992), 15.

2. Ibid., 16.

3. In the nineteenth and early twentieth centuries, producerism was a powerful political ethic that valorized the sweated labor of farmers and workingmen who produced tangible wealth. These Americans were understood as true stewards of Republican virtue and national character. Michael Kazin, *The Populist Persuasion: An American History* (Ithaca: Cornell University Press, 1995), 13–17.

4. The phrase "little white slaver" was popularized by Henry Ford, who published a four-volume treatise against cigarettes between 1914 and 1916. Henry Ford, *The Case Against the Little White Slaver* (Detroit: 1914).

5. Lizabeth Cohen, *Making a New Deal: Industrial Workers in Chicago, 1919–1939* (New York: Cambridge University Press, 1990), esp. chapter 1; Elizabeth Sanders, *Roots of Reform: Farmers, Workers, and the American State, 1877–1917* (Chicago: University of Chicago Press, 1999); Nelson Lichtenstein, *State of the Union: A Century of American Labor* (Princeton: Princeton University Press, 2002); Ellis Hawley, *The New Deal and the Problem of Monopoly: A Study in Economic Ambivalence* (Princeton: Princeton University Press, 1966); Hawley, ed., *Herbert Hoover as Secretary of Commerce: Studies in New Era Thought and Practice* (Iowa City: University of Iowa Press, 1981); Robert H. Zieger, "Labor, Progressivism, and Herbert Hoover in the 1920's," *Wisconsin Magazine of History* 58, No. 3 (1975): 196–208.

6. "Tobacco Trust Worst Cormorant, He Asserts," *New York Times,* May 29, 1906.

7. Ibid.

8. Allan Brandt, *The Cigarette Century: The Rise, Fall, and Deadly Persistence of the Product That Defined America* (New York: Basic Books, 2007), 39–41; "An Illegal Trust Legalized," *World Today,* 21 (December 1911): 1440–1441.

9. Robert F. Durden, *The Dukes of Durham,* 1865–1929 (Durham: Duke University Press), 10–12.

10. Ibid., 12.

11. Robert Proctor, *Golden Holocaust: Origins of the Cigarette Catastrophe and the Case for Abolition* (Berkeley: University of California Press, 2011), 31–35.

12. As Nan Enstad has pointed out, "the story of entrepreneurial innovation in the US cigarette industry properly begins with Ginter rather than Duke." Nan Enstad, *Cigarettes, Inc.: An Intimate History of Corporate Imperialism* (Chicago: University of Chicago Press, 2018), 16.

13. Nannie Mae Tilley, *The Bright Tobacco Industry, 1860–1929* (Chapel Hill: UNC Press, 1948), 559.

14. Leonard Rogoff, *Homelands: Southern Jewish Identity in Durham–Chapel Hill and North Carolina* (Tuscaloosa: University of Alabama Press, 2001), 42; Joseph C. Robert, *The Story of Tobacco in America* (New York: Knopf, 1949), 141.

15. Rogoff, *Homelands,* 43.

16. Quoted in Enstad, *Cigarettes, Inc.,* 63.

17. Ibid.

18. For a history of the ascendancy of the industrial logic on U.S. farms, see Deborah Fitzgerald, *Every Farm a Factory: The Industrial Ideal in American Ag-*

riculture (New Haven: Yale University Press, 2003); Alan Olmstead and Paul Rhode, "An Overview of California Agricultural Mechanization, 1870–1930," *Agricultural History* 62, No. 3 (1988): 89.

19. Bonsack was never awarded the prize money, as Lewis Ginter judged his machine too unreliable. Enstad, *Cigarettes, Inc.,* 59.

20. Cassandra Tate, *Cigarette Wars: The Triumph of the "Little White Slaver"* (New York: Oxford University Press, 1999), 15.

21. The tax reduction, which had been debated in front of Congress sporadically since 1880, passed in 1883. Duke responded by immediately cutting the price of cigarettes in half, to 5 cents a package. This gave him an immediate foothold in the market, despite selling at a loss for several months. Tate, *Cigarette Wars,* 14.

22. Enstad, *Cigarettes, Inc.,* 63.

23. Tate, *Cigarette Wars,* 16; Proctor, *Golden Holocaust,* 39; Jordan Goodman, *Tobacco in History and Culture: An Encyclopedia* (Detroit: Thomson Gale, 2005), 42; Richard B. Tennant, *The American Cigarette Industry: A Study in Economic Analysis and Public Policy* (New Haven: Yale University Press, 1950), 41.

24. As Enstad notes, historians have also long attributed the success of the American Tobacco Company to Duke's genius for innovation, manifested in his use of the Bonsack cigarette machine. Enstad, *Cigarettes, Inc.,* 52–53, 58.

25. Quoted in Kluger, *Ashes to Ashes: America's Hundred Year Cigarette War, the Public Health, and the Unabashed Triumph of Philip Morris* (New York: Knopf, 1996), 25.

26. Enstad, *Cigarettes, Inc.,* 67–68; Charles McCurdy, "The Knight Sugar Decision of 1865 and the Modernization of American Corporation Law, 1869–1903," *Business History Review* 53, No. 3 (1979): 304–342; Naomi R. Lamoreaux, *The Great Merger Movement in American Business, 1895–1904* (New York: Cambridge University Press, 1985), 1; Jonathan Levy, *Freaks of Fortune: The Emerging World of Capitalism and Risk in America* (Cambridge, MA: Harvard University Press, 2012), 276–277.

27. Santa Clara County v. Southern Pacific Railroad Company, 118 U.S. 394 (1886); Enstad, *Cigarettes, Inc.,* 75–76. As Enstad notes, what was significant about the creation of corporate personhood was the way in which it augured a shift in the public imagination of the corporation as a private rather than public entity.

28. Enstad, *Cigarettes, Inc.,* 67.

29. Brandt, *Cigarette Century,* 32–36.

30. P. G. Porter, "Origins of American Tobacco Company," *Business History Review* 43, No. 1 (1969): 59–60.

31. Brandt, *Cigarette Century,* 38; Tennant notes that "the total return on $1,000 invested in 1890 without withdrawal and also without reinvestment of dividends would have been $35,197." *American Cigarette Industry,* 39.

32. Lamoreaux, *The Great Merger Movement in American Business.*

33. Porter, "Origins of American Tobacco Company," 66–67.

34. Kluger, *Ashes to Ashes*, 37.

35. Enstad, *Cigarettes, Inc.* 82.

36. Enstad, *Cigarettes, Inc.*; Nan Enstad, "To Know Tobacco: Southern Identity in China in the Jim Crow Era," *Southern Cultures* 13, No. 4 (2007): 6–23.

37. Emily Rosenberg, *Spreading the American Dream: American Economic and Cultural Expansion* (New York: Macmillan, 1982).

38. Morton Keller, *Regulating a New Economy: Public Policy and Economic Change in America, 1900–1933* (Cambridge, MA: Harvard University Press, 1990), 23.

39. William Leuchtenberg, *The American President: From Teddy Roosevelt to Bill Clinton* (New York: Oxford University Press, 2015), 23.

40. Keller, *Regulating a New Economy*, 27–28.

41. Robert Wiebe, *The Search for Order, 1877–1920* (New York: Hill and Wang, 1967).

42. United States. Department of Justice, *The United States of America, appellant, v. the American tobacco company and others: The American tobacco company and others, appellants, v. the United States of America . . . Brief for the United States* (Washington, D.C.: Government Printing Office, 1910).

43. United States v. American Tobacco Company 221 U.S. 106 (1911).

44. Tate, *Cigarette Wars*, 7.

45. Leonard Rogoff, "Jewish Proletarians in the New South: The Durham Cigarette Rollers," *American Jewish History* 82, No. 1/4 (1994): 141–157.

46. See ibid., Table 2.

47. For a history of Italian cigarette consumption see Carl Ipsen, *Fumo: Italy's Love Affair with the Cigarette* (Palo Alto: Stanford University Press, 2016), especially 15–25; "Murder over Cigarettes," *New York Times*, April 2, 2011; "Necklace of Dynamite, Novel Suicide Method," *Washington Post*, June 18, 1922.

48. Tate, *Cigarette Wars*, 6.

49. This narrative is suggested by a number of historians. Duke's sympathetic biographers, Alfred Chandler's machine-centered account of the rise of business management, and critical accounts of the tobacco industry share a teleological conception of the cigarette's eventual triumph over other forms of consumption. Referring to the historiography of Duke's Tobacco Trust, one historian has deemed this tendency the "Whig fable of American Tobacco." See Leslie Hannah, "The Whig Fable of American Tobacco," *Journal of Economic History* 66, No. 1 (2006): 42–43.

50. Ibid,, 45.

51. Tate, *Cigarette Wars*, 4.

52. Ibid., 130.

53. "Letters to the Editor," *Journal of Education*, August 15, 1907, 156.

54. For more on the association of the cigarette and male effeminacy, see Enstad, *Cigarettes, Inc.*, 39–42.

55. Tate, *Cigarette Wars*, 21.

56. Quoted in ibid., 18.

57. Ibid.

58. Ford, *The Case against the Little White Slaver*, 27.

59. Quoted in Tate, *Cigarette Wars*, 125.

60. Ibid., 66.

61. Ibid.; Brandt, *Cigarette Century*, 51; Michael Schudson, *Advertising, the Uneasy Persuasion: Its Dubious Impact on American Society* (New York: Basic Books, 1984), 186.

62. Although tobacco had long been associated with war, the centrality of cigarettes was novel. Previous wartime rations had only included pipe and smoking tobacco. See Tate, *Cigarette Wars*, 81.

63. Quoted in ibid., 73.

64. "They've Had a Lot of Tobacco," *New York Times*, May 24, 1918; Tate, *Cigarette Wars*, 83.

65. *Don't Forget the Smoke* (Monographic, 1918), Notated Music, https://www.loc.gov/item/2009440254/.

66. William H. Nicholls, *Price Policies in the Cigarette Industry: A Study of "Concerted Action" and Its Social Control, 1911–1950* (Nashville: Vanderbilt University Press), 18.

67. Tate, *Cigarette Wars*, 151.

68. William Leach, *Land of Desire: Merchants, Power, and the Rise of a New American Culture* (New York: Pantheon, 1993); Roland Marchand, *Advertising the American Dream: Making Way for Modernity* (Berkeley, Los Angeles, and London: University of California Press, 1985).

69. Nicholls, *Price Policies in the Cigarette Industry*, 59–61.

70. Brandt, *Cigarette Century*, 73–75.

71. Tate, *Cigarette Wars*, 117.

72. The True Inwardness of the Tobacco Situation," *Progressive Farmer*, September 25, 1920, 16.

73. Historian Evan Bennett has cautioned against nostalgia for historical tobacco production practices. Evan P. Bennett, "Dubious Heritage: Tobacco, History, and the Perils of Remembering the Rural Past," *Agricultural History* 86, No. 2 (2012): 23–40.

74. Samuel Huntington Hobbs, *North Carolina: Economic and Social* (Chapel Hill: UNC Press, 1930), 119.

75. Evan Bennett, *When Tobacco Was King: Families, Farm Labor, and Federal Policy in the Piedmont* (Gainesville: University Press of Florida, 2014), 63.

76. Tilley, *Bright Tobacco Industry*, 356–357.

77. Tobacco buyers relied on a complicated set of gesticulations to signal their purchase to the auctioneer. For an excellent atmospheric description of the process, see Pete Daniel, *Breaking the Land: The Transformation of Cotton, Tobacco, and Rice Cultures since 1880* (Urbana: University of Illinois Press, 1985); Thomas Jackson Woofter, *The Plight of Cigarette Tobacco* (Chapel Hill: UNC Press, 1931), chapter 4.

78. Daniel, *Breaking the Land*, 209; Bennett, *When Tobacco Was King*, 37–38; Tilley, *Bright Tobacco Industry*, 205.
79. Quoted in Daniel, *Breaking the Land*, 27.
80. Quoted in Tilley, *Bright Tobacco Industry*, 305.
81. Woofter, *Plight of Cigarette Tobacco*, 42.
82. Tilley, *Bright Tobacco Industry*, 205.
83. Woofter, *Plight of Cigarette Tobacco*, 45.
84. *Report of the Federal Trade Commission on the Tobacco Industry* (Washington, DC: Government Printing Office, 1921), 53.
85. Ibid., 144.
86. Quoted in ibid., 26.
87. G. Cullom Davis, "The Transformation of the Federal Trade Commission, 1914–1929," *Mississippi Valley Historical Review* 49, No. 3 (1962): 437–455.
88. William Nicholls, *Price Policies in the Cigarette Industry*, 207.
89. Ibid., 214; *Report of the Federal Trade Commission*, 120; Reavis Cox, *Competition in the American Tobacco Industry, 1911–1932* (New York: Columbia University Press, 1933), 146.
90. Woofter, *Plight of Cigarette Tobacco*, 48.
91. "The True Inwardness of the Tobacco Situation," *Progressive Farmer*, September 25, 1920, 16.
92. The literature on land tenure and credit markets in the rural South is vast. See Gavin Wright *Old South–New South: Revolutions in the Southern Economy since the Civil War* (New York: Basic Books, 1986); Harold D. Woodman, *New South–New Law: The Legal Foundations of Credit and Labor Relations in the Postbellum Agricultural South* (Baton Rouge: Louisiana State University Press, 1995). Scholars have demonstrated that a lack of rural credit facilities exacerbated tenancy rates across the South. To finance a tobacco harvest, landowners, tenants and sharecroppers had to borrow money at high interest rates. Heavily indebted, farmers faced both subtle and outright pressure to settle outstanding notes as soon as possible. From a farmer's perspective, quick cash was the main advantage of the auction system—and the only way he could borrow more money to finance the next year's crop.
93. Hawley, *New Deal and the Problem of Monopoly*; Gabriel Kolko, *The Triumph of Conservatism: A Re-Interpretation of American History* (New York: Free Press of Glencoe, 1963); Louis Galambos, "The Emerging Organizational Synthesis in Modern American History," *Business History Review* 44, No. 3 (1970): 279–290; Galambos, "Technology, Political Economy, and Professionalization: Central Themes of the Organizational Synthesis," *Business History Review* 57, No. 4 (1983): 471–493; Gerhard Lehmbruch and Philippe C. Schmitter, eds., *Patterns of Corporatist Policy-Making* (London: Sage, 1982).
94. Throughout the 1920s, no less than 46 percent, and as much as 57 percent of the entire bright leaf tobacco crop was exported yearly, primarily to the United Kingdom. See Tilley, *Bright Tobacco Industry*, 338.
95. *Yearbook of Agriculture 1921* (Washington, DC: Government Printing Office, 1922), 4–12.

96. James H. Shideler, *Farm Crisis, 1919–1923* (Berkeley: University of California Press, 1957), 46.

97. Ibid., 190.

98. As farmers throughout the United States floundered during the farm crisis of the 1920s, there were several attempts to pass comprehensive farm legislation. The most influential of these attempts was the McNary-Haugen Plan, which was first proposed in 1924, but was not passed for another three years. The bill stipulated that commodities in surplus of domestic demand were to be purchased at the domestic price by a government corporation, which would sell the surplus abroad at the world price. Farmers would finance the losses sustained by the surplus corporation through a tax, or "equalization fee," assessed on each unit of the commodity purchased by the corporation. The two most interventionist aspects of the legislation, the "equalization fee" and the government storage and loan corporation, were the direct antecedents of the "processing tax" and stabilization agencies passed as part of the New Deal's agricultural policy. The most extensive work on the agricultural politics of the 1920s, especially the McNary-Haugen legislation, remains Gilbert Fite, *George N. Peek and the Fight for Farm Parity* (Norman: University of Oklahoma Press, 1954).

99. For more on the USDA as an incubator of assertive public policy, see Daniel Carpenter, *The Forging of Bureaucratic Autonomy: Reputations, Networks, and Innovation in Executive Agencies, 1862–1928* (Princeton: Princeton University Press, 2001). Indeed, the USDA's reputation for scientific expertise was cemented by the tenure of Gifford Pinchot as the chief of the Division of Forestry at the USDA, which began in 1898. See Brian Balogh, "Scientific Forestry and the Roots of the Modern American State: Gifford Pinchot's Path to Progressive Reform" in *The Associational State: American Governance in the Twentieth Century* (Philadelphia: University of Pennsylvania Press, 2015).

100. As some scholars and participants in the BAE's founding have pointed out, the establishment of the bureau was actually an act of administrative preemption against Hoover's designs on transferring "the marketing work of the Department of Agriculture to the Department of Commerce." See Harry C. McDean, "Professionalism, Policy and Farm Economists in the Early Bureau of Agricultural Economics," *Agricultural History* 57, No. 1 (1983): 77; see also Lloyd S. Tenny, "The Bureau of Agricultural Economics, The Early Years," *Journal of Farm Economics* 29, No. 4 (1947): 1017–1026. For the history of the BAE, see David E. Hamilton, *From New Day to New Deal: American Farm Policy from Hoover to Roosevelt, 1928–1933* (Chapel Hill: UNC Press, 1991), 20–25; Carpenter, *The Forging of Bureaucratic Autonomy*, 323–325; Shideler, *Farm Crisis*, 133–135. Many scholars have noted that some of the most innovative policy solutions of the New Deal were incubated at the BAE: see Richard S. Kirkendall, *Social Scientists and Farm Politics in the Age of Roosevelt* (New York: Columbia University Press, 1966); Jess Gilbert, "Eastern Urban Liberals and Midwestern Agrarian Intellectuals: Two Group Portraits of Progressives in the New Deal Department of Agriculture,"

Agricultural History 74, No. 2 (2000): 162–180; Jess Gilbert and Ellen Baker, "Wisconsin Economists and New Deal Agricultural Policy: The Legacy of Progressive Professors," *Wisconsin Magazine of History* 80, No. 4 (1997): 280–312.

101. Shideler, *Farm Crisis,* 141–151; Hamilton, *From New Day to New Deal,*133.
102. Joan Hoff Wilson, "Herbert Hoover's Agricultural Policies, 1921–1928," in *Herbert Hoover as Secretary of Commerce,* 121.
103. Shideler, *Farm Crisis,* 141–151; Joseph G. Knapp, *The Advance of American Cooperative Enterprise: 1920–1945* (Danville, IL: Interstate Printers and Publishers, 1973), 32.
104. John Mark Hansen, *Gaining Access: Congress and the Farm Lobby, 1919–1981* (Chicago: University of Chicago Press, 1991), 46–70; Philip A. Grant, "Southern Congressmen and Agriculture, 1921–1932," *Agricultural History* 53, No.1 (1979): 339.
105. Bennett, *When Tobacco Was King,* 63–64.
106. Hutcheson to Taylor, November 22, 1920, Folder 1, Box 1, Tobacco Growers' Cooperative Association (TGCA) Records, Southern Historical Collection (SHC), Louis Round Wilson Special Collections Library, University of North Carolina at Chapel Hill, Chapel Hill, North Carolina.
107. Hanna, "Agricultural Cooperation in Tobacco," 303. For a full account of the Tobacco Wars of 1904–1906, see Tracy Campbell, *The Politics of Despair: Power and Resistance in the Tobacco Wars* (Lexington: University Press of Kentucky, 2005).
108. 62 Cong. Rec. 2057 (1922).
109. Grace H. Larsen and Henry E. Erdman, "Aaron Sapiro: Genius of Farm Cooperative Promotion," *Mississippi Valley Historical Review* 49, No. 2 (1962): 242–268. For an extensive analysis of the way that cooperative marketing laws shaped agricultural development, see Victoria Saker Woeste, *The Farmer's Benevolent Trust: Law and Agricultural Cooperation in Industrial America, 1865–1945* (Chapel Hill: UNC Press, 1998).
110. Julie A. Hogeland, "The Economic Culture of U.S. Agriculture Cooperatives," *Culture and Agriculture* 28, No. 2 (2006): 68.
111. Ibid. For an illuminating analysis of the role of trade associations and cooperatives in creating new understandings of market fairness and competition, see Laura Philips Sawyer, *American Fair Trade: Capitalism, Corporatism, and the "New Competition," 1890–1940* (Cambridge: Cambridge University Press, 2018).
112. Victoria Saker Woeste, "Insecure Equality: Louis Marshall, Henry Ford, and the Problem of Defamatory Antisemitism, 1920–1929," *Journal of American History* 91, No. 3 (December 2004): 877–905; Woeste, *Henry Ford's War on Jews and the Legal Battle against Hate Speech* (Palo Alto: Stanford University Press, 2012).
113. "North Carolina Tobacco Farmers Organize," *Progressive Farmer,* October 2, 1920, 21.

114. Ibid.
115. Hamilton, *From New Day to New Deal,* 25. Farmers were not strangers to organizing for business. As historian Charles Postel has argued, the Populist movement of the late nineteenth century was sought to "adapt the model of large-scale enterprise to their own needs of association and marketing." Postel, *The Populist Vision* (New York: Oxford University Press, 2007), 4. As Evan Bennett has pointed out, the roots of cooperative organizing ran deep in the tobacco belt, with decades of (faltering) attempts at organizing against the auction system beginning in the 1870s with the Patrons of Husbandry. Bennett, *When Tobacco Was King,* 48–62.
116. See, for instance, "Cooperative Marketing Has Grown Tremendously," *Progressive Farmer,* July 4, 1925, 4; "Brightening Outlook for Tobacco Marketing Associations," *Progressive Farmer,* August 22, 1925, 4.
117. For more on the transatlantic world of agricultural reform in the Progressive era, see Daniel Rodgers, *Atlantic Crossings: Social Politics in a Progressive Age* (Cambridge, MA: Harvard University Press, 1998), 318–340.
118. Clarence Poe to J. Y. Joyner, 19 November 1920, Folder 24, Box 2, TGCA Records, SHC.
119. Quoted in Woeste, *Farmer's Benevolent Trust,* 198.
120. Ibid., 195.
121. Ibid., 194.
122. Undated, Folder 6, Box 1, Ralph Waldo Green Papers, Special Collections Library, North Carolina State University (NCSU), Raleigh, North Carolina.
123. Hanna, "Agricultural Cooperation in Tobacco," 305.
124. Quoted in Woeste, *Farmer's Benevolent Trust,* 199.
125. "News Letter," November 23, 1922, Folder 35, Box 3, TGCA Records, SHC. Emphasis in original.
126. "News Letter," April 2, 1923, Folder 40, Box 3, Folder, TGCA Records, SHC.
127. Tobacco Growers' Co-op. Association v. Jones, 185 N. C. 265, 117 S.E. 174 (1923).
128. Tilley, *Bright Tobacco Industry,* 456.
129. Woeste, *Farmer's Benevolent Trust,* 206.
130. Daniel, *Breaking the Land,* 36; Hanna, "Agricultural Cooperation in Tobacco," 313.
131. Credit, Credit Union, Folder, "War Finance Corporation," Box 7, General Correspondence, Records of the Bureau of Agricultural Economics, Record Group 83, National Archives and Records Administration–II, College Park, Maryland (NARA-II). BAE records indicate that livestock co-ops borrowed 99.9 million; cotton co-ops 81.8 million; tobacco co-ops 52.5 million; grain co-ops 36.79 million, and sugar beet co-ops 11.46 million.
132. Oliver Sands to John Hutcheson, May 13, 1921, Folder 20, Box 2, TGCA Records, SHC.
133. *Tri-State Tobacco Grower,* June 1922, 1. Emphasis and capitalization in the original.

134. Tilley, *Bright Tobacco Industry,* 152–154.
135. Indeed, flue-cured tobacco cultivation was spreading particularly rapidly in South Carolina during the years of the TGCA's operation. See Eldred E. Prince and Robert R. Simpson, *Long Green: The Rise and Fall of Tobacco in South Carolina* (Athens: University of Georgia Press, 2000).
136. Quoted in Nathaniel Browder, *The Tri-State Tobacco Growers Association, 1922–1925* (Raleigh: 1983), 8.
137. W. T. Joyner to A. J. Davis, 12 December 1922, Folder 38, Box 3, TGCA Records, SHC.
138. John R. Hutcheson to M. O. Wilson, 19 November 1921, Folder 24, Box 2, TGCA Records, SHC.
139. Tilley, *Bright Tobacco Industry,* 469–472.
140. Hanna, "Agricultural Cooperation in Tobacco," 319; ibid., 468.
141. "Tobacco Association Goes Forward," *Progressive Farmer,* January 17, 1925, 4.
142. Tilley, *Bright Tobacco Industry,* 462–463.
143. "American Tobacco Profits a Record," *New York Times,* March 18, 1927, 33.
144. United States, Federal Trade Commission, *The American Tobacco Company and the Imperial Tobacco Company. Message from the President of the United States transmitting the Report of the Federal Trade Commission of its investigation of charges against the American Tobacco Company and the Imperial Tobacco Company*... (Washington, DC: Government Printing Office, 1926), 3.

2. Tobacco's New Deal

Epigraphs: Samuel Huntington Hobbs Jr., *North Carolina: Economic and Social* (Chapel Hill: UNC Press, 1930), 117; "Southern Tobacco Farmer, Prosperous Again Pays Off Old Debts," *Wall Street Journal,* December 28, 1934.

1. Henry A. Wallace, *New Frontiers* (New York: Reynal and Hitchcock, 1934), 162. For a sympathetic biography of Wallace, see John C. Culver and John Hyde, *American Dreamer: The Life and Times of Henry A. Wallace* (New York: Norton, 2000).
2. Quoted in David T. Bazelon, "The Faith of Henry Wallace: The Populist Tradition in the Atomic Age," *Commentary,* April 1, 1947.
3. United States, Agricultural Adjustment Administration, *Agricultural Adjustment: A Report of Administration of the Agricultural Adjustment Act, May 1933 to February 1934* (Washington, DC: Supt. of Docs., GPO, 1934), 3.
4. Federal Reserve Bank of Richmond, Research Department, *Flue-Cured Tobacco: An Economic Survey* (Richmond: Author, 1952).
5. Anthony Badger, *Prosperity Road: The New Deal, Tobacco, and North Carolina* (Chapel Hill: UNC Press, 1980), 23.
6. Henry Wallace credited Rex Tugwell, Mordecai Ezekiel, Jerome Frank, Chester Davis, George Peek, and Charles Brand with the drafting of the 1933 Agricultural Adjustment Act. See Wallace, *New Frontiers,* 163.
7. Ellis Hawley, *The New Deal and the Problem of Monopoly: A Study in Economic Ambivalence* (Princeton: Princeton University Press, 1966); Brian Balogh, *The Associational State: American Governance in the Twentieth Century* (Philadelphia:

University of Pennsylvania Press, 2015), 147; Theda Skocpol and Kenneth Finegold, "State Capacity and Economic Intervention in the Early New Deal," *Political Science Quarterly* 97, No. 2 (1982): 264; Arthur Schlesinger, *The Coming of the New Deal* (Boston: Houghton Mifflin, 1958), 97.

8. Donald Brand, *Corporatism and the Rule of Law: A Study of the National Recovery Administration* (Ithaca: Cornell University Press, 1988), 266.

9. Laura Philips Sawyer, *American Fair Trade: Proprietary Capitalism, Corporatism, and the New Competition 1890–1940* (New York: Cambridge University Press, 2018), 266–289; Peter H. Irons, *The New Deal Lawyers* (Princeton: Princeton University Press, 1982), 17; Hawley, *The New Deal and the Problem of Monopoly;* Charles Frederick Roos, *NRA Economic Planning* (Bloomington, IN: Principia Press, 1937), 36–50.

10. James Morone, *The Democratic Wish: Popular Participation and the Limits of American Government* (New Haven: Yale University Press, 1990).

11. Hugh Johnson, *The Blue Eagle from Egg to Earth* (Garden City, NY: Doubleday, Doran, 1935), 263.

12. Though as Sawyer notes, "little NRAs" continued to exist at the state level. See Sawyer, *American Fair Trade,* 293. For more on the court's invalidation of the NRA, see Barry Cushman, *Rethinking the New Deal Court* (New York: Oxford University Press, 1998), 156–159; Irons, *The New Deal Lawyers,* 86–107.

13. Brand, *Corporatism and the Rule of Law,* 290; Hawley, *The New Deal and the Problem of Monopoly,* 130.

14. Tugwell was more favorably impressed with the "pragmatic government" of the Russians than he was with the "backwardness of rural life" that he saw sentimentalized in French culture. See Rexford G. Tugwell, "The Agricultural Policy of France I," *Political Science Quarterly* 45, No. 2 (1930): 221; Tugwell, "Experimental Control in Russian Industry," *Political Science Quarterly* 43, No. 2 (June 1928): 161–187.

15. Sawyer, *American Fair Trade,* 256.

16. The term *parity* was not used in the law until the Agricultural Adjustment Act of 1938, but the concept was present in the 1933 legislation.

17. Agricultural Adjustment Act of 1933, PL 73-10, Section 2.1.

18. Murray R. Benedict and Oscar C. Stine, *The Agricultural Commodity Programs: Two Decades of Experience* (New York: Twentieth Century Fund, 1956), 52.

19. Howard Wiarda describes the WIB as "essentially corporatist" in its "tripartite (business, labor, state) arrangement to protect against strikes during the war and to ensure the necessary massive and uninterrupted production." See Wiarda, *Corporatism and Comparative Politics: The Other Great "Ism,"* (Armonk, NY: M. E. Sharpe, 1997).

20. Willard W. Cochrane, *The Development of American Agriculture: A Historical Analysis* (Minneapolis: University of Minnesota Press, 1979), 118.

21. George Peek and Hugh Johnson, *Equality for Agriculture,* 2nd ed. (Moline, IL: Moline Plow Company, 1922), 32.

22. See Gilbert Fite, *George N. Peek and the Fight for Farm Parity* (Norman: University of Oklahoma Press, 1930); Cochrane, *Development of American Agriculture,* 118.

23. Lloyd Teigen, *Agricultural Parity: Historical Review and Alternative Calculations* (Washington, DC: USDA ERS, 1987).

24. United States, *Agricultural Adjustment*, 1.

25. Ibid., 74.

26. Ibid., 77.

27. For more on the Smith-Lever Act, which connected the land grant universities to rural areas, see Murray R. Benedict, *Farm Policies of the United States, 1790–1950: A Study of Their Origins and Development* (New York: Twentieth Century Fund, 1953), 153–154; Alfred True, *A History of Agricultural Extension Work in the United States, 1785–1923,* Miscellaneous Publication no. 15 (Washington, DC: USDA, 1928), 108–127; Wayne D. Rasmussen, *Taking the University to the People: Seventy-Five Years of Cooperative Extension* (Ames: Iowa State University Press, 1989), 48–94; Christopher Loss, *Between Citizens and the State: The Politics of Higher Education in the Twentieth Century* (Princeton: Princeton University Press, 2012), 64–66.

28. For the intertwined growth of the Farm Bureau and the Extension Service, see Christiana Campbell, *The Farm Bureau and the New Deal: A Study of Making of National Farm Policy, 1933–40* (Urbana: University of Illinois Press, 1962), 10; Adam D. Sheingate, *The Rise of the Agricultural Welfare State: Institutions and Interest Group Power in the United States, France, and Japan* (Princeton: Princeton University Press, 2001), 99–102; Oliver Merton Kile, *The Farm Bureau through Three Decades* (Baltimore: Waverly Press, 1948), 36–57. For a national overview of the use of the Extension Service offices as the field agents of the New Deal agriculture programs, see Loss, *Between Citizens and the States,* 66–68.

29. *Progressive Farmer,* February 1933, 24.

30. Though both discuss the network of agricultural policy planners who created and implemented farm legislation, neither Kirkendall nor Saloutos give more than passing mention to Hutson. Agricultural sociologist Jess Gilbert, who has written extensively on the geography and character of "urban liberal" and "Midwestern agrarian" policy circles, has also not devoted much discussion to Hutson's role in the Administration. See Richard S. Kirkendall, *Social Scientists and Farm Politics in the Age of Roosevelt* (Columbia: University of Missouri Press, 1966); Theodore Saloutos, *The American Farmer and the New Deal* (Ames: Iowa State University Press, 1982); Jess Gilbert, *Planning Democracy: Agrarian Intellectuals and the Intended New Deal* (New Haven: Yale University Press, 2015).

31. Hutson's own professional route into the heart of the New Deal agriculture circles ran straight through the Bureau of Agricultural Economics, the most significant source of agricultural policymaking of the 1920s. There he absorbed a faith in planning and a reverence for administration from his boss, Howard Tolley, whom sociologist Jess Gilbert has described as favoring "a developmentalist state, national economic planning, and the self-organization of labor as well as agriculture." See Jess Gilbert, "Eastern Urban Liberals and Midwestern Agrarian Intellectuals: Two Group Portraits

of Progressives in the New Deal Department of Agriculture," *Agricultural History* 74, No. 2 (2000): 176.

32. *Reminiscences of John B. Hutson,* 102, in the Columbia Oral History Collection (COHC), New York, New York.

33. Quoted in Badger, *Prosperity Road,* 46.

34. Ibid., 47.

35. Ibid.

36. Badger, *Prosperity Road,* 43–44.

37. I. O. Schaub to J. C. B. Ehringhaus, April 8, 1933, Folder, "NCSC, Extension Division," Box 12, Papers of Governor J. C. B. Ehringhaus (Ehringhaus Papers), North Carolina Division of Archives and History (NCDAH), Raleigh, N.C.

38. Badger, *Prosperity Road,* 50–51.

39. "Resolution," August 31, 1933, Folder, "Correspondence 9/1933," Box 107, Ehringhaus Papers, NCDAH.

40. Lionel Weil to J. C. B. Ehringhaus, August 3, 1933, Folder, "Correspondence 9/1933," Box 107, Ehringhaus Papers, NCDAH.

41. J. I. Hayes, *South Carolina and the New Deal* (Columbia: University of South Carolina Press), 124.

42. Badger, *Prosperity Road,* 52.

43. Ibid., 53.

44. In an uncanny coincidence, a Hollywood actor with the same name was the third to portray the Marlboro Man.

45. Daniel Carpenter, *The Forging of Bureaucratic Autonomy: Reputations, Networks, and Policy Innovations in Executive Agencies, 1862–1928* (Princeton: Princeton University Press, 2001); Kenneth Finegold and Theda Skocpol, *State and Party in America's New Deal* (Madison: University of Wisconsin Press, 1995).

46. Hutson, *Reminiscences,* 134, COHC.

47. For an overview of the evolution of scholarly perspectives on state power, which now stress public-private hybridity and the creative tension between state and private actors, see Balogh, *The Associational State,* 9–18. For an analysis of the New Deal as an exercise in associational governance see Balogh, *The Associational State,* 139–171.

48. Keel and Long to J. C. B. Ehringhaus, September 6, 1933, Folder, "Corresp. 9/1933," Box 107, Ehringhaus Papers, NCDAH.

49. "Tobacco Sign-Up at 95%," *Wall Street Journal*, March 6, 1934; Badger, *Prosperity Road,* 55–57.

50. For all commodities, securing the assent of processors was the result of intense negotiations. For Wallace's recollections of USDA deliberations with other commodity processors, see Wallace, *New Frontier,* pp. 190–195. For a systematic analysis of agricultural programs, including negotiations among producers, processors, and the USDA, see Benedict and Stine, *The Agricultural Commodity Programs.*

51. J. C. B. Ehringhaus to Franklin Roosevelt, October 6, 1933, Folder, "Corresp. 10/1933," Box 107, Ehringhaus Papers, NCDAH.

52. Franklin Roosevelt to J. C. B. Ehringhaus, October 14, 1933, Folder, "Corresp. 10/1933," Box 107, Ehringhaus Papers, NCDAH.
53. Badger, *Prosperity Road,* 63.
54. Quoted in ibid., 58.
55. Ibid., 63.
56. Ibid., 65.
57. "Southern Tobacco Farmer, Prosperous Again Pays Off Old Debts," *Wall Street Journal,* December 28, 1934.
58. *Progressive Farmer,* December 1933, 18.
59. Wallace, *New Frontier,* 199.
60. Kerr had some political capital to regain in his old Belt district after missing the vote on the original 1933 Agricultural Adjustment Act.
61. Advocates of compulsory control repeatedly used the word "chiseler" to describe potential overproducers. See Badger, *Prosperity Road,* 76, 78.
62. Ibid., 75–76.
63. Ibid., 78.
64. The "grassroots democracy" of the agriculture programs bore a striking resemblance to the "grassroots democracy" of the Tennessee Valley Authority (TVA). For acreage restriction programs and TVA's development programs, the language of grassroots participation justified iron-clad governing arrangements with local elites. See Balogh, *The Associational State,* 161–163; Philip Selznick, *TVA and the Grass Roots: A Study in the Sociology of a Formal Organization* (Berkeley: University of California Press, 1949).
65. North Carolina Department of Agriculture and North Carolina Agricultural Experiment Station, *Annual Report* (Raleigh, NC: 1935), 5.
66. Ibid.
67. United States, *Agricultural Adjustment,* 183.
68. Ibid., 206–207.
69. Adrienne Petty, *Standing Their Ground: Small Farmers in North Carolina since the Civil War* (New York: Oxford University Press, 2013), 99.
70. Ibid.
71. Quoted in Badger, *Prosperity Road,* 95.
72. Adrienne M. Petty, "Standing Their Ground: Small Farm Owners in North Carolina's Tobacco Belt, 1920–1982" (PhD diss., Columbia University, 2004), 34–35.
73. *Progressive Farmer,* March 1934; See also, Petty, *Standing Their Ground,* 103–106.
74. *Progressive Farmer,* October 1934.
75. Harold B. Rowe, *Tobacco under the AAA* (Washington, DC: Brookings Institution, 1935), 160–161.
76. Badger, *Prosperity Road,* 167–169.
77. Adrienne Petty's careful social history of small-scale North Carolina farmers reveals the sharp racial disparities of the tobacco program. See Petty, *Standing Their Ground,* 112.
78. Hutson, *Reminiscences,* 142–143, COHC.

79. The literature on the New Deal's role in accelerating southern agricultural change is vast. See Gilbert Fite, *Cotton Fields No More: Southern Agriculture, 1865–1980* (Lexington: University of Kentucky Press, 1984); Pete Daniel, *Breaking the Land: Transformation of Tobacco, Cotton, and Rice Cultures since 1880* (Urbana: University of Illinois Press, 1985); Jack Temple Kirby, *Rural Worlds Lost: The American South, 1920–1960* (Baton Route: Louisiana State University Press, 1987). Bruce Schulman, *From Cotton Belt to Sunbelt: Federal Policy, Economic Development, and the Transformation of the South, 1938–1980* (Durham: Duke University Press, 1994).

80. As Pete Daniel notes, the AAA in tobacco was more sympathetic to small growers than it was for cotton, "awarding tenants a greater share of government money." Pete Daniel, "The Crossroads of Change: Cotton, Tobacco, and Rice Cultures in the Twentieth-Century South," *Journal of Southern History* 50, No. 3 (1984): 441.

81. Badger, *Prosperity Road,* 203.

82. Ibid.

83. For transformations in cotton culture during the New Deal, see Daniel, *Breaking the Land,* 91–109; Fite, *Cotton Fields No More;* Donald H. Grubbs, *Cry from the Cotton: The Southern Tenant Farmers' Union and the New Deal* (Chapel Hill: UNC Press, 1971); Sidney Baldwin, *Poverty and Politics: The Rise and Decline of the Farm Security Administration* (Chapel Hill: UNC Press, 1968).

84. Congressional Record H11,802 (July 24, 1935) (statement of John Flannagan).

85. Ibid.

86. The echoes of the Populist criticism of discriminatory freight rates are unmistakable. Nearly a half-century earlier earlier, farmers decried the railroads' use of preferential rates for large shippers. See Lawrence Goodwyn, *The Populist Moment: A Short History of the Agrarian Revolt in America* (New York: Oxford University Press, 1978), 48; Charles Postel, *The Populist Vision* (New York: Oxford University Press, 2007), 43; Steven Hahn, *The Roots of Southern Populism: Yeoman Farmers and the Transformation of the Georgia Upcountry* (New York: Oxford University Press, 1983), 168.

87. Congressional Record H11,808 (July 24, 1935) (statement of Bayard Clark).

88. Badger, *Prosperity Road,* 122–123.

89. *Congressional Record,* 74th Congress, 2nd Session (1936), 2570.

90. Quoted in Badger, *Prosperity Road,* 122.

91. United States v. Butler 297 U.S. 1 (1936).

92. Ibid.

93. John W. Holmes, "The Federal Spending Power and State Rights: A Commentary on United States v. Butler," *Michigan Law Review* 34, No. 5 (1936): 637–649.

94. "Agricultural Adjustment and Marketing Control," *Yale Law Journal* 46, No. 1. (1936): 138–139.

95. Benedict and Stine, *The Agricultural Commodity Programs,* 78.

96. Section 314 of the 1938 Agricultural Adjustment Act.

97. Campbell, *The Farm Bureau and the New Deal,* 56.

98. Ibid., 3–5.

99. Ibid., 7–8.

100. Badger, *Prosperity Road,* 137–139.

101. "1936 Minutes," n.d., Folder 14. Box 9, Records of the North Carolina Farm Bureau Federation (NCFB Records), Special Collections Library, North Carolina State University (NCSU), Raleigh, North Carolina.

102. Badger, *Prosperity Road,* 139.

103. Ibid., 138.

104. Quoted in ibid., 158.

105. "Flue Cured Tobacco Vote Lessons," *Progressive Farmer,* January 1939, 6.

106. Badger, *Prosperity Road,* 162–164.

107. "Flue Cured Tobacco Vote Lessons," *Progressive Farmer,* January 1939, 6.

108. Cushman, *Rethinking the New Deal Court,* 190.

109. "Oral History Interview #9—J. Con Lanier," March 19, 1973, East Carolina Manuscript Collection, Digital Collections, East Carolina University, https://digital.lib.ecu.edu/text/10923.

110. Lanier later claimed to have been wrong in opposing the Inspection Act. See ibid.

111. Hughes was drawing upon the Progressive-era precedent of the Shreveport rate cases, decisions concerning Interstate Commerce Commission (ICC) rate regulation for railroads. See Currin v. Wallace at 11. For a discussion of the doctrinal history of Currin, see Cushman, *Rethinking the New Deal Court,* 190–193.

112. Currin v. Wallace at 14.

113. Currin v. Wallace at 15.

114. Ibid. Right to the present day, the use of referenda in agriculture regulations has been continually contested as the abuse of a minority by the (economically empowered) majority. See Milov, "Promoting Agriculture: Farmers, the State, and Checkoff Marketing," *Business History Review* 90, No. 3. (2016): 505–536.

115. The referendum approval of tobacco inspection was at over 90 percent. See also Evan P. Bennett, *When Tobacco Was King: Families, Farm Labor, and Federal Policy in the Piedmont* (Gainesville: University Press of Florida, 2014), 73.

116. Emphasis added. Brief for the *United States in Mulford v. Smith* at 39. For an in-depth discussion of the doctrinal implications of *Mulford v. Smith,* see Cushman, *Rethinking the New Deal Court,* 197–206.

117. *Mulford v. Smith* at 47.

118. Ibid., at 48.

119. *Progressive Farmer,* November 1939.

120. During that same period, the United States consumed an average of 302 million pounds yearly. Joseph W. Hines, "Recent Trends and Developments

in the Flue-Cured Tobacco Export Trade," *Southern Economic Journal* 18, No. 3 (1952): 382.

121. Badger, *Prosperity Road,* 179–180.

122. And, in fact, the vast majority of these tobacco stocks were sold to the Lend-Lease Administration. See Benedict and Stine, *The Agricultural Commodity Programs,* 68.

123. Quoted in Badger, *Prosperity Road,* 186.

124. Allan M. Brandt, *The Cigarette Century: The Rise, Fall, and Deadly Persistence of the Product that Defined America* (New York: Basic Books, 2007), 88–89.

125. Federal Reserve Bank of Richmond, *Flue-Cured Tobacco,* 134.

126. Ibid., 135.

127. Benedict and Stine, *The Agricultural Commodity Programs,* 70. "Flue-Cured Ceiling Raised on Tobacco," *New York Times,* July 8, 1945.

3. Cultivating the Grower

1. "The Story of the TGIC—Tobacco Growers Are Fighting Back," April 24, 1959, R. J. Reynolds Records, University of California at San Francisco (UCSF) Library, https://www.industrydocumentslibrary.ucsf.edu/tobacco/docs/sppv0099.

2. Untitled Speech at Washington, D.C.," n.d. (1947), Folder "Speech Folder," Box 1, Papers of J. Con Lanier (Lanier Papers), East Carolina University (ECU), Greenville, N.C.

3. Brian Balogh, *The Associational State: American Governance in the Twentieth Century* (Philadelphia: University of Pennsylvania Press, 2015), 141.

4. The literature documenting a change in Americans' conception of citizenship around the idea of consumption is vast. For the now-classic argument that the postwar period inaugurated a fundamental transformation in American society around private consumption and property ownership, see Lizabeth Cohen, *A Consumers' Republic: The Politics of Mass Consumption in Postwar America* (New York: Knopf, 2003); see also Gary Cross, *An All-Consuming Century: Why Commercialism Won in Modern America* (New York: Columbia University Press, 2000). Meg Jacobs argues similarly that activist politics of consumption were shunted to the sidelines of American politics after the Second World War. See Jacobs, *Pocketbook Politics: Economic Citizenship in Twentieth Century America* (Princeton: Princeton University Press, 2005), 252. Tracey Deutsch narrates a similar story of the declining power of women shoppers amid the consolidation of grocery chains in the postwar period. See Deutsch, *Building a Housewife's Paradise: Gender, Politics, and American Grocery Stores in the Twentieth Century* (Chapel Hill: UNC Press, 2010).

5. For more on agricultural productivity after the Second World War, see Paul Conkin, *A Revolution Down on the Farm: The Transformation of American Agriculture since 1929* (Lexington: University Press of Kentucky, 2008); Alan L.

Olmstead and Paul W. Rhode, *Creating Abundance: Biological Innovation and American Agricultural Development* (Cambridge: Cambridge University Press, 2008).

6. Edward L. Schapsmeier and Frederick H. Schapsmeier, "Eisenhower and Ezra Taft Benson: Farm Policy in the 1950s," *Agricultural History* 44, No. 4 (1970): 373.

7. "Tobacco Future Is Meeting Topic," *Raleigh News and Observer,* September 29, 1945; Folder "Clippings," Box 55, North Carolina Department of Agriculture Records (NCDA), North Carolina Division of Archives and History (NCDAH), Raleigh, N.C. Of course, tobacco farmers did not anticipate that India would very shortly be removed from the scope of the British Empire with its declaration of independence in 1947. See Federal Reserve Bank of Richmond, Research Department, *Flue-Cured Tobacco: An Economic Survey* (Richmond: Author, 1952), 48.

8. "The Price Outlook for Flue-Cured Tobacco," *Progressive Farmer,* June 1947, 82.

9. James T. Sparrow, *Warfare State: World War II Americans and the Age of Big Government* (Oxford: Oxford University Press, 2011), 247.

10. On the paradigm of scarcity in the early New Deal, see Robert Collins, *More: The Politics of Growth in Postwar America* (Oxford: Oxford University Press, 2000), 6–8; Alan Brinkley, "The New Deal and the Idea of the State," in *The Rise and Fall of the New Deal Order, 1930–1980,* Steve Fraser and Gary Gerstle, eds. (Princeton: Princeton University Press, 1989), 105–108. On the doctrine of growth in the immediate postwar period, see Collins, *More,* 17–39.

11. These goals were articulated in the Employment Act of 1946: "The Congress hereby declares that it is the continuing policy and responsibility of the federal government to use all practicable means consistent with its needs and obligations . . . to promote maximum employment, production, and purchasing power." See Employment Act of 1946, PL 79–304, ch. 33, 60 Stat. 23 (1946); see also Collins, *More,* 16.

12. Collins, *More,* 20–21.

13. Harry S. Truman: "Annual Message to the Congress on the State of the Union," January 5, 1949; online in Gerhard Peters and John T. Woolley, *The American Presidency Project,* http://www.presidency.ucsb.edu/ws/?pid =13293.

14. Nelson Lichtenstein, *Most Dangerous Man in Detroit: Walter Reuther and the Fate of American Labor* (New York: Basic Books, 1995), 221; Collins, *More,* 23.

15. Lichtenstein, *Most Dangerous Man in Detroit,* 220.

16. In October 1945, Governor R. Gregg Cherry named Scott the chairman of a "special committee" to "promote the welfare of tobacco in North Carolina." Others named to the committee included the state's Grange master, the Farm Bureau president, a former statewide AAA committee chair, a former governor, and two professors—one from Duke and one from North Carolina State. See R. Gregg Cherry to W. Kerr Scott, October 2, 1945, Folder "Correspondence," Box 55, NCDA, NCDAH.

17. "Agricultural Review," April 1, 1946, Folder "Clipping File," Box 55, NCDA, NCDAH; W. Kerr Scott to Dr. W. E. Colwell, July 19, 1946, Folder "Clippings," Box 55, NCDA, NCDAH.

18. Balogh, *The Associational State*, chapter 5.

19. Tobacco Associates, Articles of Incorporation, 1947; North Carolina Department of the Secretary of State, http://www.secretary.state.nc.us/search /CorpFilings/4645662.

20. Robert Proctor, *Golden Holocaust: Origins of the Cigarette Catastrophe and the Case for Abolition* (Berkeley: University of California Press, 2011), 32–33. Tobacco that has been flue-cured has a higher sugar content and is far less alkaline than pipe or cigar smoke. This "mildness" of taste is what makes cigarette smoke so dangerous. Flue-cured tobacco smokers can inhale more easily and with less coughing. Inhaled smoke encounters a large surface area in the lungs, which become the site of nicotine absorption, and therefore addiction. At the same time, the inhalation of tobacco smoke over this large surface area exposes the body to diseases of the lungs, such as cancer, bronchitis, and emphysema.

21. Historians of tobacco and public-health scholars point to the 1980s as the era in which modern tobacco companies became transnational, citing regulatory pressures at home and liberalized trade relations with Asia and Europe. See Allan M. Brandt, *The Cigarette Century: The Rise, Fall, and Deadly Persistence of the Product that Defined America* (New York: Basic Books, 2007), 450. By contrast, Nan Enstad has recently argued that at the turn of the twentieth century, the American Tobacco Company represented one of the first truly multinational corporations. Enstad, *Cigarettes, Inc.: An Intimate History of Corporate Imperialism* (Chicago: University of Chicago Press, 2018).

22. Federal Reserve Bank of Richmond, quoted in *Flue-Cured Tobacco,* 19.

23. Richard B. Tennant, *The American Cigarette Industry: A Study in Economic Analysis and Public Policy* (New Haven: Yale University Press, 1950), 393; F. S. Everts and E. M. Evans, "Export and Import Trade of the United States in Manufactured Tobacco," U.S. Department of Commerce, Office of International Trade, World Trade in Commodities 6, Pt. 8, No. 16 (October 1948), 4.

24. R. Flake Shaw to Gentlemen, February 19, 1947, Folder 1, Box 1, North Carolina Farm Bureau Records (NCFB Records), Special Collections Library, North Carolina State University (NCSU), Raleigh, N.C.

25. "U.N. and City Hail Gen. Bor as Hero," *New York Times,* May 25, 1946, 9. "Gromyko Protests Welcome to Bor by Official of U.N.," *New York Times,* May 26, 1946, 1; "Lie to Reorganize U.N. Cabinet Soon," *New York Times,* June 21, 1946, 1; *Reminiscences of John B. Hutson,* 501–504, Columbia Oral History Collection (COHC), New York, New York.

26. "Memorandum in Connection with Meeting of Producers," February 17, 1947, Folder 1, Box 1, NCFB Records, NCSU.

27. TA domesticated in South Carolina, Virginia, Georgia, and Florida the following year, where referenda were also held.

28. Interview with Frank Jeter, April 28, 1947, Folder 1b, Box 1, Papers of John B. Hutson (Hutson Papers), Special Collections Division, J. Y. Joyner Library, East Carolina University (ECU), Greenville, North Carolina.

29. Ibid.

30. "Farmers Cast Votes in Leaf Referendum Today," *Dispatch* (Lexington, NC), July 23, 1949, 1.

31. See, for instance, "Leaf Growers Will Vote on Assessment," *Loris Sentinel* (Conway, SC), December 10, 1958, 1.

32. 94 Cong., 2nd sess., part 4, 5341 (1976).

33. J. Bradford De Long and Barry Eichengreen, "The Marshall Plan: History's Most Successful Structural Adjustment Program," Discussion Paper 634 (May 1992), 3.

34. Daniel Sargent, *A Superpower Transformed: The Remaking of American Foreign Relations in the 1970s* (Cambridge, MA: Harvard University Press, 2014), 17. For the U.S. role in establishing the postwar order, see Elizabeth Borgwardt, *A New Deal for the World: America's Vision for Human Rights* (Cambridge, MA: Harvard University Press, 2005).

35. After all, tobacco was not one of the necessities shipped to Europe through the United Nations Relief and Rehabilitation Administration (UNRRA) during the three years of that program's aid work. For more on UNRRA, see William I. Hitchcock, *The Bitter Road to Freedom: A New History of the Liberation of Europe* (New York: Free Press, 2008), 212–214.

36. Cooley held the chairmanship of the House Agricultural Committee from 1949 until the Democrats lost control of the house in 1953. He again served from 1955 until he lost his House seat in 1967.

37. "Lucius Clay Dies," *New York Times,* April 17, 1978.

38. J. Con Lanier Oral History Interview, March 19, 1973, Special Collections, ECU. Lanier, an exporter and TA affiliate, as well as Hutson's old lieutenant in the tobacco section of the AAA, was present at the negotiations with Clay, Hutson, and Cooley.

39. The best history of the Marshall Plan remains Michael Hogan, *The Marshall Plan: America, Britain, and the Reconstruction of Western Europe, 1947–1952* (Cambridge: Cambridge University Press, 1987). For an account that emphasizes the role of European officials in shaping the priorities of the Marshall Plan, see Alan Milward, *The Reconstruction of Western Europe, 1945–1951* (Berkeley: University of California Press, 1984).

40. Federal Reserve Bank of Richmond, *Flue-Cured Tobacco,* 62; U.S. Department of State, Committee of European Economic Cooperation, "Technical Reports, July–September 1947," Vol. 2 (Washington, DC, October 1947), 39.

41. "The Marshall Plan: A Summary Prepared by J. B. Hutson of Tobacco Associates," n.d. (1947), Folder 1b, Box 1, Hutson Papers, ECU.

42. Ibid.

43. Hutson did not always think that his activities rose to the level of lobbying as defined in the Lobby Reorganization Act of 1946. During 1947–1948, the

years in which the ECA package was being put together, Hutson did not register as a lobbyist. He noted in his oral history that his goal in the Marshall Plan package was to remedy what the "tobacco people" saw as a historic discrimination against tobacco by the crop's exclusion from UNRRA aid. See Hutson, *Reminiscences,* 530.

44. Lanier Oral History, ECU.
45. In 1951, as Marshall Plan operations were drawing to a close, FitzGerald and Cooley once again worked together to bolster the American tobacco trade in West Germany. They authorized a trade mission to rectify the "falling off in tobacco exports to Germany" in spite of a "demonstrated preference on the part of German consumers for American tobacco products." See "Tobacco Trade Mission to Germany," May 5, 1951, Folder 1359, Box 33, Papers of Harold D. Cooley (Cooley Papers), SHC.
46. "Remarks of J. B. Hutson before Board of Governors, Tobacco Association of the United States," January 30, 1948, Folder 1c, Box 1, Hutson Papers.
47. John Flannagan, "Tobacco and the European Recovery Program in General," Cong. Rec.,80th Cong., 2nd sess. (March 31, 1948), H3881. See also Federal Reserve Bank of Richmond, *Flue-Cured Tobacco,* 60.
48. Federal Reserve Bank of Richmond, *Flue-Cured Tobacco,* 69.
49. John Flannagan, "Tobacco and the European Recovery Program in General," Cong. Rec., 80th Cong., 2nd sess. (March 31, 1948), H3881.
50. Proctor, *Golden Holocaust,* 46.
51. Hutson, "Maintaining Agricultural Exports," Address of J. B. Hutson, 29th Annual Convention of American Farm Bureau Federation, December 15, 1947, Folder 1b, Box 1, Hutson Papers, ECU.
52. Ibid.
53. *New York Times,* December 16, 1947, 8.
54. Robert N. Proctor, *The Nazi War on Cancer* (Princeton: Princeton University Press, 1999), 228. For an analysis of German public health attempts to deal with the postwar upsurge in smoking during the 1960s and 1970s, see Rosemary Elliott, "Inhaling Democracy: Cigarette Advertising and Health Education in Postwar West Germany, 1950s–1975," *Social History of Medicine* 28, No. 3 (August 2015): 509–531.
55. Rosemary Elliott, "Smoking for Taxes: The Triumph of Fiscal Policy over Health in Postwar Germany, 1945–1951," *Economic History Review* 65, No. 4 (2012): 1458–1460.
56. "Tabakwaren Ausverkauft," *Der Spiegel,* November 12. 1948.
57. Joseph W. Hines, "Recent Trends and Developments in the Flue-Cured Tobacco Export Trade," *Southern Economic Journal* 18, No. 3 (1952): 386–388, esp. appendix, fig. 4.2, and fig. 4.3.
58. "Bei aller Dankbarkeit," *Der Spiegel,* August 13, 1952, 19.
59. Éric Godeau, *Le tabac en France de 1940 à nos jours: Histoire d'un marché* (Paris: Presses Paris Sorbonne, 2008), 58.
60. Lanier Oral History, ECU.

61. Godeau, *Le tabac en France de 1940 à nos jours,* 119.
62. "Untitled Speech at Washington, N.C.," n.d. (1947), Folder "Speech Folder," Box 1, Lanier Papers, ECU.
63. Ibid.
64. Ibid.
65. For more on the partisan politics of PL 480, see Edward L. Schapsmeier and Frederick H. Schapsmeier, *Ezra Taft Benson and the Politics of Agriculture: The Eisenhower Years, 1953–1961* (Danville, IL: Interstate Printers and Publishers, 1975), 98–100. Indeed, the primary opponents of PL 480 were not congressional Democrats but the members of Eisenhower's own State Department. Secretary of State John Foster Dulles feared that U.S. commodity disposal abroad would weaken the economies of friendly governments and endow recipient states with bargaining leverage vis-à-vis the United States. See "Public Law 480: 'Better Than a Bomber,'" *Middle East Report* 145 (March–April 1987).
66. Robert R. Sullivan, "The Politics of Altruism: An Introduction to the Food-for-Peace Partnership between the United States Government and Voluntary Relief Agencies," *Western Political Quarterly* 23, No. 4 (1970): 763; Mitchel B. Wallerstein, *Food for War / Food for Peace: United States Food Aid in a Global Context* (Cambridge, MA: MIT Press, 1980).
67. At first, the United States refused to engage in trade with bloc countries. However, in 1955 Eisenhower embraced the idea of "net advantage," reasoning that if communist countries were going to import commodities, the United States might as well benefit from their trade. See Schapsmeier and Schapsmeier, *Ezra Taft Benson and the Politics of Agriculture,* 110.
68. *Policies and Operations under Public Law 480, Hearings before the Subcommittee on Agriculture and Forestry,* United States Senate, 85th Cong., 1st sess., 512 (1957).
69. "The Public Law 480 Market Development Program," July 11, 1958, Folder 1g, Box 1, Hutson Papers, ECU.
70. *Policies and Operations under Public Law 480,* 668.
71. United States, Foreign Agricultural Service, *New Markets for U.S. Agricultural Commodities: A Pictorial Report of Foreign Market Development* (Washington, DC: U.S. Dept. of Agriculture, 1958), 16.
72. Tobacco Institute, "Tobacco Associates Annual Report," February 25, 1969, UCSF Library, http://legacy.library.ucsf.edu/tid/kor59b00/pdf.
73. Ibid.
74. Tobacco Institute, "Tobacco Associates Annual Report," March 7, 1961, UCSF Library, http://legacy.library.ucsf.edu/tid/qor59b00.
75. "What Tobacco Associates Is Doing in Leipzig," *Tobacco Reporter,* January 1967, 34–35.
76. Stephen Gross, "Selling Germany in South-Eastern Europe: Economic Uncertainty, Commercial Information, and the Leipzig Trade Fair, 1920–40," *Contemporary European History* 21, No. 1 (2012): 29–30.
77. David F. Crew, ed., *Consuming Germany in the Cold War* (New York: Berg, 2003).

78. "What Tobacco Associates Is Doing in Leipzig," 35.

79. Ibid.

80. Tobacco Institute, "Tobacco Associates Annual Report," March 2, 1971, http://legacy.library.ucsf.edu/tid/mro6aa00.

81. Tobacco Institute, "Tobacco Associates Annual Report," February 25, 1969.

82. Tobacco Institute, "Tobacco Associates Annual Report," March 7, 1967, http://legacy.library.ucsf.edu/tid/mor59b00/pdf.

83. "USDA Trade Mission Reports on Overseas Markets," *Tobacco Reporter,* February 1969, 70.

84. *Farm Policy: The Politics of Soil, Surpluses and Subsidies* (Washington, DC: Congressional Quarterly, 1984), 118; USDA Economic Research Service, *Tobacco Situation 1959–1960* (Washington, D.C.: USDA, 1960), 5.

85. Wayne D. Rasmussen and Gladys L. Baker, "Price-Support and Adjustment Programs From 1933 through 1978: A Short History," Agriculture Information Bulletin, No. 424 (Washington, D.C.: USDA, 1979), 20; Schapsmeier and Schapsmeier, *Ezra Taft Benson and the Politics of Agriculture,* 85.

86. North Carolina Dept. of Agriculture, *North Carolina Tobacco Report* (Raleigh, NC: North Carolina Dept. of Agriculture, 1959), 19.

87. Ibid., 5.

88. USDA Economic Research Service, *Tobacco Situation 1959–1960,* 6.

89. Brandt, *Cigarette Century,* 136–148.

90. John Fischer, "The Country Slickers Take Us Again," *Harper's Magazine,* December 1955.

91. The reporter quoted, Harrison Salisbury, was the *New York Times* longtime Russian affairs correspondent most famous for reporting on the "Kitchen Debate" between Nixon and Khrushchev a few years later. His observations of the Iowa farm visit were quoted by Fischer, the editor of *Harper's,* in the "Country Slickers" article cited in note 90.

92. *Farm Policy,* 113.

93. "Public Found Divided on Farm Subsidy," *Los Angeles Times,* August 28, 1953.

94. United States, Bureau of the Budget, *The Federal Budget in Brief* (Washington, DC: Government Printing Office, 1952).

95. *Farm Policy,* 110.

96. Louis Galambos and Joseph Pratt, *The Rise of the Corporate Commonwealth* (New York: Basic Books, 1988), 153.

97. Ibid., 143.

98. Quote from Franklin Delano Roosevelt, Madison Square Garden Speech, October 31, 1936.

99. Marver Bernstein, "The Regulatory Process: A Framework for Analysis," *Law and Contemporary Problems* 26, No. 2 (1961): 329–346.

100. Galambos and Pratt, *Rise of the Corporate Commonwealth,* 144–153.

101. Karl Polanyi, *The Great Transformation: The Political and Economic Origins of Our Time* (1944; reprint, Boston: Beacon, 2001), 147.

102. For more on the politics and ideology of economic growth during the postwar years, see Collins, *More*. For the business-supported construction of the "American Way," see Wendy Wall, *Inventing the "American Way": The Politics of Consensus from the New Deal to the Civil Rights Movement* (New York: Oxford University Press, 2008).

103. For more on the relationship between the land grant colleges, the Extension Service, and the USDA, see Wayne D. Rasmussen, *Taking the University to the People: Seventy-Five Years of Cooperative Extension* (Ames: Iowa State University Press, 1989), and Roy Scott, *The Reluctant Farmer: The Rise of Agricultural Extension to 1914* (Chicago: University of Chicago Press, 1970).

104. Margaret Pugh O'Mara, *Cities of Knowledge: Cold War Science and the Search for the Next Silicon Valley* (Princeton: Princeton University Press, 2004); Fred Block, "Swimming against the Current: The Rise of a Hidden Developmental State in the United States," *Politics and Society* 36, No. 2 (June 2008): 169–206. For universities as intermediaries between citizens and state bureaucracy, see Christopher Loss, *Between Citizens and State: The Politics of American Higher Education in the Twentieth Century* (Princeton: Princeton University Press, 2012), esp. chapter 3; Balogh, *The Associational State*, 155–157. For more on the expansion of federal funding for science at universities during the Cold War, see Stuart W. Leslie, *The Cold War and American Science: The Military-Industrial-Academic Complex at MIT and Stanford* (New York: Columbia University Press, 1993); Rebecca Lowen, *Creating the Cold War University: The Transformation of Stanford* (Berkeley: University of California Press, 1997).

105. Block, "Swimming against the Current," 7–8.

106. Ibid.

107. Balogh, *The Associational State,* chapter 5. For a general theory of why Americans are so frequently ignorant of government programs, see Suzanne Mettler, *The Submerged State: How Invisible Government Policies Undermine American Democracy* (Chicago: University of Chicago Press 2011).

108. "When I became Secretary and surveyed the patchwork price support program I had inherited and was expected to administer for the welfare of agriculture and the nation, I thought of the words of the Master as related by Mark: 'No man also seweth a piece of new cloth on an old garment: else the new piece that filled it up taketh away from the old, and the rent is made worse.'" See Ezra Taft Benson, "Benson and Brannan Debate the Farm Issue," in *The Paradox of Plenty,* Robert Branyan and A. Theodore Brown, eds. (Dubuque, IA: William C. Brown, 1968), 106.

109. Edward L. Schapsmeier and Frederick H. Schapsmeier, "Eisenhower and Ezra Taft Benson: Farm Policy in the 1950s," *Agricultural History* 44, No. 4 (1970): 369–378.

110. Quoted in Barry Riley, *The Political History of American Food Aid: An Uneasy Benevolence* (New York: Oxford University Press, 2017), 180.

111. "Farm Surplus Hot Issue of Election Year," *Chicago Daily Tribune*, February 28, 1960, A8.

112. During and immediately after his tenure as secretary of agriculture, Benson authored a number of books elaborating his views on the spiritual and moral dimensions of efficient, free-marketing farming. See Ezra Taft Benson as told to Carlisle Bargeron, *Farmers at the Crossroads* (New York: Devin-Adair, 1956); Benson, *Freedom to Farm* (Garden City, NY: Doubleday, 1960); Benson, *Cross Fire: The Eight Years with Eisenhower* (Westport, CT: Greenwood Press, 1962).

113. Schapsmeier and Schapsmeier, *Ezra Taft Benson and the Politics of Agriculture*, 244–246.

114. "Farm Surplus Hot Issue of Election Year," *Chicago Daily Tribune*, February 28, 1960, A8.

115. Folder 2140, Box 51, Cooley Papers, SHC.

116. Reuel Schiller, "Enlarging the Administrative Polity: Administrative Law and the Changing Definition of Pluralism, 1945–1970," *Vanderbilt Law Review* 53, No. 5 (2000): 1389.

117. Alice Sturgis, *Your Farm Bureau* (New York: McGraw Hill, 1958), 3.

118. For a discussion of the intellectual history of interest group pluralism, see Schiller, "Enlarging the Administrative Polity," 1399–1410.

119. Earl Latham, *The Group Basis of Politics: A Study in Basing-Point Legislation* (Ithaca: Cornell University Press, 1952), 14–15.

120. Ibid., 36.

121. Ibid., 37. David Truman, *The Governmental Process: Political Interests and Public Opinion* (New York: Knopf, 1951), esp. 26–32.

122. C. Wright Mills, *The Power Elite* (New York: Oxford University Press, 1956), 355.

123. Political scientist E. E. Schattschneider memorably indicted interest group theory's naively blinkered approach to power. "The vice of the groupist theory is that it conceals the most significant aspects of the system," Schattschneider wrote in 1960. "The flaw in the pluralist heaven is that the heavenly chorus sings with a strong upper class accent." See Schattschneider, *The Semisovereign People: A Realist's View of Democracy in America* (New York: Holt, Rinehart, and Winston, 1960), 35.

124. Schiller, "Enlarging the Administrative Polity," 1411.

125. Grant McConnell, *Private Power and American Democracy* (New York: Vintage Books, 1966), 341–343. In applying this idea to American associational life, McConnell drew upon German sociologist Robert Michels, who asserted the law in his 1915 *Political Parties: A Sociological Study of the Oligarchical Tendencies of American Democracy*, trans. Eden and Cedar Paul (New York: Hearst's International Library Co., 1915).

126. Wesley McCune, *Who's Behind Our Farm Policy?* (New York: Praeger, 1956), 16.

127. Quoted in ibid., 17.

128. Ibid., 5.

129. Ibid., 7.

130. Ibid.

131. "R. Flake Shaw to Harold Cooley," November 26, 1951, Folder 1362, Box 33, Cooley Papers, SHC.

132. The NCFB shared with the AFBF an antipathy to organized labor. Indeed, the AFBF was a driving force behind the passage of right-to-work laws across the country. See, for example, McCune, *Who's Behind Our Farm Policy?*, 24–25; *John G. Schott, How "Right-to-Work" Laws Are Passed: Florida Sets the Pattern* (Washington, DC: Public Affairs Institute, 1956), pp. 26–30.

133. "Answers to Questions Farmers Ask about Farm Bureau," ca. 1955, Folder 17, Box 18, NCFB Records, NCSU.

134. "You Ought to Join the Farm Bureau," ca. 1955, Folder 17, Box 18, NCFB Records, NCSU.

135. Ibid.

136. "Resolutions Adopted at 18th Annual Convention, North Carolina Farm Bureau Federation, Raleigh, N.C., November 16, 1953," Folder 2, Box 16, NCFB Records, NCSU.

137. Ibid.

138. "Resolutions Adopted at the 19th Annual Convention Annual Convention, North Carolina Farm Bureau Federation, Asheville, N.C., November 24, 1954," Folder 2, Box 16, NCFB Records, NCSU.

139. For more on the expansion of white suburbs, see David Freund, *Colored Property: State Policy and White Racial Politics in Suburban America* (Chicago: University of Chicago Press, 2007).

140. Shane Hamilton, "Agribusiness, the Family Farm, and the Politics of Technological Determinism in the Post-World War II United States," *Technology and Culture* 55, No. 3 (2014): 571.

141. "1968 Policies, Resolutions, and Recommendations: North Carolina Farm Bureau Federation, Greensboro, N.C.," Folder 3, Box 16, NCFB Records, NCSU. The position of the Farm Bureau resonates with Ira Katznelson's reinterpretation of New Deal social welfare policies as beneficial to whites at the expense of African Americans—an in-built system of white racial privilege that Katznelson calls "affirmative action for whites." See Ira Katznelson, *When Affirmative Action Was White: An Untold Story of Racial Inequality in Twentieth Century America* (New York: W. W. Norton, 2005). See also Pete Daniel, *Dispossession: Discrimination against African American Farmers in the Age of Civil Rights* (Chapel Hill: UNC Press, 2013).

142. "North Carolina Policies and Recommendations to the American Farm Bureau Federation, Charlotte, North Carolina, November 21, 1956," Folder 3, Box 16, NCFB Records, NCSU.

143. "1959 Policies, Resolutions, and Recommendations: North Carolina Farm Bureau Federation, Greensboro, N.C.," Folder 3, Box 16, NCFB Records, NCSU.

144. Ibid.

145. "N.C. Lawmaker's 'Jokes' Offend, Listeners Walk-Out," *New Journal and Guide,* May 26, 1951.

146. Ibid. A handful of letters sent to the congressman, presumably written by African Americans (either present at the talk, or having read the coverage in the black media), reveal the depth of outrage at his comments.

147. David Westfall, "Agricultural Allotments as Property," *Harvard Law Review* 79, No. 6 (April 1966): 1181.

148. *Acreage-Poundage Marketing Quotas for Tobacco: Hearings on S.821, a Bill to Amend the Agricultural Adjustment Act of 1938, as Amended, to Provide for Acreage-Poundage Marketing Quotas for Tobacco*, 89th Con., 1st sess. 126 (February 9, 1965, and February 19, 1965).

149. "To Honorable W. R. Poage," 1/2/74, Folder K, Box 287, Walter B. Jones Papers (Jones Papers), Special Collections, ECU.

150. Randal R. Rucker, Walter N. Thurman, and Daniel A. Sumner, "Restricting the Market for Quota: An Analysis of Tobacco Production Rights with Corroboration from Congressional Testimony," *Journal of Political Economy* 103, No. 1 (February 1995): 160.

151. Harold Cooley, "The Real Peril to the Farm Program," ca. 1955, Folder 2119, Box 49, Cooley Papers, SHC.

152. See, for example, Sturgis, *Your Farm Bureau*, 2–4.

153. "Cancer by the Carton," *Reader's Digest*, December 1952, 7–8; "Medicine: Beyond Any Doubt," *Time*, November 30, 1953, 60–61; "Smoke Gets in the News," *Life*, December 31, 1953, 20–21.

154. National Institutes of Health, "Appendix: Cigarette Smoking in the United States, 1950–1978," https://profiles.nlm.nih.gov/ps/access/nnbcph.pdf.

155. Kelly Bedard and Olivier Deschenes, "The Long-Term Impact of Military Service on Health: Evidence from World War II and Korean War Veterans," *American Economic Review* 96, No. 1 (2006): 176–194.

156. Brandt, *Cigarette Century*, 105. For a discussion of the industry's use of health claims, see Brandt, *Cigarette Century*, 105–114.

157. For more on the use of doctors in cigarette advertising, see Martha Garnder and Allan Brandt, "The Doctor's Choice Is America's Choice: The Physician in Cigarette Advertisements," *American Journal of Public Health* 96, No. 2 (2006): 222–232.

158. Evarts A. Graham, "Foreword" in Alton Ochsner, *Smoking and Cancer: A Doctor's Report* (New York: Messner, 1954), viii. For a summary of the medical profession's increasing confidence in the cigarette-cancer link, see Brandt, *Cigarette Century*, 131–157.

159. Alton Ochsner, *Smoking and Cancer: A Doctor's Report* (New York: Julian Messner, Inc., 1954), 3.

160. National Institutes of Health, "Appendix," A-5.

161. Thomas R. Marshall, *Public Opinion, Public Policy, and Smoking: The Transformation of American Attitudes and Cigarette Use, 1890–2016* (Lanham, MD: Lexington Books, 2016), 52.

162. Proctor, *Golden Holocaust*, 260. For an in-depth history of the founding and operation of TIRC in the 1950s, see Brandt, *Cigarette Century*, 163–183.

163. The participation of farmers in the Big Tobacco lobby has largely been over-looked by historians of Big Tobacco. For example, Jack Hutson's presence at the Plaza meeting is not mentioned in Brandt's chapter on the industry's construction controversy in the 1950s. See Brandt, *Cigarette Century*, chapter 6.

164. "Notes on Minutes of the Tobacco Industry Research Committee Meeting—December 28 1953," Brown & Williamson Records, https://www.industry documentslibrary.ucsf.edu/tobacco/docs/spdx0225.

165. Brandt, *Cigarette Century*, 170–171.

166. Robert Proctor's *Golden Holocaust* contains the most extensive compendium of the manifold strategies of doubt utilized by the tobacco industry from the 1950s through the early 2000s. Proctor, *Golden Holocaust*, 260–288.

167. Brandt, *Cigarette Century*, 171.

168. Proctor, *Golden Holocaust*, 261.

169. "Board of Directors and Endorsing Organizations of the Tobacco Growers Information Committee, Inc." n.d. (1960), Uncategorized Binder Collection of TGIC Minutes, Tobacco Growers Information Committee Records (TGIC Records), Duke Homestead Historic Site (Duke Homestead), Durham, North Carolina.

170. "Carl T. Hicks, Leaf Co-op," 1973, Tobacco Institute, http://legacy.library .ucsf.edu/tid/lft58b00.

171. Tobacco Institute, "From the Desk of Tobacco Growers' Information Committee," October 14, 1968, http://legacy.library.ucsf.edu/tid/yro93b00.

172. "Tobacco Growers Information Committee Meeting Minutes," November 17, 1960, Uncategorized Binder Collection of TGIC Minutes, TGIC Records, Duke Homestead; "Board of Directors and Endorsing Organizations of the Tobacco Growers Information Committee," n.d. (ca. 1960), TGIC Records, Duke Homestead.

173. For the organization's 1960–1961 budget of $52,000, $25,000 was to come from Tobacco Associates, $25,000 from the Tobacco Institute, and $2,000 from unspecified member donations. See "Tobacco Growers Information Committee, Inc. Proposed Budget, November 1, 1960–October 31, 1961," TGIC Records, Duke Homestead.

174. Radio was a particularly important medium in tobacco-producing regions—not only because farmers were less likely to own televisions than other Americans, but also because of Jesse Helms's early popularity on the Raleigh-based Tobacco Radio Network. For an example of the industry emphasis on "facts" versus opinions, see "Tobacco Growers Information Committee News," August 1958, R. J. Reynolds Records, UCSF Library, http://legacy.library.ucsf.edu/tid/lws23a00.

175. Tobacco Growers Information Committee News, December 1958, R. J. Reynolds Records, UCSF Library, https://www.industrydocumentslibrary.ucsf .edu/tobacco/docs/tkgf0003.

176. "Tobacco Growers Information Committee News," August 1958.

177. Chambliss Pierce, "Abingdon Market One of Oldest," Tobacco Institute, UCSF Library, http://legacy.library.ucsf.edu/tid/jpl19a00.

178. Bold emphasis in original; "Virginia: The First American Heritage," File "American Heritage," Uncategorized File Cabinets, TGIC Records, Duke Homestead.

179. TIRC, "Confidential Report: Tobacco Industry Research Committee Meeting," 9 May 9, 1957, Council for Tobacco Research, UCSF Library, http://legacy.library.ucsf.edu/tid/uwr30a00.

180. Harold Cooley, "A Positive Public Relations Program for Farmers," June 15, 1955, Folder 2119, Box 49, Cooley Papers, SHC.

181. Ibid..

182. "Tobacco Growers Information Committee News," 1960, Philip Morris Records, Morris Records. UCSF Library, https://www.industrydocuments library.ucsf.edu/tobacco/docs/fkby0141.

4. The Challenge of the Public Interest

1. First epigraph: "Hubert Says His Foes Have Dirty Souls," *Chicago Tribune*, October 29, 1964. Second epigraph: "Sacrifice Profits, Business Is Asked," *Washington Post*, May 5, 1970.

2. "Smoking Banned at News Parley," *New York Times*, January 12, 1964.

3. Ibid.; see also Allan M. Brandt, *The Cigarette Century: The Rise, Fall, and Deadly Persistence of the Product that Defined America* (New York: Basic, 2007), 229.

4. Surgeon General's Advisory Committee on Smoking and Health, *Smoking and Health: Report of the Advisory Committee to the Surgeon General of the Public Health Service* (Washington, DC: U.S. Department of Health, Education, and Welfare, Public Health Service, 1964), 31.

5. Ibid., 323.

6. Ibid., 301.

7. "Cigarettes Peril Health, US Report Concludes," *New York Times*, January 12, 1964.

8. The literature on the role of expertise and the vaunted place of scientific experts in the postwar United States is vast. For accounts that highlight role of the Cold War in consolidating scientific and social scientific expertise within the federal government, see Audra Wolfe, *Competing with the Soviets: Science, Technology, and the State in Cold War America* (Baltimore: Johns Hopkins University Press, 2012); Brian Balogh, *Chain Reaction: Expert Debate and Public Participation in American Commercial Nuclear Power, 1945–1975* (Cambridge: Cambridge University Press, 1991); Don K. Price, *The Scientific Estate* (Cambridge, MA: Belknap Press, 1965).

9. Brandt, *Cigarette Century*, 218.

10. Ibid., 219–220.

11. Hugh Heclo, "The Sixties' False Dawn: Awakenings, Movements, and Postmodern Policy-Making," in *Integrating the Sixties: The Origins, Structures, and*

Legitimacy of Public Policy in a Turbulent Decade, Brian Balogh, ed. (University Park: Penn State University Press, 1996), 49–50.

12. Adam Rome, *Bulldozer in the Countryside: Suburban Sprawl and the Rise of American Environmentalism* (New York: Cambridge University Press, 2001), 5.

13. Laura Kalman, *The Strange Career of Legal Liberalism* (New Haven: Yale University Press, 1996), 49.

14. Charles Reich, "The New Property," *Yale Law Journal* 73, No. 5 (1964): 754.

15. Karen Tani, *States of Dependency: Welfare, Rights and American Governance* (New York: Cambridge, 2016); Karen Tani, "Flemming v. Nestor: Anti-Communism, the Welfare State, and the Making of New Property," *Law and History Review* 26, No. 2 (2008): 379–414.

16. Reich, "The New Property," 761–764.

17. Ibid., 770.

18. Ibid., 767.

19. Ibid., 778.

20. Ibid., 786.

21. Goldberg v. Kelly, 397 US 254 (1970).

22. See Charles A. Horsky, *The Washington Lawyer* (Boston: Little Brown, 1952).

23. For an analysis of Reich's contribution to the campaign for welfare rights, see Martha Davis, *Brutal Need: Lawyers and the Welfare Rights Movement, 1960–1973* (New Haven: Yale University Press, 1993), 82–86, 104; Rodger D. Citron, "Charles Reich's Journey from the *Yale Law Journal* to the *New York Times* Best-Seller List: The Personal History of *The Greening of America,*" *New York Law Review* 52 (2007 / 2008): 397.

24. Laura Kalman, *Yale Law School and the Sixties: Revolt and Reverberations* (Chapel Hill, UNC Press, 2005).

25. Ibid., 68.

26. Charles Reich, "The Public and the Nation's Forests," *California Law Review* 50, No. 3 (1962): 391.

27. "The New Public Interest Lawyers," *Yale Law Journal* 79, No. 6 (1970): 1069–1152.

28. Paul Sabin, "Environmental Law and the End of the New Deal Order," *Law and History Review* 33, No. 4 (2015): 1–39.

29. William J. Novak, " A Revisionist History of Regulatory Capture," in Carpenter and David Moss, eds., *Preventing Regulatory Capture: Special Interest Influence and How to Limit It* (Cambridge: Cambridge University Press, 2013); Reuel Schiller, "Enlarging the Administrative Polity: Enlarging the Administrative Polity: Administrative Law and the Changing Definition of Pluralism, 1945–1970," *Vanderbilt Law Review* 53 (2000): 1389–1453. For a left critique of interest groups, see Gabriel Kolko, *The Triumph of Conservatism: A Reinterpretation of American History, 1900–1916* (New York: Free Press of Glencoe, 1963); James Weinstein, *Corporate Ideal in the Liberal State, 1900–1918* (Boston: Beacon Press, 1968); Martin J. Sklar, *The Corporate Reconstruction of American Capitalism, 1890–1916: The Market, the Law, and Politics* (Cambridge: Cambridge University Press, 1988). On the right, see Samuel P. Huntington,

"The Marasmus of the ICC: The Commission, The Railroads, and the Public Interest," *Yale Law Journal* 61, No. 4 (1952): 467–509; Marver H. Bernstein, *Regulating Business by Independent Commission* (Princeton: Princeton University Press, 1955). For the classic formulation of the "Chicago school" approach to public choice economics, see George J. Stigler, "The Theory of Economic Regulation," *Bell Journal of Economics and Management Science* 2 (1971): 3–21.

30. Scenic Hudson Preservation Conference v. Federal Power Commission, 354 F.2d 608 (2nd Cir. 1965).

31. Schiller, "Enlarging the Administrative Polity."

32. Pat Ortmeyer and Arjun Makhijani "Worse Than We Knew," *Bulletin of the Atomic Scientists,* November–December 1997; Scott Kirsch, "Harold Knapp and the Geography of Normal Controversy: Radioiodine in the Historical Environment," *Osiris,* 2nd Series, 19 (2004): 167–181.

33. Rome, *Bulldozer in the Countryside,* 107.

34. Linda Lear, "Bombshell in Beltsville: The USDA and the Challenge of 'Silent Spring,'" *Agricultural History* 66, No. 2 (1992): 151–170.

35. The literature on the 1960s organizing strategies of social movements is voluminous. For an introduction to the post-1960s consumer movement, see Mark V. Nadel, *The Politics of Consumer Protection* (Indianapolis: Bobbs-Merrill, 1971).

36. Samuel P. Hayes, *Beauty, Health, Permanence: Environmental Politics in the United States, 1955–1985* (Cambridge: Cambridge University Press, 1989), 474.

37. A. Lee Fristschler, *Smoking and Politics: Policymaking in the Federal Bureaucracy* (Michigan: 1969), 29.

38. Ironically and tragically, the micronite filter in use between 1952 and 1956 contained asbestos, increasing a smoker's risk for mesothelioma.

39. "Head of FTC Confirms Accord on Shifting Cigarettes' Ad Pitch," *New York Times,* February 6, 1960.

40. Edward Finch Cox, Robert C. Fellmeth, and John E. Schulz, *The Nader Report on the Federal Trade Commission* (New York: R. W. Baron, 1969).

41. This was a criticism made by Oregon Senator Maurine Neuberger when she introduced legislation immediately after the *Report.* See "Sen. Neuberger Seeks U.S. Cigarette Controls. 1964," *Los Angeles Times,* January 12, 1964.

42. For a discussion of the "tar derby," see *The Cigarette Papers,* Stanton Glantz and Lisa Bero, eds. (Berkeley: University of California Press, 1996), 27–29.

43. Paul Rand Dixon Oral History Interview, August 7, 1968, John F. Kennedy Presidential Library and Museum, http://archive1.jfklibrary.org/JFKOH /Dixon,%20Paul%20Rand/JFKOH-PRD-01/JFKOH-PRD-01-TR.pdf.

44. Dixon quoted in Fritschler, *Smoking and Politics,* 73–74.

45. Richard Kluger, *Ashes to Ashes: America's Hundred-Year Cigarette War, the Public Health, and the Unabashed Triumph of Philip Morris* (New York: Vintage, 1997), 268–269.

46. "Leaf Farmers Request No Labeling," *Durham Morning Herald,* April 10, 1964.

47. Fritschler, *Smoking and Politics,* 98–99.

48. Herbert Marcuse, *One Dimensional Man: Studies in the Ideology of Advanced Industrial Society* (Boston: Beacon, 1964; reprint, 1966), 242.

49. *Hearings, Interstate and Foreign Commerce*, 88th Cong., sess. 2, Vol. 1 (1964): 76.

50. Brandt, *Cigarette Century*, 254–256.

51. Elizabeth Drew, "The Quiet Victory of the Cigarette Lobby: How it Found the Best Filter Yet—Congress," *Atlantic Monthly*, September 1965, 76.

52. Joseph Califano, *Inside: A Public and Private Life* (New York: Public Affairs, 2005), 168; "Tobacco: Administration Showing Little Enthusiasm for Follow-Up on Public Health Service Report," *Science* 143, No. 3613 (March 27, 1964): 1418.

53. Nancy Tomes, *Remaking the American Patient: How Madison Avenue and Modern Medicine Turned Patients into Consumers* (Chapel Hill: UNC Press 2017), 262. For more on the participatory ideal about Office of Economic Opportunity (OEO) community health clinics see Alice Sardell, *US Experiment in Social Medicine: The Community Health Center Program, 1965–1986* (Pittsburgh: University of Pittsburgh Press, 1988).

54. Silber, *With All Deliberate Speed: The Life of Philip Elman, An Oral History Memoir* (Ann Arbor: University of Michigan Press, 2004), 349.

55. Cabell Phillips quoted in Laura Kalman, *Abe Fortas: A Biography,* reprint (New Haven: Yale University Press, 1992), 114.

56. Ibid., 3.

57. Judith Stein, *Pivotal Decade: How the United States Traded Factories for Finance in the Seventies* (New Haven: Yale University Press, 2010).

58. Kalman, *Abe Fortas,* 152–162.

59. Kluger, *Ashes to Ashes,* 289.

60. Kalman, *Abe Fortas*, 163.

61. "US Silence Gives Jitters to Tobacco Men," *Advertising Age,* June 15, 1964.

62. Kluger, *Ashes to Ashes,* 279–280.

63. "Cigarette Code Stirs a Debate," *New York Times*, April 29, 1964.

64. Sam Blum, "An Ode to the Cigarette Code," *Harper's Magazine*, March 1966, 61.

65. "The Cigarette Ad Code: Will FTC Buy It?" *Sponsor Magazine,* April 5, 1964, 25–28.

66. "US Silence Gives Jitters to Tobacco Men," *Advertising Age,* June 15, 1964.

67. National Association of Broadcasters, "TV Code Review Board Acts on Cigarette Advertising," October 7, 1966, Liggett & Myers Records, source unknown, University of California at San Francisco (UCSF) Library, https://www.industrydocumentslibrary.ucsf.edu/tobacco/docs/#id =frff0014; "Code Board Authorizes Cigaret Ad Guidelines," *Advertising Age,* October 10, 1966.

68. Daniel L. Brenner, "The Limits of Broadcast Self-Regulation under the First Amendment," *Stanford Law Review* 27, No. 6 (July 1975): 1528–1529, see especially 1552–1553.

69. See Green v. American Tobacco Company, 304 F. 2d 70 (1962).

70. Kalman, *Abe Fortas*, 153.

71. "Conference at the Department of Justice Concerning Antitrust Clearance for Cigarette Advertising," June 12, 1964, Lorillard Records, source unknown, UCSF Library, https://www.industrydocumentslibrary.ucsf.edu /tobacco/docs/xhxf0191.

72. Ibid.

73. Ibid. For the New Deal-era precedent, see Panama Refining Co. v. Ryan, 293 US 388 (1935).

74. W. H. Orrick, Department of Justice, June 17, 1964, Lorillard Records, source unknown, UCSF Library, https://www.industrydocumentslibrary.ucsf.edu /tobacco/docs/pfcl0010.

75. Ralph Nader, *Unsafe at Any Speed: The Designed-in Dangers of the American Automobile* (New York: Grossman Publishers, 1965), ix, iv.

76. "G.M. Apologies for Harassment of Critic," *New York Times,* March 23, 1966.

77. Schiller, "Enlarging the Administrative Polity," 1414.

78. "Conservationists Press Fight against Pesticides," *New York Times,* November 26, 1967.

79. Adam Rome, *The Genius of Earth Day: How a 1970 Teach-In Unexpectedly Made the First Green Generation* (New York: Hill and Wang, 2014), 194–195; Yannacone quoted in Rome, The Genius of Earth Day 197.

80. The Genius of Earth Day.

81. Sabin, "Environmental Law and the End of the New Deal Order." See also Hayes, *Beauty, Health Permanence,* 458–463; Christopher J. Bosso, *Environment, Inc.: From Grassroots to Beltway* (Lawrence: University Press of Kansas, 2005), 39–44.

82. Sabin, "Environmental Law and the End of the New Deal Order," 969.

83. Reuel Schiller has provided the most extensive history of the emergence of judicial oversight over administrative agencies. See Schiller, "Enlarging the Administrative Polity," especially 1415–1416. *Gideon's Trumpet* popularized the idea of the Warren Court as a refuge for the dispossessed. See Anthony Lewis, *Gideon's Trumpet* (New York: Knopf, 1964).

84. Ben F. Waple, "In the Matter of Television Station WCBS," September 1967, R. J. Reynolds Records, source unknown, UCSF Library, https://www .industrydocumentslibrary.ucsf.edu/tobacco/docs/fqpb0086.

85. "Minutes of the Commission Meetings and Hearings, June 2, 1967–June 14, 1967," Box 1211, Federal Communications Commission Archives, Record Group 173, National Archives and Records Administration (NARA-II), College Park, MD; FCC, *Federal Communications Commission Reports: Decisions, . . . 2nd,* Vol. 9 (1967): 925.

86. FCC, *Federal Communications Commission Reports,* 925–928.

87. Ibid., 948–950.

88. "Memorandum Opinion, September 8, 1967, Minutes of Commission Meetings and Hearings, Sept. 6, 1967–Sept. 20, 1967," Box 1218, Federal Communications Commission Archives, Record Group 173, NARA-II.

89. "Concurring Opinion of Commissioner Lee Lovinger in the Matter of Cigarette Advertising, Memorandum Opinion, September 8, 1967, Minutes of

Commission Meetings and Hearings, Sept. 6, 1967–Sept. 20, 1967," Box 1218, Federal Communications Commission Archives, Record Group 173, NARA-II.

90. "Minutes of the Commission Meetings and Hearings, June 2, 1967–June 14, 1967," Box 1211, Federal Communications Commission Archives, Record Group 173, NARA-II; FCC, *Federal Communications Commission Reports*, 933.

91. "Advertising: Top Spenders for Network TV," *New York Times,* February 2, 1968.

92. "Computer Program Copyrighted for First Time," *New York Times,* May 8, 1964.

93. U.S. Congress, House, Committee on the Judiciary, Subcommittee No. 3 (1966), *Copyright Law Revision: Hearings,* Eighty-Ninth Cong., 1st sess. (Washington, DC: U.S. Govt. Print. Off.), 1144–1150.

94. John F. Banzhaf, "Weighted Voting Doesn't Work: A Mathematical Analysis," *Rutgers Law Review* 19 (1965): 317–343; Banzhaf, "Multi-Member Electoral Districts. Do They Violate the 'One Man, One Vote' Principle?" *Yale Law Journal* 75, No. 8 (1966): 1309–1338.

95. "Professor John F. Banzhaf III—Major Professional Accomplishments," accessed September 10, 2016. http://banzhaf.net/accom.html.

96. "John Banzhaf, the So-Called 'Nader of the Tobacco Industry,'" *Washington Post,* March 15, 1970.

97. Ibid.

98. Sabin, "Environmental Law and the End of the New Deal Order," 972.

99. "John Banzhaf, the So-Called 'Nader of the Tobacco Industry'"; "Cigaret Commercial Ban Won't Halt Fight, Says Smoking Foe," *Los Angeles Times,* February 8, 1969.

100. "John Banzhaf, the So-Called 'Nader of the Tobacco Industry.'" Recent scholarship in political science has highlighted a similar dynamic of private enforcement of civil rights law, highlighting the relationship between private attorneys and administrative agencies. See Lynda G. Dodd, ed., *The Rights Revolution Revisited: Institutional Perspectives on the Private Enforcement of Civil Rights in the United States* (New York and Cambridge: Cambridge University Press, 2018).

101. In editorials objecting to the ruling, comparisons to Nazi Germany and Orwell's dystopian *1984* abound. See Hill & Knowlton, "Editorial Comment on FCC 'Fairness Doctrine' Ruling," July 21, 1967, Liggett & Myers Records, UCSF Library, https://www.industrydocumentslibrary.ucsf.edu/tobacco/docs/jykd0014.

102. FCC, *Federal Communications Commission Reports*, 949.

103. Kluger, *Ashes to Ashes,* 305–307. Banzhaf filed his appeal not because he disagreed with the FCC ruling but because he wanted it to stand. He appealed on the thin ground that the FCC had not granted him the requested "equal airtime."

104. Banzhaf v. FCC, 405 F.2d 1082 (D.C. Cir., 1968).

105. 90 Cong. Rec. H8242 (June 28, 1967).

106. H&K (Hill & Knowlton), "Further Developments in FCC Ruling," June 12, 1967, Liggett & Myers Records, https://www.industrydocumentslibrary.ucsf.edu/tobacco/docs/rjjd0014.

107. See, for example, "A Nonsensical Ruling," *Pueblo* (Co.) *Chieftain,* June 22, 1967, Brown & Williamson Records, https://www.industrydocumentslibrary.ucsf.edu/tobacco/docs/glwm0054.; B. D. Shaffer, "Speaking Out for Liberty," June 19, 1967, American Tobacco Records, UCSF Library, https://www.industrydocumentslibrary.ucsf.edu/tobacco/docs/llcg0147.

108. "A Nonsensical Ruling," *Pueblo* (Co.) *Chieftain,* June 22, 1967, Brown & Williamson Records, https://www.industrydocumentslibrary.ucsf.edu/tobacco/docs/glwm0054.

109. "A Word from Our Anti-Sponsor," June 17, 1967, American Tobacco Records, UCSF Library, https://www.industrydocumentslibrary.ucsf.edu/tobacco/docs/xhcc0015.

110. "How Far Can Fairness Go?," *Broadcasting,* June 12, 1967, Brown & Williamson Records, UCSF Library, https://www.industrydocumentslibrary.ucsf.edu/tobacco/docs/gldn0124.

111. James J. Kilpatrick, *The Sovereign States: Notes of a Citizen of Virginia* (Chicago: Henry Regnery, 1957).

112. James Hustwit, *James J. Kilpatrick: Salesman for Segregation* (Chapel Hill: UNC Press, 2013).

113. Quote from William Anderson (Tobacco Growers Information Committee), "Tobacco Industry Fear Being Taxed to Death," *Richmond News Leader,* February 24, 1969.

114. D. T. Frederickson, "Action on Smoking and Health," January 26, 1968, R. J. Reynolds Records, UCSF Library, https://www.industrydocumentslibrary.ucsf.edu/tobacco/docs/mfkx0096.

115. Amanda Amos and Margaretha Haglund, "From Social Taboo to 'Torch of Freedom': The Marketing of Cigarettes to Women," *Tobacco Control* 9 (2009): 3–8; Edward L. Bernays, *Biography of an Idea: Memoirs of Public Relations Counsel Edward L. Bernays* (New York: Simon and Schuster, 1965), 382–395.

116. "Smoking, the Destruction of Self," *New England Journal of Medicine* 279, No. 5 (August 1, 1968): 267–268.

117. "Group Will Spur Suits against Cigarette Makers," *New York Times,* January 29, 1969.

118. "Consumer Groups Test Regulatory Agencies," *Washington Post,* November 23, 1969; "GW Law School Group Hits Unfair Collection Practices," *Washington Post,* January 8, 1970.

119. "Students Waging Consumer Battle," *New York Times,* December 2, 1969.

120. "Tempest in a Soup Can: BBDO Exec Recalls Landmark Legal Battle between Campbell, the FTC, and 5 Law Students," *Ad Age,* October 17, 1994; "John Banzhaf, the So-Called 'Nader of the Tobacco Industry.'"

121. Indeed, it was precisely at this moment that economist Mancur Olson published his *Logic of Collective Action* (1965), which expounded a straightforward explanation for why some groups organized and other groups did not.

Groups that represented relatively small numbers of voters—such as those composed of tobacco-dependent industries—were more likely to organize than groups representing the far larger mass of Americans who would have preferred to see greater regulation of cigarettes, but who did not feel as intensely about the matter, or have the kind of short-term financial stakes.

122. Kluger, *Ashes to Ashes,* 285.

123. Ibid.

124. See, for example, Kennedy's embrace of hunger and malnutrition as a political issue, as described in Rachel Moran, *Governing Bodies: American Politics and the Shaping of the Modern Physique* (Philadelphia: University of Pennsylvania Press, 2017), 116–120. In his advocacy of free food stamps, Kennedy departed with the Johnson administration's continued support of the USDA's administration of the food stamp program.

125. *World Conference on Smoking and Health: A Summary of the Proceedings, September 11–13* (n.p.: National Interagency Council on Smoking and Health, 1967), 9.

126. Ibid.

127. "Advertising: An Ex-Smoker's Exit," *Time,* September 25, 1964.

128. *World Conference,* 245.

129. Ibid.

130. Ibid., 237.

131. "Novice Lawyer Shakes an Industry," *National Observer,* September 18, 1967, 16.

132. "Letters to the Editor: Dead Letter Ruling?" *Washington Post,* August 27, 1967.

133. "The Law Professor behind ASH, SOUP, PUMP and CRASH," *New York Times,* August 23, 1970.

134. Ibid.

135. Hugh Heclo has argued that many of the movement politics of the 1960s took on the organizational, bureaucratic logic of their times. See Heclo, "The Sixties False Dawn."

136. Brandt, *Cigarette Century,* 268.

137. "The Law Professor behind ASH, SOUP, PUMP and CRASH."

138. Ibid.

139. *World Conference on Smoking and Health,* 243. For a discussion of the changing understandings of risk and consent that shaped cigarette regulation, see Allan M. Brandt, "Blow Some My Way: Passive Smoking, Risk and American Culture," in *Ashes to Ashes: The History of Smoking and Health,* Stephen Lock, Lois Reynolds, and E. M. Tansey, eds. (Amsterdam: Rodopi, 1998), 164–167.

140. "Banzhaf Shoots at WNBC-TV," April 1968, Tobacco Institute Records, Source: Roswell Park Cancer Institute (RPCI), https://www.industrydoc umentslibrary.ucsf.edu/tobacco/docs/jhfk0148.

141. Page, "The Law Professor behind ASH, SOUP, PUMP and CRASH."

142. ASH Newsletters, Folder 13, Box 6, Luther Terry Papers (Terry Papers), National Library of Medicine (NLM), Bethesda, M.D.

143. G. A. Giovino et al., "Surveillance for Selected Tobacco-Use Behaviors—United States, 1900–1994," *Morbidity and Mortality Weekly Report Surveillance Summaries* 43, No. 3 (1994), https://www.cdc.gov/mmwr/preview/mmwrhtml/00033881.htm; Brandt, *Cigarette Century*, 237–238; Laverne Creek, Tom Capehart, Verner Grise, *U.S. Tobacco Statistics, 1935–1992* (Washington: Economic Research Service, U.S. Department of Agriculture, 1994), 14. The per capita declines began in 1973.

144. Kluger, *Ashes to Ashes*, 325.

145. *Health Consequences of Smoking—50 Years of Progress: A Report of the Surgeon General* (Atlanta: Centers for Disease Control and Prevention, 2014), https://www.ncbi.nlm.nih.gov/books/NBK294310/.

146. Kluger, *Ashes to Ashes*, 326.

147. For an example of outrage, see Unprocessed marketing papers, North Carolina Division of Archives and History (NCDAH), 3133–3134; *Tobacco Reporter*, March 1968, 62.

148. Sam Ervin (NC), "A Study in Governmental Brainwashing," 90 Cong. Rec. S937 (February 6, 1968).

149. Elizabeth Drew, "The Cigarette Companies Would Rather Fight Than Switch," *New York Times Magazine*, May 4, 1969.

150. "Bess Myerson Is Sworn In as the City's Consumer Aide," *New York Times*, March 5, 1969.

151. Richard J. Leighton, "Consumer Protection Agency Proposals: The Origin of the Species," *Administrative Law Review* 25, No. 3 (Summer 1973): 287. Leighton argues that proposals for cabinet-level consumer agencies had been around since the 1930s.

152. Ibid., 299; Richard Nixon: "Special Message to the Congress on Consumer Protection," October 30, 1969, accessed online in Gerhard Peters and John T. Woolley, *The American Presidency Project*, http://www.presidency.ucsb.edu/ws/?pid=2299.

153. Drew, "The Cigarette Companies Would Rather Fight Than Switch."

154. "Report of the President to the Members and Directors at the Sixth Annual Meeting TGIC," 2 November 1964, TGIC Meetings and Minutes, Duke Homestead, Durham, NC.

155. Julian Zelizer, *On Capitol Hill: The Struggle to Reform Congress and Its Consequences* (New York: Cambridge University Press, 2004), 63–69.

156. Ibid., 73. For an account of Cooley's loss as a result of his fealty to agriculture at the expense of North Carolina's diversifying economy, see John Mark Hansen, *Gaining Access: Congress and the Farm Lobby* (Chicago: University of Chicago Press, 1991), 184–185.

157. 88 Cong. Rec. S4335 (March 4, 1964).

158. Alexander Holmes, "Delaware Galahad," *Los Angeles Times*, January 19, 1954.

159. 88 Cong. Rec. S4336 (March 4, 1964)..

160. "Kill Tobacco Support Program," *Knoxville News Sentinel*, March 4, 1964.

161. "Flue-Cured Tobacco Cooperative Stabilization Corporation," Folder-Tobacco Resources, Uncategorized Collections, Duke Homestead.

162. "Acreage-Poundage Marketing Quotas for Tobacco: Hearings to Amend the Agricultural Adjustment Act of 1938," 88th Congress (February 9, 1965, and February 19, 1965) 14.

163. "Subsidy Hunters Swooping Down on Washington," *New York Times*, September 8, 1968.

164. "Tobacco Price Supports Cost Taxpayers Least of All Crops," *New York Times*, October 4, 1964.

165. L. H. Fountain, House Interstate and Foreign Commerce Committee, Cigarette Labeling and Advertising, 91st Congress, 1st sess., 26 (April 15, 1969). Discrepancies in the figures cited by tobacco supporters and others reflect supporters' neglect of the cost of export subsidies, Food-for-Peace, tobacco grading services, and administration.

166. See, for example, "The Tobacco Subsidy," *New York Times*, March 15, 1964.

167. "Troubles Beset Tobacco Areas," *New York Times*, October 4, 1964.

168. Tobacco Associates, "Annual Report—1965," March 2, 1965, Tobacco Institute Records, https://www.industrydocumentslibrary.ucsf.edu/tobacco/docs/yjlv0041.

169. Brianna Rego, "The Polonium Brief: A Hidden History of Cancer, Radiation, and the Tobacco Industry," *Isis* 100, No. 3 (2009): 453–484.

170. "Immediate Release—Cooley Introduces Acreage-Poundage Bill," February 8, 1964, "Miscellaneous Files From the Commissioner's Office, 1965," North Carolina Department of Agriculture, NCDAH.

171. "Acreage-Poundage Marketing Quotas for Tobacco," 14.

172. Ibid., 66–68.

5. Inventing the Nonsmoker

1. National Commission on Smoking and Public Policy, "Catalog of Themes and Anti-Smoking Recommendations," March 22, 1977, Liggett & Myers Records, University of California at San Francisco (UCSF) Library, https://www.industrydocumentslibrary.ucsf.edu/tobacco/docs/ypyy0011.

2. Glenn Goldberg, "Legal Aspects of Non-Smokers' Rights or 'If We Are Not for Ourselves, Then Who Will Be for Us?'" in *Smoking and Health: Proceedings of the Third World Conference on Smoking and Health, New York City, June 2–5 1975* (Bethesda, M.D.: U.S. Dept. of Health, Education, and Welfare, Public Health Service, National Institutes of Health, National Cancer Institute, 1976), 363.

3. This articulation of an equal and opposite right underscores what legal scholar Mark Tushnet has called the "indeterminacy" of rights talk, providing "only momentary advantages in ongoing political struggles." See Mark Tushnet, "An Essay on Rights," *Texas Law Review* 62 (1984): 1371.

4. "The Rights of the Nonsmoker," 1976, Folder 6, Carton 1, Americans for Nonsmokers' Rights (ANR) Records, University of California at San Francisco (UCSF), San Francisco, C.A.

5. See, for example, Lily Geismer's excellent analysis of knowledge professionals that reshaped liberalism along the Route 128 corridor in Massachusetts: Geismer, *Don't Blame Us: Suburban Liberals and the Transformation of the Democratic Party* (Princeton: Princeton University Press, 2015).

6. Daniel Rodgers, *Age of Fracture* (Cambridge, MA: Belknap Press, 2011).

7. Martha Dirthick and Paul Quirk, *The Politics of Deregulation* (Washington, DC: Brookings Institution, 1985).

8. Samuel Hayes has argued that environmentalists during the 1960s and 1970s sought and found assistance from state governments. In the realm of air pollution control specifically, localities enlisted the expertise of the federal government for leverage against industrial polluters. See Samuel P. Hayes, *Beauty, Health, and Permanence: Environmental Politics in the United States, 1955–1985* (Cambridge: Cambridge University Press, 1989), 433–445. Brian Balogh has argued that interests expressed at the state level opposed nuclear reactor projects developed by the federal Atomic Energy Commission on public-health grounds in the late 1950s. See Brian Balogh, *Chain Reaction: Expert Debate and Public Participation in American Commercial Nuclear Power, 1945–1975* (New York: Cambridge University Press, 1991), 159–170.

9. Geismer, *Don't Blame Us*.

10. Steven H. Leleiko, "The Clinic and NYU," *Journal of Legal Education* 24, No. 4 (1972): 429–461.

11. "Faculty Profile—John Banzhaf," *Amicus Curiae* (George Washington Law School), October 14, 1968.

12. Paul Sabin, "Environmental Law and the End of the New Deal Order," *Law and History Review* 33, No. 4 (November 2015): 965–1003.

13. Joseph Sax, *Defending the Environment: A Handbook for Citizen Action* (Vancouver, WA: Vintage, 1970), xviii.

14. Ibid., 59.

15. Arthur F. McAvoy, "Environmental Law and the Collapse of New Deal Constitutionalism," *Akron Law Review* 46, No. 4 (2013): 896.

16. Jack Anderson, "Washington Merry Go-Round: Consumer Advocates Eye Cola Drinks," *Washington Post*, February 17, 1971, C19.

17. "FCC Orders Closed Captioning," *The GW Advocate*, August 2, 1976; "DEAFWATCH," *The GW Advocate*, June 8, 1975.

18. *Aviation Daily*, December 19, 1969, American Tobacco Records, UCSF Library, https://www.industrydocumentslibrary.ucsf.edu/tobacco/docs/zhbl0075.

19. Ralph Nader, Petitioner to Honorable John H. Shaffer, December 7, 1969, R. J. Reynolds Records, UCSF Library, https://www.industrydocumentsli brary.ucsf.edu/tobacco/docs/nfhf0003.

20. John F. Banzhaf III., "Action on Smoking and Health to Honorable John A. Volpe," March 31, 1970, R. J. Reynolds Records, https://www.industrydoc umentslibrary.ucsf.edu/tobacco/docs/nyyv0101.

21. Ibid.

22. Ann Landers, *Washington Post*, January 8, 1970, C8.

23. Warren Burger to John H. Shaffer, December 18, 1969, R. J. Reynolds Records, UCSF Library, https://www.industrydocumentslibrary.ucsf.edu /tobacco/docs/yxck0086; *Wall Street Journal*, January 29, 1970.

24. "Nader Seeks Bar on Bus Smoking," *Washington Post*, February 10, 1970.

25. Ibid.

26. *Federal Register* 36, No. 239 (November 12, 1971): 23638.

27. "Justice Beefs, Metroliner Cuts Smoking," *Washington Post*, December 14, 1972.

28. "Pan-Am to Offer Seats Just for Nonsmokers," *New York Times*, January 27, 1970; "3d Airline, American, Begins 747 Service," *New York Times*, March 3, 1970; "All TWA Jets Will Have Sections for Nonsmokers," *New York Times*, March 10, 1970.

29. "Pan Am to Offer Seats Just for Nonsmokers," *New York Times*, January 27, 1970, 85.

30. "No Smoking: Pressure Builds to Curb Smokers in Airlines," *Wall Street Journal*, January 29, 1970, 1.

31. HEW, FAA, Department of Transportation, National Institute for Occupational Safety, "Health Aspects of Smoking in Transport Aircraft," December 1971, R. J. Reynolds Records, UCSF Library, https://www .industrydocumentslibrary.ucsf.edu/tobacco/docs/pybk0086.

32. Ibid.

33. Ibid.

34. J. P. Jeblee, "Proposed C.A. Ruling," November 27, 1972, Philip Morris Records, UCSF Library, https://www.industrydocumentslibrary.ucsf.edu /tobacco/docs/szbf0122.

35. "Smoking Is Hazardous to Passengers' Comfort," *New York Times*, December 31, 1972.

36. Edwin L. Bierman to Federal Aviation Administration, April 24, 1970, Lorillard Records, UCSF Library, https://www.industrydocumentslibrary .ucsf.edu/tobacco/docs/pnff0121.

37. Gerald A. Ahronheim to James F. Rudolph, April 27, 1970, R. J. Reynolds Records, UCSF Library, https://www.industrydocumentslibrary.ucsf.edu /tobacco/docs/qnyv0101.

38. "Caution: Smoking Is Hazardous to Passengers' Comfort," *New York Times*, December 31, 1972.

39. AJ Stevens, n.d., Philip Morris Records, UCSF Library, https://www .industrydocumentslibrary.ucsf.edu/tobacco/docs/mmcp0119.

40. Docket No. 21708, November 13, 1972, Philip Morris Records, UCSF Library, https://www.industrydocumentslibrary.ucsf.edu/tobacco/docs /fmcp0119.

41. Ibid.

42. Ibid.

43. Ibid.

44. Lorillard, Docket No. 21708, January 30, 1973, Philip Morris Records, https://www.industrydocumentslibrary.ucsf.edu/tobacco/docs/smcp0119.

45. "ASH Breaks Logjam at Cab," *ASH Newsletter,* May–June 1978; "CAB Moves on ASH Complaints," July–August 1978, Folder 15, Box 6, Terry Papers, NLM.

46. David Moss, "Reversing the Null: Regulation, Deregulation, and the Power of Ideas," in *Challenges to Business in the Twenty-First Century,* Gerald Rosenfelt, Jay W. Lorsch, and Rakesh Khurana, eds. (Cambridge, MA: American Academy of Arts and Sciences, 2011).

47. "Regulators and the Polls," *Regulation* 6, No. 2 (November–December 1978): 11.

48. Phillip J. Cooper, *The War against Regulation: From Jimmy Carter to George W. Bush* (Lawrence: University Press of Kansas, 2009), 16.

49. Thomas K. McCraw, *Prophets of Regulation: Charles Francis Adams, Louis D. Brandeis, James M. Landis, Alfred E. Kahn* (Cambridge, MA: Belknap Press, 1984), 219.

50. Susan E. Dudley, "Alfred Kahn, 1917–2010," *Regulation* 34, No. 1 (Spring 2011): 9–11.

51. Rodgers, *Age of Fracture,* 60–62.

52. "CAB Requests Input on Smoking, Approves Waivers," *ASH Newsletter,* September–October 1980, Tobacco Institute Records, UCSF Library, https://www.industrydocumentslibrary.ucsf.edu/tobacco/docs/zshv0051.

53. Gail Appleson, "Fired-Up Nonsmokers Take Cab to Court," *American Bar Association Journal* 68, No. 12 (December 1982): 1556.

54. Peggy Lopipero and Lisa Bero, "Tobacco Interests or the Public Interest: 20 Years of Industry Strategies to Undermine Airline Smoking Restrictions," *Tobacco Control* 15, No. 4 (August 2006): 326–327.

55. Hugh Heclo captures the skeptical yet dependent posture of public interest lawyers toward the regulatory state. See Heclo, "The Sixties' False Dawn: Awakenings, Movements, and Postmodern Policy-Making," in *Integrating the Sixties: The Origins, Structures, and Legitimacy of Public Policy in a Turbulent Decade,* Brian Balogh, ed. (University Park: Penn State University Press, 1996), xx.

56. "Sue the CAB Again?" *ASH Newsletter,* July 1984, Folder 16, Box 6, Papers of Luther L. Terry, National Library of Medicine (NLM).

57. There were some variations on the group's name. The College Park GASP chapter began as Group Against Smokers' Pollution, but then changed its name to the less accusatory Group Against Smoking Pollution. Other GASPs stood for Group Against Smoke and Pollution.

58. "The First GASP," February 28, 2006, in author's possession. Brandt notes that the framing of children as innocent victims of tobacco smoke helped to reshape "the moral calculus of cigarette smoking." Allan M. Brandt, "Blow Some My Way: Passive Smoking, Risk and American Culture," in *Ashes to Ashes: The History of Smoking and Health,* Stephen Lock, Lois Reynolds, and E. M. Tansey, eds. (Amsterdam: Rodopi, 1998), 171.

59. "The First GASP," February 28, 2006, in author's possession.

60. "Co-Op Bans Smoking in Some Areas," *Oakland Post,* October 7, 1971, 10.

61. "The First GASP," February 28, 2006, in author's possession.

62. "Campaign for Their Rights: A New Militancy Gets Results," *Los Angeles Times,* October 25, 1973; "Where There's Smoke, There's Ire," *Houston Post,* February 2, 1975; "GASP Tries to Clear Air of Smokers," *Pasadena Evening Star News,* August 20, 1977.

63. See, for example, *GASP Update* (Georgia), Folder 8, Carton 1, Peter Hanauer Tobacco Control Papers (Hanauer Papers), UCSF.

64. "Speak Up: Every Victory Counts," *GASP News,* October 1976, Folder 2, Carton 1, Hanauer Papers, UCSF.

65. Michael Novak, *The Rise of the Unmeltable Ethnics: Politics and Culture in the Seventies* (New York: Macmillan, 1972).

66. Carrie Menkel-Meadow, "The Causes of Cause Lawyering: Toward an Understanding of the Motivation and Commitment of Social Justice Lawyers," in *Cause Lawyering: Political Commitments and Professional Responsibilities,* Austin Sarat and Stuart Scheingold, eds. (New York: Oxford University Press, 1998), 43.

67. Thomas Frank, *The Conquest of Cool: Business Culture, Counterculture, and the Rise of Hip Consumerism* (Chicago: University of Chicago Press, 1997), 155–156.

68. Pamphlet, "GASP: Non-Smokers Have Rights Too," January 1975, in author's possession.

69. For examples of "assertiveness training" workshops see GASP, *Nonsmoker's Voice* (Denver, Colorado), Folder 5, Carton 3, Donna Shimp Papers and Environmental Associates Records (Shimp Papers), UCSF. For the support switchboard, see *GASP Bulletin* (Berkeley, California), 1972, Folder 13, Carton 1, Hanauer Papers, UCSF.

70. Sarah Evans, *Personal Politics: The Roots of Women's Liberation in the Civil Rights Movement and the New Left* (New York: Knopf, 1975), 134.

71. "Where There's Smoke, There's Ire," *Sun Magazine,* August 27, 1972.

72. "Nonsmokers' Liberation Ceremony: Birthday of Abraham Lincoln," February 12, 1975, in author's possession.

73. Serena Mayeri, *Reasoning from Race: Feminism, Law, and the Civil Rights Revolution* (Cambridge, MA: Harvard University Press, 2011).

74. "Civil Rights and the Non-Smokers' Movement," Folder 18, Carton 1, Hanauer Papers, UCSF.

75. Grace Elizabeth Hale argues that by the 1960s, middle-class Americans had appropriated the status of marginalized African Americans to fashion their own identities. See Hale, *A Nation of Outsiders: How the White Middle-Class Fell in Love with Rebellion in Postwar America* (New York: Oxford University Press, 2011).

76. Christopher Sellers, *Crabgrass Crucible: Suburban Nature and the Rise of Environmentalism in Twentieth-Century America* (Chapel Hill: University of North Carolina Press, 2012).

77. Geismer, *Don't Blame Us,* 120–121.

78. *Non-Smokers' Liberation Guide,* 1973, in author's possession.

79. The first use of "NIMBY" was in a 1980 *Christian Science Monitor* article on toxic waste disposal. The article noted that within the waste disposal in-

dustry, the term was already in circulation. See Emilie Travel Livezey, "Hazardous Waste," *Christian Science Monitor,* November 6, 1980.

80. *Philadelphia Bulletin,* April 1978, Tobacco Institute Records, UCSF Library, https://www.industrydocumentslibrary.ucsf.edu/tobacco/docs/ltnx0026.

81. James Longhurst, *Citizen Environmentalists* (Medford, MA: Tufts University Press, 2010), 49.

82. Jack Oppenheimer, "Administering the Air Quality Act of 1967," *Natural Resources Lawyer* 2, No. 1 (1969): 17.

83. Longhurst, *Citizen Environmentalists,* 47–49.

84. 42 U.S. Code §7401.

85. Quoted in Longhurst, *Citizen Environmentalists,*18–19.

86. Hayes, *Beauty, Health, and Permanence,* 484.

87. Sierra Club v. Morton, 405 U.S. 727 (1972).

88. Joseph Sax observed that the Court's opinion "explicitly states that a plaintiff who is an actual user of an area" would have standing to sue on the grounds that "they affect his aesthetic and recreational enjoyment of the area" and could also "assert the interests of the general public." See Joseph Sax, "Standing to Sue: A Critical Review of the Mineral King Decision," *Natural Resources Journal,* January 1973, 79.

89. United States v. Students Challenging Regulatory Agency Procedures 412 U.S. 669.

90. Antonin Scalia, "The Doctrine of Standing as an Essential Element of the Separation of Powers," *Suffolk Law Review* 17 (1983): 898. Scalia argued that in accepting the students' attenuated claims to injury, the Supreme Court had violated the separation of powers, wading into territory that rightfully belonged to the other branches. Scalia prophesied a post-*SCRAP* era in which courts would reject "breathlessly broad" grants of standing. Indeed, he helped to usher in such an era as a Justice, authoring a series of decisions in the 1990s limiting standing by requiring more precise articulations of legal injury for environmental groups that brought suit. See Jonathan Z. Cannon, *Environment in the Balance: The Green Movement and the Supreme Court* (Cambridge, MA: Harvard University Press, 2015), 150.

91. Reuel Schiller, "Enlarging the Administrative Polity: Administrative Law and the Changing Definition of Pluralism, 1945–1970," *Vanderbilt Law Review* 53, No. 5 (2000): 1442.

92. For a deft analysis of the relationship between poverty lawyers and welfare activists in the 1960s, see Martha F. Davis, *Brutal Need: Lawyers and the Welfare Rights Movement, 1960–1973* (New Haven: Yale University Press, 1993).

93. *SCRAP* was also heralded as a landmark by environmental lawyers in the 1970s. "Ecological Suits Reported Eased," *New York Times,* February 19, 1974.

94. Richard A. Harris and Sidney M. Milkis, *Politics of Regulatory Change: A Tale of Two Agencies* (New York: Oxford University Press, 1989), 240–243.

95. Jesse Steinfeld, oral history interview with Alexandra Lord, September 20, 2005, NLM.

96. Ibid.

97. Mark Nadel, *The Politics of Consumer Protection* (Indianapolis: Bobbs-Merrill, 1971), 50; Richard Nixon, "Special Message to the Congress on Consumer Protection," October 30, 1969, online in Gerhard Peters and John T. Woolley, *The American Presidency Project,* http://www.presidency.ucsb.edu/ws/?pid =2299.

98. Lizabeth Cohen, *A Consumers' Republic: The Politics of Mass Consumption in Postwar America* (New York: Knopf, 2003), 346.

99. "Consumer Bill of Rights," *New York Times,* November 1, 1969; "AMA Rejects 'Health Care Bill of Rights,'" *Washington Post,* June 25, 1970.

100. Marc Galanter, "Why the 'Haves' Come Out Ahead: Speculations on the Limits of Legal Change," *Law and Society Review* 9, No. 1 (1974): 95–160.

101. John Stuart Mill, *On Liberty* (1859; reprint, Mineola, NY: Dover Thrift Edition, 2002), 8.

102. This analogy to sex was a favorite among nonsmokers' rights activists. See, for example, "Can Other People's Smoking Hurt You?" *Kiplinger's,* September 1975, 11; Alden Stahr, 1987, Folder 67, Carton 7, Shimp Papers, UCSF; Stan to Board, "Mike Pertschuk's piece on nonsmokers' rights," May 16, 1984, Folder 40, Carton 1, ANR Records, UCSF.

103. Brian Balogh, "Making Pluralism 'Great': Beyond a Recycled History of the Great Society," in *The Great Society and the High Tide of Liberalism,* Sidney M. Milkis and Jerry Mileur, eds. (Amherst: University of Massachusetts Press, 2005), 145–182.

104. Nancy C. Doyle, "Involuntary Smoking—Health Risks for Nonsmokers," 1987, Folder 35, Carton 3, Shimp Papers, UCSF. Having made a rhetorical mark upon the anti-tobacco movement, Roisman would soon leave its orbit for the Justice Department. But Roisman's early partner in public interest law, Gladys Kessler, indelibly shaped the history—and historiography—of tobacco. As a judge for the DC Circuit, Kessler issued a landmark 1,683-page ruling holding the tobacco companies liable for fraud under the Racketeer Influenced and Corrupt Organizations (RICO) Act. See U.S. v. Philip Morris, 449 F.Supp. 2d 1 (DDC 2006). As part of the remedy, Kessler required the online disclosure of internal industry documents produced by smoking litigation. These documents have formed some of the evidentiary trove for recent historians of tobacco. See Edward Berlin, Anthony Z. Roisman, and Gladys Kessler, "Public Interest Law," *George Washington Law Review* 38 (1970): 647–693.

105. Allan M. Brandt, *The Cigarette Century: The Rise, Fall, and Deadly Persistence of the Product that Defined America* (New York: Basic Books), 292. Elsewhere, Brandt has argued that rendering the environmental tobacco smoke as a risk "was powerfully influenced by a range of social and moral factors" articulated by the nonsmokers' rights movement. Brandt, "Blow Some My Way," 170.

106. United States Public Health Service, Office of the Surgeon General, National Clearinghouse for Smoking and Health, *The Health Consequences of Smoking* (Washington, DC: United States Public Health Service, Office of the Surgeon General, 1972), 111.

107. Ibid., 127–131.
108. Ibid., 131.
109. Philip H. Abelson, "A Damaging Source of Air Pollution," *Science* 158, No. 3808 (December 22, 1967): 1527.
110. Brandt, *Cigarette Century,* 293.
111. Historical National Ambient Air Quality standards can be found at https://www.epa.gov/pm-pollution/table-historical-particulate-matter -pm-national-ambient-air-quality-standards-naaqs.
112. National Commission on Smoking and Public Policy, "Catalog of Themes and Anti-Smoking Recommendations," March 22, 1977, Liggett & Myers Records, UCSF Library, https://www.industrydocumentslibrary.ucsf.edu /tobacco/docs/#id=ypyy0011.
113. National Cancer Institute, Office of Cancer Communications, *The Smoking Digest: Progress Report on a Nation Kicking the Habit* (Bethesda, MD: National Cancer Institute, 1977), 24.
114. Ibid.
115. "Smokey the Boor," *Village Voice,* April 25, 1974.
116. "Safer Cigarettes for Those Who Can't Quit Asked by Official," *Los Angeles Times,* January 10, 1972.
117. "Smoking to Be Banned on Staten Island Ferry," *New York Times,* January 27, 1971.
118. Jesse Steinfeld, oral history interview with Alexandra Lord, September 20, 2005, NLM.
119. Mike Stobbe, *Surgeon General's Warning: How Politics Crippled the Nation's Doctor* (Berkeley: University of California Press, 2014), 144; Richard Kluger, *Ashes to Ashes: America's Hundred-Year Cigarette War, the Public Health, and the Un- abashed Triumph of Philip Morris* (New York: Knopf, 1996), 366–367.
120. Stobbe, *Surgeon General's Warning,* 144.
121. Ibid., 153.
122. "Jesse L. Steinfeld, Former Anti-smoking U.S. Surgeon General Dies at 87," *Washington Post,* August 6, 2014.
123. "Fact Sheet on H.R. 10748," December 2, 1975, American Tobacco Records, UCSF Library, https://www.industrydocumentslibrary.ucsf.edu/tobacco /docs/lxgl0075.
124. "If You Love Someone Who Smokes, Do Something," *Raleigh News and Ob- server,* August 7, 1973.
125. Kluger, *Ashes to Ashes,* 374.
126. R. J. Reynolds, "The Facts about Public Smoking," 1971, R. J. Reynolds Rec- ords, UCSF Library, https://www.industrydocumentslibrary.ucsf.edu /tobacco/docs/gzcw0003; Brandt, *Cigarette Century,* 288.
127. "Anti-Smoking Claims and the Minnesota Clean Indoor Air Act," 1975, To- bacco Institute Records, UCSF Library, https://www.industrydocumentsli brary.ucsf.edu/tobacco/docs/jmcl0004.
128. Transcript, "State of Minnesota House of Representatives Health Subcom- mittee of the Health and Welfare Committee," February 22, 1974, Deposi- tions and Trial Testimony, Tobacco Deposition and Trial Testimony Archive

(DATTA), UCSF Library, https://www.industrydocumentslibrary.ucsf.edu
/tobacco/docs/qjfp0034.

129. "Anti-Smoking Claims and the Minnesota Clean Indoor Air Act," 1975,
Tobacco Institute Records, UCSF Library, https://www.industrydocuments
library.ucsf.edu/tobacco/docs/jmcl0004.

130. Office of Cancer Communications, *Smoking Digest*, 83–86.

131. In a quantitative survey of anti-tobacco legislation passed between 1975 and
2000, political scientists Charles R. Shipan and Craig Volden found evidence
of "bottom-up federalism"—or diffusion of anti-smoking laws from the
local to the state level—when states contained powerful health organizations
and professionalized legislatures. See Shipan and Volden, "Bottom-Up Federalism: The Diffusion of Antismoking Policies from Cities to States,"
American Journal of Political Science 50, No. 4 (October 2006): 825–843.

132. For the 1978 Proposition 5 see, Folders 90–96, Carton 3, ANR Records,
UCSF. For activists' strategy on the 1980 Proposition 10, see Folders 115–
120, Carton 3, ANR Records, UCSF; see also Stanton A. Glantz and Edith D.
Balbach, *Tobacco War: Inside the California Battles* (Berkeley: University of
California Press, 2000), 10–21.

133. "Number of Local Actions on Smoking Restrictions, 1971–1976," October 1976, Tobacco Institute Records, UCSF Library, https://www
.industrydocumentslibrary.ucsf.edu/tobacco/docs/ppwl0004.

134. Horace R. Kornegay, "Remarks—TI Spring Meeting," 1974, Philip Morris
Records, UCSF Library, https://www.industrydocumentslibrary.ucsf.edu
/tobacco/docs/ytgc0107.

135. "Smoking Ban Has Berkeley Residents Smoldering," *Chicago Tribune*, August 21, 1977.

136. Francis Ward, "Chicago Antismoking Law: Smokers Court Punishes Public
Puffers," *Los Angeles Times,* May 2, 1976, G4. Although African-American
men smoked at higher rates than white men—55 percent versus 42 percent
in 1974—behavioral discrepancies could not account for the demography
of smokers' court. See "Smoking and Health: A Report of the Surgeon General: Appendix: Cigarette Smoking in the United States, 1950–1978" (U.S.
Public Health Service, Office on Smoking and Health, 1979), A-15.

6. From Rights to Cost

1. First epigraph quotation: Alton Ochsner, *Smoking: Your Choice between Life and
Death* (New York: Simon and Schuster, 1954; reprint, 1970), 20. Second epi-
graph quotation: Robert F. Schilling II, Lewayne D. Gilchrist, and Steven
Paul Schinke, "Smoking in the Workplace: Review of Critical Issues," *Public
Health Reports* 100, No. 5 (1985): 474.

2. Bureau of National Affairs, *Where There's Smoke: Problems and Policies Con-
cerning Smoking in the Workplace*, ASPA-BNA Survey No. 50 (Washington,
DC: Bureau of National Affairs, 1986); "US Sets Goal to End Smoking by
Year 2000," *Los Angeles Times,* May 21, 1984; Koop quotation: "Smoke-Free
Society by the Year 2000!!!," *Smoking and Health Reporter* 1, No. 4 (1984): 2.

3. "Smokers Fume about Bans in the Office," *Washington Post,* November 18, 1990; D.C. Kent and L. Cenci, "Smoking and the Workplace: Tobacco Smoke Health Hazards to the Involuntary Smoker," *Journal of Occupational Medicine* 24, No. 6 (1982): 469.

4. "Workplace Smoking: Corporate Practices & Developments," *BNA Employee Relations Weekly,* October 23, 1989.

5. Administrative Management Society Smoking Policies Survey, 1989, Tobacco Institute Records, University of California San Francisco (UCSF) Library, https://www.industrydocumentslibrary.ucsf.edu/tobacco/docs/qgmk0135.

6. Nancy MacLean, *Freedom Is Not Enough: The Opening of the American Workplace* (Cambridge, MA: Harvard University Press, 2008); Katherine Turk, *Equality on Trial: Gender and Rights in the Modern American Workplace* (Philadelphia: University of Pennsylvania Press, 2016); Sophia Z. Lee, *The Workplace Constitution: From the New Deal to the New Right* (New York: Cambridge University Press, 2014); Serena Mayeri, *Reasoning from Race: Feminism, Law, and the Civil Rights Revolution* (Cambridge, MA: Harvard University Press, 2011); Margot Canaday, *Pink Precariat: LGBT Workers in the Shadow of Civil Rights* (forthcoming), chapter 6.

7. By the late 1980s, antidiscrimination law covered not only women and racial minorities, but also the disabled, pregnant women, and, in Reagan's one contribution to the expansion of antidiscrimination law, older Americans. At the same time, Katherine Turk argues, the "conceptual terrain" of what constituted sex equality dramatically contracted in the 1980s and 1990s. See Turk, *Equality on Trial.*

8. Frank Dobbin, *Inventing Equal Opportunity* (Princeton: Princeton University Press, 2009). For more on the ethical world of corporate managers, see Robert Jackall, *Moral Mazes: The World of Corporate Managers* (New York: Oxford University Press 1988; reprint, 20th Anniversary Edition, 2010). For a recent business history of the postwar corporation, see Louis Hyman, "Rethinking the Postwar Corporation: Management, Monopolies, and Markets," in *What's Good for Business: Business and American Politics since World War II,* Kim Phillips-Fein and Julian E. Zelizer, eds. (New York: Oxford University Press, 2012), 195–211.

9. Daniel Rodgers, *Age of Fracture* (Cambridge, MA: Harvard University Press, 2012), 44.

10. Ibid., 58.

11. Donna Shimp to Luther Terry, February 6, 1976, Folder 1, Box 7, Terry Papers, NLM.

12. Marjorie Stockford, *The Bellwomen: The Story of the Landmark AT&T Sex Discrimination Case* (New Brunswick, NJ: Rutgers University Press, 2004), 16.

13. Donna Shimp, Alfred Blumrosen, and Stuart B. Finifter, *How to Protect Your Health at Work: A Complete Guide for Making the Workplace Safe* (Salem, NJ: Environmental Improvement Associates, 1976), 18.

14. Ibid., 67.

15. For more on citizen activism, particularly in the fields of health and the environment in the 1970s, see Christopher Sellers, *Crabgrass Crucible: Suburban Nature and the Rise of Environmentalism in Twentieth Century America* (Chapel Hill: UNC Press, 2013); James Longhurst, *Citizen Environmentalists* (Lebanon: Tufts University Press, 2010).

16. See, for instance, Constance Nathanson, *Disease Prevention as Social Change: The State, Society and Public Health* (New York: Russell Sage Foundation, 2007), 118.

17. *The Health Consequences of Smoking: A Report of the Surgeon General* (Washington, DC.: U.S. Public Health Service, 1972), 121–131.

18. Office on Smoking and Health, United States Public Health Service, *Smoking and Health: A Report of the Surgeon General—Appendix: Cigarette Smoking in the United States, 1950–1978*, A-10, https://profiles.nlm.nih.gov/ps/access/nnbcph .pdf. Gender discrepancies in smoking prevalence were consistent regardless of occupational type, although men and women clerical workers smoked at the most similar rates: 40 percent and 34 percent, respectively.

19. "Creative and Media Proposals for a Continuation and Extension of the Existing Advertising Program of the Tobacco Industry, June 1978, Tobacco Institute Records, UCSF Library, https://www.industrydocumentslibrary .ucsf.edu/tobacco/docs/ytkv0060.

20. Gregory Wood, *Clearing the Air: The Rise and Fall of Smoking in the Workplace* (Ithaca: Cornell University Press, 2016), 130.

21. Shimp, Blumrosen, and Finister, *How to Protect Your Health at Work,* 92–95

22. Ibid.

23. Nonsmokers like Shimp tapped into concern with rising health-care costs during the 1970s. Such concerns led to a variety of actual and attempted reforms, from Health Management Organizations (HMOs), legalized in 1973, to multiple unsuccessful attempts to pass universal health care. See Christy Ford Chapin, *Ensuring America's Health: The Public Creation of the Corporate Healthcare System* (New York: Cambridge University Press, 2015), 237–242.

24. For more on the role of the courts in the 1960s in acknowledging individual rights over the group rights of unions, see Reuel Schiller, "From Group Rights to Individual Liberties: Post-War Labor Law, Liberalism, and the Waning of Union Strength," *Berkeley Journal of Employment and Labor Law* 20, No. 1 (1999): 57–73.

25. Shimp, Blumrosen, and Finister, *How to Protect Your Health at Work,* 37–38; Alfred W. Blumrosen, Donald M. Ackerman, Julie Kligerman, and Peter VanSchiak, "Injunctions against Occupational Hazards: The Right to Work under Safe Conditions," *California Law Review* 42, No. 3 (1976): 702–731. For more on the role of private litigation in enforcing employment law, see Sean Farhang, *The Litigation State: Public Regulation and Private Lawsuits in the United States* (Princeton: Princeton University Press, 2010). Farhang notes that Blumrosen was present at the founding of the civil litigation system for discrimination law, serving as the EEOC's first chief of conciliations. Farhang, *The Litigation State,* 109–111.

26. Shimp v. New Jersey Bell Tel. Co., 368 A.2d 408 (N.J. Super. Ch. 1976).

27. "Nonsmoker Honored for Efforts," *New York Times,* December 23, 1976; "Court Says Employee Has Right to Work in Smoke-Free Area," *Wall Street Journal,* December 22, 1976.

28. E.F. Roberts, "The Right to a Decent Environment; E=MC2: Environment Equals Man Times Courts Redoubling Their Efforts," *Cornell Law Review* 55, No. 5 (1970): 674–706; Dave Sive, "Some Thoughts of an Environmental Lawyer in the Wilderness of Administrative Law," *Columbia Law Review* 70, No. 4 (1970): 612–651; William D. Kirchick, "The Continuing Search for a Constitutionally Protected Environment," *B.C. Environmental Affairs Law Review* 4, No. 3 (1975): 515–558; "Where There's Smoke There's Ire: The Search for Legal Paths to Tobacco-Free Air," *Columbia Journal of Environmental Law* 3, No. 1 (1976): 62–111.

29. Gasper v. Louisiana Stadium and Exposition District, 577 F.2d 897 (5th Cir. 1978). For a discussion of the arguments developed by nonsmokers in the Gasper case, see John M. Barth, "The Public Smoking Controversy: Constitutional Protection v. Common Courtesy," *Journal of Contemporary Health Law & Policy* 2, No. 1 (1986): 215–230.

30. "Amicus Curiae of Action on Smoking and Health," March 20, 1978, Brown & Williamson Records, UCSF Library, https://www.industrydocuments library.ucsf.edu/tobacco/docs/nfgn0132.

31. Federal Employees for Non-Smokers' Rights v. US, 446 F.Supp. 181 (D.D.C., Mar. 01, 1978).

32. "Nonsmoking Employees' Suit a Government in Trouble," *ASH Newsletter,* March–April 1978; "FENSR Suit Dismissed: ASH Preserves Principle," *ASH Newsletter,* May–June 1978, Folder 13, Box 6, Terry Papers, NLM.

33. In 1983, a nonsmoking plaintiff discovered this once again. In *Kensell v. State of Oklahoma,* an employee of the Oklahoma Department of Human Services sued the state for permitting smoking in the workplace. The plaintiff claimed that his First Amendment "right to think" was harmed by his workplace conditions. Such a right had been found in a case that concluded that patients at state mental institutions had a right to refuse the forcible administration of mind-altering drugs. The Tenth Circuit found that environmental tobacco smoke at the workplace was "far cry from forcible injections of mind altering drugs." Kensell v. Oklahoma, 716 F.2d 1350, p. 6.

34. "Paul Smith v. Western Electric," Folders 54–55, Carton 9, Shimp Papers, UCSF.

35. Radio/TV Reports, "Indoor Air Pollution Caused by Cigarette Smoke: Morning Edition," March 10, 1981, Tobacco Institute Records, UCSF Library, https://www.industrydocumentslibrary.ucsf.edu/tobacco/docs/jhbm0087.

36. John Rupp to Alfred Pollard, January 26, 1981, Tobacco Institute Records, UCSF Library, https://www.industrydocumentslibrary.ucsf.edu/tobacco/docs/zpnv0037.

37. Affidavit of James Repace, Case Number 446121.,Paul Smith v. Western Electric Company, November 4, 1980, Tobacco Institute Records, UCSF

Library, https://www.industrydocumentslibrary.ucsf.edu/tobacco/docs/rtxx0062.

38. John Rupp to Alfred Pollard, January 26, 1981, Tobacco Institute Records, UCSF Library, https://www.industrydocumentslibrary.ucsf.edu/tobacco/docs/zpnv0037.

39. Smith v. A. T. & T. Technologies, No. 4461221, St. Louis County Circuit Court, April 23, 1985, Tobacco Institute Records, UCSF Library, https://www.industrydocumentslibrary.ucsf.edu/tobacco/docs/ssvv0060.

40. Irene Parodi v. Merit Systems Protection Board, 702 F.2d 743.

41. "Tobacco Companies Are Facing Many Days in Court," *New York Times,* October 6, 1985.

42. In Harriet Brooks v. Trans World Airlines & Liberty Mutual Insurance, a flight attendant was paid workers' compensation because "she sustained an industrial injury" caused by an allergic reaction to cabin smoke. A New Mexico appeals court awarded a technician workers' compensation after he passed out due to tobacco smoke at work. See Schober v. Mountain Bell Telephone, 630 P. 2d 1231 (N.M. 1980). In California, a woman was awarded unemployment insurance after her workplace failed to enforce a no-smoking policy that triggered her tobacco smoke allergy. See McCrocklin v. Employment Development Dept. 156 Cal. App. 3d 1067. In Linda Apell v. Moorestown Board of Education a secretary was awarded unemployment compensation after leaving a job where the constant presence of tobacco smoke left her with eye irritation and headaches.

43. "ALA Article Legal," n.d., Folder 20, Carton 2, Shimp Papers, UCSF.

44. "Environmental Improvement Associates: Constitution and By-Laws," n.d., Carton 1, Folder 30, Shimp Papers, UCSF.

45. Tasty Baking, 1977, Folder 87, Carton 7, Shimp Papers, UCSF. Donna Shimp to Henry Simpson, 1 June 1981, Folder 51, Box 6, Terry Papers, NLM.

46. Donna Shimp to Oscar Austad, January 30, 1980, Folder 36, Carton 4, Shimp Papers, UCSF.

47. "To All Advisory Council Members," n.d., Folder 2, Carton 7, Terry Papers, NLM.

48. Ruth Milkman, *On Gender, Labor, and Inequality* (Urbana: University of Illinois Press, 2016), 171–180.

49. "To All Advisory Council Members," n.d., Folder 2, Carton 7, Terry Papers, NLM.

50. See, for example, Mary Kathleen Benet, *The Secretarial Ghetto* (New York: McGraw-Hill, 1972); Wendy Stevens, "Women Organizing the Office," *Off Our Backs* 9, No. 4 (1979): 10.

51. Christopher McKenna, *The World's Newest Profession: Management Consulting in the Twentieth Century* (New York: Cambridge University Press, 2006). For a discussion of the commodification of "corporate culture" in the 1980s, see especially chapter 9. See also Jackall, *Moral Mazes,* 145; Hyman, "Rethinking the Postwar Corporation," 205–209.

52. Jackall, *Moral Mazes,* 148.

53. Robert Jackall, "Moral Mazes: Bureaucracy and Managerial Work," *Harvard Business Review* 61, No. 5 (September 1983): 129.

54. Donna Shimp to Luther Terry, 1981, Folder 41, Box 2, Terry Papers, NLM.

55. "An invitation to corporate personnel and medical directors," December 1, 1977, Folder 2, Box 7, Terry Papers, NLM.

56. Smokefree Day at Work, January 11, 1978, Folder 41, Box 1, Shimp Papers.

57. MacLean, *Freedom Is Not Enough,* 64.

58. "MIT-Philip Morris Round Table," February 5, 1981, Philip Morris Records, UCSF Library, https://www.industrydocumentslibrary.ucsf.edu/tobacco/docs/pjny0124.

59. "*Good Morning America*," Radio TV Reports, January 10, 1978, Tobacco Institute Records, UCSF Library, https://www.industrydocumentslibrary.ucsf.edu/tobacco/docs/qnjl0043.

60. "To All Advisory Council Members," March 8, 1978, Folder 32, Carton 1, Shimp Papers, UCSF.

61. Ibid.

62. Donna Shimp, "Nonsmokers Rights in the Work Environment: A New Look—An Address before the Annual Meeting of the American Lung Association," May 15, 1978, Folder 1, Carton 2, Shimp Papers, UCSF.

63. William L. Weis, "Profits Up in Smoke," *Personnel Journal,* March 1981; "Can You Afford to Hire Smokers?" *Personnel Administrator,* May 1981; "Smoking: Burning a Hole in the Balance Sheet," *Personnel Management,* May 1981; "No Ifs, ands, or Butts—Why Workplace Smoking Should Be Banned," *Management World,* September 1981; "Cold Shouldering the Smoker," *Supervisory Management,* September 1981; "Workplace Smoking Revisited," *Personnel Administrator,* October 1982. "Warning—Smoking Is Dangerous to Your Career," *Listen Magazine,* May 1984; "Giving Smokers Notice: Going Public with Policies against Hiring Smokers," *Management World,* 1984; "Debate over Smoking at Work: End of the Smoking Era," *Business and Society Review,* Fall 1984.

64. For an in-depth analysis of the political economy of the 1970s, see Judith Stein, *Pivotal Decade: How the United States Traded Factories for Finance in the Seventies* (New Haven: Yale University Press, 2010). For an overview of the process and cultural significance of deindustrialization see Jefferson Cowie and Joseph Heathcott, eds., *Beyond the Ruins: The Meanings of Deindustrialization* (Ithaca: Cornell University Press, 2003). For the canonical work that enshrined "deindustrialization" as part of the American lexicon, see Barry Bluestone and Bennett Harrison, *Deindustrialization of America: Plant Closings, Community Abandonment, and the Dismantling of Basic Industry* (New York: Basic Books, 1982).

65. William L. Weis and Nancy Wick, "Smokeless Office: America's Bosses Clear the Air," *American Health,* April 1985; William L. Weis, "Profits Up in Smoke," *Personnel Journal,* March 1981, 162.

66. Weis, "'No Ifs, ands or Butts,'—Why Workplace Smoking Should Be Banned," *Management World,* September 1981, 39; Weis and Wick, "Smokeless Office," *American Health,* April 1985, 18–19.

67. Weis, "Profits Up in Smoke," 164.

68. Quoted in William L. Weis and Bruce W. Miller, *The Smoke-Free Workplace* (Buffalo: Prometheus Books, 1985), 31.

69. "Smoking Is Costly for Employers as Well as Employees," *Employee Health and Fitness,* August 1987, 1.

70. Weis, "Profits Up in Smoke," 164.

71. Weis and Miller, *The Smoke-Free Workplace,* 37.

72. Stanton Glantz to Ms. Roland, November 7, 1984, Folder 41, Carton 1, ANR Records, UCSF.

73. Weis and Miller, *The Smoke-Free Workplace,* 23.

74. "ASH to Seek Lower Health Insurance Rates for Nonsmokers," *ASH Smoking and Health Review,* November 1984, Folder 13, Box 6, Terry Papers, NLM.

75. Helen Halpin Schauffler, "Health Insurance Policy and the Politics of Tobacco," in *Smoking Policy: Law, Politics, and Culture,* Robert L. Rabin and Stephen D. Sugarman, eds. (New York: Oxford University Press, 1993), 184–206; H. H. Schauffler and D. Gentry, "Smoking Control Policies in Private Health Insurance in California: Results of a Statewide Survey," *Tobacco Control* 3, No. 2 (1994).

76. Robert E. Leu and T. Schaub, "Does Smoking Increase Medical Care Expenditure," *Social Science and Medicine* 17, No. 23 (1983): 1907–1914.

77. United States, Public Health Service, Office of the Surgeon General, Office on Smoking and Health, and Surgeon General's Advisory Committee on Smoking and Health, *Smoking and Health: A Report of the Surgeon General* (Rockville, MD, and Washington, DC: U.S. Dept. of Health, Education, and Welfare; Public Health Service; Office of the Assistant Secretary for Health; Office on Smoking and Health, 1979), ii.

78. James Repace, *Enemy No. 1:Waging the War on Secondhand Smoke* (Amazon: Repace Associates, Inc., 2019), 32–40; James B. Sullivan, "Working with Citizens' Groups," *Physics Today* 27, No. 6 (June 1974): 32–37.

79. Repace, *Enemy No. 1,* 36–39.

80. Ibid., 50–59.

81. James Repace and Alfred Lowrey, "Indoor Air Pollution, Tobacco Smoke, and Public Health," *Science* 208, (May 2, 1980): 471.

82. "Tobacco Smoke: An Occupational Health Hazard," n.d., Folder 1, Carton 2, Shimp Papers, UCSF.

83. Repace and Lowrey, "Indoor Air Pollution, Tobacco Smoke, and Public Health," 471.

84. Richard Kluger, *Ashes to Ashes: America's Hundred-Year Cigarette War, the Public Health, and the Unabashed Triumph of Philip Morris* (New York: Knopf, 1996), 496.

85. For a fascinating exploration of the gendered dynamics of the quest for indoor occupational health, see Michelle Murphy, *Sick Building Syndrome and the Problem of Uncertainty: Environmental Politics, Technoscience, and Women Workers* (Durham: Duke University Press, 2006).

86. Notably, Repace's work was part of a brief submitted on behalf of a Nevada prisoner whose case appeared before the Supreme Court in 1994. In a 7-2

decision, *Helling v. McKinney* held that the Eighth Amendment protected against future harm to the inmate that might result from environmental tobacco smoke.

87. Repace, *Enemy No. 1,* 101-107.

88. Kluger, *Ashes to Ashes,* 497-498; Susan M. Stuntz, "Repace Rebuttal," June 6, 1985, Tobacco Institute Records, RPCI Tobacco Institute and Council for Tobacco Research Records, UCSF Library, https://www.industrydocuments library.ucsf.edu/tobacco/docs/nhkh0047; Colucci and Kloepfer, "Repace," February 19, 1985, R. J. Reynolds Records, UCSF Library, https://www .industrydocumentslibrary.ucsf.edu/tobacco/docs/qgdn0093.

89. Quoted in Kluger, *Ashes to Ashes,* 498.

90. For citations, see J. F. Banzhaf, "Testimony of Action on Smoking and Health," July 10, 1985, R. J. Reynolds Records, UCSF Library, https://www .industrydocumentslibrary.ucsf.edu/tobacco/docs/stkk0087. For a concise history of Americans' understandings of risk and cigarette smoking, see Allan Brandt, "The Cigarette, Risk, and American Culture," *Daedalus* 119, No. 4 (1990): 155-176.

91. Takeshi Hirayama, "Non-Smoking Wives of Heavy Smokers Have a Higher Risk of Lung Cancer: A Study from Japan," *British Medical Journal* 282, No. 6259 (1981): 183-185; D. Trichopoulos, A. Kalandidi, L. Sparros, and B. MacMahon, "Lung Cancer and Passive Smoking," *International Journal of Cancer* 27, No. 1 (1981): 1-4. See also Allan M. Brandt, *The Cigarette Century: The Rise, Fall, and Deadly Persistence of the Product that Defined America* (New York: Basic, 2007), 284-286.

92. "Study Says Cancer Risk Is High for Smokers' Wives," *Chicago Tribune,* January 17, 1981; "'Wives' Lung Cancer Linked to Mates' Smoking," *Los Angeles Times,* January 17, 1981; "Cancer Study Reports High Risk for Wives of Smoking Husbands," *New York Times,* January 16, 1981; "How to Enjoy a Healthy Marriage: Don't Smoke," *New York Times,* January 18, 1981.

93. "Tobacco Associates Annual Report," March 2, 1971, Tobacco Institute Records, UCSF Library, https://www.industrydocumentslibrary.ucsf.edu /tobacco/docs/jjlv0041.

94. For an analysis of the rising influence of "social cost" and market-talk in the 1980s, see Rodgers, *Age of Fracture,* 54-60.

95. Donna Shimp to Mr. and Mrs. Jesperson, July 26, 1975, Folder 44, Carton 4, Shimp Papers, UCSF.

96. For more on the changing nature of unions in the 1970s, see Nelson Lichtenstein, *State of the Union: A Century of American Labor* (Princeton, NJ: Princeton University Press, 2002), 212-245. For more on the Quality of Work Life movement, see Robert Wechsler, "Unions and the Quality of Work Life," *International Labor and Working Class History* 22 (1982): 60-62. For an analysis of the Quality of Work Life as an anti-union crusade, see Guillermo Grenier, *Inhuman Relations: Quality Circles and Anti-Unionism in American Industry* (Philadelphia: Temple University Press, 1988). For a discussion of

organized labor's lassitude in cataloguing instances of occupational disease, see Amy Fairchild, Ronald Bayer, and James Colgrove, *Searching Eyes: Privacy, the State and Disease Surveillance in America* (Berkeley: University of California Press, 2007), 92–93.

97. Fairchild, Bayer, and Colgrove, *Searching Eyes,* 98–99.
98. Ibid.
99. Labor historian Gregory Wood has made this argument forcefully. See Wood, *Clearing the Air: The Rise and Fall of Smoking in the Workplace* (Ithaca: Cornell University Press, 2016).
100. Ibid., 97–101.
101. A. L. Holm and R. M. Davis, "Clearing the Airways: Advocacy and Regulation for Smoke-Free Airlines," *Tobacco Control* 13, No. 1 (March 2004): i30–i36; Jocelyn Pan et al., "Smokefree Airlines and Organized Labor: A Case Study," *American Journal of Public Health* 95, No. 3 (2005): 398–404.
102. "Foreword," n.d., Folder 61, Carton 2, Shimp Papers, UCSF.
103. Bureau of National Affairs, *Where There's Smoke,* 68.
104. Donna Shimp to Mr. Richard Earl, March 18, 1982, Folder 15, Carton 4, Shimp Papers, UCSF.
105. "Proposed Plan of Activities for 1977–1978" and "Activity Report 1979 and 1980," Folder 33, Carton 1, Shimp Papers, UCSF.
106. Paul Brodeur, *Expendable Americans* (New York: Viking, 1973); Rachel Scott, *Muscle and Blood* (New York: Dutton, 1974); Susan Daum and Jeanne Stellman, *Work is Dangerous to Your Health* (New York: Vintage, 1973). See also Fairchild, Bayer, and Colgrove, *Searching Eyes,* 94.
107. Robert L. Rabin, "A Sociolegal History of the Tobacco Tort Litigation," *Stanford Law Review* 44, No. 4 (1992): 853–878.
108. Irving J. Selikoff, E. Cuyler Hamond, and Jacob Churg, "Asbestos Exposure, Smoking and Neoplasia," *Journal of the American Medical Association* 204, No. 2 (1968): 106–112. By 1979, the relationship between cigarette smoking and occupational exposures in increasing lung cancer risks was well established. See *Smoking and Health: A Report of the Surgeon General* (Washington: United States Department of Health Education and Welfare, Public Health Service, Office of the Assistant Secretary for Health, Office on Smoking and Health, 1979), 19; John A. Jenkins, *The Litigators: Inside the Powerful World of America's High Stakes Trial Lawyers* (New York: St. Martins, 1989), 119.
109. Johns-Manville Sales Corporation v. International Association of Machinists Local Lodge 1609, 621 F.2d 756. (5th Cir. 1980).
110. Charles Noble has pointed out that organized labor was relatively indifferent to issues of health and occupational safety for much of the postwar period. "Unions bargained away safety and job control for productivity-based wage gains, health programs, pension plans, and unemployment insurance." See Noble, *Liberalism at Work: The Rise and Fall of OSHA* (Philadelphia: Temple University Press, 1986), 52.
111. Morrison v. Burlington Industries, 304 N.C. 1, 282 S.E. 2d 458 (1981).

112. National Health Interview Surveys revealed that between 1975 and 1985, education level replaced gender as the major predictor of smoking status. That is, smoking had become a heavily classed phenomenon.

113. Tom McQuiston quoted in BNA, *Where There's Smoke,* 26.

114. Fairchild, Bayer, and Colgrove, *Searching Eyes,* 94.

115. Susan M. Daum to Donna Shimp, December 19, 1977, Folder 30, Carton 5, Shimp Papers.

116. "Press Conference for the 1985 Report on the Health Consequences of Smoking," December 5, 1985, Folder 4, Carton 125, Papers of C. Everett Koop (Koop Papers), NLM.

117. BNA, *Where There's Smoke,* 25.

118. "Worker's Rights and Legal Climate Concerning Indoor Air Quality and Workplace Smoking," n.d., Folder 17, Carton 4, Shimp Papers, UCSF.

119. BNA, *Where There's Smoke,* 25.

120. "Resolution No. 24. Opposition to Anti-Smoking Campaigns," 1980, Brown & Williamson Records, source unknown, UCSF Library, https://www.industrydocumentslibrary.ucsf.edu/tobacco/docs/gxfh0138. For the industry's satisfaction at this resolution, see "Tobacco Institute Newsletter," December 11, 1979, Tobacco Institute Records, https://www.industrydocumentslibrary.ucsf.edu/tobacco/docs/rfcv0048.

121. "Cigarette Smoke and the Non-Smoker: Issue Analysis and Program Recommendations Draft," May 29, 1985, Ness Motley Law Firm Litigation Documents, UCSF Library, https://www.industrydocumentslibrary.ucsf.edu/tobacco/docs/xznc0040.

122. "Minutes of the State Activities Policy Committee," March 30, 1984, Brown & Williamson Records, UCSF Library, https://www.industrydocumentslibrary.ucsf.edu/tobacco/docs/frfx0137.

123. There are several excellent histories of the struggles for union recognition at R. J. Reynolds in the 1940s—a struggle that ultimately ended in defeat for unionists. The best place to start is Robert Korstad, *Civil Rights Unionism: Tobacco Workers and the Struggle for Democracy in the Mid-Twentieth-Century South* (Chapel Hill: UNC Press, 2003). Korstad argues that tobacco workers waged a multipronged attack on "economic exploitation, political disfranchisement, and racial discrimination," illustrating deep linkages between union organizing and civil rights organizing. For an overview of the union organizing drive at Winston-Salem that is sympathetic to R. J. Reynolds, see, Nannie Mae Tilley, *The R. J. Reynolds Tobacco Company* (Chapel Hill: UNC Press, 1985), 373–414. For an oral history conducted with black tobacco workers in Durham, see Beverly W. Jones, "Race, Sex, and Class: Black Female Tobacco Workers in Durham, North Carolina, 1920-1940, and the Development of Female Consciousness," *Feminist Studies* 10, No. 3 (Autumn, 1984), 441–451. For an analysis of the intersection of gender and race in a short-lived, black female–led local, see Larry J. Griffin and Robert R. Korstad, "Class as Race and Gender: Making and Breaking a Labor Union

in the Jim Crow South," *Social Science History* 19, No. 4 (1995): 425–454; and also Dolores Janiewski, "Seeking 'a New Day and New Way': Black Women and Unions in the Southern Tobacco Industry" in *"To Toil the Livelong Day": America's Women at Work, 1780–1980*, Carol Groneman and Mary Beth Norton, eds. (Ithaca: Cornell University Press, 1987).

124. United States, Congress, Senate, Committee on Governmental Affairs, Subcommittee on Civil Service, P. Office. *Non-Smokers Rights Act of 1985: Hearings before the Subcommittee on Civil Service, Post Office, and General Services of the Committee on Governmental Affairs,* United States Senate, Ninety-Ninth Congress, first session, on S. 1440 . . . September 30, October 1 and 2, 1985. Washington, DC: U.S. GPO (1986).

125. Christina V. Mangurian and Lisa A. Bero, "Lessons Learned from the Tobacco Industry's Efforts to Prevent the Passage of a Workplace Smoking Regulation," *American Journal of Public Health* 90, No. 12 (December 2000): 1926–1930.

126. Edith Balbach, Elizabeth Barbeau, et al., "Political Coalitions for Mutual Advantage: The Case of the Tobacco Institute's Labor Management Committee," *American Journal of Public Health* 95, No. 6 (June 2005): 985–993.

127. "Final Copy for the BC&T," August 31, 1984, Tobacco Institute Records, UCSF Library, https://www.industrydocumentslibrary.ucsf.edu/tobacco /docs/sfch0026.

128. "Speech Given at the Legislative Conference for Unions in the Tobacco Industry," February 5, 1985, Brown & Williamson Records, UCSF Library, https://www.industrydocumentslibrary.ucsf.edu/tobacco/docs/ hkbx0138.

129. D. Fishwick et al., "Smoking Cessation in the Workplace," *Occupational Medicine* 63, No. 8 (2013): 526–536.

130. William N. Evans, Matthew C. Farrelly, and Edward Montgomery, "Do Workplace Smoking Bans Reduce Smoking?" NBER Working Paper Series (National Bureau of Economic Research, 1996), 3–4, 31–34.

131. William N. Evans, Matthew C. Farrelly, and Edward Montgomery, "Do Workplace Bans Reduce Smoking?" *American Economic Review* 89, No. 4 (1999): 728–747.

132. Quoted in BNA, *Where There's Smoke,* 89.

7. Shredding a Net to Build a Web

Epigraph: "Helms Exhorts Tobacco Bloc to Fight Budget Cuts," *New York Times,* March 21, 1981.

1. For an examination of the role of commodity subcommittees, see Bill Winders, *The Politics of Food Supply: US Agricultural Policy in the World Economy* (New Haven: Yale University Press, 2009); John Mark Hansen, *Gaining Access: Congress and the Farm Lobby, 1919–1981* (Chicago: University of Chicago Press, 1991).

2. *Public Citizen Report*, 1975, p. 9, Box 420, David Newton Henderson Papers (Henderson Papers), Duke University Special Collections, Durham, NC.

3. Michael McCann, *Taking Reform Seriously: Perspectives on Public Interest Liberalism* (Ithaca: Cornell University Press, 1986).

4. "Nader Group Says Tobacco Price Supports Spur Cancer Deaths," *New York Times*, August 10, 1975; "Nader Calls for End to Tobacco Aid," *Washington Post*, August 10, 1975.

5. For a provocative analysis of the ways in which the "false neutrality" health discourse serves to hide the structural causes of disparities in well-being, see Jonathan M. Metzel and Anna Kirkland, eds., *Against Health: How Health Became the New Morality* (New York: New York University Press, 2010).

6. "Cancer Society Seeks End to Aid for Tobacco," *Los Angeles Times*, January 14, 1977.

7. Quoted in McCann, *Taking Reform Seriously*, 125.

8. Quoted in ibid., 63.

9. "News Release," October 13, 1976, Folder C, Box 288, Walter B. Jones Papers, ECU.

10. "Why They Love Earl Butz," *New York Times*, June 13, 1976.

11. "Butz: The Maverick Rider," *Washington Post*, December 3, 1974.

12. "Earl L. Butz, Secretary Felled by a Racial Remark, Is Dead at 98," *New York Times*, February 3, 2008.

13. John Dean, "Rituals of the Herd," *Rolling Stone*, October 7, 1976.

14. "Prepared for West Central Community Center . . . Democratic Rally by NC Commissioner of Agriculture Jim Graham," Commissioners Office, Correspondence File "A-N, 1976," NCDA, NCDAH.

15. "Jimmy Carter and Tobacco," *Flue Cured Tobacco Farmer*, November 1978, 7–10.

16. Richard Kluger, *Ashes to Ashes: America's Hundred-Year Cigarette War, the Public Health, and the Unabashed Triumph of Philip Morris* (New York: Knopf, 1996), 436–438; Joseph Califano, *Inside: A Public and Private Life* (New York: Public Affairs, 2004), 355–358.

17. "Califano, Blumenthal Are Fired from Cabinet," *Washington Post*, July 20, 1979; "Carter Replaces Bell, Blumenthal, Califano," *New York Times*, July 20, 1979.

18. *Flue Cured Tobacco Farmer*, January 1979, 10–11.

19. "Zigzagging in Search of Identity," *Washington Post*, July 15, 1984.

20. Julian E. Zelizer, *On Capitol Hill: The Struggle to Reform Congress and Its Consequences, 1948–2000* (Cambridge: Cambridge University Press, 2004), 157.

21. Kluger, *Ashes to Ashes*, 541.

22. Ibid.

23. "Two Conflicts of Interest," *New York Times*, February 4, 1979.

24. Quoted in Kluger, *Ashes to Ashes*, 549.

25. "RJR Officials Were Charged with Making $90,000 in Illegal Campaign Contributions to Republican Presidential Candidates from 1964 to 1972." See Kluger, *Ashes to Ashes,* 386.

26. *Tobacco Observer,* May 1977, Tobacco Institute Records, UCSF Library, https://www.industrydocumentslibrary.ucsf.edu/tobacco/docs/kjfk0146; Irvin Molotsky, "This Odd Couple Focuses on Health," *New York Times,* September 14, 1984.

27. John Sledge, "To Presidents of Flue-Cured Tobacco Counties," July 1, 1977, Folder 7, Box 2, NCFB Records, NCSU.

28. "How a Tobacco Subsidy Got 'Beet-en' Down," *Washington Post,* July 27, 1977.

29. PL 97-98, Sec. 1109.

30. "The Tobacco Family Assesses Its Representation," October 1981, Tobacco Institute Records; RPCI Tobacco Institute and Council for Tobacco Research Records, UCSF Library, https://www.industrydocumentslibrary .ucsf.edu/tobacco/docs/fnmd0002.

31. Tobacco Institute, "On Smoking," 1978, Lorillard Records, source unknown, UCSF Library, https://www.industrydocumentslibrary.ucsf.edu /tobacco/docs/khnn0104. The family farm also played a prominent role in the Tobacco Institute's "Tobacco History Series"—booklets that filtered state history through a pro-tobacco lens.

32. "Farmers Edgy," *Los Angeles Times,* October 13, 1978, 1.

33. This tension between commitments to American producers and Cold War–driven development aid is fruitfully explored in Judith Stein, *Pivotal Decade: How the United States Traded Factories for Finance in the Seventies* (New Haven: Yale University Press, 2010).

34. PL 74-320, § 31, 49 Stat. 773 (1935).

35. Winders, *The Politics of Food Supply,* 142.

36. North Carolina Grange, "To the Honorable Frederick Dent," October 31, 1975, Box 420, Henderson Papers, Duke. John Sledge, "To County Presidents of Flue-Cured and Burley Tobacco Counties," October 31, 1975, Folder 20, Box 1, NCFB Records, NCSU.

37. Economic Research Service, TS-178, December 1981. Although the practice was not known to the general public until the 1970s, since the 1950s tobacco companies had added "reconstituted" tobacco to cigarettes. Reconstituted tobacco is a pressed sheet comprised of the parts of the tobacco plant that had previously been considered trash. The chemicals added to reconstituted tobacco deliver a more potent dose of nicotine—augmenting consumer desire for cigarettes while simultaneously lowering amount of tobacco leaf input. See Robert N. Proctor, *Golden Holocaust: Origins of the Cigarette Catastrophe and the Case for Abolition* (Berkeley: University of California Press, 2012), 397–399; David Kessler, "From the US Food and Drug Administration: The Control and Manipulation of Nicotine in Cigarettes," *Tobacco Control* 3, No. 4 (1994): 362–369.

38. "Probe of Tobacco Imports Threatens to Run Away with Its Backers," *Washington Post*, May 27, 1981.

39. "Trade Commission Opposes Quotas on Imports of Flue-Cured Tobacco," *Washington Post*, August 5, 1981; "Vote on Tobacco Quota," *New York Times*, August 6, 1981.

40. John Sledge, "Dear Mr. Stockman," February 27, 1981, Folder 1, Box 33, NCFB Records, NCSU.

41. "Five-Year Austerity Plan," *Progressive Farmer*, April 1984, 11; "Farm Policy Disaster for Reagan," *Washington Post*, March 25, 1984.

42. "In the Nation, The Ugliest Campaign," *New York Times*, October 19, 1984.

43. "ITC Rejects Tobacco Bar," *New York Times*, February 2, 1985, 38.

44. General Accounting Office, *Tobacco Program's Production Rights and Effects on Competition: Report* (Washington, DC: U.S. General Accounting Office, 1982), iii.

45. Ibid., i.

46. "The Referendum—Why You Should Vote Yes," *Flue-Cured Tobacco Farmer*, November 1979, 14.

47. The historiography of tobacco industry denialism is extensive: see Proctor, *Golden Holocaust*; Naomi Oreskes and Erik Conway, *Merchants of Doubt: How a Handful of Scientists Obscured the Truth on Issues from Tobacco Smoke to Global Warming* (New York: Bloomsbury, 2010); Proctor, "Agnotology: A Missing Term to Describe Ignorance (and Its Study)," in *Agnotology: The Making and Unmaking of Ignorance*, Robert Proctor and Londa Schiebinger, eds. (Palo Alto: Stanford University Press, 2008).

48. "Helms Exhorts Tobacco Bloc to Fight Budget Cuts," *New York Times*, March 21, 1981, 1. The discrepancy between this figure and the ones cited by tobacco's opponents lay in the fact that as a loan program, tobacco that went unsold above the floor price was, more often than not, sold at a profit later.

49. "Repeal of Programs Concerning Price Support for and the Marketing of Tobacco," 97 Cong. Rec. 24724–24725 (1981).

50. Charles R. Pugh, "The Structure of Flue-Cured Tobacco Farms," in *Farm Structure: A Historical Perspective on the Changes in the Number and Size of Farms* (Washington, DC: US GPO, 1980), 351.

51. "An Endangered Crop," *Washington Post*, April 13, 1980.

52. Fred Bond, "Flue-Cured Tobacco Stabilization Statement for International Trade Commission, Washington D.C.," June 24, 1981, Brown & Williamson Records, UCSF Library, https://www.industrydocumentslibrary.ucsf.edu/tobacco/docs/plld0052.

53. Brent Cebul, *The American Way of Growth* (Philadelphia: University of Pennsylvania Press, forthcoming).

54. *Economic Value of Present Tobacco Program: Hearing before the Subcommittee on Tobacco of the Committee on Agriculture*, 95th Congress, 1st session, October 6, 1977 (Washington, DC.: US GPO, 1977), H21.

55. Ibid., 6. For more on the way in which New Deal economists hoped to generate a greater property tax base through welfare programs, see Cebul, *American Way of Growth.*

56. "Future of 2 Southern Industries Raises Concern," *New York Times,* December 9, 1984.

57. Statement by T. C. Blalock, *Economic Impact of Tobacco Program: Hearings before the Subcommittee on Tobacco of the Committee on Agriculture, House of Representatives,* Ninety-Fifth Congress, second session, July 21, 1978, Valdosta, Ga.; August 4, 1978, Smithfield, N.C.; September 15, 1978, Marion, S.C. (Washington, D.C.: US GPO, 1978), 43–44.

58. "Tobacco Quotas Leased Like Land," *Los Angeles Times,* May 22, 1980, 8.

59. "Tobacco Allotment Club Feeling the Heat of Subsidy Opponents," *Washington Post,* April 18, 1981, A5.

60. There are several excellent political biographies of Jesse Helms, all of which describe his embattled relationship with congressional colleagues—including colleagues from North Carolina like Charlie Rose—over the tobacco program. See William A. Link, *Righteous Warrior: Jesse Helms and the Rise of Modern Conservatism* (New York: St. Martins, 2008); Ernest B. Ferguson, *Hard Right: The Rise of Jesse Helms* (New York: Norton, 1986); William D. Snider, *Helms and Hunt: The North Carolina Senate Race, 1984* (Chapel Hill: UNC Press, 1985).

61. "Program: Update It Quick," *Flue-Cured Tobacco Farmer,* April 1979, 8.

62. "Another Point of View: Who Benefits from Lease and Transfer," *Flue-Cured Tobacco Farmer,* February 1981, 45.

63. Political scientist Jacob Hacker has dubbed the fraying of the American social safety net "the great risk shift" as the "fragile balance sheets of American families" now must absorb risks once shouldered by the government and corporate America. See Hacker, *The Great Risk Shift: The New Economic Insecurity and the Decline of the American Dream* (New York: Oxford University Press, 2006).

64. "Statement of Harry Bell before the Joint House-Senate Committee Hearing on Tobacco," Raleigh, NC, February 12, 1982, Folder 9, Box 7, NCFB,NCSU.

65. "Farmers Back Tobacco Plan They Would Finance," *New York Times,* March 1, 1982.

66. "From the Office of Congressman L. H. Fountain," June 1982, Tobacco Institute Records, UCSF Library, https://www.industrydocumentslibrary.ucsf.edu/tobacco/docs/ltnl0004.

67. "In Newest Subsidy Dispute, Old Tobacco Road Allies Are Divided," *Washington Post,* April 1, 1983.

68. Stan Boman to Robert Hanrahan, March 21, 1983. Tobacco Institute Records, UCSF Library, https://www.industrydocumentslibrary.ucsf.edu/tobacco/docs/zspd0002.

69. Ibid.

70. Gene Ainsworth to G. Dee Smith and R. E. Clements, March 21, 1983, R. J. Reynolds Records, source unknown, UCSF Library, https://www.industrydocumentslibrary.ucsf.edu/tobacco/docs/pkxp0100.

71. Kluger, *Ashes to Ashes*, 511.

72. T. Capehart and A. L. Clauson, *Flue-Cured Tobacco Farms: Selected Characteristics*. (Washington, DC: U.S. Dept. of Agriculture, Economic Research Service, 1991), 2.

73. John Fraser Hart and Ennis L. Chestang, "Rural Revolution in East Carolina," *Geographical Review* 68, No. 4 (1978): 446–448; Charles Pugh, "The Structure of Flue-Cured Tobacco Farms," in *Farm Structure: A Historical Perspective on Changes in the Number and Size of Farms* (Washington, DC: GPO, 1980), 352–356.

74. Heather Gerken, "A New Progressive Federalism," *Democracy Journal* 24 (Spring 2012), https://democracyjournal.org/magazine/24/a-new-progressive-federalism/.

75. "The Legacy of Dr. Koop," *New York Times*, October 9, 1988.

76. "Reagan Nominee for Surgeon General Runs into Obstacles on Capitol Hill," *New York Times*, 7 April 7, 1981, A16; "Anti-Abortion Groups Run into Snags," *Los Angeles Times*, April 19, 1981, A4.

77. "Anti-Abortion Groups Run into Snags"; "Health Official Sees Abortion Leading to Euthanasia," *Washington Post*, May 9, 1981.

78. "Time for New Surgeon General," May 26, 1981, *New York Times*. See also "Koop: Bad Medicine," *Los Angeles Times*, June 8, 1981; "Dr. Unqualified," *New York Times*, April 9, 1981.

79. "Koop Promises Job Won't be a 'Pulpit,'" *New York Times*, October 2, 1981; "Senate Likely to Confirm Koop as Surgeon General," *Los Angeles Times*, October 2, 1981.

80. Mike Stobbe, *Surgeon General's Warning: How Politics Crippled the Nation's Doctor* (Berkeley: University of California Press, 2014), 169.

81. Kluger, *Ashes to Ashes*, 539.

82. George Will, "A Cloud of Smoke Covers the Reagan Team's Blushes," *Los Angeles Times*, March 25, 1982.

83. Kluger, *Ashes to Ashes*, 539, 549.

84. Although it won him few fans in the tobacco belt, Koop did notably part with health organizations like the American Academy of Pediatrics and the Coalition on Smoking or Health in refusing to call for the abolition of the tobacco program. Treading lightly, Koop called price supports "an agricultural and economic issue" not a matter of public health. "Surgeon General Lengthens List of Tobacco Dangers," *New York Times*, February 28, 1982, E6.

85. For more on the significance of the names used to characterize secondhand smoke, see Allan M. Brandt, "Blow Some My Way: Passive Smoking, Risk and American Culture," in *Ashes to Ashes: The History of Smoking and Health*, Stephen Lock, Lois Reynolds, and E. M. Tansey, eds. (Amsterdam: Rodopi, 1998), 168.

86. U.S. Public Health Service, Office on Smoking and Health, *The Health Consequences of Smoking: Cancer: A Report of the Surgeon General* (Washington, DC: U.S. Public Health Service, Office on Smoking and Health, 1982), 241.

87. Ibid., 244.

88. Ibid., 251.

89. C, Everett Koop and Joanne Luoto, "The Health Consequences of Smoking: Cancer, Overview of a Report of the Surgeon General, *Prevention* 97, No. 4 (July–August 1982): 323.

90. Ibid.

91. Nicholas J. Wald, Kir'an Nananchal, Simon G. Thompson, and Howard S. Cuckle, "Does Breathing Other People's Tobacco Smoke Cause Lung Cancer?" *British Medical Journal* 293 (November 8, 1986): 1217–1222.

92. Emphasis in the original. C. Everett Koop, "Julia M. Jones Lecture," May 20, 1984, Philip Morris Records, UCSF Library, https://www.industrydocumentslibrary.ucsf.edu/tobacco/docs/gxpm0114.

93. Ibid; Emphasis in the original. See also C. Everett Koop, "The 'New Federalism' and Public Health," *Health Values* 6, No. 5 (1982): 36–39.

94. C. Everett Koop, "Julia M. Jones Lecture," May 20, 1984, Philip Morris Records, UCSF Library, https://www.industrydocumentslibrary.ucsf.edu/tobacco/docs/gxpm0114.

95. Ibid.

96. Stanton Glantz to Matthew Myers, July 20, 1984, Folder 40, Carton 1, ANR Records, UCSF.

97. James Miller, who chaired the FTC during Reagan's first term, called Pertschuk "a chronic complainer." See "The Iconoclast," *New York Times*, September 16, 1984; Pertschuk quotation found in Stan to Board, "Mike Pertschuk's piece on nonsmokers' rights," May 16, 1984, Folder 40, Carton 1, ANR Records, UCSF.

98. Stan to Board, "Mike Pertschuk's piece on nonsmokers' rights," May 16, 1984, Folder 40, Carton 1, ANR Records, UCSF.

99. Karen Krzanowski to C. Everett Koop, June 25, 1986, Folder 10, Box 51, Koop Papers, NLM.

100. From Denis Muchmore, Mike Spaniolo, Walt Maner to Mr. Bill Trisler, February 14, 1986, R. J. Reynolds Records, https://www.industrydocumentslibrary.ucsf.edu/tobacco/docs/xxdx0087.

101. Stan to Board, "Mike Pertschuk's piece on nonsmokers' rights," May 16, 1984, Folder 40, Carton 1, ANR Records, UCSF.

102. *Non-Smokers Rights Act of 1985: Hearings before the Subcommittee on Civil Service, Post Office, and General Services of the Committee on Governmental Affairs, United States Senate,* Ninety-Ninth Congress, first session, on S. 1440, September 30, October 1 and 2, 1985 (Washington D.C.: U.S. G.P.O, 1986), 225.

103. Ibid., 225–241.

104. Ibid., 221.

105. "Smoking Restrictions Tightened," *Washington Post,* December 6, 1986, A1.

106. See George Latimer to C. Everett Koop, March 3, 1988; Kurt L. Schmoke to C. Everett Koop, March 8, 1988; Gerald L. Baliles to C. Everett Koop, March 4, 1988; Bill Clinton to C. Everett Koop, March 3, 1988; Edward Koch

to C. Everett Koop, March 15, 1988; Folder: "Sequential File," Box 62, Koop Papers, NLM.

107. United States Public Health Service, Office on Smoking and Health, *The Health Consequences of Involuntary Smoking: A Report of the Surgeon General* (Washington, DC: U.S. Public Health Service Office on Smoking and Health, 1986), x.

108. Kluger, *Ashes to Ashes,* 503–504.

109. Irvin Molotsky, "Surgeon General, Citing Risks, Urges Smoke-Free Workplaces," *New York Times,* December 17, 1986.

110. Phillip Morris Legal Department, "Project Down Under—Conference Notes; Summary of Meeting in Hilton Head," June 14, 1987, Ness Motley Law Firm Documents, UCSF Library, https://www.industrydocumentslibrary.ucsf .edu/tobacco/docs/frmy0042.

111. Amanda Fallin, Rachel Grana, and Stanton A. Glantz, "To Quarterback behind the Scenes, Third-Party Efforts': The Tobacco Industry and the Tea Party," *Tobacco Control* 23, No. 4 (2014): 322–331.

112. Phillip Morris Legal Department, " Project Down Under," 4.

113. Ibid.

114. Ibid, 15–16.

115. Ibid.

116. Allan M. Brandt, *The Cigarette Century: The Rise, Fall, and Deadly Persistence of the Product that Defined America* (New York: Basic Books), 294.

117. Quoted in Ibid.

118. For a superb study of the material, political, and gendered construction of Sick Building Syndrome, see Michelle Murphy, *Sick Building Syndrome and the Problem of Uncertainty: Environmental Politics, Technoscience, and Women Workers* (Durham, NC: Duke University Press, 2006).

119. Scientific Witnesses Appearances 1987. Tobacco Institute Records, UCSF Library, https://www.industrydocumentslibrary.ucsf.edu/tobacco /docs/ggnj0146; P. G. Sparber, "Public Communications Program 1987," Tobacco Institute Records, UCSF Library, https://www.industrydocu-mentslibrary.ucsf.edu/tobacco/docs/hrgk0146.

120. *Choice* 1, No. 2 (1987), R. J. Reynolds Records, https://www.industrydocuments library.ucsf.edu/tobacco/docs/jqbg0079.

121. A parallel process occurred in the realm of resource management. The "Sagebrush Rebellion" of the late 1970s and early 1980s sought state control over federally managed lands. See Samuel P. Hays, *Beauty, Health, Permanence: Environmental Politics in the United States, 1955–1985* (Cambridge: Cambridge University Press, 1987), 498–502. ALEC was also instrumental in that fight. See Christopher Ketcham, "The Great Republican Land Heist," *Harper's Magazine,* February 2015.

122. Although scholars have noted the extent to which Charles Reich and Ralph Nader animated Powell's defense of free enterprise, his reaction to the fairness ruling has gone unremarked upon. For a succinct explication of the Powell Memo, see Kim Philips-Fein, *Invisible Hands: The Making of the*

Conservative Movement from the New Deal to Reagan (New York: Norton, 2009), 156–165.

123. G. Weissman, "Lewis Powell Recommendations Re: Cigarette Industry Environment", September 22, 1969, Philip Morris Records, https://www.industrydocumentslibrary.ucsf.edu/tobacco/docs/yngb0131.

124. "Cigarette Industry Environment," n.d., Philip Morris Records, https://www.industrydocumentslibrary.ucsf.edu/tobacco/docs/pngb0131.

125. K. Teague, American Legislative Exchange Council, December 28, 1979, Tobacco Institute Records, UCSF Library, https://www.industrydocumentslibrary.ucsf.edu/tobacco/docs/gnlv0134.

126. Memorandum from Angle Walker, December 10, 1981, Tobacco Institute Records, UCSF Library, https://www.industrydocumentslibrary.ucsf.edu/tobacco/docs/gzjb0033.

127. P. Bergson, "RJR Public Affairs Status Report," July 25, 1986, R. J. Reynolds Records, UCSF Library, https://www.industrydocumentslibrary.ucsf.edu/tobacco/docs/gllk0087.

128. ALEC, *Legislative Policy,* 1984, Folder 49, Carton 4, ANR Records, UCSF.

129. Recent accounts of the influence of right-wing lobbies in state legislatures include Nancy MacLean, *Democracy in Chains: The Deep History of the Radical Right's Stealth Plan for America* (New York: Viking, 2017); Jane Mayer, *Dark Money: The Hidden History of the Billionaires behind the Rise of the Radical Right* (New York: Doubleday, 2016); Jeffrey A. Nesbit, *Poison Tea: How Big Oil and Big Tobacco Invented the Tea Party and Captured the GOP* (New York: Thomas Dunne Books, 2016). For an analysis of the strategy of business lobbying in the 1970s, see Benjamin Waterhouse, *Lobbying America: The Politics of Business from Nixon to NAFTA* (Princeton: Princeton University Press, 2013), esp. chapter 5.

130. Athena Mueller to Constance Heckman, January 15, 1987, Philip Morris Records, UCSF Library, https://www.industrydocumentslibrary.ucsf.edu/tobacco/docs/qkcy0009

131. "To: TI State and Local Legislative Counsel," 5 February 5, 1987, Tobacco Institute, UCSF Library, https://www.industrydocumentslibrary.ucsf.edu/tobacco/docs/mzhl0039.

132. Eric Gorovitz, James Mosher, and Mark Pertschuk, "Preemption or Prevention? Lessons from Efforts to Control Firearms, Alcohol, and Tobacco," *Journal of Public Health Policy* 19, No. 1 (1998): 36–50.

133. Kurt L. Malmgren to Samuel Chilcote, November 30, 1992, Philip Morris Records, UCSF Library, https://www.industrydocumentslibrary.ucsf.edu/tobacco/docs/tlnh0111. See also Stanton Glantz and Edith Balbach, *Tobacco War: Inside the California Battles* (Berkeley: University of California Press, 2000), 212–215.

134. Kathleen Sylvester, "The Tobacco Industry Will Walk a Mile to Stop an Anti-Smoking Law," *Governing,* May 1989, 40.

135. Tobacco Control Legal Consortium, "Preemption: The Biggest Challenge to Tobacco Control," online at http://www.publichealthlawcenter.org/sites

/default/files/resources/tclc-fs-preemption-tobacco-control-challenge
-2014.pdf.

136. Sylvester, "The Tobacco Industry Will Walk a Mile," 39.
137. "Preemptive State Tobacco-Control Laws—United States, 1982–1998," *Morbidity and Mortality Weekly Report* 47, Nos. 51/52 (January 8, 1999): 1112–1114.
138. A. L. Holm and R. M. Davis "Clearing the Airways: Advocacy and Regulation for Smoke-Free Airlines," *Tobacco Control* 13 (2004): i30–i36.
139. "Senate Compromises on Airline Smoking Ban," *Chicago Tribune,* October 30, 1987, 3.
140. Holm and Davis, "Clearing the Airways," 33. In 1987, when the American Association for Respiratory Care asked more than 33,000 airline passengers if they favored a total ban on in-flight smoking, 64 percent said they did—which represented 74 percent of nonsmokers and 30 percent of smokers. See American Association for Respiratory Care, "AARC Airline Smoking Survey," October 13, 1987, Tobacco Institute Records, UCSF Library, https://www.industrydocumentslibrary.ucsf.edu/tobacco/docs/yxgx0062
141. *Washington Forum,* "Smoking Clippings," Folder 10, Box 55, Koop Papers, NLM.
142. "Three Year Plan, 1989–1991," 1989, American Tobacco Records, UCSF Library, https://www.industrydocumentslibrary.ucsf.edu/tobacco/docs/fxkg0136

Conclusion

1. "On Tobacco Road, A Generation Gap," *New York Times,* May 30, 1996.
2. Marth Derthick, *Up in Smoke: From Legislation to Litigation in Tobacco Politics* (Washington, D.C.: Congressional Quarterly Press, 2002), 62–67.
3. William J. Clinton: "Address before a Joint Session of the Congress on the State of the Union," January 19, 1999; online in Gerhard Peters and John T. Woolley, *The American Presidency Project,* https://www.presidency.ucsb.edu/node/230240.
4. Derthick, *Up in Smoke,* 110–114.
5. James Repace and Alfred Lowrey, "Indoor Air Pollution, Tobacco Smoke, and Public Health," *Science* 208 (1980): 464–472; Repace and Lowrey, "A Quantitative Estimate of Nonsmokers' Lung Cancer Risk from Passive Smoking," *Environment International* 11, No. 1 (1985): 3–22; National Research Council, *Environmental Tobacco Smoke: Measuring Exposures and Assessing Health Effects* (Washington, DC: National Academy Press, 1986); J. M. Samet, M. C. Marbury, and J. D. Spengler, "Health Effects and Sources of Indoor Air Pollution," *American Review of Respiratory Disease* 136, No. 6 (1987): 1486–1506; A. Judson Wells, "An Estimate of Adult Mortality in the United States from Passive Smoking," *Environment International* 14, No. 3 (1988): 249–265.
6. Stanton Glantz and William Parmley, "Passive Smoking and Heart Disease: Epidemiology, Physiology, and Biochemistry," *Circulation* 83, No. 1 (1991): 1–12.

7. "Secondhand Tobacco Smoke a Serious Cancer Threat, EPA Declares," *Chicago Tribune*, January 8, 1993; "Will OSHA's IAQ Rule Go Up in Smoke?" *Occupational Hazards*, March 1995; Philip Morris Records, UCSF Library, https://www.industrydocumentslibrary.ucsf.edu/tobacco/docs/rfxh0093.

8. "The War on Workplace Smoke Goes Nationwide," *Washington Post*, September 18, 1994.

9. Occupational Health and Safety Administration, "Indoor Air Quality," proposed rule, 59 Fed. Reg. 15968–16039 (April 5, 1994), https://www.osha.gov/laws-regs/federalregister/1994-04-05.

10. M. Upton, Dinwiddie County. "OSHA Public Hearing—Proposed Standard for Indoor Air," October 28, 1994, Depositions and Trial Testimony (DATTA), UCSF Library, https://www.industrydocumentslibrary.ucsf.edu/tobacco/docs/jtcp0034.

11. "OSHA Flooded with Angry Mail Opposing Workplace Smoking Ban," *Washington Post*, August 13, 1994.

12. Derthick, *Up in Smoke*, 65.

13. Richard L. Barnes, S. Katherine Hammond, and Stanton A. Glantz, "The Tobacco Industry's Role in the 16 Cities Study of Secondhand Tobacco Smoke: Do the Data Support the Stated Conclusions," *Environmental Health Perspectives* 114, No. 2 (2006): 1890–1897. For more on the industry's approach to the OSHA hearings, see Katherine Bryan-Jones and Lisa Bero, "Tobacco Industry Efforts to Defeat the Occupational Safety and Health Administration Indoor Air Quality Rule," *American Journal of Public Health* 93, No. 4 (2003): 585–592.

14. Andrew L. Roth, Joshua Dunsby, and Lisa Bero, "Framing Processes in Public Commentary of US Federal Tobacco Control Regulation," *Social Studies of Science* 33, No. 1 (2003): 7–44.

15. FDA v. Brown & Williamson Tobacco Corp., 529 U.S. 120 (2000).

16. Heather Steiner, "Food and Drug Administration v. Brown & Williamson Tobacco Corp.," *Ecology Law Quarterly* 28, No. 2 (2001): 355–376; Michael R. McPherson, "The Denial of FDA Jurisdiction over Tobacco in Brown & Williamson Tobacco Corp. v. FDA: A Step in the Wrong Direction," *Quinnipiac Health Law Journal* 3 (1999–2000): 133–163.

17. Action on Smoking and Health, "ASH Nixes OSHA Suit to Prevent Harm to Movement," December 17, 2001, Philip Morris Records, UCSF Library, https://www.industrydocumentslibrary.ucsf.edu/tobacco/docs/ghnk0057.

18. "Some Businesses Already Moving Closer to Bans," *Wall Street Journal*, January 7, 1993.

19. Allan M. Brandt, *The Cigarette Century: The Rise, Fall, and Deadly Persistence of the Product that Defined America* (New York: Basic Books, 2007), 401–402; Tobacco on Trial, Norma Broin v. Philip Morris, accessed July 27, 2018, http://www.tobaccoontrial.org/?page_id=592.

20. Brandt, *Cigarette Century*, 404.

21. American Nonsmokers' Rights Foundation, accessed July 26, 2018, https://no-smoke.org/.

22. Center for Disease Control, "Vital Signs: Disparities in Nonsmokers' Exposure to Secondhand Smoke—United States, 1999-2012," *Morbidity and Mortality Weekly Report* 64 (February 6, 2016): 103-105, https://www.cdc.gov/mmwr/pdf/wk/mm6404.pdf.

23. Peter D. Jacobson and Lisa M. Zapawa, "Clean Indoor Air Restrictions: Progress and Promise," in *Regulating Tobacco,* Robert Raban and Stephen Sugarman, eds. (New York: Oxford University Press, 2001), 222; Tobacco Control Legal Consortium, "Preemption: The Biggest Challenge to Local Control," accessed July 26, 2018, http://www.publichealthlawcenter.org/sites/default/files/resources/tclc-fs-preemption-tobacco-control-challenge-2014.pdf.

24. Brandt, *Cigarette Century,* 413.

25. Ibid., 414.

26. Derthick, *Up in Smoke,* 78.

27. Michele Bloch, Richard Daynard, and Ruth Roemer, "A Year of Living Dangerously," *Public Health Reports* 113 (1998): 488-497; Michael Givel and Stanton Glantz, "The 'Global Settlement' with the Tobacco Industry: 6 Years Later," *American Journal of Public Health* 94, No. 2 (2004): 218-224. Richard Kluger described opposition to the settlement as foolish overreach by the anti-tobacco forces. Michael Pertschuk shares this assessment. See Pertschuk, *Smoke Gets in Their Eyes: Lessons in Movement Leadership from the Tobacco Wars* (Nashville: Vanderbilt University Press, 2001), 255-279.

28. "Kessler and Koop Urge Congress to Do Away with the Tobacco Settlement," *New York Times,* July 30, 1997.

29. Quoted in Derthick, *Up in Smoke,*123.

30. Brandt, *Cigarette Century,* 428.

31. "Senate Drops Tobacco Bill with '98 Revival Unlikely," *New York Times,* June 18, 1998.

32. Tobacco Control Legal Consortium, "Master Settlement Agreement: An Overview," created 2015, accessed July 31, 2018, http://www.publichealthlawcenter.org/sites/default/files/resources/tclc-fs-msa-overview-2015.pdf..

33. United States v. Philip Morris, 449 F. Supp. 2d 1 (DDC 2006). The legal battle between the Department of Justice and the tobacco companies is chronicled in Sharon Eubanks and Stanton Glantz, *Bad Acts: The Racketeering Case against the Tobacco Industry* (Washington, DC: American Public Health Association, 2012).

34. Brandt, *Cigarette Century,* 432-434.

35. Ibid., 435-435; "States' Tobacco Settlement Has Failed to Clear the Air," *Los Angeles Times,* November 9, 2003.

36. "On Tobacco Road, a Generation Gap," *New York Times,* May 30, 1996.

37. "Tobacco Farmers Feel the Heat," *Washington Post,* January 2, 1999.

38. "False Friends: Report Details U.S. Cigarette Companies' Betrayal of American Tobacco Growers," https://www.tobaccofreekids.org/press-releases/id_0007.

39. Ibid.

40. Peter Benson, *Tobacco Capitalism: Growers, Migrant Workers, and the Changing Face of a Global Industry* (Princeton: Princeton University Press, 2012), 122.

41. Ibid, 129.

42. John Fraser Hart, "The Initial Impact of the Tobacco Buyout Program," *Geographical Review* 101, No. 3 (2011): 451.

43. Brandt, *Cigarette Century*, 449–458.

44. Benson, *Tobacco Capitalism*, 172; Ariel Ramchandani, "The Overlooked Children Working in America's Tobacco Fields," *Atlantic Monthly*, June 21, 2018. Human Rights Watch, "Teens of the Tobacco Fields," December 9, 2015, accessed July 13, 2018, https://www.hrw.org/report/2015/12/09/teens-tobacco-fields/child-labor-united-states-tobacco-farming; Sarah Milov and Gabriel Rosenberg, "Opinion: Back to School—or Back to the Fields?" thehill.com, 8, accessed July 31, 2018, http://thehill.com/blogs/congress-blog/labor/250774-back-to-school-or-back-to-the-fields. Accessed July 31, 2018.

45. Contracting between buyers and a minority of growers predated the end of the tobacco program. "Tobacco Auctions Are Going . . . Going," *Washington Post*, August 11, 2001.

46. Centers for Disease Control, "Current Cigarette Smoking among Adults in the United States," updated February 15, 2018, accessed July 31, 2018, https://www.cdc.gov/tobacco/data_statistics/fact_sheets/adult_data/cig_smoking/index.htm; Brandt, *Cigarette Century*, 449.

47. American Cancer Society, "Study: 50 Years of Anti-Smoking Efforts Have Saved 8 Million Lives," January 7, 2014, accessed July 31, 2018, https://www.cancer.org/latest-news/study-50-years-of-anti-smoking-efforts-have-saved-8-million-lives.html.

48. Benjamin W. Chaffee, Shannon Lea Watkins, and Stanton A. Glantz, "Electronic Cigarette Use and Progression from Experimentation to Established Smoking," *Pediatrics* 141, No. 4 (2018).

49. Centers for Disease Control, "Cigarette Smoking and Tobacco Use among People of Low Socioeconomic Status," updated February 3, 2017, accessed July 31, 2018, https://www.cdc.gov/tobacco/disparities/low-ses/index.htm.

50. D. Yu, N. A. Peterson, M. A. Sheffer, R. J. Reid, and J. E. Schneider, « Tobacco Outlet Density and Demographics: Analysing the Relationships with a Spatial Regression Approach," *Public Health* 124, No. 7 (2010): 412–416; C. G. Brown-Johnson, L. J. England, S. A. Glantz, and P. M. Ling, "Tobacco Industry Marketing to Low Socioeconomic Status Women in the USA," *Tobacco Control* 24 (2015): 505–508.

51. Gregory Wood, *Clearing the Air: The Rise and Fall of Smoking in the Workplace* (Ithaca: Cornell University Press, 2016), 195.

52. Benjamin Alamar and Stanton A. Glantz, "Effect of Increased Social Unacceptability of Cigarette Smoking on Reduction in Cigarette Consumption," *American Journal of Public Health* 96, No. 8 (2006): 1359–1363.

53. Jennifer Stuber, Sandro Galea, and Bruce Link, "Stigma and Smoking: The Consequences of Our Good Intentions," *Social Service Review* 83, No. 4 (2009): 585–609.

54. Gallup, "Tobacco and Smoking," accessed July 31, 2018, https://news.gallup.com/poll/1717/tobacco-smoking.aspx.

55. B. Houle and M Siegel, "Smoker-Free Workplace Policies: Developing a Model of Health Consequences of Workplace Policies Barring Employment to Smokers," *Tobacco Control* 18 (2009): 64–69; "Company's Smoking Ban Means Off Hours Too," *New York Times,* February 8, 2005; ACLU National Task Force on Civil Liberties in the Workplace, "Lifestyle Discrimination in the Workplace: Your Right to Privacy under Attack," accessed August 1, 2018, https://www.aclu.org/other/lifestyle-discrimination-workplace-your-right-privacy-under-attack.

Acknowledgments

I've imagined writing these acknowledgments for the past five years. What I did not imagine was that I'd be writing them during the time of blissed-out sleep deprivation that is the early postpartum period. As any new mother will tell you, this time is one of emotional extremes and late-night (or early-morning) ruminations. When not facing the immediacy of my daughter's needs, I've thought frequently about my place in the chain that connects the generations. As I've wrestled with anxieties and doubts, I've been overwhelmed with gratitude for those who have come before me, and those who help me now. Giving birth is nothing like writing a book. Having a baby is a humbling experience like no other—one that has made me reevaluate the myriad ways in which I am indebted to the assistance of colleagues, mentors, friends, and family. Perhaps postpartum is the ideal time in which to pen acknowledgments after all?

This project took shape with the help of many people in many places. In graduate school at Princeton, I found a supportive and intellectually stimulating environment. Before he was a Twitter celebrity, Kevin Kruse was a model adviser. Kevin read countless drafts of the initial paper and, later, of the manuscript. But more importantly, Kevin has been an exemplar of how to make a life within the academy with grace and wit. Daniel Rodgers read my work with a sharp eye, and I will be forever thankful to him for asking probing questions and nurturing the impulse to make big, synthetic connections. I am grateful to Dirk Hartog for many things, especially for introducing me to the world of legal history. The community of Historians of Science at Princeton—especially Angela Creager, Michael Gordin, Erika Milam, and Keith Wailoo—provided important suggestions along the way, even when I was an interloper into Program Seminar. Margot Canaday has been a mentor, cheerleader, and friend, setting a standard as a scholar and as a human that I aspire toward. In seminars, workshops, and conversations in between, I benefited from the insights of fellow graduate students Dan Bouk, Jennifer Jones, and Dael Norwood.

The Corcoran Department of History at the University of Virginia has been the ideal place to finish this book and grow as a scholar. From the moment I arrived in Charlottesville, Brian Balogh has been an incredible colleague, generously reading the entire manuscript at a key stage. I could not ask for a better, more gracious colleague than Andrew Kahrl, whose dedication to scholarship, teaching, and social justice is an inspiration. I treasure all of the stimulating conversations I've had on long runs with Grace Hale, and I look forward to more of them. I am grateful for the support and encouragement that Fahad Bishara, Risa Goluboff, Paul Halliday, Claudrena Harold, Justene Hill, Will Hitchcock, Mel Leffler, Erik Linstrum, Jim Loeffler, David Singerman, and Liz Varon have provided. Nau Hall would be a much worse place without them. And without Kathleen Miller it might cease to run at all.

Many others have shaped this book at critical stages. Although my time in San Francisco was brief, my fellowship at the Center for Tobacco Control Research and Education at the University of California–San Francisco was extraordinarily fruitful, allowing me to explore an entirely new dimension of tobacco's history. Stanton Glantz and Rachel Grana-Mayne helped me make the most of my time. A year-long fellowship at the Virginia Foundation for the Humanities (now Virginia Humanities) gave me the space and time I needed to finish writing the book.

I am lucky that numerous colleagues have devoted their time to engaging with my work. Daniel Ernst, Lily Geismer, Joanna Grisinger, Shane Hamilton, Meg Jacobs, Louis Kyriakoudes, Sophia Lee, Alison Lefkovitz, Jon Levy, Michelle McKinley, Julia Ott, Gautham Rao, Laura Phillips Sawyer, Reuel Schiller, Christopher Schmidt, Sarah Seo, Bryant Simon, Lauren Thompson, Victoria Saker Woeste, and Rebecca Woods have made this book better with their comments and suggestions.

I am also grateful for the thoughtful engagement of participants at conferences and workshops where I presented portions of this project, including the American Society for Legal History, the Policy History Conference, the American Society for Environmental History, the American Bar Foundation, the History of Science Society, the Virginia Foundation for the Humanities, the University of Virginia Legal History Workshop, the History of Capitalism workshop at the University of Georgia, and the History of Science colloquium at the University of California–San Diego. At UVA, financial assistance from the Dean of the College and Graduate School of Arts and Sciences and the Vice President for Research was essential to the completion of this book. My editor at Harvard University Press, Andrew Kinney, believed in this book for many years before seeing anything resembling the final product. I am deeply appreciative to him and his editorial assistant, Olivia Woods, for patiently guiding the manuscript toward completion.

This book would not have been possible without the help of many librarians and archivists. I would like to thank the knowledgeable and helpful professionals at the Southern Historical Collection and North Carolina Collection at University of North Carolina–Chapel Hill; the Joyner Special Collections at East Carolina University; the Special Collections Research Center at North Carolina State University; the David M. Rubenstein Rare Book and Manuscript Library, Duke University; the Duke Homestead Historic Site; the Archives and Special Collections at the University of North Carolina–Pembroke; the Archives and Special Collections at the University of California–San Francisco; the Small Special Collections at the University of Virginia; the Columbia Center for Oral History; the National Library of Medicine; and the National Archives and Records Administration at College Park. The assistance of interlibrary loan services at the University of Virginia was also timely and crucial. Two veterans of the anti-smoking battles of the 1970s, Clara Gouin and James Repace, graciously shared their time and memories with me. Several of their photographs and anti-tobacco ephemera appear in this book.

Portions of Chapter 6 were first published in "Cleaning the Air and Counting Costs: *Shrimp v. New Jersey Bell* and the Tragedy of Workplace Smoking" in *Shaped by the State*, edited by Brent Cebul, Lily Geismer, and Mason B. Williams, © 2019 by University of Chicago Press, and are reprinted here with permission.

It is a pleasure when intellectual community blends with lasting friendships. Henry Cowles, Rohit De, William Deringer, Catherine Evans, Evan Hepler-Smith, Zack Kagan-Guthrie, Jamie Kreiner, Hanna Lee, Ronny Regev, Padraic Scanlan, Margaret Schotte, Chris Shannon, Kelly Swartz, and Anne Twitty helped me think about tobacco. But more importantly they helped me forget about it. Niki Hemmer, Mary Kuhn, and Lisa Messeri have added immeasurably to my time in Charlottesville. Claire Edington and Dan Navon did the impossible by making a Cambridge winter feel positively warm. Brent Cebul deserves special mention for keeping me on task during the summer of 2017, when we both would rather have been glued to the news.

Regardless of whether writing, research, or teaching is going well, old friends have reminded me that there is much more to life than the ivory tower. Jessie Greenberg and Katie Rodgers are my oldest friends, and I treasure the decades of memories we've made in Florida, Boston, New York, and Atlanta. Charley McNamara was a most hospitable host throughout graduate school during overnight trips to New York. Margaret Ho has always checked in on the book's progress but with a light touch that is surely a testament to her skills as an editor. All these years later, the language that David and Matt Lebowitz and I share continues to be impenetrable to outsiders—which is probably a good thing.

Finally, my deepest debts will always be to my family. The odds of my finding a job at the same institution as my in-laws were vanishingly slim. But somehow it happened, and I am glad for it. Katya Makarova and Krishan Kumar have been generous with their good cheer and good wine. My thanks go to the Florida Milovs who have provided diversion and respite during my visits back to the state that I still consider home. Best of all, they've avoided asking too frequently when the book would be done. Thanks to my father, David Milov, for years of love and support that I've never questioned. For thirty-two years, including two when we overlapped at Princeton, my sister, Joelle Milov, has been a support and a distraction when I needed it most; her partner, Will Shuck, has only added to the fun. I met Kyrill Kunakhovich during my first days of graduate school. Happily, my life hasn't been the same since. Kyrill has seen this book (and its author) in various states of disarray and confusion. And he has put both back together a hundred times over. His editorial skill; his unending patience; and, above all, his love made it possible. Except for its flaws, this book is as much his as it is mine. One month ago, our daughter, Vivian, was born. It is hard to think about much besides her—except, maybe, for the idea of motherhood itself, and for my own mother, Elizabeth Estrada. A book's acknowledgments feel somehow a canvas entirely too small in which to express my love and wonder at the depths of our bond. But it is what I have. This book is for her.

Index

Note: Page numbers in italics indicate figures.

abortion, 261–262, 268–269
Addison, Rita, *229*
administrative agencies: costs of regulation and, 275–276; as job-killers, 127–128; judicial review of, 123, 339n83; public interest movement's focus on, 122–125, 143–154, 160–163; regulatory capture dynamics and, 9, 47–48, 122–127, 129–134, 160–163, 216, 280; rights talk and, 122, 163–172; rule-making prerogatives of, 280–285; Sherman Act and, 21–22; smoking's regulation in, 3, 125–129, 279–285. *See also specific agencies*
advertising: American agricultural exports and, 85–95; class identity and, 231–232; consumerism and, 13, 81–85, 109–118; Fairness Doctrine and, 136–139, 147–151; First World War and, 22–23; gender and, 28; health claims and, 109–112, 125–128, 132, 138, 142; Labor Management Committee and, 238–239; New Deal policies and, 76–77; nonsmoker rights activism and, 179–181; public interest movement and, 134–154; regulation of, 125–126, 131–132, 134–136, 288; tobacco producers' defense of, 27–28, 152–159. *See also* cigarettes; tobacco program; *and specific companies*
AFBF (American Farm Bureau Federation), 35–36, 69–71, 76, 88, 97, 101–104, 244–245, 332n132

AFL-CIO, 101, 130, 232, 235–238, 274
African Americans: auction system and, 31; farmers' interest groups and, 106–108; policing of, 199–200; smoking rates and, 287. *See also* farmers (of tobacco); Jim Crow regime; New Deal; race
Agricultural Adjustment Act (1933), 48–53, 58, 65–71, 74, 258
Agricultural Adjustment Act (1938), 69, 71, 73–74, 98, 251, 292–293, 317n16
Agricultural Adjustment Administration, *51*, 51–65, 72–77, 84–85, 103, 133, 324n16
Agriculture Trade Development and Assistance Act (1954), 91
AHA (American Heart Association), 119, 146, 266, 275
AIDS, 268–270
Airline Deregulation Act, 174
airlines, 3, 164–165, 168, 171–175
Air Quality Act (1967), 185–186
alcohol, 23–24
ALEC (American Legislative Exchange Council), 272–273
Allen & Ginter, 16
AMA (American Medical Association), 119, 189, 242, 275
American Academy of Pediatrics, 366n84
American Airlines, 168
American Association for Respiratory Care, 371n140
American Cancer Society, 119, 136, 146, 148, 150–151, 264, 266

American Lung Association, 146, 148, 209, 214, 220, 233, 264, 266, 275
American Nonsmokers' Rights Association, 287
Americans for Non-Smokers' Rights, 268, 275
Americans United for Life, 261
Annual Reports (Extension Service), 62
Anti-Cigarette League, 24
Anti-Saloon League, 24
antiwar activism, 119, 140
Arizona, 196
Arkansas, 65
Arnold, Fortas & Porter, 129–130
Arnold, Thurman, 137
Arnold and Porter, 122
Aronow, Wilbert, 193
asbestos, 233–234
ASH (Action on Smoking and Health), 143–152, 160–172, 191, 196, 200, 207, 212–213, 224, 242, 273–275
Ashcroft, John, 289
Ashes to Ashes (Kluger), 305n40
ASH v. Civil Aeronautics Board, 174–175
associationalism, 4, 13–14, 34, 41, 124–125, 129–135, 257–260, 300n17
Association of American Railroads, 104
Association of Growers, 11
ATC (American Tobacco Company), 11–14, 19–22, 27–33, 44–45, 76–77, 110–111, 125–126. *See also* Tobacco Trust
Atomic Energy Commission, 124, 345n8
auction system, 28–33, *30,* 30–45, 53–56
Austern, Tommy, 131

BAE (Bureau of Agricultural Economics), 34–35, 55, 58, 87, 313n100
Bailey, Josiah, 38
Baker v. Carr, 139
Balogh, Brian, 345n8
Bandits (Banzhaf's), 144, 175
Banzhaf, John, 135–154, 162–179, 186–188, 195, 204, 215–219, 227, *229,* 240, 270–275, 281, 285–287
Baruch, Bernard, 48
BAT (British American Tobacco), 20
Bay Area Tuberculosis and Respiratory Disease Association, 199
Beef Trust, 14
"Be Kind to Non-Smokers" week, 177
Bell, Daniel, 101

Bell System, 99. *See also* deregulation movement; New Jersey Bell Telephone
Bennett, Evan, 311n73, 315n115
Benson, Ezra Taft, 79, 100–101, 244, 331n112
Bernays, Edward, 28, 144
Big Tobacco (figure), 8–10, 79, 111, 269–278, 306n45, 334n163. *See also* tobacco program; *and specific corporations*
Black, Hugo, 122
Black Patch Tobacco Wars, 36
Block, John, 252
Blue Eagle emblem, 49, *49*
Blumrosen, Alfred, 210–211, 354n25
Bogart, Humphrey, 109
Bonsack, James, 17, 19
Bonsack Cigarette Machine, 17, *18,* 309n24
Brandeis, Louis, 14
Brandt, Allan, 305n40
Brennan, William, 122
Britain, 74–77
British Doctors Study, 110
British Medical Journal, 228
Broadcasting, 142–143
Broin, Norma, 286
bronchitis, 1, 118–119, 165, 214, 325n20
Brotherhood of Carpenters and Joiners, 238
Brotherhood of Firemen and Oilers, 238
Brown & Williamson (firm), 8, 111, 239, 280
Brown v. Board of Education, 122, 143, 219
Buchanan, Benjamin and James, 15
Bureau of National Affairs, 233
Burger, Warren, 167–168
Burley Growers Cooperative, 113
business case against smoking, 6, 203, 209, 221–225, 230, 240, 261–265, 277–278
buttons, 181, *182*
Butz, Earl, 244–245
Byrnes, James, 55
byssinosis, 235

CAB (Civil Aeronautics Board), 3, 99, 170, 173–175, 275
Califano, Joseph, 129, 196–200, 218, 224–225, 246–249, 263
California, 196
Californians for Clean Indoor Air, 194, 198
Californians for Non-Smokers' Rights, 223, 266. *See also* GASP (Group Against Smoking Pollution)
"California Plan," 37

"A Call to Arms" (brochure), 115
Canada, 75
Cantwell, Henry, 52
Capper, Arthur, 36–37
Capper-Volstead Act, 12, 36, 39, 50
capture (regulatory), 9, 47–48, 122–127,
    129–135, 161–163, 216, 280
Carnes, Betty, 196, 215–216, 265
Carson, Rachel, 134, 154
Carter, Jimmy, 131, 173, 195, 243, 245–249,
    251–252
The Case against the Little White Slaver (Ford),
    25
CBT (International Confectionery, Bakers,
    and Tobacco Workers Union), 236,
    238–239
CCC (Commodity Credit Corporation), 84,
    100, 155
CDC (Centers for Disease Control),
    275–276
CEEC (Committee of European Economic
    Cooperation), 86–88
Center for Indoor Air Research (CIAR), 271,
    283, 290
Center for the Study of Responsive Law,
    134
Center for Tobacco Research, 271
Chamber of Commerce, 101
Chandler, Alfred, 310n49
Chemical Workers Union, 235
Cherry, R. Gregg, 324n16
Chevron v. Natural Resources Defense Council,
    285
Chilcote, Samuel, 272
China, 20–21
chiseling, 61–62, 320n61
Cigarette Advertising Code, 131–135
Cigarette Country (Brandt), 305n40
Cigarette Labeling Act, 130–131, 151
cigarettes: consumerism and, 78–101,
    127–128, 134–143; demand for, 9–10,
    22–33; e-cigarettes and, 294–295;
    foreignness of, 23, 25–26, 109; labor
    unrest and, 16–22, 361n123; as little
    white slavers, 13, 308n4; manufacturers
    of, 13–14, 16–22, 59–61, 96–101, 108–118,
    242–243, 250–251, 255, 270, 277;
    marketing of, 8–9, 20–28, 78–79, 81–85,
    96–101, 125–129, 134–154, 288; Master
    Settlement Agreement and, 8, 113,
    279–280, 287–291; patriotism and, 13,
    22–28, 74–77, 88, 311n62; temperance

movement and, 13, 24–25, 142–143, 190;
    toxins in, 5–6, 191–193; unions and,
    231–240. *See also* advertising; non-
    smokers; smoking; tobacco program;
    and specific manufacturers
Cigarettes, Inc. (Enstad), 306n45
citizenship: consumer power and, 200,
    323n4; economic efficiency and, 6–7, 10,
    194–195, 295; farmer-, 104–108; health
    claims and, 194, 307n52; the nonsmoker
    figure and, 2, 295; participation in
    government and, 5; producerism and,
    3–8, 12–14; rights talk and, 2, 189–195.
    See also associationalism; consumerism;
    government (federal); nonsmokers;
    public interest movement; rights
City Bank of New York, 41
Civil Rights Act (1964), 208
civil rights movement, 2, 4, 119, 140,
    160–161, 178, 183–184, 232, 280, 303n31,
    340n100
Clark, J. Bayard, 67, 72
class: advertising and, 231–232; farmers
    and, 253–257, 291–295; nonsmokers and,
    230–240, 276–277; smoking habits and,
    230–240, 276–277, 291–295. *See also*
    democracy; farmers (of tobacco); gender;
    race; unions
Clay, Lucius, 86
Clayton Act, 36
Clean Air Act, 135, 186, 207
Clean Indoor Air Act (Michigan), 266,
    268
Clean Indoor Air Act (Minnesota), 197
Clearing the Air at Work (Shimp), 220
Clements, Earle, 113, 130–131
Clinton, Bill, 279–280, 283
Clinton, Hillary, 279
Coalition on Smoking or Health, 266,
    366n84
Cold War, 9–10, 83, 98–99, 119, 251
collective bargaining, 36–45, 230–240,
    293–294, 303n31
Collins, Robert, 81
collusion, 22, 31–32, 67, 132, 144
Commission on Consumer Affairs, 151–152
Communication Act, 99
Community Action Program, 125, 186
compensatory federalism, 297n9
Congressional Farm Bloc, 35–37, 51–52
Connecticut, 114, 196
consciousness-raising, 219–220

consumerism: advertising and, 127–128, 134–143; citizenship and, 200, 323n4; European reconstruction and, 85–95; overproduction's relation to, 79; producer resentment and, 96–101; rights talk and, 189–195, 244–245; tobacco program's turn to, 78–79. *See also* business case against smoking; free enterprise ethos; rights

Consumer Protection and Safety Act (1972), 274

Consumer Protection Safety Commission, 5

Conway, Erik, 305n44

Cooley, Harold Dunbar, 68, 86–87, 96, 101–108, 116–117, 153–158, 242, 327n45

Coolidge, Calvin, 52

coronary artery disease, 1, 5, 118–119

cotton, 20, 29, 36, 41–43, 47, 50, 54, 59, 65, 87, 97, 100, 153

Council for Tobacco Research, 145–146

"The Country Slickers Take Us Again" (article), 96

Covington and Burling, 131, 213, 270

CRASH (Citizens to Reduce Airline Smoking Hazards), 145, 164

Currin, D. T., 72–73

Currin v. Wallace, 72–74

Curtis, Tony, 150–151

CWA (Communications Workers of America), 209–211, 231–233

"A Damaging Source of Air Pollution" (article), 191–192

Daniel, Pete, 321n80

Daum, Susan, 216

Davis, Chester, 56–57

DDR (Deutsche Demokratische Rupublik), 93–94

DDT, 135, 140

DEAFWATCH (Demanding Equal Access to Facts and Warnings Aired on Television for Citizens who are Hearing-impaired), 164

Dean, James, 109

Dean, John, 245

debt (farmers'), 32–36, 43

deButts, John, 208

Decline of Agrarian Democracy (McConnell), 103

Defense Logistics Agency, 213–214

Delaney Amendment (1958), 197

Demarest, Eleanor, 216

democracy, 61–66, 69, 77, 84–85; associationalism and, 3, 13–14, 34, 41, 124–135, 257–260, 300n17; capitalism and, 129–130; citizenship forms and, 2–10, 12–14, 104–108, 189–195, 200, 295, 307n52, 323n4; deregulation movement and, 161–162, 173–175, 249–253, 277; litigation and, 140, 148–149, 161–163, 186–187, 204, 210–211, 233–234, 270; localism and, 260–278, 285–287, 297n9; participatory ideal and, 120–125, 184–188. *See also* deregulation movement; free enterprise ethos; New Deal

Department of Commerce, 35

Department of Justice, 133–134

Depression of 1893, 19–20

deregulation movement, 161–162, 173–175, 249–253, 263

Der Spiegel, 89

Dirksen, Everett, 109

disability (legal category), 213–214, 234–235

Dixon, Paul Rand, 126

"Don't Be a Slacker, Send Some Tobaccer" (song), 27

"Don't Forget the Smoke" (song), 27

dose-response studies, 263–265

doubt-mongering, 110–118, 260–265, 270–271, 281–282, *282,* 286–287, 305n44

Drew, Elizabeth, 2–3, 128–129, 151

Drinan, Robert, 195, 215, 248

Duke, James B., 11, 14–22, 248

Duke, Washington, 14–15, 17, 309n21

Dulles, John Foster, 328n65

DuPont, 20

Durbin, Dick, 275–276

Earhart, Amelia, 28

Earth Day, 135, 152

Eastern Airlines, 172

East Germany, 93–94

ECA (Economic Cooperation Administration), 87, 326n43

e-cigarettes, 294–295

E. C. Knight decision, 21

Economic Opportunity Act (1964), 129

economists, 34–35, 46–61, 85, 99, 173. *See also specific economists*

EDF (Environmental Defense Fund), 135, 149

Edison, Thomas, 25, 222

EEOC (Equal Employment Opportunity
Commission), 204, 210
Ehringhaus, J. C. B., 57–58, 60, 63
EIA (Environmental Improvement
Associates), 215–221, 232–233, 235
Eighteenth Amendment, 142
Eisenhower, Dwight D., 98, 100, 155,
328n67
Ellender, Allen, 158
Elman, Philip, 129
emphysema, 1, 118–119, 165, 279, 325n20
Employment Act (1946), 324n11
Enstad, Nan, 306n45, 308n12, 309n24,
325n21
environmental impact statements, 163, 187,
225–226, 280
environmental movement, 5, 120–125,
135–143, 159–163, 184–192, 211–214,
306n48, 345n8
EPA (Environmental Protection Agency),
5, 149, 207–208, 213, 227–229, 268, 281,
286
Equality for Agriculture (Wallace and
Cantwell), 51–52
Ervin, Sam, 151, 158
Europe, 85–95
Evans, Sarah, 182
expertise, 34–35, 46–61, 85, 99, 118–120,
173, 260–265, 300n16, 313n99, 335n8.
See also specific economists
Extension Service, 38, 54–56, 58, 61–65,
69–71, 76, 84, 107

FAA (Federal Aviation Administration),
145, 164–170
Fair and Equitable Tobacco Reform Act,
292
Fairness Doctrine, 136, 138–139, 141–144,
147, 149
Family Smoking Prevention and Tobacco
Control Act, 280
FAMRI (Flight Attendant Medical
Research Institute), 286
Farm and Ranch Magazine, 115
farmers (of tobacco): as AAA advisors,
58–61, 76–77; auction system and, 28–45,
53–56; cigarette manufacturers and,
11–14, 291–295; class and, 253–257,
291–295; collective action of, 12–14,
29–33, 36–45, 127–128, 145–146,
152–159, 341n121; crop selection and,
42–43; government action on behalf of,

33–36, 243–249; indebtedness of, 32–36,
43, 312n92; leaf buyers and, 20, 22,
28–33, 258–259; parity and, 51–56, 104,
317n16; as patriotic figure, 249–253;
producerism and, 12–14, 96–101,
258–260; public relations and, 104–117;
race and, 12–15, 63–65, 106–107, 301n22;
referenda mechanisms and, 61–66, 69, 77,
84–85; supply control mechanisms and,
55–56, 61–65, 75–76, 95–101, 107–108,
154–158, 241–260; tenancy and, 29,
42–44, 64–65, 312n92. *See also* cigarettes;
class; quota system
Farm Security Administration, 103
FCC (Federal Communications Commission), 99, 136–151, 162–163
FDA (Food and Drug Administration), 164,
279, 283–285
FDA v. Brown and Williamson Tobacco Corp.,
280, 284–285
Federal Air Quality Standards, 193–194
Federal Aviation Act, 164
Federal Power Commission, 124–125
"Federal Support against the Public
Health" (Public Citizen), 241–243
feminism, 216–217, 230–232
FENSR (Federal Employees for Non-
Smokers' Rights), 212
Fifth Amendment, 121, 211
filters, 125–126
First Amendment, 121, 141, 355n33
"The First American Heritage" (brochure),
115–116
First World War, 12–13, 22–28, *26,* 26–28,
52, 81
Fisher, Irving, 25
FitzGerald, Dennis, 87, 327n45
Flannagan, John, 67, 87–88
Florida, 74, 82, 114, 196, 288
flue-cured tobacco: Brazilian-produced,
250–251, 259, 277, 291–292; demise of,
259–260; global preference for, 33–34, 56,
79–95, 158, 291–292, 325n20; health
risks and, 229–230; supply controls on,
3–8, 61–65, 75–76, 95–101, 107–108,
154–158, 241–253, 258–260, 299n13
Flue-Cured Tobacco Farmer, 246, 257
Flue-Cured Tobacco Stabilization
Cooperative Corporation, 84, 155–157,
258–260
Food, Drug, and Cosmetics Act (FDCA),
197, 283–285

Food for Peace program, 91–95, 229–230, 241, 248. *See also* PL 480
Food Retailers Committee, 104
Food Stamp Program, 239
Foote, Emerson, 147
Forbes, 217
Ford, Gerald, 231, 244
Ford, Henry, 25, 222, 308n4
Fortas, Abe, 129–134, 148–149
Fountain, Lawrence, 156, 258
Fourteenth Amendment, 19, 211
Fourth Amendment, 121
France, 89–90
Frank, Jerome, 60
"Frank Statement to Cigarette Smokers," 111, *112,* 116
Frederickson, Donald, 144
free enterprise ethos, 6, 203, 209, 221–225, 230, 240, 244–249, 258–265, 277–278, 304n34, 331n112, 369n122
Freeman, Orville, 127
Freud, Sigmund, 28
FTC (Federal Trade Commission), 22, 31–32, 125–132, 145, 151, 243–244, 266, 268

Gallaher, 158
Gardner, James, 153
Garn, Jake, 248
GASP (Group Against Smoking Pollution), 161–162, 175–189, 191, 198–200, 204, 206, 213, 216, 223, 226, 233, 240, 242, 266, 275, 347n57
Gasper v. Louisiana Stadium and Exposition District, 211–212
Gaston, Lucy Page, 24, 27, 109
GATT (General Agreement on Tariffs), 251
Gauloises, 90
GDR (East Germany). *See* East Germany
gender: cigarette manufacturing and, 17, 28; feminism and, 216–217, 230–232; nonsmoker rights movement and, 161–162, 175–184, 206–207, 215–221; public interest movement and, 4, 176–178, 181, 188, 195–199, 213, 221–222, 265; smoking's association with, 24–25. *See also* nonsmokers; women; workplaces
General Electric, 20
General Motors, 28, 130, 134
George Washington University, 143–152, 163
Georgia, 74, 82

Gerken, Heather, 260
Gilbert, Jess, 318n30
Ginsberg, Allen, 8
"Give Earth a Chance" (Seeger), 135
Glantz, Stanton, 265–266
Goldberg, Glenn, 160
Golden, Terence, 267
"Golden Fleece Award," 154
Golden Holocaust (Proctor), 305n40
Gompers, Samuel, 231
Good Morning America, 219
Goodwin & Company, 16
Gore, Al, 279
Gouin, Clara, 176–177, *177,* 178, 181, 188, 195–196, 199, 213, 221–222, 264
government (federal): associationalism and, 3–4, 13–14, 34, 41, 101–104, 124–135, 257–260, 300n17; citizen participation in, 5, 195–200; deregulation and, 161–162, 173–175; environmental protections and, 5, 149, 163, 185–188, 207–208, 213, 225–229, 268, 281, 286; expert policymaking and, 34–35, 46–61, 85, 99, 173, 300n16, 313n99; interstate commerce and, 21, 49–50, 67–68, 72–74; lobbying power and, 3, 9–10, 101–104, 123–125, 130, 139–140, 152–159, 161–162, 173, 195; localism and, 260–269; private partnerships with, 4, 58–59, 82, 85–95, 122; public interest movement and, 5, 119–125, 135–143; race and, 301n22; regulatory capture and, 9, 47–48, 122–127, 129–135, 161–162, 280; Sherman Act and, 20–22, 36; tobacco program and, 2, 7–10, 12–14, 33–36, 57–61, 85–95, 153–154, 169–172, 241–249
government (local): associationalism and, 3, 13–14, 34, 41, 257–260; nonsmoker rights efforts and, 161–162, 260–269; smoking's regulation by, 3, 177, 198–199, 203–204, 269–278, 285–287
government (state): ALEC and, 272–278; farmers' power within, 105–108; local preemption laws and, 287; nonsmoker rights efforts and, 161–162; North Carolina's tobacco legislation and, 4; smoking regulations by, 196–200, 269–278
Graham, James, 245–246
Great Britain, 20, 33, 74–77, 80, 96, 109–110, 151, 228

Great Merger Movement, 20–21
The Greening of America (Reich), 122
Griswold, Erwin, 132
The Group Basis of Politics (Latham), 102
Gruccio, Phillip, 204, 211
GSA (General Services Administration), 267–268

Hacker, Jacob, 99, 366n63
Hahn, Paul, 110
Hale, Grace Elizabeth, 348n75
Hall, Claude, 70, 76
Hall of Columns, 2
Hanna, Mark, 21
Harriet Brooks v. Trans World Airlines & Liberty Mutual Insurance, 356n42
Hart, Gary, 247
Hartford Times, 142
Harvard Business Review, 217
Hatch, Orrin, 248
Hatfield, Mark, 248
Hayes, Samuel, 345n8
health care, 165, 196, 222–225, 279, 288, 295, 354n23
heart disease. *See* coronary artery disease
Heckman, Constance, 273
Heclo, Hugo, 342n135
Helling v. McKinney, 358n86
Helms, Dorothy, 255–257
Helms, Jesse, 242–243, 252–257, 262, 275, 334n174, 366n60
HEW (Department of Health, Education, and Welfare), 151, 169, 194–196, 198, 218, 246
Hicks, Carl, 114, 157
Hill, George Washington, 28
Hill & Knowlton, 110, 113, 115
Hirayama, Takeshi, 228–229, *229,* 230
Hiss, Alger, 55
Hogan, Michael, 301n18
Homestead Act, 99
Hoover, Herbert, 34–36, 41, 313n100
House Committee on Agriculture, 101, 153, 242, 248–249
House Subcommittee on Health and the Environment, 247, 279–280, 283–284
"How Far Can Fairness Go?," 143
Howl (Ginsberg), 8
How to Protect Your Health at Work (Shimp), 281
Hughes, Charles Evans, 73, 322n111
Humphrey, Hubert, 247–249

Hunt, James, 246, 252
Hutson, Jack, 55–60, 65, 75–76, 83–90, 92–93, 111, 318nn30–31, 326n43, 334n163
Hyman, Louis, 306n47

ICC (Interstate Commerce Commission), 3, 167, 186–187
Illinois, 196
IMF (International Monetary Fund), 85
Immigration Act (1924), 28
Imperial Tobacco Company, 20, 44, 75, 158
Import-Export Bank, 85
"Improve Productivity Overnight" (Weis), 222
Indianapolis News, 142
INFANTS (Interested Future Attorneys Negotiating for Tot Safety), 164
inflation, 161, 173, 221, 245–253
The Insider (film), 280
Interagency Council on Smoking and Health, 146–147, 188, 190–191
interest groups, 9, 47–48, 101–117, 122–123, 134–143, 300n17. *See also* democracy; public interest movement; tobacco program
International Association of Machinists, 234
Iowa, 96–97
"I Quit" campaign, 150–151
IRS (Internal Revenue Service), 153–154
ITC (International Trade Commission), 252–253

Jackson, Scoop, 243–244
Jaffe, Louis, 144
Japan Tabacco Monopoly, 94–95
Jews and Jewishness, 23, 37, 44, 194–195
Jim Crow regime, 31, 45, 63–64, 106, 153
Joe Camel, 290
Johns-Manville, 233–234
Johnson, Hugh, 48–49, 52
Johnson, James, 248–249
Johnson, Lyndon, 1, 109, 113, 128–131, 155
Jones, Walter, 141, 244
Jordan, Everett, 107–108, 158
Journal of Education, 24
Joyner, W. T., 114
judicial review (of administrative agencies), 123, 339n83

judicial standing, 5, 123, 186–188, 349n90
The Jungle (Sinclair), 14
juvenile delinquency, 24, 109

Kahn, Alfred, 174
Kahn, Phyllis, 197
Katznelson, Ira, 332n141
Keller, Morton, 21
Kellogg, John Harvey, 24
Kennedy, John F., 1
Kennedy, Robert, 146
Kennedy, Ted, 173, 247
Kensell v. State of Oklahoma, 355n33
Kerr, John, 61–62, 320n60
Kerr-Smith Tobacco Act, 61–62, 64–65, 69
Kessler, David, 279, 283–284, 288–289
Kessler, Gladys, 290, 350n104
Kilpatrick, James J., 143
King, Martin Luther, Jr., 239
Kingston *Free Press,* 70
Kinter, Earl, 126
Kluger, Richard, 305n40
Knoxville *News-Sentinel,* 154
Koch, Edward, 144
Komorowski, Tadeusz, 83
Koop, C. Everett, 201–202, 235–236,
    261–269, 275–278, 288–289, 366n84
Korean War, 97
Kornegay, Horace, 113, 199

LABEL (Law Students Association for
    Buyers' Education in Labeling), 164
labor: cigarette manufacturing and,
    15–22; collective bargaining and, 36–45,
    230–240, 293–294, 303n31; farmer
    organization and, 37–45; gender and, 17;
    race and, 14–15, 20–21; workplace safety
    and, 360n110. *See also* unions
Labor Management Committee, 238
Lambda Legal, 179
Landers, Ann, 166, 168
Lanier, Con, 59, 72–73, 76, 86–87, 90–91,
    114, 322n110, 326n38
Lasker, Albert, 28, 147
Las Vegas, 287
Latham, Earl, 102
Legal Activism (course), 163
legal clinics, 162–163
Legislative Policy, 273
Leipzig Trade Fair, 93–94, *94*
Lend-Lease program, 76, 323n122
Lie, Trygve, 83

Liggett & Myers, 14, 27–28, 44
Lincoln, Abraham, 24
Lindsay, John, 151
Lipset, Seymour Martin, 101
litigation. *See* sue the bastards ethos
Little, Clarence Cook, 116
Lobby Reorganization Act (1946), 326n43
localism, 260–278, 285–287, 297n9
Logic of Collective Action (Olson), 341n121
Lorillard, 14, 27–28, 111, 125–126, 152, 171
Lovinger, Lee, 137–138
Lowrey, Al, 226–228, 280
loyalty oaths, 121
lung cancer, 5, 110; 1964 *Surgeon General's
    Report* and, 1–2

Machinists and Aerospace Workers, 238
Magnuson, Warren, 131, 243
Marcuse, Herbert, 128
Marketing Act, 40–41
Marlboro Man, 138, 207, 318n44
Marshall, George, 87
Marshall, Thurgood, 109
Marshall Plan, 86–89, 326n43, 327n45
Maryland Growers Association, 113
Massachusetts, 196, 288
Master Settlement Agreement (MSA),
    8, 113, 279, 287–295
Mayeri, Serena, 184
McCain, John, 289
McCann, Michael, 302n23
McCann-Erickson, 147
McConnell, Grant, 103–104, 117, 301n22
McCune, Wesley, 103, 117
McGovern, George, 244
McKinley, William, 21
McNary-Haugen bill, 35, 51–52, 313n98
Merit Systems Protection Board, 214
Merle Norman Cosmetics, 220
Merryman, Walker, 274
Mexican American Legal Defense and
    Education Fund, 179
Meyner, Robert, 132
Michels, Robert, 331n125
Michigan, 196
Milkman, Ruth, 216
Mill, John Stuart, 190
Mills, C. Wright, 102, 104
minimum wages, 48, 50–51, 287, 293
Minnesota, 197–198, 288
Minnesota Restaurant and Food Service
    Association, 197

Missouri, 213
mixed economy, 95–101
Moline Plow Company, 52
Monroe, Marilyn, 109
"More Doctors Smoke Camels Than Any
    Other Cigarette," 109–110
Morgan, J. P., 14, 22
Morill Land Grant College Act, 99
Morris, Dick, 279
Moss, Frank, 146–147
Motor Vehicle Safety Act, 142
Mueller, Athena, 273
Mulford v. Smith, 72–74
Mussolini, Benito, 49
Myers, Matthew, 266
Myerson, Bess, 151

NAACP (National Association for the
    Advancement of Colored People), 109,
    123, 179
NAB (National Association of Broad-
    casters), 132
Nader, Ralph, 134–135, 140–145, 151,
    164–175, 189–190, 241–243, 248–250,
    275, 369n122
NAS (National Academy of Sciences), 268,
    275
Nation, Carrie, 190, 195, 207
National Association of Broadcasters,
    141
National Association of Manufacturers,
    101
National Cancer Institute, 193
National Environmental Policy Act, 135
National Health Survey (1967), 165
National Institutes of Health, 99, 144
National Press Club, 168
National Right to Life Committee, 261
National Safety Council, 233
National Science Foundation, 99
National Tuberculosis Association, 119,
    148
Naval Research Laboratory, 225, 227
NCFB (North Carolina Farm Bureau),
    69–70, 76, 82–84, 96, 100–108, 114, 117,
    158, 252, 258, 332n132
Nebraska, 196
Nelson, Gaylord, 151–152
neoliberalism (definition), 304n34
NEPA (National Environmental Policy
    Act), 186–187
Neuberger, Maurine, 144, 337n41

New Deal: agricultural regulations of, 3–8,
    12–13, 53–65; bureaucratic machinery of,
    55–61, 113; Cold War administrative
    agencies and, 129–134; consumerism
    and, 80–95; Great Depression and,
    46–48; New Right's rise and, 3–4, 9–10;
    NIRA and, 48–53, 66–69, 72; postwar
    planning and, 95–101; race and, 63–65,
    332n141; Second World War and, 74–77;
    supply control and, 45–48, 53–56, 61–65,
    244–260. *See also* tobacco program; *and
    specific judicial decisions and legislative acts*
New England Journal of Medicine, 144
New Jersey Bell Telephone, 204–211,
    214–215, 218–219, 231
"The New Property" (Reich), 120–125
New Times, 245
New York City, 287
New York State, 196
New York State Regulatory Commission,
    174
New York Times, 86, 96–97, 135, 139, 148,
    229, 242–243, 261–262
Night Rider (Warren), 11–12
Nightwatch, 219
NIMBY (not in my backyard), 185, 226,
    348n79
Ninth Amendment, 211
NIRA (National Industrial Recovery Act),
    48–53, 66, 68–69, 72
Nixon, Richard, 2–3, 100, 152, 173, 180,
    188, 194–195, 206, 231, 244–245
Noble, Charles, 360n110
No Net Cost Tobacco Act (1982), 249–253,
    257–260, 277
nonsmokers: business case against smoking
    and, 6, 203, 209, 221–225, 230, 240,
    261–265, 277–278; as citizen identity, 2,
    4–6, 185–188, 219–221, 230; civil rights
    movement and, 2, 160–162, 178–179,
    183–184, 232; class and, 230–240,
    276–277, 291–295; consumer power of,
    195–196, 200; dining sections and, 175,
    177, 197; disease risk of, 165, 169 172,
    176, 191–195, 197–198, 203, 211–214,
    223–225, 263–278, 280–287; environ-
    mental movement and, 5, 120, 191–192,
    211–214, 345n8; gender and, 161–162,
    175–184; localism and, 260–269,
    285–287; New Right and, 278; quality of
    life discourse and, 184–188, 230–231,
    306n48; race and, 161–162, 183–184,

nonsmokers (*continued*)
199–200; rights claims based upon, 10, 160–162, 169–175, 188–200, 208–214, 269–271, 306n48; state and local governments and, 161–162; tobacco industry's federalism and, 5, 242–243; unions and, 6, 230–240; virtuous citizenship of, 6, 194–195, 295; workplace rights of, 6, 201–211, 220–225, 230–240, 286–287. *See also* environmental movement; pollution; public interest movement; rights; sue the bastards ethos
"Nonsmoker's Bill of Rights," 189–191
Nonsmokers' Liberation Guide, 179–180, 185
Non-Smokers Rights Act (1985), 237–238, 267
Norma R. Broin v. Philip Morris, 286–287
North Carolina Grange, 79–85
North Carolina Railroad, 15
North Carolina Tobacco Growers Association, 61
North Carolina Tobacco Report, 95–96
Northern Securities decision, 22
NRA (National Recovery Administration), 49–52, 58, 60, 72–73, 98, 133, 174

Occupational Health and Safety Act, 207, 231
Ochsner, Alton, 110, 144
O'Connor, Sandra Day, 284–285
Ogden (company), 20
Oil, Chemical and Atomic Workers International Union, 231
Olson, Mancur, 341n121
One Dimensional Man (Marcuse), 128
O'Neill, Tip, 246
On Liberty (Mill), 190
"Operation Down Under," 270–271
Oppenheimer, Robert, 109
Oreskes, Naomi, 305n44
Orrick, William, 132–133
OSHA (Occupational Health and Safety Administration), 5–6, 186, 207–208, 281, 283, 285–287
overproduction issues, 33, 47–54, 61, 69, 79, 97–101, 154. *See also* supply control policies

Palmer, John, 93, 158
Pan Am airlines, 168
parity, 51–56, 104, 317n16
Parodi, Irene, 213–214

participatory democracy ideal, 120–125, 184–188. *See also* public interest movement
passive smoking. *See* nonsmokers; secondhand smoke
Patrons of Husbandry, 315n115
Peek, George, 51–52, 60
Pershing, John J., 26
Pertschuk, Michael, 243, 266, 268
PETA (People for the Ethical Treatment of Animals), 273
Petri, Thomas, 249
Petty, Adrienne, 320n77
Philip Morris, 111, 130, 141, 180, 238–239, 248, 259–260, 270, 272, 294
PHS (Public Health Service), 118, 151, 209
Pierson, Paul, 99
Pinchot, Gifford, 313n99
pinhookers, 66
PL 89-12, 159
PL 480, 91–92, 248, 328n65. *See also* Food for Peace program
pluralism (political), 101–104
PNB (Pacific Northwest Bell), 201–204
Poe, Clarence, 38, 44, 63, 76
Poland, 83, 93
Polanyi, Karl, 99
policing, 199–200
Political Parties (Michels), 331n125
pollution, 5–6, 225–230, 233–234, 247, 281–285
Pontiac Stadium, 193
populism, 38, 57–58, 67, 135, 173, 197, 293, 321n86
Postel, Charles, 315n115
Powell, Lewis, 272, 369n122
preemption laws, 274–275, 278, 287, 290
Preyer, L. Richardson, 247
price supports (for tobacco), 3–8, 13–14, 34–36, 48–61, 66, 79, 95–101, 108, 155–156, 244–257, 299n13
Private Power and American Democracy (McConnell), 103
Proctor, Robert, 111, 305n40
producerism, 3–8, 44–45, 53–56, 67, 95–101, 152–159, 229–230, 253–257, 306n47, 308n3. *See also* populism
"Profits Up in Smoke" (Weis), 221
Progressive Era, 23–24
Progressive Farmer, 32, 38, 61, 63, 71, 81, 115, 252

property (tobacco acreage allotments as), 108, 120–125, 252–257
Proposition 13, 198
protectionism (in trade), 33
Proxmire, William, 154
Public Citizen, 241–243
public comment periods, 167, 169, 171, 185–187, 283
Public Health Cigarette Smoking Act, 274
public interest movement: administrative agencies and, 122–125, 143–154, 160–163; advertising and, 134–154; anti-associationalism and, 124–125; civil rights movement and, 4; democracy's visions and, 120–125; environmental movement and, 5, 123–125, 135–143, 161–163; expertise and, 118–120; regulatory capture and, 129–134, 161–162, 175; rights claims and, 121–122, 164–172; tobacco interests' mimicry of, 171–172; women's leadership of, 4, 176–178, 181, 188, 195–199, 213, 221–222, 265
Pueblo Chieftain, 142
PUMP (Protests Unfair Marketing Practices), 145

Quaker Oats Company, 104
quality of life discourse, 184–188, 230–231, 306n48
quota system, 12, 69–77, 82–85, 107–108, 249–260, 292–293

race: auction system and, 31; cigarette's associations with, 25; entitlement programs and, 253–257; Jim Crow and, 31, 45, 63–64, 106, 153, 301n22; New Deal structures and, 63–65, 332n141; nonsmoker rights and, 161–162; policing and, 199–200; slavery and, 14–15. See also Jim Crow regime
Raleigh News and Observer, 68, 115
Ralston Purina, 244–245
Raytheon, 286
"Reach for a Lucky Instead of a Sweet" campaign, 28
Reader's Digest, 109
Reagan, Ronald, 7, 173, 201–202, 221–225, 236, 251–252, 261–265, 353n7
red herring research, 111. See also doubt-mongering
Reemtsma, 158

referenda, 61–66, 69, 77, 84–85
Reich, Charles, 120–125, 284, 369n122
Reich, Robert, 281
Repace, James, 225–230, 280, 358n86
Reynolds v. Sims, 139
Richardson, Elliott, 195
Richmond, Julius, 195
Richmond Times-Dispatch, 115
RICO act, 290
Riggs, "Speed," 30
rights: administrative agencies and, 122, 163; business logic and, 209–211; consumerism and, 143–145, 159, 189–195; gendered activism and, 175–184; localism and, 260–269, 285–287; "New Property" and, 121–125; nonsmokers as protected class and, 2–3, 10, 160–162, 173–175, 188–200, 211–214, 232, 306n48; paradoxes of, 160–162; quality of life discourse and, 184–188, 230–231, 306n48; race and, 199–200; unions and, 232–240; workplace battles and, 201–221
right to work laws, 332n132
R. J. Reynolds, 14, 23, 27–28, 44, 60–61, 109–111, 195, 237, 259–260, 271, 273, 282, 283, 290–291, 294
Robertson, Gary, 271
Rockefeller, John D., 14
Rodgers, Daniel, 203
Roisman, Anthony, 190–191, 350n104
Roosevelt, Franklin D., 46, 49–50, 67, 155
Roosevelt, Teddy, 21
Rose, Charlie, 219, 248–249, 258, 366n60
Royal College of Physicians, 1
Royster, Fred, 127
Ruckelshaus, William, 268
Rupp, John, 270–271, 273

Salisbury, Harrison, 328n91
Sapiro, Aaron, 37–44
Sargent, Daniel, 85
Sax, Joseph, 163, 187, 349n88
Scalia, Antonin, 187–188, 349n90
Scenic Hudson Preservation Conference v. Federal Power Commission, 124
Schattschneider, E. F., 331n123
Schaub, Ira, 56–58, 69–70
Schechter Poultry Corp. v. United States, 49–50, 66–69, 72
Schiller, Reuel, 339n83
Schlesinger, Arthur, Jr., 101

scientific evidence: expert policymaking
    and, 34–35, 46–61, 85, 99, 118–120, 173,
    335n8; initial emergence of, 96;
    nonsmoker figure's risk and, 5–6, 165,
    191–192, 229, 263–265, 269–270,
    280–282; public relations campaigns
    and, 109; tobacco companies' research
    and, 8–10, 110–119, 145–146, 196,
    260–265, 270–271, 281–282, *282*,
    286–287, 305n44. *See also* secondhand
    smoke
scrap, 251–252
SCRAP (Students Challenging Regulatory
    Agency Procedures), 186, 188
Sears, Roebuck, 104
secondhand smoke, 5–6, 165–170, 191–197,
    203–206, 211, 269, 280–287, 294, 303n28
Second World War, 27, 74–77, 103
Securities and Exchange Act, 98
Seeger, Pete, 135
SEITA (Société Nationale d'Exploitation
    Industrielle des Tabacs et Allumettes),
    89–90
Senate Committee on Agriculture and
    Forestry, 154, 242
Senate Subcommittee on Health, 247
Service Employees International Union,
    235
shading up, 31, 44
Shaffer, John, 165
Shamansky, Robert, 249
sharecropping, 42–44, 64
Sheet Metal Workers, 238
Sherman Anti-Trust Act, 12, 14, 19–21, 36
Shimp, Donna, 202–211, *206*, 212, 214–222,
    227, 230–234, 240, 281, 354n23
Shimp v. New Jersey Bell, 202, 204–211,
    213–215, 231
"Should Trees Have Standing?" (Stone), 123
Sick Building Syndrome, 271
Sierra Club v. Morton, 186–187
Silent Spring (Carson), 134, 154
Sinclair, Upton, 14
Sir Walter Raleigh Hotel, 79–85
"16 Cities Study," 283
Smith, Paul, 212–213
"Smokefree day at Work," 217–219
"The Smoke Free Workplace" (Weis), 230
The Smoke-Free Workplace (Weis), 223–224
smoking: airlines and, 164–172, 275–276,
    286, 356n42; citizenship and, 2–8, 295;
    class and, 230–240, 276–277, 291–295;

consumerism and, 95–96; costs to
    employers of, 208–211, 217–225, 240,
    260–265; disease and, 96, 110, 118–120,
    153–154, 164–165, 170–172, 197–198,
    260–269; employers and, 2–3, 201–211,
    217–221, 230–240; federal regulation of,
    3–7, 125–129; on flights, 3, 164–168,
    171–175; lung cancer and, 1–2; non-
    smoker figure and, 160–162, 263–265; as
    pollution, 5–6, 225–230, 233–234, 247,
    281–285; public interest campaigns and,
    120–125, 136–143; rates of, 2, 9–10, 109,
    206–207, 239–240, 276–277, 322n120;
    smokers' rights and, 160–162, 166–168,
    170, 173–175, 189–195, 210–211, 269–271,
    274–278; state legislation and, 263,
    267; tobacco lobby's power and, 2–3;
    workplaces and, 201–211, 230–240,
    279–287. *See also* cigarettes; nonsmokers;
    tobacco program
Smoking and Health, 224
social science, 34–35, 38, 56–61
Social Security Administration, 212
Social Security Amendments of 1965, 129
SOUP (Students Opposing Unfair
    Practices), 145
South Carolina, 82
South Dakota, 196
Soviet Union, 50, 83, 91–97, 291
Stabilization. *See* Flue-Cured Tobacco
    Stabilization Cooperative Corporation
Standard Oil, 14, 20, 22
standing (judicial), 5, 349n90
The State Factor (ALEC), 273
Steinfeld, Jesse, 2–3, 188–191, 193–197, 206,
    226
Stevens, Ted, 237, 267
Stewart, Potter, 187
Stockman, David, 252
Stone, Christopher, 123
subsidies. *See* government (federal); supply
    control policies; tobacco program
sue the bastards ethos, 140, 148–149,
    161–163, 186–187, 204, 210–211, 233–234,
    270
Sullivan, John, 25
Sundquist, Don, 228
Superdome, 211
supply control policies, 3–8, 61–65, 75–76,
    95–101, 107–108, 154–158, 241–253,
    258–260, 299n13
Supreme Court. *See specific decisions*